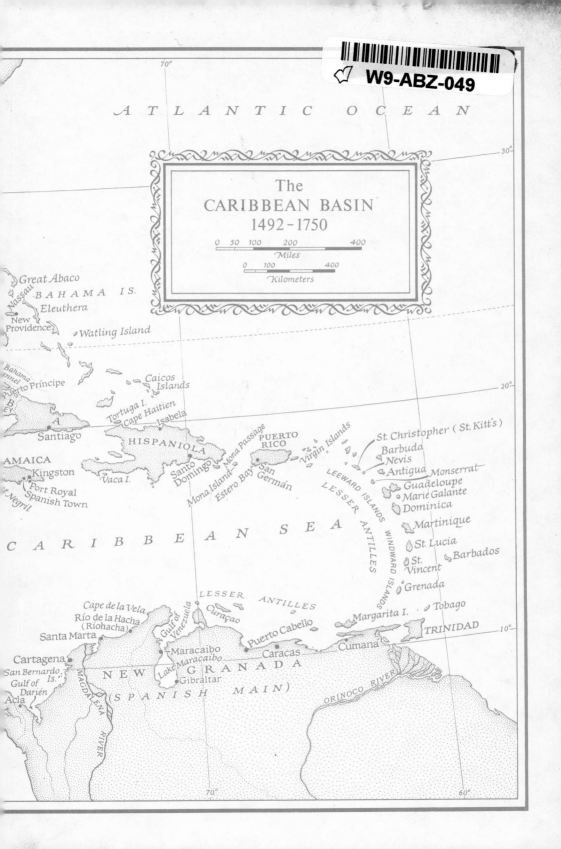

ATLANTIC OCEAN

The CARIBBEAN BASIN 1492–1750

Miles
0 50 100   200   400

Kilometers
0   100   400

30°

20°

10°

70°

60°

Great Abaco
Nassau
BAHAMA IS.
Eleuthera
New Providence
Watling Island

Bahama Channel
Puerto Príncipe
Caicos Islands
B[Y]
[B]EY
Santiago
Tortuga I.
Cape Haitien
Isabela
HISPANIOLA
JAMAICA
Kingston
Port Royal
Spanish Town
Vaca I.
Santo Domingo
Negril
PUERTO RICO
Mona Island
Mona Passage
Estero Bay
San Germán
Virgin Islands
St. Christopher (St. Kitt's)
Barbuda
Nevis
Antigua   Monserrat
LEEWARD ISLANDS
Guadeloupe
Marie Galante
Dominica
LESSER   ANTILLES
Martinique
St. Lucia
WINDWARD ISLANDS
St. Vincent   Barbados
Grenada

CARIBBEAN   SEA

Cape de la Vela
Río de la Hacha (Ríohacha)
Santa Marta
LESSER ANTILLES
Curaçao
Gulf of Venezuela
Margarita I.   Tobago
Puerto Cabello
Cumaná
TRINIDAD
Cartagena
San Bernardo Is.
Gulf of Darien
Acla
MAGDALENA RIVER
Maracaibo
Lake Maracaibo
Caracas
NEW GRANADA
Gibraltar
(SPANISH   MAIN)
ORINOCO RIVER

THE FUNNEL OF
GOLD

THE FUNNEL OF GOLD

Mendel Peterson

LITTLE, BROWN AND COMPANY
BOSTON-TORONTO

FIRST EDITION

T11/75

The author is grateful to the following publishers and magazines for permission
to quote from previously copyrighted materials:

The Historical Association of Southern Florida, for the *Memoir of Hernando
d'Escalente Fontaneda Respecting Florida*, edited by David O. True. Copyright
1944 by the University of Miami and the Historical Association of Southern
Florida.

The University Presses of Florida, for *Laudonnière and Fort Caroline* by
Charles E. Bennett. Copyright © 1964 by the Board of Commissioners of State
Institutions of Florida.

The Bermuda Historical Quarterly, Vol. 18, No. 1 (Spring 1961), for the article
"Shipwrecked Spaniards 1639: Grievances Against Bermudians." Translated from
the Spanish by Lawrence Dudley Gurrin.

Farrar, Straus & Giroux, Inc., for *The Discovery and Conquest of Mexico,
1517–1521* by Bernal Díaz del Castillo, translated by A. P. Maudslay. Copyright ©
1956 by Farrar, Straus and Cudahy.

LIBRARY OF CONGRESS CATALOGING IN PUBLICATION DATA

Peterson, Mendel L
  The funnel of gold.

  Bibliography: p.
  Includes index.
    1. Caribbean area—History.   2. Pirates—Caribbean
area.   I. Title.
F2161.P5   972.9   75-19457
ISBN 0-316-70300-1

Designed by Susan Windheim

*Published simultaneously in Canada
by Little, Brown & Company (Canada) Limited*

PRINTED IN THE UNITED STATES OF AMERICA

To:
L.,T.,V., M., G., H., B., and C.

Contents

Maps

Acknowledgments

I wish to thank the many people whose help made this book possible. The financial support of Ed Link and George R. Wallace provided for the research on which parts of this book are based. The encouragement and above all patience of Ned Bradford, who waited and waited and waited for my manuscript, enabled me to finish it during a busy career that carried me all over Europe and America. The gracious help of the many librarians and archivists in Seville and London and in the larger libraries of Washington and New England enabled me to consult the necessary sources. Miss Flora Murray, for many years my secretary at the Smithsonian, helped in innumerable ways, particularly in securing source materials and typing the early chapters. To my good diving companions I owe a debt I can never adequately repay: Barney and Jane Crile, Teddy Tucker, Robert Canton, Arthur McKee, Tom Gurr, Ed Reimard, Peter Stackpole, Alan Albright, and all the others who have shared the experiences that contributed to the chapters on shipwreck. And I wish especially to thank my family for their support and tolerance. Most of all I thank my wife, Trudy, for her patient work in unscrambling my involved syntax and preparing the manuscript in its final form.

M. P.

THE FUNNEL OF GOLD

I

The Gate Is Opened

... they passed to Havana and came out of the Bahama Channel, and with prosperous wind arrived at Spain, being the first who made that navigation.
—Juande Torquemada, *Monarchía Yndiana*

 EARLY IN THE MORNING of October 12, 1492, a seaman named Rodrigo, from Triana, a suburb of Seville, looked out from the mast top of a sleek caravel called the *Pinta* and saw a thin white line on the horizon glowing in the light of the moon in its third quarter. He was looking at a tiny speck of a new world, the existence of which had been known definitely to only a few Norsemen and perhaps some Breton fishermen. Surely this was one of the great moments in the history of mankind, one that was to transform completely old economic, political, and social institutions and give a new life and a new direction to the evolution of Western civilization.

The exact point at which the New World was discovered is still a matter of dispute. We know that the landfall was in the Bahamas area, very likely on either Watling Island or on one of the islands in the Caicos group to the south, but while speculation about the site of the landfall is interesting, it is really not of great significance. The important thing is that through the courage, determination, and faith of one of the great men of history, a new world was found.

Columbus remained at Guanahaní, as the natives called their island, a short time, renaming it San Salvador, and then in a fever of excitement, pushed on, convinced that he at last had come to the fabled East and would soon visit the courts of oriental rulers and trade for their gold and spices. He sailed to three other islands, naming them Santa María de la Concepción, Fernandina, and Isabela. Then, hearing from the natives reports of a large island to the southwest, Columbus went in that direction. The natives called the island Cuba; Columbus believed it to be Cipango (Japan).

This decision to sail southwest probably changed importantly the later development of Spanish America, for it carried Columbus away from the coast of Florida, and the straits with their mighty current, leaving them to be discovered a generation later. In exploring the coasts of Cuba and Hispaniola,* Columbus was impressed by the size and fertility of the islands, and even if the loss of the *Santa María* had not forced him to found a settlement of the men whom the smaller *Pinta* and *Niña* could not carry home to Spain, he would have un-doubtedly advocated settlement on the islands in any case.

Thus it was that Columbus was led away from the straits that were to become the gateway from the New World to the Old, from the continent of North America, and from the possible discovery of the civilization of Mexico. It was his destiny to spend the remainder of his life searching the Caribbean to the south: discovering new islands, defining the West Indies and the northern coast of South America for posterity, but never finding those fabulous kingdoms and courts of which he dreamed.

On Columbus's return to Palos in March 1493, he was received with the honor due him and word of the greatest discovery of the age swept Europe. The discovery not only presented Spain with claims to vast new lands but with stupendous problems as well. The political, moral, and legal puzzles arising from the discovery were to occupy the best minds of the nation for generations. Spain claimed title by right of discovery, but she could expect these rights to be recognized only in those areas the Spanish explorers actually touched—which was not enough. The Spanish Crown wanted to obtain exclusive title to the entire new world, not only to those areas already discovered but to those yet unknown. To accomplish her aim, Spain applied to the Pope for sanction: he was the closest approximation to an international court existing at that time. Although the temporal powers of the papacy had declined greatly since the days when an emperor of Germany abased himself before Pope Gregory VII, the papacy was still considered the supreme power of Christendom.

Papal sanction of conquests of heathen peoples harked back to the Crusades and was based on a medieval concept in canon law. One

---

* The island now comprising the Dominican Republic and Haiti. Columbus called it La Isla Española, but the name was soon latinized to Hispaniola. Santo Domingo, the name of the town and colony that Columbus ordered established after his second voyage—now Ciudad Trujillo—later came to be applied to the whole island.

An imaginative view of the landing of Columbus in the
Bahamas. An engraving by Théodore de Bry, late sixteenth
century. De Bry has clothed Columbus and his men in cos-
tumes of the late Tudor period

Christopher Columbus. Wood engraving after an idealized early portrait

fourteenth-century authority, Heinrich Suso, reasoned that when Christ became King of the Earth, all heathen peoples lost title to their possessions. Peter, the Apostle, inherited Christ's dominion over the earth, and the Popes inherited it from Peter. It was on this obtuse reasoning that Spain attempted to establish her claim to exclusive possession of the New World.

After applying to Pope Alexander VI, the Spanish sovereigns received a bull dated May 3, 1493, which granted them sovereignty over the new lands already discovered and to be discovered. Portugal, however, claimed that she had prior rights in the new lands under the Treaty of Alcaçovas of 1479, which recognized her sphere of influence as extending westward into the unknown. The bull of May 3, 1493, also drew a line between the Spanish and the Portuguese colonial territories: the famous Line of Demarcation, which ran north–south one hundred leagues west of the Azores. All territory east of the line was Portugal's, all that west of the line was Spain's. Thus getting the jump on all the other nations of Europe, including Portugal, Spain then negotiated from a position of strength with her neighbor and under the Treaty of Tordesillas signed June 7, 1494, secured recognition by agreeing to extend the Line of Demarcation to a meridian three hundred and seventy leagues to the west of the Cape Verde Islands. Unknown to either party to the treaty, it gave Portugal claim to Brazil, the existence of which was not discovered until six years later. Thus, without so much as a word to the other Christian princes of Europe, the sovereigns of Spain and Portugal simply divided the New World between them while the Pope in effect beamed and blessed the bargain between his favorite children.

While Spain was thus mending her legal fences, less theoretical considerations were not neglected and feverish preparations were begun to send the Admiral of the Ocean Sea back for more discoveries. Secure in his claims and honors, Columbus now sailed on September 25, 1493, with a fleet of three large carracks and fourteen caravels, carrying some twelve hundred men and animals and supplies for colonization in the new lands.

Proceeding down the northern coast of Hispaniola, he founded, at a poorly selected location, the town of Isabela. The colonists were also poorly selected: they proved to be arrogant, mutinous, overly proud, and unwilling to work with their hands. This must have puzzled the son of an Italian woolcomber, their admiral. Columbus was learning more and more about Spanish individualism.

Anxious to be off for further discoveries, Columbus delegated his authority to his brother Diego and a council, and set sail toward the southwest. Before this, however, in his dispatch of February 2, he had suggested the enslavement of the cannibal Carib Indians and their sale in Spain, a suggestion which may be said to have established slave trading in the New World. This principle, when extended to forced native labor in the gold mines, was to bring death to millions of native Americans and to depopulate whole countries, including the Bahamas, whose gentle and handsome poeple had welcomed Columbus at the moment of his discovery.

The admiral sailed along the southern coast of Cuba, and sweeping the waters south of that island, discovered Jamaica, naming it Santiago. Returning to Cuba he sailed along the southern coast westward until he was convinced he had discovered a continent. Turning eastward, he sighted the Isle of Pines and again touched at Jamaica. From here he stood northeastward and touched at Mona Island. Then exhaustion overtook him and he sailed for Isabela, the settlement on Hispaniola. Stricken by serious illness on the way, he lay near death there for several months.

Columbus, like many men of great vision, was impatient of details. Great leaders often make poor bookkeepers and Columbus delegated the routine duties to others less devoted if more systematic. The condition of the colony fell to a very sad state. The illness of the admiral had prevented his devoting even an impatient supervision to its affairs. Word of the wretched state of things leaked back to Spain and the sovereigns sent out an agent to investigate. His arrival did not please the admiral and Columbus resolved to return to Spain to protect his interests. Here he was received cordially at court. His explanations satisfied Ferdinand and Isabella and he was given a new fleet to push his discoveries. With this he sailed for the New World on May 30, 1498. The fleet, taking a more southerly route, discovered Trinidad and coasted along the northern coast of South America before sailing on to Hispaniola. On the way over, the great virtues of the trade winds were undoubtedly recognized by the admiral, his officers and men, and their course became the one by which later fleets sailed to America.

On reaching the city of Santo Domingo (the capital had moved there from Isabela), Columbus found a revolt. He restored order as best he could but word of the new outbreak and jealous enemies at court secured the appointment of Francisco de Bobadilla as governor and judge. After an investigation, Bobadilla, to the lasting shame of the Spanish nation, placed Columbus in chains and sent him home in confinement. Thus was a jealous, small-minded petty tyrant able to disgrace one of the truly great men of history.

This regrettable occurrence rallied support for Columbus and he

Wrought-iron naval guns, 1490–1550. Above: the swivel gun, designed to fire on enemy ships from short range as they closed to board or to resist boarders. The gun fired everything from lead balls to pebbles and scrap iron. Below: breech-loading gun on a stock carriage. The guns on Columbus's ships were similar. Photographs of models in the Smithsonian Institution

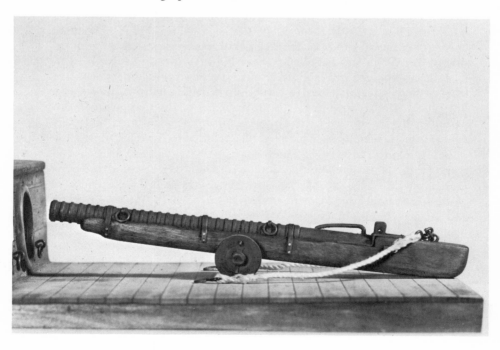

was received at court. Here the sovereigns promised compensation for his losses and redress of his grievances. But while Ferdinand and Isabella could repay him for the actual monetary loss inflicted by their contemptible servant, they could never erase from the admiral's memory the bitterness which Spanish ingratitude had engendered. To the day of his death Columbus kept his shackles hanging in his chambers as a reminder of the reward bestowed by the petty on the great.

A new governor was sent out to replace Bobadilla and Columbus was given a new fleet with which to push further explorations. He sailed in May 1502 with orders to avoid Hispaniola. Enduring great hardships, the small fleet coasted along Central America, further delineating the main features of the southern Caribbean basin. Here rumors of a great kingdom were heard from the natives but it was not for Columbus to discover the civilization of Mexico and he returned to Spain in November 1504, ill and even more bitter. Still he dreamed of returning once again, but death is no respecter of ambitions and hopes no matter how worthy they may be. The admiral died on May 30, 1508, his hope of reaching the East unrealized.

The voyages of Columbus had opened the Caribbean, had defined most of its coastline, and had discovered many of its islands. Other daring and less idealistic leaders were to spread Spanish dominion over the entire Caribbean basin and onto the continents surrounding it. The conquest of the Caribbean was of remarkable rapidity when we consider the difficulties that faced the conquistadores—tropical jungle and swamps, long stretches of uncharted water studded with coral reefs and shoals that spelled disaster for their comparatively small vessels, odd and curious diseases that were completely unknown to the Europeans, and, in some places, savage, warlike, and well-armed natives in large numbers.

To meet the challenge, the Spaniard of the fifteenth century brought a character peculiarly appropriate to the difficulties he faced. Centuries of warfare against the Moors in Spain had molded the Spanish soldier into a superb fighting man most proficient in the use of the sword in hand-to-hand combat, and of the horse and the lance. Completely convinced of his own skill, haughty and full of self-righteousness, greedy and cruel for the love of it, the Spanish soldier was a formidable foe in Europe, and in America facing native troops, unconquerable.

Within one generation of Columbus's discovery the Spanish had pushed onto the larger islands of the Caribbean, settled Panama, conquered Mexico, had begun to define the northern limits of the Gulf of Mexico, and were preparing to push down the western coast of South

Above: Spaniards attacked by hostile Indians. Below: A Carib cannibal feast. Engravings by Théodore de Bry, late sixteenth century

Spanish infantry of the early sixteenth century. From a painting of the period

America from their settlements in Panama. The colony of Santo Domingo, settled in 1493, was for a time the center of Spanish colonial administration, but the more restless conquistadores, particularly those without land grants or mining rights on the island, quickly pushed on to other fields, thirsty for the gold which they hoped lay just over the horizon. Panama and Puerto Rico in 1508, Jamaica in 1509, Cuba in 1511, the islands off Venezuela in 1515, Mexico in 1519—this was the sequence of conquest.

Very early in the first years of settlement the Spanish probably were aware of the existence of a large land mass north of Cuba and west of the Bahamas. There is a possibility that the Cabots had visited the Florida coast in 1497. The Cantino map, which was probably drawn in 1502, shows a Florida-like peninsula in a relatively correct position and very likely was based on actual exploration by someone, although some students believe the land mass shown on it to be a cartographical error. The La Cosa map, which may have been drawn two years earlier than the Cantino, shows a long vague coastline to the northwest of Cuba. It is presumable that land to the north of Cuba was sighted by Spanish skirting the northern coast of Cuba. Thus, before Ponce de León sailed on his great voyage, there was undoubtedly a vague knowledge of a land mass to the north.

Juan Ponce de León had come to America with the fleet which Columbus brought on his second voyage. No mention of his participation in the disputes between the admiral and the dissident colonists is found in the Spanish histories. Ponce, ever a careful and wise proprietor, was in all likelihood just minding his business and working at establishing his position in the new colony. He came from an ancient family that claimed descent from one of the kings of León. While his birthplace is known to have been the village of San Servos, León, the exact year of his birth is unknown.

Ponce received the usual training in the use of arms as a page in the household of a local nobleman. During the wars in Granada he served as a squire. Later he went to Hispaniola with Columbus on the second voyage in 1493 and thereafter busied himself with making his mark in the first years of his stay. He became prominent under Governor Nicolásde Ovando, who had replaced Bobadilla, in his successful pacification of rebellious natives in the northeastern part of the island. For these services he was made the local commander of the area. During his administration there Ponce began to interest himself in the island of Puerto Rico, getting information about it from natives who frequently called at the eastern end of Hispaniola for trading. As a result Ovando ordered Ponce to explore the island and found a settlement. Ponce set

Juan Ponce de Léon, and Ponce fighting with Indians on the Florida coast. From a woodcut published in Madrid, 1726

out on June 12, 1508. On the way, he stopped off at Mona Island and
provided for planting cassava there to supply his new colony. In this
Ponce showed more foresight than many of the conquistadores who
depended largely on foraging for their food. After proving the existence of gold and selecting a site for settlement, Ponce returned to
Hispaniola, where Ovando appointed him governor and chief justice of
the newly explored island. Ponce returned to his new proprietorship
and went ahead with the development of the colony. His administration was both wise and firm, and in it he proved himself to be a man of
promise.

While the development of the infant colony was progressing, events
were taking place in Spain which were to change drastically the course
of Ponce's life and the early history of Spanish America. After the
death of Columbus, his son Diego began a suit to establish his rights as
heir to the concessions made to his father by the Spanish Crown. Diego
was successful, the courts deciding that he was indeed the rightful heir.
The Crown approved the decision but limited the rights to those lands
which actually had been discovered by the admiral. Diego sailed for his
patrimony in July 1509. Upon his arrival, he removed Ponce from the
governorship of Puerto Rico and put two of his own party in charge.
Ovando, having returned to Spain, secured the reappointment of
Ponce. Once back in office, Ponce again had to suppress bloody rebellion of the natives, which had occurred as a result of the abuses perpetrated by the two protégés of Diego. These two, Juan Cerón and
Miguel Díaz, were sent to Spain in chains, but the courts decided they

had been illegally removed and reinstated them. Seeing the fruits of his wise management of the island being destroyed through official stupidity, and facing removal from office for a second time, Ponce resolved to seek his fortune elsewhere.

As a result of Ponce's treatment and because of the urgings of Ovando at court, Ferdinand determined to reward the explorer for his services. A cedula was issued on July 25, 1511, to the Treasurer General of the Indies, directing that Ponce's interests be preserved and that new explorations by him be looked on with favor, and further directing the Treasurer General to discuss these matters with Ponce. As a result Ponce was given permission to search for the island of Bimini to the north.

Ponce's principal objective was the discovery of lands not discovered by Columbus and, therefore, regions to which Diego could have no claim. In Puerto Rico Ponce had again proved himself to be an able organizer and administrator. His greatest desire must have been to reestablish his fortunes in a land where he could be sole proprietor without the danger of losing his labor to some court favorite. Perhaps the legend of the Fountain of Youth played some part in his decision to explore to the north for Bimini. Even the serious literature of the period is full of such tales, and the otherwise realistic Ponce can be excused for having believed that a mirage was the truth. In so believing, he was in tune with the age in which he lived.

With all the preliminary paperwork accomplished and with supplies assembled and men recruited, Ponce set sail from San Germán, Puerto Rico, in March 1513. Within a week they were in the Bahamas, and on the fourteenth reached San Salvador, the site of Columbus's discovery. Running to the northwest, they passed several islands without stopping and on April 2 (Easter) they landed on a coast which they named Florida.* Though it extended out of sight in each direction, they believed it to be another island.

During the next five months Ponce's party explored the coast to the north and then southward, rounding the end of the peninsula. They discovered that remarkable line of small islands, the Florida Keys, and to them gave the name of Los Mártires because they were reminded of a row of early Christian martyrs tied to their stakes as they suffered death from the flames. This name was to remain on the charts through the eighteenth century.

On their run southward they observed for the first time the Florida Current, which flows northward at a pace of two to three knots. They

---

* After Pascua Florida, the Spanish term for Easter.

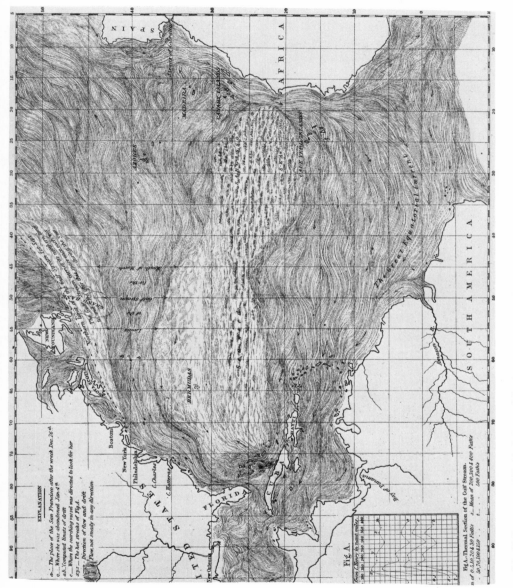

"Gulf Stream and Drift." From Matthew Fontaine Maury's *Physical Geography of the Sea* (1855)

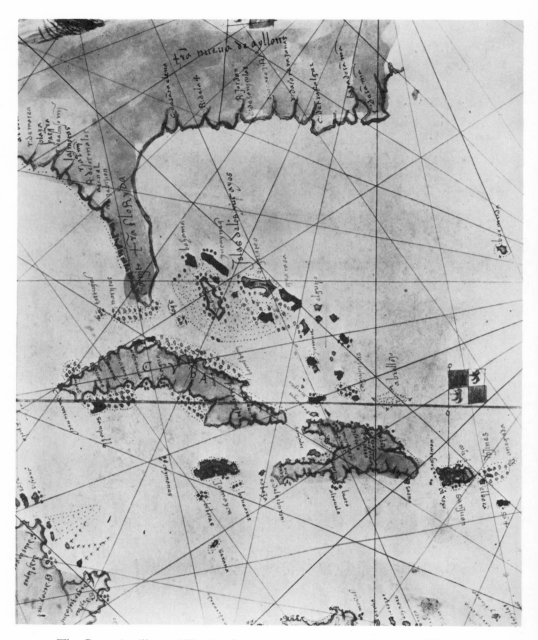

The Great Antilles and Florida, from the map of the world by Juan Vespucci, 1526. The map is reprinted courtesy of the Hispanic Society of America, New York

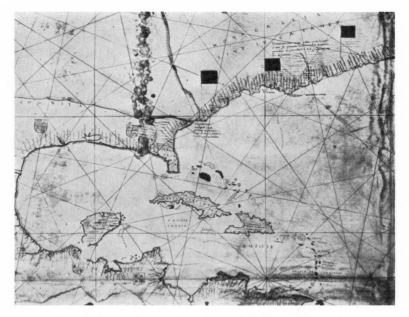

The West Indies and a portion of North America from the Verrazano map of 1529. After just a generation the entire Caribbean
basin and the eastern coast of North America had been almost
completely defined

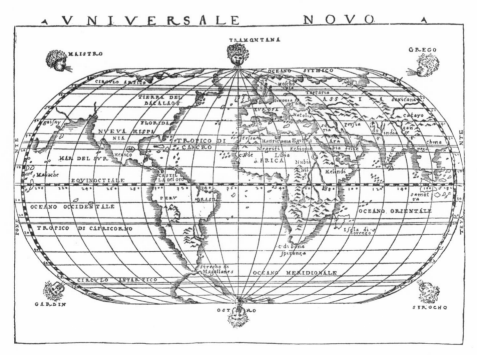

Map of the world by Gastaldi from the first Italian edition of
Ptolomy's *Geography*, 1548

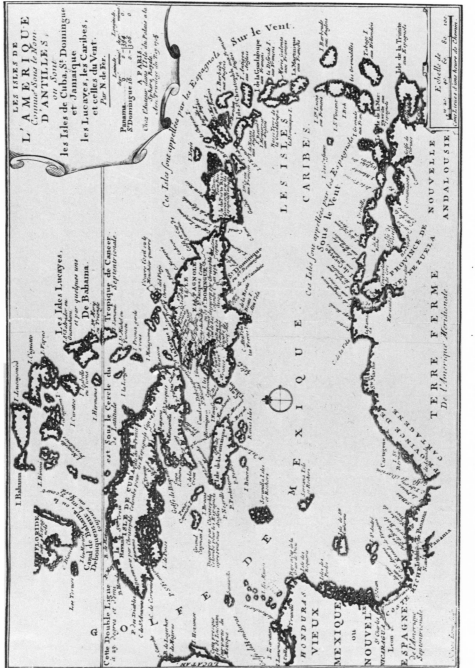

The West Indies, showing the Straits of Florida as "Debouquement la Mer." From a map published in Paris, 1705

had crossed it at night on their voyage to the Florida coast from the Bahamas but were not conscious of it since they could not observe the coast and thus calculate their drift. Herrera says, "And the day following, all three vessels following the sea, they saw a current that, notwithstanding they had a strong wind, they could not go forward." Since they were close enough to shore to sight reference points, it was evident that the current flowed with great force. Two of the ships were able to anchor but lay straining at their cables while the mighty flood rushed past. The brigantine, unable to anchor, was carried back over the horizon. Ponce and his party realized that they had discovered a major ocean current. Although Ponce probably did not realize the significance of this discovery, one of his pilots, Antón de Alaminos, was to remember it on a later voyage as pointing the way to a new and better course from the Indies to Spain. Completing his explorations of the southwestern coast of Florida, Ponce returned to Puerto Rico through the Bahamas. He had learned of the savage Indians of Florida, had determined the great size and fertility of the country, had discovered the Keys, had observed the Florida Current, and was now determined to colonize the new land. He never discovered that Florida was a peninsula and not an island.

Upon his return to Puerto Rico, Ponce resolved to go to Spain and present his claims to Florida at court. A fortunate connection secured him an audience with King Ferdinand, who was favorably impressed with him and his plans for the development of his claim. He was knighted, given a coat of arms, and appointed governor of Bimini and Florida. At the same time the King asked Ponce to undertake an expedition to the island of Guadeloupe to subdue the Caribs there who had been raiding the native settlements of Puerto Rico.

Ponce sailed from Cádiz in the fall of 1514. At Guadeloupe the crafty Caribs succeeded in making off with some laundresses and a small contingent of soldiers sent ashore to guard them. Ponce dared not pursue them without trained guides and dogs. Soon the captives were furnishing the pièce de résistance to a Carib feast and Ponce sailed on to Puerto Rico embarrassed by his poor showing but not as disturbed as the victims had been.

The next seven years saw him busy with his affairs in Puerto Rico, and not until 1521 was he able to mount his expedition for the settlement of his new lands. Now sixty years old but undaunted in spirit, Ponce set out with a well-supplied expedition. But the fates had decided against him and in a battle with the Indians, probably near Estero Bay on the southwestern coast, he was wounded in the thigh. Carried aboard his ship, he was taken to Cuba where he died, probably from infection. Before his death, Ponce, still the practical proprietor, directed that his estate be converted into cash and the cash used to purchase livestock, which should be taken to Mexico and sold to the Cortés party. The profits were to be divided among his heirs. But this man, who had in life suffered from the hostility of dishonest and small characters, was wronged even in death, for the executors of his estate ran off with the money.

Great changes had occurred between 1513, when Ponce discovered Florida, and 1521, when he attempted to settle the land. Other adventurers had been pushing out to the west of Cuba. In February 1517, Captain Francisco Hernández de Córdoba sailed from Ajaruco and, after twenty-one days, touched Yucatan at Cape Catoche. Here he and his party were received by the natives with showers of arrows and rocks. Skirting the Yucatan peninsula they reached Champotón, where disaster struck: fierce native troops attacked and killed forty-eight Spaniards, captured two, and wounded all the rest, including Bernal Díaz del Castillo, whose pen recorded the event for us. The chief pilot was Antón de Alaminos, who had been with Ponce de León at the discovery and exploration of the Florida coast. His presence proved to be most fortunate for the battered Córdoba party: his knowledge permitted him to set a course for Havana by way of Florida, thus avoiding the easterly winds that blow along the northern coast of Cuba and pointing the way to the course which became standard. The survivors arrived in Cuba wounded, exhausted, suffering from malnutrition and extreme thirst, and discouraged beyond measure.

The voyage of Córdoba had indicated the existence of a superior native civilization on the mainland opposite Cuba and soon another expedition was organized. This time it was led by Juan de Grijalva, but it included veterans of the Córdoba expedition, one of whom was Bernal Díaz del Castillo. It left Matanzas Bay in April 1518, proceeded to Cozumel Island off the Yucatan coast and then on to Champotón, where the Spanish again were bloodied in a battle with the natives. From here the party pushed northward up the coast of Mexico to the area north of Tuxpan. Not all the natives were in search of battle and the expedition amassed gold and jewels worth 20,000 pesos. The chief pilot of the expedition was again Antón de Alaminos.

The arrival of the Grijalva expedition at Santiago on October 5 created a stir in Cuba and the governor, Diego Velásquez, was very much impressed by the gold and jade which was displayed, even though some of the "gold" proved to be copper. Bernal Díaz del Castillo describes the arrival: "When the Governor saw the gold that we brought, which was four thousand dollars [pieces of eight] and with that which had already been brought by Pedro de Alvarado, amounted in all to twenty thousand dollars, he was well contented. Then the officers of the King took the Royal Fifth, but when the six hundred axes which we thought were low-grade gold were brought out, they were all rusty like copper which they proved to be, and there was a good laugh at us, and they made great fun of our trading."[1] Velásquez resolved then and there to send a large expedition to Mexico to get the treasure he had seen such fascinating samples of.

As the leader of the new venture the governor chose Hernando Cortés. This young man of thirty-three had already held responsible positions in the colonial governments of Santo Domingo and Cuba, having served in Santiago as an *alcalde.** Cortés was handsome, of pleasing personality, skilled in the military arts, and in the amorous as well. In Spain, while waiting for the expedition of Ovando to sail, Cortés, whom Ovando had appointed a member of his company, was injured when he fell from a wall he was scaling to keep an appointment with a young lady. At the time, this talented lover was just seventeen. Finally he was able to join a fleet which sailed from Sanlúcar de Barrameda in 1504.

Cortés's obvious abilities won him immediate favor in the colonies and Ovando gave him several positions of responsibility and honor. In Cuba Cortés had served Governor Velásquez well and they had become friends. Later this friendship was marred by a violent quarrel about which there are many contradictions in the contemporary accounts. Las Casas, who was there, said that Cortés plotted against the governor and was discovered. Gómara, writing twenty-five years later, after Cortés was famed and powerful, declared that the trouble began over a beautiful lady, Catalina Xuárez, the sister of Cortés's partner, and that Cortés refused to marry her after having exacted favors from her. Perhaps both the stories were true. The second certainly is in keeping with the character of Cortés. Whatever the cause of the quarrel, it was deep and bitter, but in the end the two men were reconciled and Cortés's fortunes in Cuba rose steadily. He amassed a comfortable fortune and lived a happy life with his Catalina, whom he married after all. This was the state of his affairs when Grijalva sailed into Santiago harbor with his loot and caused an epidemic of gold fever.

Velásquez, who is characterized as an avaricious, egotistical, pompous, though altogether faithful, servant of the King, had been sent to Cuba by Diego Columbus to develop that island as an adjunct of His-

---

* A municipal official with both administrative and judicial functions.

Hernándo Cortés, from an early engraving

paniola. After securing his position, he had begun to act like an independent official and in most matters had become such, thus adding disloyalty to the list of his dubious qualities.

Velásquez' choice of Cortés was made after several other candidates had been considered and eliminated. Of all of them, Cortés stood out in popularity, ability, and personality. He was well liked and respected, and there was no doubt about his ability to recruit and lead an expedition. In choosing him, Velásquez was to find that he had served the King exceptionally well but himself very poorly, for Cortés was to give the governor the same treatment he had given Diego Columbus.

Cortés had both friends and enemies in the governor's official family. His friends had helped him secure the appointment; now his enemies attempted to deprive him of it. His energy in organizing the expedition and the strength of personality he began to display apparently raised some doubts in Velásquez' mind. The governor was quite perplexed by his problem. Having double-crossed his patron, he feared the same treatment at the hands of his newly chosen captain. Yet, without Cortés's forceful leadership, the expedition might accomplish no more than Grijalva's had. The governor's doubts were increased by the constant prodding of Cortés's enemies. When Cortés's secret friends learned of the governor's doubts, they immediately sent word of them to the expedition. Cortés knew now that he must get away as quickly as possible and rushed his preparations. The future conqueror of Mexico had no intention of relinquishing his command under any circumstances. He had invested his entire fortune in the expedition and would face financial ruin as well as complete disgrace if he submitted to the governor's probable intentions. The expedition sailed from Santiago on November 18, 1518. Soon after the departure, Velásquez finally decided to remove Cortés and issued instructions for his arrest and return to Santiago. But Cortés's friends and the loyalty of his men and officers allowed him to get clear of Cuba after several stops for more supplies.

On March 4, 1519, the expedition landed on the coast of Mexico. In three years of fighting, often against tremendous armies of natives, against intrigue in his own ranks, and against the efforts of the infuriated Velásquez to remove him, Cortés proved himself to be a consummate general and statesman. Now striking terror into the hearts of native enemies, now conciliating them, he was able to form alliances with tribes that were traditional enemies of Montezuma. That ruler, terrified at the strangeness of the enemies he faced and fearing that they were indeed gods, attempted to bribe Cortés to leave the country. The Spanish leader had long since resolved to conquer the new coun-

A knight of the early sixteenth century, by Albrecht Dürer. The mounted, armored troops of Cortés wrought terror and havoc among the native Mexican warriors. From the Biblioteca Ambrosiana, Milan

el Grande Templo de Mexico

A great temple in Mexico after an Italian engraving of the sixteenth century

try or lose all in the attempt. Montezuma's rich gifts merely whetted the appetites of the Spanish for more treasure and strengthened their determination to conquer the entire country.

Bernal Díaz del Castillo, that veteran of the Córdoba and Grijalva expeditions and now with Cortés, described the arrival of the ambassador and presentation of the gifts:

> when these people arrived and came before our Captain they first of all kissed the earth and then fumigated him and all the soldiers who were standing around him, with incense which they brought in braziers of pottery. Cortés received them affectionately and seated them near himself, and that chief who came with the present had been appointed spokesman together with Tendile [Teuhtlilli, a local governor under Montezuma]. After welcoming us to the country and after many courteous speeches had passed he ordered the presents which he had brought to be displayed, and they were placed on mats over which were spread cotton cloths. The first article presented was a wheel like a sun, as big as a cartwheel, with many sorts of pictures on it, the whole of fine gold, and a wonderful thing to behold, which those who afterwards weighed it said was worth more than ten thousand dollars. Then another wheel was presented of greater size made of silver of great brilliancy in imitation of the moon with other figures shown on it, and this was of great value as it was very heavy—and the chief brought back the helmet full of fine grains of gold,* just as they are got out of the mines, and this was worth three thousand dollars. This gold in the helmet was worth more to us than if it had contained twenty thousand dollars, because it showed us that there were good mines there. Then were brought twenty golden ducks, beautifully worked and very natural looking, and some [ornaments] like dogs, and many articles of gold worked in the shape of tigers and lions and monkeys, and ten collars beautifully worked and other necklaces; and twelve arrows and a bow with its string, and two rods like staffs of justice, five palms long, all in beautiful hollow work of fine gold. Then there were presented crests of gold and plumes of rich green feathers, and others of silver, and fans of the same materials, and deer copied in hollow gold and many other things I cannot remember.[2]

The Spaniards were enthralled at the sight of this exotic, beautiful, and priceless array. Here before them were the best artistic products of a civilization undreamed of just a few months before. The unfortunate Montezuma, hoping to buy the departure of the Spanish men-gods

---

* Previously, when Tendile had taken the Spaniards' presents to Montezuma, Cortés had lent him a helmet that Tendile thought Montezuma would be interested in seeing and had asked that it be returned full of grains of gold.

from his territory, had only sharpened their greed and had, with his generosity, assured his own destruction and the collapse of his empire. The Spanish resolved to march inland at the earliest possible moment. Before he left, Cortés knew he must make some overture to the Spanish Crown to secure favor at court. His position was completely without legal foundation. His commission had been revoked by Velásquez, and he had resisted attempts to place him under arrest and to remove him from his command. His eloquence, and the eloquence of the wealth they had seen, won over those Spaniards sent to take him in the name of the governor of Cuba. Cortés had himself proclaimed captain general of the colony he established at Vera Cruz. All of his acts were approved by his company and he was very careful to preserve a record of all matters of public concern. His acts were a betrayal of Velásquez—this cannot be denied. Neither can it be denied that a man of lesser courage, resourcefulness, and determination probably would have failed.

To inform Charles V of the events which had occurred, Cortés, with characteristic thoroughness, penned the first of five letters to the emperor. This letter has been lost, but fortunately, at the same time Cortés wrote, so did the "Judiciary and Municipal Authorities" of the city of Vera Cruz, officials who had been duly elected when Cortés founded the city. Undoubtedly the two letters gave the same account of events that had occurred since Cortés's departure from Cuba, so we do know what Cortés must have said. The officials gave the king an account of the previous attempts to explore and trade and a thorough description of the Cortés expedition. They informed the king of the first meetings with the natives and described the cities they had seen and the customs of the Mexicans. All through the letter they took notice of the base qualities of Velásquez and his efforts to thwart their exertions. In effect they said that Velásquez was for Velásquez, and they were for the King (the sixteenth-century Spaniard was an accomplished throatcutter). They then informed the King:

> Some of those noble persons who came in this armada, gentlemen, and sons of gentlemen, zealous in the service of our Lord, and of Your Royal Highnesses, and desirous for the exaltation of your royal crown, and the extension of your dominions, and the increase of your revenues, assembled and spoke with the Captain Fernando Cortés, saying that this land was good and that, judging by the sample of gold which that cacique had brought, it was reasonable to believe that it must be very rich, and that he and all his Indians were well disposed towards us. For these reasons, it seemed to us that it was not advantageous for Your Majesties' service to do as Diego Velásquez had ordered the said Cap-

n Fernando Cortés to do, which was to trade for all the gold we could, and, having obtained it, to return to the island of Fernandina, in order that the said Diego Velásquez, and the said Captain might profit exclusively by it, and that it seemed better to all of us that a town should be founded and peopled there in the name of Your Royal Highnesses. In this, there should be a court of justice, so that you would have your jurisdiction in this country just as in your kingdom and dominions. . . .

Having decided this, we all agreed with one accord and mind, and we made a requirement to the said Captain in which we told him that, as he saw how agreeable it would be to the service of God, Our Lord, and of Your Majesties, that this country should be peopled . . . we required him to cease trading, as he was doing, inasmuch as it was equivalent to destroying the country to a great extent, and that Your Majesties would thus be but poorly served; and that, for the same reason, we asked and required him to name alcaldes, and municipal authorities, in the name of Your Royal Highnesses, for the town which was to be founded and built by us. . . . This requirement having been made to the said Captain, he replied that he would give his answer the next day; and the said Captain, having seen how all that we had asked him to do would be profitable to the service of Your Royal Highnesses, answered us the next day, saying that he was exclusively devoted to the service of Your Majesties, and that, without considering the profit which might result to him from carrying on the trading as planned, so as to recover the great expenses which had been sustained out of his property in fitting out that armada with the said Diego Velásquez, but rather putting aside everything else, he was glad and satisfied to do whatever we had asked him to do, inasmuch as it was advantageous to the service of Your Royal Highnesses. Immediately, therefore, he began with great diligence to found and people a town, to which the name was given of Rica Villa de la Vera Cruz. He named those of us who will sign at the end alcaldes and municipal officers of the said town receiving from us the oath in the name of Your Royal Highnesses, with the solemnity customary in such cases; after which we assembled the next day in our council and assembly chamber, and, being thus assembled, we sent to summon the Captain Fernando Cortés, and we asked him in the name of Your Royal Highnesses to show us the powers and instructions, which the said Diego Velásquez had given him for coming to these parts. He immediately sent for these, and showed them to us, and, having been seen and read by us, and well examined according to the best of our understanding, it seemed to us that, by those powers and instructions, the said Captain Fernando Cortés, had no longer any authority, and that, they having expired, he could no longer exercise the office of justice or of captain.

It seemed to us, Very Excellent Princes, that, for the sake of peace

and concord among us, and in order to govern us well, it was necessary
to install a person for Your Royal service to act in the name of Your
Majesties in the said town, and in these parts as Chief Justice, and
Captain, and head, whom we could all respect and obey until we might
give account of everything to Your Royal Highnesses, so that you
could provide as best suited your service. Recognizing that to no one
could we better give such a charge than to the said Fernando Cortés,
because, besides being a most suitable person, he is moreover very
zealous in the service of Your Majesties, as well as being very experienced in these parts and islands, of which he has always given good
proofs, for having spent all that he possessed to serve Your Majesties in
this armada, and heeded so little . . . his possible gains and profits from
continuing to trade, we therefore elected him, in the name of Your
Royal Highnesses, to the office of Justice and Superior Alcalde, receiving from him the oath which is required in such cases. And, having
done this as profitable to the service of Your Majesties, we received
him in Your Royal name in our Council and Assembly Chamber, as
Chief Justice and Governor of Your Royal arms, and thus he is, and will
continue, until Your Majesties provide what is best for your service.[3]

Thus, by a face-saving legal farce, Cortés had resigned the power
given him by Velásquez, had placed that power in the hands of a
council which he appointed, and then was in turn elected chief justice
and captain by the council. By this device he had severed his connections with Velásquez, had established an independent colony with himself as its head, and by reporting all of this in great detail to Charles
through his letter and that of the council, had placed the decision for
the future of the colony directly in the hands of the King, thus elimi-
nating Velásquez from the picture. To assure a kind ear from the
Crown, Cortés and his lieutenants punctuated their communications
with the treasure which had been sent by Montezuma:

Having done as stated, and, being all assembled in our Council Chamber, we agreed to write to Your Majesties, and to send you, in addition
to the one-fifth part which belongs to your rents, according to Your
Royal prescriptions, all the gold, and silver, and valuables which we
have obtained in this country, on account of its being the first, and
above which we keep nothing for ourselves, we place this at the disposi-
tion of Your Highnesses, as a proof of our very good will for your
service, as we have heretofore done with our persons and property.

Alonso Hernández Puetocarrero and Francisco de Montejo were
selected as the emissaries to carry the letters and treasure to Spain.
Then "the best ship in the fleet was got ready, and two pilots were

appointed, one of these being Antón de Alaminos who knew the passage through the Bahama Channel, for he was the first man to sail through it."

Thus, the trickle of treasure that began with the first voyage through the Straits of Florida was, within a generation, to become a flood. And yet while the straits were to become a kind of pipeline through which treasure flowed to Spain, they were left unprotected. To the west lay the peninsula of Florida, peopled by savage and war-like tribes who would fight at the sight of an European. To the east lay the Bahamas, by the time of the conquest of Mexico almost deserted, having been the target of Spanish slave raiders who carried off the island peoples to the mines of Hispaniola and Cuba and the pearl fisheries of Margarita Island. A little over a century after their discovery, the Bahamas were a void, stripped of their population and forests by the Spanish, who took no permanent interest in them.

This neglect the Spanish would come to regret. In the fever of history's greatest treasure hunt, they were too occupied to appreciate the vulnerable position of the route by which that treasure moved to Spain. The later attempts to settle Florida seem to have been unrelated to the question of the protection of the route, and so the fleets sailed along hundreds of miles of coastline that was unoccupied and unfortified. Not until a direct threat was made by the enemies of Spain was any serious effort made to guard the route by establishing a stronghold in Florida.

II

Treasure

Yet it is a thing worth of consideration, that the wisdom of the
Eternall Lord would inrich those partes of the World which
are most remote, and which are peopled with men of lesse
civilitie and governement, planting there great store of mines,
and in the greatest abundance that ever were, thereby to invite
men to search out those lands, and to possesse them to the end
that by this occasion, they might plant religion.
  —José de Acosta,
  The Natural and Moral History of the Indies, 1590

 IT HAS BEEN SAID that "gold, glory and gospel" brought the
Spanish to America. While thirst for glory, desire for adventure and exaltation of the Church and the Holy Faith were important
factors in the Spanish conquest of America, we may safely assume that
cupidity was the principal motivation. Even though such clever thinkers
as Father Acosta sought to adorn the Spanish motive with the trappings
of religion and to ignore the tremendous price in blood which "men of
lesse civilitie and governement" paid for the wealth which flowed into
Spanish coffers, the fact remains that the treasure of America was the
product of human suffering on a vast scale.

The sum total of treasure which the Spanish extracted from the
New World was enormous. Not, perhaps, as great as the gossip of the
time proclaimed or the later writers were wont to believe, but sufficient to alter materially the economy of Europe: "Increasing production of gold and silver was the most important cause of the price
revolution of the sixteenth and seventeenth centuries. As by far the
greater part of this metallic wealth came from America, the function
of Spain in the movement was a very significant one. She became the
distributor of the precious metals to the rest of Europe. And since she
'produced little and manufactured less' she performed this function
with an efficiency which startled even the Spaniard."[1] It is significant
that dollar-size silver coins, rarely struck in the late fifteenth and early
sixteenth centuries, were by 1560 being issued by many principalities

of Europe. The medieval silver penny and the four-penny piece or groat had given way to a system based on the dollar or crown.

It would be impossible today to determine the exact amount of gold, silver, pearls, and emeralds that went to Spain from the Indies. The amounts stated by the more reliable sixteenth-century writers are probably correct. Later authors undoubtedly exaggerated the figures. The trickle of gold which began to flow from the islands of Hispaniola and Cuba became a respectable stream with the wealth that came from the conquest of Mexico.

The first treasure Cortés had sent to Emperor Charles V and Queen Joanna, his mother, with the pilot Antón de Alaminos and two of his other officers arrived safely in Spain, was received by the Casa de Contratación de las Indias (House of Trade of the Indies) in Seville, and sent on to the Emperor in Valladolid. It was described as follows:

A gold necklace composed of seven pieces, with 185 small emeralds set in it, and 232 gems, like rubies, from which hung 27 small bells of gold, and some pearls.

Another necklace of four pieces of gold, with 102 red gems, like rubies, 172 emeralds, 10 fine pearls, set in it, and 26 little golden bells pendant.

Two wheels, one of gold representing the sun, the other of silver bearing the image of the moon, 28 hands in circumference, and bearing various figures of animals, and other devices, beautifully worked in relief.

A head-dress of wood, decorated with gold and gems, with 25 golden bells pendant; instead of a plume it had a green bird, whose eyes, beak, and feet, were of gold.

A gold bracelet; a small sceptre with two rings of gold, set with pearls at the ends.

Four tridents, tied with feathers of different colours, and pearl points tied with gold thread.

Several deerskin shoes, sewn with gold thread, and having soles of brilliant blue and white stones.

A shield of wood and leather, decorated with hanging bells of gold, and having gold plates in the centre, carved with the figure of the god of war, surrounded by four heads of a lion, a tiger, an eagle, and an owl, represented with their hair and feathers.

Several skins, tanned with the hair and feathers on them.

Twenty-four curious and beautiful golden shields, decorated with feathers and small pearls, four others of feathers and silver.

Four fish, two ducks, and other birds, made of gold.

Two sea-shells, imitated in gold, and a large crocodile, girt with golden threads.

A large mirror, and several small ones, of gold.

Several head-dresses, and crowns of feathers and gold, ornamented with pearls and gems.

Several large plumes of beautiful feathers, of various colours, spangled with gold and small pearls.

Several fans; some of gold and feathers, others of feathers alone, but all very rich.

A variety of cotton robes; some all white, others chequered white and black, or red, green, yellow, and blue, the outside being shaggy, and the inside smooth, without colour.

A number of coats, handkerchiefs, bedcovers, tapestries, and carpets of cotton stuffs.

There were several Mexican books, written in hieroglyphics, on their paper, which was about the consistency of light pasteboard. Peter Martyr describes them as folding tablets, and says of the writing, "*Sunt characteres a nostris valde dissimilis, Egypteas fere formas aemu-lantur*" (*De Insulis nuper inventis*).

Gómara says the paper was made of cotton, and a kind of gum, or paste; sometimes also of aloe leaves; Peter Martyr describes it as made of fine crushed bark, kneaded together with a gum.[2]

After the conqueror had entered Mexico City and had taken Montezuma prisoner, he persuaded that unfortunate ruler to turn over to him the entire treasure of the Mexican Crown. Bernal Díaz describes the scene:

> After some more polite conversation, Montezuma at once sent his Mayordomos to hand over all the treasure and gold and wealth that was in that plastered chamber [in the Royal Palace], and in looking it over and taking off all the embroidery with which it was set, we were occupied for three days, and to assist us in undoing it and taking it to pieces, there came Montezuma's goldsmiths from the town named Azcapotzalco, and I say that there was so much, that after it was taken to pieces there were three heaps of gold, and they weighed more than six hundred thousand pesos, as I shall tell further on, without the silver and many other rich things, and not counting in this the ingots and slabs of gold, and the gold in grains from the mines. We began to melt it down with the help of the Indian goldsmiths and they made broad bars of it, each measuring three fingers of the hand across. . . .
>
> The gold I have spoken about was marked with an iron stamp, and the stamp was the royal arms. The mark was not put on the rich jewels which it did not seem to us should be taken to pieces.[3]

Can one estimate the loss to the world of this priceless art? Much of it was lost in the ensuing retreat from the city but the successful subjugation of all of Mexico brought into the empire of Charles V one of the richest colonies in the history of man, with gold and enormous silver deposits yet to be discovered.*

The pattern of exploitation was pretty much the same whether it was Hispaniola, Cuba, Panama, Mexico, or Peru. First, the invading Spaniards looted the natives of any gold or silver they might possess, killing them if necessary. Then the graves and temples were systematically stripped of any precious offerings or ornament. In the process of conquest the population of the country was decimated and the native leaders killed; even the unresisting ones were often put to the sword. After the country was subjugated, the remaining Indians, in the name of Christian education, were apportioned out to the Spanish soldiers according to the rank of the soldier, and were then forced to work the placed deposits of gold. Many of them were literally worked to death. The last stage consisted of locating and mining the lodes which fed the placer deposits. Here the natives suffered most. Accustomed to living free and comparatively sedentary lives, they died by the thousands in the dank mines.

The first stages of exploitation were developed during the subjugation of Mexico by Cortés. The working of the placer deposits and the establishment of mines soon followed. After looting the natives and the temples, the Spanish were greatly disappointed to find that the Mexican placer deposits were quite poor. The great amounts of gold Montezuma and his followers possessed had apparently represented the fruits of many generations of labor and had deceived the Spaniards, who naturally assumed the native deposits to be very rich. Had it not been for the discovery of extremely rich silver mines Mexico might have been spared the attention of the Spanish miners and have become a purely agricultural nation in which the lot of the native would have been much better.

The first mines opened were those near the capital city and had probably been worked superficially by the natives. Taxco, Zultepec and Pachuca were opened before 1532. By 1558, Zacatecas, Vetagrande, San Luis Potosí, Sombrerete and Guanajuato were producing. During the seventeenth century few new silver deposits were opened but in the following century many new and rich mines were discovered.

---

* The Emperor's share of the main treasure of Mexico sent to Spain in 1522 was captured by French corsairs and fell into the hands of Francis I. The objects in the first shipment found their way into collections in Florence, Italy, and Vienna, where some of them can be seen today.

Indians surrendering treasure to the Spanish conquerors,
a fanciful engraving by Théodore de Bry, late sixteenth
century

The silver mines at Potosí in Upper Peru (Bolivia). The "silver mountain"
is in the background. From an anonymous painting of the sixteenth century

With the conquest of Peru, Colombia and Chile, additional wealth of enormous value flowed into Spain. As in Mexico, the golden ransom of the King of the Incas was of great value—$4,500,000; and the result was the same, the death of the prince after the ransom was paid. As in Mexico, the natives of South America had obtained most of their gold from deposits in the gravel of stream beds or easily worked surface veins. They had little silver. Mining was only the superficial scratching of the outcroppings. The natives left alive after the pillaging of their nation were set to work in the mines which the Spanish opened in great numbers. In 1539 Francisco Pizarro sank a shaft at Porco. Shortly thereafter, the rich mines of Potosí began to produce and the greatest flood of silver the world had ever seen flowed into Spain and the rest of Europe.

The deposits of Chile, from the invasion of Pedro de Valdivia in 1540 to the end of Spanish rule in 1818, furnished an estimated $125 million in gold alone to the Spanish. Added to this was the gold and silver of Central America, the pearls of Margarita, the emeralds of Colombia, rare woods, and drugs and other natural products, including dyestuffs.

In 1503 the Casa de Contratación was organized to control all the trade with the Spanish colonies in America and from that year the records of royal income show a steady increase:

Year	Maravedís*	Equivalent in Ducats
1503	3,000,000	8,000
1505	22,000,000	58,660
1512	34,000,000	88,640
1518	46,000,000	122,600
1535	119,000,000	317,250

* Under laws dated 1475 and 1497, the maravedí, a copper coin, was tariffed at 375 to the ducat, which was gold.

In 1535 the system of treasure fleets started and treasure began to be accumulated in large shipments. The fleet of Blasco Núñez Vela, which sailed in 1538, carried on the fleet treasurer's account 989,086 ducats. Of this, 750,000 ducats belonged to the King. The Peruvian treasure constituted the bulk: 268,750 ducats in gold and 335,000 in silver. The treasure from Cartagena was valued at almost 80,000 ducats, including 208 ducats worth of pearls from Margarita and a giant gold nugget weighing over fourteen pounds and valued at 1,630 ducats. The balance of the treasure came from the islands of Central America. In 1543 the fleet of Martín Alonso brought 573,000 ducats of Peruvian and Mexican gold and silver and over 9,000 ducats in pearls. In 1550 Pedro de la Gasca returned to Spain with 1,500,000 ducats for the King's account alone. By 1600 the Crown's annual receipts from the Indies averaged 2,000,000 ducats a year.

Father Acosta in his *Natural and Moral History of the Indies* says that the fleet of 1585, with which he returned to Spain, carried 12 chests of gold each weighing a hundred pounds; 11,000,000 silver coins, most probably pieces of eight; two chests of emeralds, each chest weighing a hundred pounds.

Antonio Vázquez de Espinosa, a barefoot Carmelite friar who traveled in America in the early seventeenth century, estimated the wealth received from the Indies up to the year 1628 at 1 billion 800 million pesos. Of the wealth from the Potosí range in Upper Peru (Bolivia) he says:

So huge is the wealth which has been taken out of this range since the year 1545, when it was discovered, up to the present year of 1628, which makes 83 years that they have been working and reducing its ores, that merely from the registered mines, as appears from an examination of most of the accounts in the royal records, 326,000,000 assay pesos have been taken out. At the beginning when the ore was richer and easier to get out, for then there were no Mita Indians and no mercury process, in the 40 years between 1545 and 1585, they took out 111,000,000 of assay silver. From the year 1585 up to 1628, 43 years, although the mines are harder to work, for they are deeper down, with the assistance of 13,300 Indians whom His Majesty has granted to the mine owners on that range, and of other hired Indians, who come there freely and voluntarily to work at days wages, and with the great advantage of the mercury process, in which none of the ore or the silver is wasted, and with the better knowledge of the technique which the miners now have, they have taken out 215,000,000 assay pesos. That, plus the 111 extracted in the 40 years previous to 1585, makes 326,000,-000 assay pesos, not counting the great amount of silver secretly taken from these mines to be registered in others paying only 10 percent tithes, the silver in the 20 percent impost, the currency circulating in those kingdoms, the silver plate and vessels of private individuals, that in the churches in the form of chalices, crosses, lamps, and other vessels for decoration and use in divine service, and that that has been taken secretly to Spain, paying no 20 percent or registry fee, and to other countries outside Spain, and to the Philippines and China, which is beyond all reckoning; but I should venture to imagine and even assert that what has been taken from the Potosí range must be as much again as what paid the 20 percent royal impost.[4]

A fair estimate of the precious metals and gems going to Spain during the period of her rule in the New World is $4 billion to $6 billion, which then represented perhaps five times the value a like sum would have today.

Father Acosta's account of the illicit silver on which payment of tax was evaded points up the serious problem the Spanish Crown had in controlling the mining and shipment of precious metals. Regulations took several forms, all directed to the same end—the maintenance of the royal monopoly through the regulation of the mining, assaying, taxing and shipping to Spain of silver and gold.

In the earliest period of the conquest the old Spanish laws governing mining were enforced in the new fields. These laws declared all deposits of precious metals the property of the Crown. In 1501 Ferdinand and Isabella specifically forbade the washing or digging for gold without their express permission. As a system for assaying, taxing and stamping was established, these laws were replaced by more liberal ones. In 1504 Spaniards were permitted to mine without royal permission if they first registered their claims and swore to bring in all their gold and silver to the royal smeltery (Casa de Fundición) for smelting, assaying, taxing and stamping. No metal could move legally in the channels of commerce without the stamps, which indicated that the royal tax had been paid. Much gold and silver undoubtedly did circulate without authority since the Spaniard was as competent a tax dodger as some of his later counterparts. The ordinance of 1504 was extended in 1526, when Indians were also given rights under it, but not until 1584 were mines made the permanent possessions of their discoverers with the right of sale or lease.

At first, the King took an enormous proportion of the metals washed or dug by the colonists, but it was soon apparent that this burden would discourage the development of deposits and the royal share was lowered. In 1500 the King's share was one half; shortly thereafter it was lowered to one third; and in 1504 it was made a fifth, the *quinto*. In areas where washing and mining presented special difficulties the royal share was often lowered to one tenth, the *diezmo*. In Mexico the *quinto* was generally in effect until 1716 and in Peru until 1735. In those years the *diezmo* replaced it. There were exceptions to these percentages throughout the entire period of Spanish rule in America, as there were generally exceptions to every Spanish law.

The methods of smelting and assaying silver in Peru are described by Antonio Vázquez de Espinosa, writing in 1628:

The mills to grind the ore are run by water, like water mills (*acenas*) or gristmills; for that purpose they have around the range or at some distance from it 16 reservoirs; the most remote, called Tavaconuno, is 3 leagues off. In these they collect the water which falls in the rainy season; the mills are all built and arranged in order, and when the grinding is to start, they let the water into a channel passing from one to another, for as soon as it issues from one, it goes into another; the whole Potosí range is like that. Most of the mills have two heads (of water), with great heavy stone hammers which pound the ore, the ones rising and the others falling, just as in a fulling mill, until the ore, hard as flint though some of it is, has been reduced to meal; then they sift it through sieves set up for that purpose; in 24 hours they will sift over 30 quintals.*

They set great store on the water in these reservoirs; as soon as one is empty, they start on another, for although they are all divided up and apportioned, they are arranged in such a way that each distributes its water to the first mill, and from that on in order. This Potosí range is the larger; most years, when the water gets low, they have processions and prayers for rain to fill the reservoirs; and according as the year is wet or dry, they run the mills a longer or shorter time, to grind the ore. The Tarapaya range is the shorter; the mills there grind with the water of a stream on which they are built.

After grinding and sifting the ore they dump it into containers for the furnaces and saturate it with brine, using for every 50 quintals of ore, 5 of salt, more or less, according to the quality of the ore, for it to eat and consume it, or part of it, and scour it. Then they put the mercury in, so that by this arrangement it may better embrace and combine with the silver, and shorten the process, and bring about a union of the mercury with the silver, having thrown salt in with it; they knead it twice a day with their feet, just as they do clay in the making of tile or brick, and they remix it with mercury twice a day; then they put the containers on furnaces and start the fires underneath in small ovens, so that the heat may cause the mercury to amalgamate more quickly with the silver.

Although the ore all comes from one range, the mines and the ore are usually of a different grade, and so different materials are necessary for their treatment; for some they put in salt and lime, and iron or copper ground up in water, for which processing they have some small mills; in others they put lead and tin; other ore—the *negrillo* (stephanite)—is first roasted in ovens for its grinding in the mills. Thus in some cases

---

* About 3,000 pounds avoirdupois.

they use all materials, in some, many, and in some, fewer, according to the need and to the grade of the ore; if low, the quicksilver is hampered in its union and amalgamation with the silver. With all this preparation and solicitude, in one case it may come to 20, in others more or less; with the fire or heat they apply, and these materials mentioned, the quicksilver absorbs the silver within 8 days.

At the moment which seems right to them, according to the ore and the treatment given it, the mercury having already absorbed the silver, they dump this ore into large tubs with water running into them. These have a device with paddles or wheels in continual motion inside the tubs, so that the ore dust is carried off by the running water, and the combined mercury and silver, being heavier, goes to the bottom and settles there in tubs. The rest of the ore, which was not well washed in these tubs or other puddling operations, they finish refining, until the silver and mercury alone are left without any dust. This lump, which is soft as dough, is put in a linen cloth and squeezed hard until they press out and separate all the mercury they can from the silver. Then they put the lumps of silver which have had the mercury squeezed out, into clay forms or pots shaped like sugar loaves, with an aperture at the end of the narrowest point, and set them in ovens specially made for the purpose; when they start the fire, the mercury goes out through the hole as vapor or smoke, but nothing is lost, thanks to the preparation made.

After the fire has severed the mercury from his friend the silver, the cone (*pina*) of pure silver comes out the size and shape of a loaf of very white sugar, for silver looks very white and spongy. Each cone is usually of 40 silver marks,* slightly more or less; that is the ordinary product from one container; but if the grade and richness of the ore permit, they may get two cones, as happened at the beginning when the rich range was first exploited; the same is true of certain new mines; but ordinarily it is only one. They make up a bar by melting two together. The silver refined by the mercury process is so fine and white that it is always above the 2,380 grade; and to make it fit for use by the silversmiths, they reduce the grade to 11 dineros and 4 grains† which is the legal sterling standard, by the addition of copper or other alloy. . . .

The silver which is extracted and collected from the ore dust is much finer than that which they get first from the ore; it is the most delicate part that runs off with the mud and ore dust in the first washings and rewashings of the ore in the tubs. Of this dust, which contains much silver that has passed through and escaped the mercury process, they treat every year more than 300,000 quintals, roasting it in

---

* The mark weighed 11 ounces; the cone, therefore, would weigh 440 ounces.
† The exact purity of the silver is unclear here. Vázquez means that the cones from the furnace are nearly pure silver and are reduced to about 925 parts fine silver to 1,000 parts metal for working by the silversmiths.

more than 200 (700?)* furnaces maintained for this purpose on the Potosí and Tarapaya ranges. Thus they recover a large amount of silver, which will amount each year to over 300,000 pesos; this is the finest and highest-grade silver of all that is handled. Together with it they recover more than 2,000 quintals of mercury carried off with it in the ore dust; this amount, plus over 6,000 more brought from the Huancavelica mines, is used up every year at Potosí alone in the reduction of the ore and the silver.

After this silver has been run into bars, the Assayer takes a bit from each and weighs it by itself to see what grade it is. He puts each bit of silver into a receptacle made of ashes from ground burnt bones, cast in a mold, each with its label; these are like the little molds used by the silversmiths in casting silver or gold. These jars or molds are used for the assay sample and when they take it for the assay, His Majesty collects his royal 20 percent.

They assay them in a jeweler's furnace at his direction; the indications are easily recognized. He applies a very hot flame which melts the metal contained in each mold; and if the silver contains copper, tin, or lead, the intensity of the flame makes it go up in smoke and disappear, leaving the silver purified and very fine. When it is in this state, even though liquid and molten, and the jar turned upside down, not a drop falls out; by this and by its color, the Assayer knows when it is refined. Then he takes the jars from the flame and with a very accurate balance reweighs each sample or bit by itself; and according to the shrinkage or loss in weight, he determines the grade of each bar; if it has lost little or nothing, its sterling quality is recognized; and others are graded according to the loss or shrinkage shown by the bit or sample. This assay and weighing is done where there is not a breath of wind or other interference that can affect the accuracy and precision of the weighing, for on that depends the determination of the grade of each bar. They always take the assay of many bars together; otherwise it would be a very hard and tiring operation. After doing this, each bar is graded and marked according to the bit taken from it, with certainty, so that by this test they know the grade, price, and value of each bar.

This is the way in which its fineness and standard are known. Before becoming a bar, it passes through and suffers great torture, for in their covetousness for it, men go where it is ever since they have made acquaintance with it; they bore into the bowels and center of the earth, bursting open the strongboxes in which Nature created it, given it for its defense and preservation. To get it out, much suffering is endured; they carry it off to the mills where they grind and pound with heavy hammers the rock and ore in which it took form; then they sift it, and after sifting it they dump it into troughs or containers with lime, salt, iron-water (*agua de hierro*), and the other materials mentioned, to

* The translator was in doubt as to the number in the manuscript.

scour it; according as is required, they knead it and tread upon it many times, going over it all again, and then they set that ferret, mercury, upon it, for him to search out and appropriate the silver in all the mud in which it lies; then they put the flame to it to help the mercury; and after the amalgamation, they wash it in tubs, as has been said. Then when the mercury and silver are clean, they give it the water-cure torture (*tormento de toca*), separating the mercury from the silver; for this they put that dough or putty of the two amalgamated metals into a linen cloth and garrot it hard, squeezing the mercury out; and since not all of it comes out, they apply fire to it, and thus they get it completely alone, severed from the mercury and from the earth which created it. And now that it has become pure, they again torture it with fire to make it into bars; it goes through so many tortures that the Holy Ghost uses it in the comparison with the righteous: Malachi III:3, "And he shall purify the sons of Levi, and purge them as gold and silver"; and Eccles. II: "Like silver purged of earth, purged sevenfold."[5]

The silver was cast into loaf-shaped bars weighing about seventy pounds, wedges weighing from two to ten pounds, or cakes of a pound or two. The assaying of gold was carried out in much the same manner but the requirements for precision in the operation were much greater. Gold was cast into bars and cakes weighing ounces instead of pounds.

As the economies of the Spanish colonies developed, it became evident that a circulating currency had to be provided. The first mint is believed to have been established on Hispaniola, where copper 4-maravedí pieces were struck. This issue apparently provided for the everyday transactions of the marketplace before the great wealth of the mainland had made its effect felt on prices. During the first years in Mexico after the conquest, the scarcity of circulating money became a serious deterrent to economic development. The Spanish met the problem by melting gold dust and nuggets and making disks marked with the weight only. Pradeau states that these disks circulated into the reign of Philip II (none of them have survived).[6] In 1526 the *cabildo* (municipal council) of Mexico City passed a resolution which permitted individuals to bring their gold to the Casa de Fundición to be made into slugs of definite purity weighing from 24 grains to 384 grains (2 tomines to 4 pesos de oro).[7]

The further development of the country made the establishment of a mint imperative. The shipment of coin from Spain and the emergency coinage of disks and slugs was completely inadequate for a rapidly growing country of great wealth. In 1535 a royal cedula was issued directing the establishment of a mint in Mexico City. The striking of silver coins began probably in the month of April 1536. From

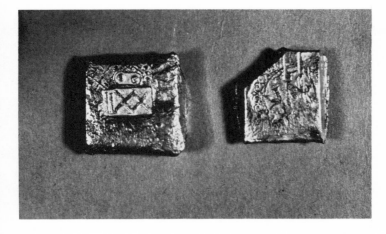

Sections of gold bar

A gold "quoit" weighing almost two pounds

Small gold bar of six ounces

1 CM.
½ IN.

this time to the end of the Spanish administration in Mexico the mint coined about 2.68 billion silver pieces of eight and its subdivisions. The first issues of Charles and Joanna were handsome well-struck coins of the value of ¼, ½, 1, 2 and 4 reales. During the reign of Philip II the mint began to produce pieces of eight or dollars. Until the end of Philip's reign the workmanship of the mint was on a comparatively high standard even though the coins were produced with sledge-hammer and simple dies. Early in the reign of Philip III demands for greater output in the mint led to the striking of crude, irregularly shaped coins known as cobs, from the Spanish *cabo de barra*, meaning "cut from a bar." These coins, though of full weight and purity, rarely show more than a portion of the royal arms and inscriptions.

The cob coinage did not supplant completely the more finely executed issues.* These continued to appear but are generally rarer than the cobs. In 1732 new mint machinery began operation. The coin blanks were now punched by machine from strips rolled in a mill and the coins were struck by a balancing screw press. The pieces were now of uniform dimensions and of high technical quality.

The mint in Mexico had begun striking gold in the reign of Charles II in 1662. Apart from a mysterious issue of quarter doubloons from the mint of Santa Fe de Bogotá, which were struck during the reign of Philip IV, the Mexican coins were the first gold issues struck in Spanish America. The technical execution of the gold ran parallel to the silver coinage; until 1732 they were cobs, along with a few well-executed pieces. The gold doubloon was also a piece of eight—eight scudos—although it was not referred to by this name but was called doubloon or onza. Its subdivisions were the four-scudo, two-scudo, scudo and half-scudo pieces. All of these denominations were not struck at all mints in all reigns. The doubloon was normally worth sixteen dollars (pieces of eight). The silver pieces of eight and its fractions and the doubloon and its divisions were the most common coins circulating in America and many other parts of the world during the period of Spanish occupation of America. These are the coins which were the money of the pirates and of legitimate business in the New World and parts of the Old, and they dominated the money markets of the world. They formed the largest part of the hard money circulating in the English-American colonies in North America and exceeded the English coinage in quantity. Their importance to the economic life of the colonies is indicated by the fact that the notes issued by the colonists before and during the Revolution and those

* It has been suggested that these were struck to pay the King's fifth (20 percent tax).

The famed pieces of eight, coined in the New World mints from the late sixteenth century through the early decades of the nineteenth. These coins spread all over the world through the channels of commerce. They became the standard currency of international trade and markedly altered the money economy of the world. The Spanish piece of eight was legal tender in the United States until 1857. Photograph from the Smithsonian Institution

issued by the Continental Congress were many times in "Spanish Milled Dollars," the new pieces of eight struck from 1733 on.*

From its establishment to 1732, the entire operation of the Mexico City mint was in the hands of private lessees. In 1732 Crown officials took over all the operations but the actual striking of the coins, which was still performed under their supervision by private contractors. In 1777 the Crown assumed control of all operations.

The rapid exploration and exploitation of Peru led to the establishment of a mint in Lima, which began operations in 1568. The discovery of the enormous silver deposits at Potosí resulted in the founding of a mint there in 1575. Mexico City, Lima and Potosí then supplied the currency of Spanish America, the Philippines, and later the English colonies to the north and in the West Indies and parts of Europe. Vázquez de Espinosa, in describing the operations of the mint of Mexico, says: "There they coin the money for the whole kingdom

* The issue of 1732 is very rare and did not circulate extensively.

and much that goes to the Philippines and to all the Windward Islands, and much that is brought over to Spain; these are the pieces of eight well-known in Spain as Mexican dollars, and in all Europe." Of the money of Potosí he remarks: "All this currency coined in the Potosí Mint circulates in the entire Kingdom, in Chile, Tucumán, Paraguay, and Buenos Ayres; Nicaragua and also in the Spanish Main, where it is brought by the traders who go down there to buy merchandise coming from Spain, and much gets to Spain which is coined in that mint."[8]

The economic expansion of other areas with increased production of metals and trade led to the opening of other mints to supply local needs for currency and to assure better control of the taxing of gold and silver: Santa Fe de Bogotá, which was established in 1622 but did not issue a large coinage; Guatemala, established in 1733; Popayán, which began coining gold in 1758; Santiago, which began coining in the mid-eighteenth century; and Cuzco, which coined briefly after 1697 and again in 1824.

While much bullion was coined in the royal mints, great quantities of silver and lesser amounts of gold were fabricated into objects of ornamentation and utility. The wealthy Spanish American loved the elegant life quite as much as his counterpart in Europe. His tastes were partially satisfied by rich and heavy silverware fabricated by Spanish-American and trained native smiths and by gold ornaments fashioned by skilled workers in the colonies. Travelers to the New World were quite overcome by the richness of ornamentation in the churches and in the homes of the wealthy. Thomas Gage, an English Dominican friar who lived in Mexico and Guatemala between 1625 and 1637, was astonished at the wealth of some of the churches: "There is in the cloister of the Dominicans [in Mexico City] a lamp hanging in the church with three hundred branches wrought in silver to hold so many candles, besides a hundred little lamps for oil set in it, every one being made with several workmanship so exquisitely that it is valued to be worth four hundred thousand ducats."[9]*

The goldsmiths' shops and the richness of the objects displayed there were a source of wonderment to the Englishman: "The streets of Christendom must not compare with those in breadth and cleanness, but especially in the riches of the shops which do adorn them. Above all the goldsmiths' shops and works are to be admired."

Not only did the wealthy Spanish American eat from silver plate and adorn his chambers with it, but he kept his coach and lavished on

---

* Gage was writing of America to inspire an attack by the government of England on the Spanish possessions but his descriptions of American wealth are probably not much exaggerated.

it the richest of materials: "To this I may add the beauty of some of the coaches of the gentry, which do exceed in cost the best of the Court of Madrid and other parts of Christendom; for there they spare no silver nor gold, nor precious stones, nor cloth of gold, nor the best silks from China to enrich them. And to the gallantry of their horses the pride of some doth add the cost of bridles and shoes of silver."

The wealth of Guatemala, while not comparable to that of Mexico, was enough to continue to impress Gage. In one church in the southern colony he describes two treasures: "a lamp of silver hanging before the high altar, so big as requires the strength of three men to hale it up with a rope; but the other is of more value, which is a picture of the Virgin Mary of pure silver, and of the stature of a reasonable [sic] tall woman, which standeth in a tabernacle made on purpose in a Chapel of the Rosary with at least a dozen lamps of silver also burning before it. A hundred thousand ducats might soon be made up of treasure belonging to that church and cloister."

Gold and silver were not the only precious metals produced in Spanish America. Unvalued at the time was a third precious metal which today has a much greater value than either silver or gold. The lack of esteem in which it was held by the early Spanish placer miners is indicated by the name they gave it: *platina*—little silver.

Platinum was discovered in the placer gold deposits of what is now the Republic of Colombia.* At first some Spanish thought it to be an alloy of gold and iron, since it had great weight but a color midway between that of silver and iron. Its high temperature of fusion made it difficult to work and its weight caused it to accumulate in the pans and riffle boards of the miners as they separated gold from the sand of the stream beds. To them it was a nuisance.

Its first use seems to have been as a material for counterfeiting gold and it was used for this purpose until the nineteenth century. Its weight and fusibility with gold made it ideal for this purpose. Not until its qualities as a chemical catalyst were discovered in the nineteenth century did it assume its present value, roughly three times that of gold.† It is possible that the Spanish used it in the later colonial period for objects of utility such as sword hilts and containers. It has been suggested that the Spanish may have used it as an alloy in their bronze guns to give them toughness. This has never been proved but it is interesting to speculate on finding a bronze tube with a hundred

---

* About the middle of the eighteenth century the metal was first introduced to Europe as *platina del Pinto*, so named from the Pinto River in the Chocó region where it was found. Sir William Watson first described it as a new metal in 1750.

† That is, as of 1970.

pounds of platinum in it. The temperature of fusion of platinum made its use as an alloy in guns unlikely since the Spanish probably found it impossible to maintain the heat necessary to fuse platinum in a mass of bronze large enough for a gun.

While the early miners considered platinum a nuisance, its good qualities were beginning to be appreciated by the beginning of the nineteenth century. Antonio de Alcedo wrote of it:

> It cannot be affected by an simple acid, or by any known solvent, except the *aqua regia;* it will not tarnish in the air, neither will it rust; it unites to the fixedness of gold, and to the property it has of not being susceptible of destruction, a hardness almost equal to that of iron, and a much greater difficulty of fusion. It is of an intermediate colour between that of iron and silver; it can be forged and extended into plates; and when dissolved in *aqua regia*, it may be made to assume, by precipitation, an infinite diversity of colours. . . . Upon the whole, from considering the advantages of the platina, we cannot but conclude that this metal deserves, at least, from its superiority to all others, to share the title King of Metals of which gold has so long been in possession.[10]

While gold and silver constituted the bulk of the treasure produced in Spanish America, emeralds and pearls of considerable value were traded throughout the colonies and shipped to Spain in large amounts. The historian Oviedo says that in the year 1547 the royal *quinto* on pearls amounted to 15,000 ducats annually. Gage describes the lavish use of pearls and other gems by the Spanish Americans in Mexico: "Both the men and women are excessive in their apparel, using more silks than stuffs and cloth. Precious stones and pearls further much this their vain ostentation; . . . a hatband of pearls is ordinary in a tradesman; nay a blackamoor or tawny young maid and slave will make hard shift but she will be in fashion with her neck-chain and bracelet of pearls, and her ear-bobs of some considerable jewels."[11]

The emeralds of America were the best of their day. Before the discovery of deposits in the Ural Mountains in 1830, the American emeralds were the world's only considerable supply and they were found regularly among the cargoes of the early treasure fleets, sometimes in unbelievable quantities. Father Acosta states that the fleet of 1587 carried home to Spain two chests of rough emeralds, each chest weighing a hundred pounds. When Pizarro went into Peru, great numbers of emeralds were taken from the natives and these formed the bulk of the stones sent to Spain in the early period. Try as they would, the Spanish never were able to discover the source of the precious stones the Incas possessed.

By the seventeenth century the old Indian emerald mines of New Granada (in what is now Colombia) had been discovered and were extensively worked by the Spanish with Indian and Negro laborers. Around the city of Trinidad in Los Muzos, Vázquez describes the mine of Itoto:

> The hill of Itoto where this rich mine is, is very high, with soil black as charcoal; the veins where the emeralds are formed, are in general soft. The way they handle them is to dig out all that earth following the veins in their search for the emeralds; they have flumes coming from the river which runs near the hill, and nearby, large tanks full of water with sluice gates, which they call *tamires*.
> When they have excavated and followed the veins enough, they raise the sluice gates and the water which has been dammed up, dashes out with such force that it carries off all the earth excavated and leaves clean what has been mined, and at once they find the emeralds in that sort of soft, black, stony covering. . . . The water of this river which flows near the city, is generally almost black, both from the soil it runs through and from the mine operations.[12]

Pearls were produced in great quantities in the oyster beds near Margarita Island (*margarita* is one of the Spanish words for pearl) lying off the coast of Venezuela. Again we are indebted to Vázquez for a description of the pearl fishing there:

> The Island of Margarita lies in 12°30′ N. It is 15 leagues long from E. to W., and 7 across from N. to S. It has the mainland to the S., 8 leagues distant . . . ; in between lie the islands of Goche and Cubagua, from which has come great wealth in pearls. . . .
> The way they fish for pearls in this district, is as follows. At the water's edge within sight of the oyster beds and pearl fishery they establish settlements which they call *rancherías* and every evening the canoes anchor there. These canoes are really sizable lateen-rigged frigates,* but although they are ships of 1,500 fanegas† capacity of wheat or corn, in this pearl-fishing trade they call them canoes. To be a canoe master, one has to have at least a dozen Negro divers, plus their captain who is a Negro expert in the profession, the canoeman (*canoero*, who is a Spanish pilot), and the superintendent; with this crew he is a canoe master, although generally there are more persons in each pearl-fishing canoe.
> When the canoe anchors near the *rancherías* at night, the Negro

---

* In this period *frigate* was the name given to a much smaller vessel than ships so named of the eighteenth and nineteenth centuries.
† Twenty-four hundred bushels. A fanega equaled 1.6 bushels.

divers come out, each presenting in his shell the pearls he has got that day; they turn in their shells and the superintendent takes them over. Now each canoe master has in his house, or *rancheria*, a room or large chamber like a hospital ward, called the prison, where the Negros have their beds and sleep under lock and key, for even in pearl fishing chastity is necessary, to such a degree that if anyone among them did otherwise, he would not be able to dive under water, but would stay on the surface like a cork.* Those who have disappointed their master in their catch of pearls, or who are contrary, they keep in these dormitories or prisons, grills, and cells, and they punish them by beating and flogging them in a cruel and savage manner, a procedure quite alien to the profession of Christianity, except that in what concerns this traffic, every possible means is required, for without it they would not do a thing.

The following day the canoe master leaves with his outfit and boards his ship, or canoe, and sets sail for the oyster beds or pearl fishery, which generally lies offshore 1½ or 2 leagues or even more, and anchors at the bed; and there are canoemen so expert and with such keen discrimination that, having purposely dropped a knife the previous evening on a certain bed, the canoeman keeps such a sure recollection of the spot where he left it that when he sees he is sailing over the place, he drops anchor and tells one of the Negroes to bring up the knife he left there the day before, and this in 8, 10, 12 and even 14 fathoms, according to the depth of the bed, and that of Macanao lies deep. When they dive under water, they carry down a little net or reticule, fastened by a rope to the canoe; and they walk about under water picking up the shells and putting them into this net or reticule; and with great speed and skill they come up this rope to the surface, and each empties out his shells into his own pile; when they have caught their breath and rested a little, they start diving again; and they continue thus till evening when their task is over and they return to their dormitory to sleep.[13]

As with gold, silver and emeralds, so it was with pearls; the Spanish depended on the exploitation of slave labor to enrich themselves and feed the pipeline of treasure to Spain.

Precious metals and gems, while the most exciting of the wealth from America, were not the only fruits of the Indies. Vegetable and animal products went to Spain in great quantity and these products formed a source of wealth of no mean value. From the middle of the sixteenth century onward, the cargoes of the treasure fleets regularly included hides, cochineal, indigo, tobacco, brazilwood, lignum vitae

---

* This idea seems to have been a carry-over from the old belief in the trial by water when that element was expected to reject sinners.

and other rare woods, vanilla beans, sarsaparilla and other drugs. The fleet of 1597 referred to by Acosta carried, in addition to gold, silver and emeralds, the following products of forest and plantation: 50 hundredweight of sarsaparilla; 1,309 hundredweight of brazilwood; 99,794 hides from Hispaniola; 22,053 hundredweight of ginger. The last may have been a transshipment from the Manila galleon trade, which ran between the Philippines and Acapulco, Mexico, for by this time the bulk of the Far Eastern products reaching Spain came by that route and the American treasure fleets.

And so the stream of treasure from the Indies to Spain flowed on, ebbing now and then as a mine or pearl fishery became exhausted but flooding as other mines were discovered and exploited and as new plantations poured forth their products.

The news of the discovery of land to the west had swept Europe. As the wealth of the Americas began to flow during the succeeding decades, news of the wealth spread by word of mouth through sailors and merchants. It was common talk in the taverns of the seaports of France and England and the legend began to grow. Not only did the swift wind of rumor carry the news, those bankers of the Spanish Crown, the Fuggers, with a direct interest in the Indies trade, regularly spread the word of the arrival of the Indies fleets through their news letters and gave details of the treasure and other cargo aboard. Soon, very soon, after the trickle became a respectable stream, French corsairs began to appear on the coast of Spain when the fleets from America were due. The years of war between Francis I of France and Charles V of Spain saw the Spanish coast swarming with French letters of marque threatening the golden route. Even in times of peace the enemies of Spain were a danger. French and English authorities looked the other way as private armed ships left their ports to sail the treasure route. After all, had they not been excluded from a share in the wealth of the Americas by the preemption of that region by Spain and Portugal with the help of the Pope?

Almost as soon as French corsairs threatened the safe arrival of treasure ships on the Spanish coast, bolder spirits invaded the Indies themselves. John Cabot met a French corsair off the coast of Brazil in 1526. The next year an English ship appeared at Santo Domingo, throwing that colony into an uproar. In 1540 an English ship captured a Spaniard laden with hides near Santo Domingo. By the time Peru had been opened and her gold and silver were flowing toward Spain, the French and English had developed an insatiable taste for Spanish treasure. Thus, almost as soon as Spain had located the treasure they sought, she was called on to defend it.

III

Galleons, Flotas, and Ships of Register

The famous harbor of Havana lies on the N. Coast of the island, WNW of the city of Santiago de Cuba, just within 23 degrees N., opposite Florida; it is there that the galleons and fleets come and unite, both from the Spanish Main and New Spain, and it is there that they outfit themselves and take on the supplies necessary to pass through the Bahama Channel and sail to Spain.
—Antonio Vázquez de Espinosa,
Compendium and Description of the West Indies, ca. 1628

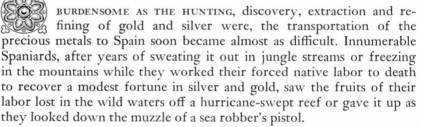 BURDENSOME AS THE HUNTING, discovery, extraction and re-fining of gold and silver were, the transportation of the precious metals to Spain soon became almost as difficult. Innumerable Spaniards, after years of sweating it out in jungle streams or freezing in the mountains while they worked their forced native labor to death to recover a modest fortune in silver and gold, saw the fruits of their labor lost in the wild waters off a hurricane-swept reef or gave it up as they looked down the muzzle of a sea robber's pistol.

Some chose to settle in the new land and pay the exorbitant prices charged by the merchants of the Spanish monopoly for the many necessities and few luxuries that came from Spain rather than risk the dangers of the passage home. But many had no choice but to return to Spain with their wealth, and of course, the King's treasures had always to be shipped home to sustain the government of Spain. Thus it was that private travelers, royal officials and officers and men of the royal service faced on every voyage the terrible risks of shipwreck, robbery and death along the treasure route.

The dons could do little to defend themselves against the tropical storms that lashed the seaways to a gray fury but they could organize for the defense of their loot against the rovers who, almost from the first, flocked to the coasts of Spain and the Indies in response to the heady smell of gold and silver.

The Spanish system of monopoly pointed the way to protection of the trade with the Indies. From the very first years of discovery the

Havana harbor, where the Spanish fleets from Panama, Honduras and New Spain joined to sail to Spain. From a seventeenth-century engraving

Spanish government had been determined to preserve the trade with the New World as a royal monopoly. They had a good example in the King of Portugal, who through royal factories and fleets completely monopolized the early spice trade with India. It was evident to Spanish officialdom that a very strict control on shipping to and from America was needed if illegal shipments of goods to the Indies and precious metals from them were to be prevented.

Even as Columbus sailed on his first two voyages, the Crown held a firm grip on his commercial activities. The instructions under which he sailed gave to the Crown complete control over trade except for some small commerce the admiral was permitted. Haring points out that in these earliest regulations were all the essential elements of control by which the Crown sought to maintain its monopoly: "There is the control exercised by the treasurer, comptroller, and royal factor, and there is the minute provision for the registration of every sailor, officer and passenger, every piece of ordnance, every package of muni-

CARLO V·IMP·

Charles V of Hapsburg (Charles I of Spain). An engraved portrait of the early seventeenth century

tions, merchandise or provisions, carried to and from the New World."[1]

By 1495 pressure by Castilians anxious to share in the discovery and exploitation of the New World led to the opening of the Americas to all the subjects of Castile. (Spanish America was considered to be the property of the kingdoms of Castile and León since they had supported the first voyages of discovery; hence, only subjects of Castile and León were considered eligible to participate in the exploitation of the new lands; even the right of the subjects of Navarre to visit Spanish America and engage in trade was disputed until the 1550's.) The tremendous burst of energy with which the Castilians accepted their new privilege must have alarmed Spanish officials, for the comparative freedom which characterized relations between Castile and the Indies lasted only a few years. In 1501 their Catholic Majesties proclaimed throughout Spain a new restriction on emigration to the Indies without specific royal authority. Thus came to an end the short period during which navigation between Spain and the Americas was comparatively free of control. Regulation soon piled on regulation, until trade with the Americas was perhaps the most strictly controlled and monopolistic of any in the history of Western Europe.

When the Casa de Contratación de las Indias was established at Seville in 1503, that city received the monopoly of all trade with the Indies. The choice was not a happy one.

Seville, the largest and richest city of Castile, was probably chosen because of its wealth and its position as the greatest port of entry for the Mediterranean trade with Castile. Historically, its claim to the monopoly was well founded. Geograhically, the selection could not be supported with logic. Seville was located some 80 miles up the Guadalquivir River, which was always partially blocked at the mouth by the bar of Sanlúcar de Barrameda. The river was tortuous and difficult to navigate: "At the mouth of the Guadalquivir the largest ships became entangled with one another, often lost cables and anchors, and drifted on the rocks. The sand bar was an added danger, captains sometimes waiting weeks for a proper conjunction of tides, winds and daylight, finally in despair taking a chance and often losing their vessels."[2]

Even in the first half of the sixteenth century larger ships could not navigate the shallow channel to Seville without unloading a large part of their cargoes some twenty-five miles below the city. Later, when the river began to silt up, the problem was even more difficult.

Upon the selection of the port an instant cry went up from the merchants of other cities in Castile and from experienced seamen, who immediately foresaw the difficulties which the port of Seville would present. The city of Cádiz was the one serious rival to Seville. It had been the usual port of departure for the early expeditions of discovery and conquest that had sailed to the Indies. It was located on a deep harbor closer to the American possessions than Seville, an important consideration in days of sail. When compared to Seville, Cádiz appears to have had so many advantages that the selection of the former city is a mystery, perhaps to be explained by facts that have not come down to us.

Having made a poor choice, the Crown now acceded to the pressures of merchants and seamen, and Cádiz was soon made a port of departure but only under the rigid control of the Casa in Seville. For the next two centuries constant disputes occurred between the two cities, the Sevillian merchants who dominated the Casa using their power to circumvent the limited trade which Cádiz was permitted to have: "for two centuries, in spite of claims of other cities, in spite of protests from the colonies, and the well-intentioned efforts of Ferdinand's grandson, the emperor Charles V, Seville retained her high distinction. The vested interests of the merchants whose prosperity depended upon the preservation of this monopoly were sufficient to beard down all opposition; and for the Crown it was much easier to maintain in a single port that rigid supervision of every detail of trade and navigation which was the Spaniard's ideal."[3] While departure points other than Seville were permitted under the strict control of the Casa, the regulations requiring the return of American fleets to the city on the Guadalquivir were regularly enforced and only in extreme cases were exceptions made.

Stiff penalties were imposed on captains and fleet commanders who put into any port other than Seville without sufficient cause. In 1623 the *Capitana* (flagship) and one other vessel of the Mexican fleet entered the port of Cádiz. For this the captain general and the owner of the merchant ship which accompanied him were each fined 2,000 ducats. By the second half of the seventeenth century the influence of the Sevillian monopolists was so great that all commanders in the American fleets were ordered to enter the Guadalquivir or be fined heavily and suffer loss of rank and exclusion from the American trade. The extreme was reached in 1671, when Don José Centeño, captain general of the fleet, and the captain of a galleon which accompanied him were fined 6,000 ducats each and sentenced to six years' imprisonment at Oran for sailing into Cádiz when Centeño found his ship too heavily laden to cross the bar at Sanlúcar and because he had heard that enemy ships were near Gibraltar.[4]

Cádiz was to have its satisfaction, however. In 1717 Bourbon logic and the arguments of geography prevailed and Philip V transferred the Casa de Contratación to that city and Seville declined into a sleepy provincial city dreaming of its past glories beside a mud-filled river.

The Casa consisted of three officials, appointed in February of 1503: a treasurer, a comptroller and a secretary. Two of them, Francisco Pinelo and Jimeno de Briviesca, had been in charge of certain of the preparations for Columbus's later voyages and therefore brought to their positions valuable experience. The Casa was the first office of the Spanish government created to attend to matters connected with the new possessions, but the roots of it lay in a royal action of ten years before. In May 1493 the Crown had requested Juan Rodríguez de Fonseca, archdeacon of Seville, to assume authority over the preparations for Columbus's second voyage. From that time until creation of the Casa, Fonseca had almost complete control over Spain's relations with her new possessions. He was a man of great ability and acquitted his office with wisdom and distinction. When the Casa assumed the administrative duties connected with the American commerce, Fonseca became a sort of colonial minister to the Crown and continued to exercise great influence in the conduct of colonial affairs.

The ordinances establishing the Casa defined its duties clearly. The Casa was directed to select with care the captains for the ships in the American trade and to send with each ship an *escribano,* or clerk, to record every article brought aboard at the port of embarkation. The lists thus prepared had to be signed by the captain and sent to the Casa. A similar record of articles shipped from the Indies to Spain was to be prepared and furnished the Casa on arrival at Seville. Every year the Casa sent the books to the King for examination.

In the first years of the Casa's existence, the Crown continued to cherish the hope that all trade with the Indies could be a royal monopoly. The magnitude of the undertaking soon became apparent as the geographical extent and great riches of the American possessions became evident and the trade was opened to Castilian merchants. "It was a task too great for a government unassisted by the inducements and initiative of private enterprise."[5]

In 1510 thirty-six new ordinances were issued to further define the functions of the Casa. They minutely prescribed its every activity and spelled out earlier regulations governing shipping to and from the Indies: "No shipowner or captain might freight for the Indies until his vessel had been examined, and its fitness and tonnage certified, by the Casa's officers. And anyone loading his vessel beyond the limit officially set was liable to severe penalties. Gold brought from America unregistered or without the royal stamp, was confiscated, the smuggler fined four times the amount seized, and his person placed at the mercy of the sovereign."[6] These ordinances hardly concern themselves with trade for royal profit and those that do mention it indicate that such trade was of unusual occurrence.

Thus by 1510 the Casa de Contratación, originally intended as an instrument of royal monopoly, had evolved into an office of the Spanish government for control of private trade between Spain and the Indies, a trade based on the mercantilist doctrines which held that a colony should trade only with the mother country to supply her material needs and that the mother country should be the exclusive recipient of the precious metals produced by the colony. The regulations of 1510 established the character which the Casa was to retain almost throughout the long period of Spanish-American rule.

As the new possessions in the Indies were settled and vast new wealth discovered, the trade with Spain showed a corresponding increase and the increasing complexity of the trade resulted in a continual growth of the Casa. By the middle of the sixteenth century the Casa had

> expanded into an elaborately organized institution, the original officers being the executive heads of departments, and enjoying honors, privileges and exemptions as high as those of the supreme courts and chancelleries of the realm. Nothing might be sent to the Indies without the consent of the Casa, nothing might be brought back and landed, either on the account of the merchants or the king himself, without its authorization. Bullion from the colonies consigned to Spanish merchants belonged to them only when the Casa permitted its release. It controlled and regulated the character of the ships, crews, and passengers. In short, it saw to the execution of all laws and ordinances relating to trade and navigation with America.[7]

During the first half of the sixteenth century a postmaster general had been added to the Casa and this official continued to supervise the transatlantic mails until the end of the Spanish rule in the New World. During its formative period the Casa was made to include also a hydrographic bureau and school of navigation under a pilot major. The first to bear this title was Amerigo Vespucci. This institution became the finest of its kind in Europe and its pattern was copied by other governments. Not the least important duties of the Casa were its judicial functions. While the Casa probably had judicial authority from its inception, this authority was formally recognized in a proclamation of the Crown in 1511. The Casa was given jurisdiction over all law suits involving contracts in the Indies commerce and certain other civil and criminal cases. With the creation of the Council of the Indies to exercise supreme legislative and judicial control over the American possessions, a court of appeal from the Casa was established. While certain cases under the jurisdiction of the Casa came to the Council for review, the Casa, for all practical purposes, maintained its control over the trade with America.

In the earliest years of the American trade the Crown, through the Casa, concerned itself principally with the protection of the trade from smuggling and other evasive practices of the merchants and mariners. Very soon, however, protection of the commerce from external enemies became an equally important consideration. No sooner had a trickle of gold begun to flow back to Spain from the West Indies than word of it flashed across Europe with astonishing speed. Soon corsairs appeared off the coast of Spain to see what was going on and the vessels of Spain's enemies to the north began to sail to the Indies

A carrack of the late fifteenth century, an early engraving based on drawings in a fifteenth-century account of a voyage to the Holy Land. This is the proto-type of the carracks that sailed in the early treasure fleets to and from America. Photograph from the Smithsonian Institution

Armed carrack from a woodcut of 1540. Photograph from the Smithsonian
Institution

themselves. Indeed, Columbus had met French corsairs near the
Canaries in 1492 and on his return from the third voyage to America
had altered his intended course to evade French vessels which lay in
wait for him near Cape St. Vincent.

In 1501 the Crown had offered a premium to owners of ships of over
150 tons if they would fit them out to chase privateers off the coast of
Spain. In 1512 the King sent armed ships to meet the Indies ships at the
Canaries. The next year he directed the Casa to send two caravels to
Cuba to guard the coasts and the Indies trade from French pirates. The
beginning of the long period of wars between Francis I of France and
Charles V in 1520 increased the danger to which the Indies ships were
subjected. Swarms of privateers now sailed off the Spanish coast with
the blessings of the French Crown. In 1521 the Sevillian merchants
were appalled to hear of the capture of two of their treasure ships by
Frenchmen. On this occasion the King hurriedly sent a small squadron
to patrol off Cape St. Vincent. To meet the expenses of this squadron
the Crown for the first time levied a special tax on all the Indies trade.
This tax, the *avería*, was to become a regular means of maintaining
ships and equipment for the protection of the trade with the Indies.

The evolution of the American treasure fleet was a gradual one. The
highly developed convoys which were characteristic of the best years

of the reign of Philip II and his immediate successor were the outgrowth of the experience of the reign of Charles V. As the danger to the Indies trade increased, measures ever more intensive were taken for protection. The very idea of rigid control of the trade had led to the sailing of merchantmen in groups as they were cleared for the voyage by the Casa. The threat of capture stimulated the same practice. In times of war or other special danger, when the threat of attack became imminent, armed escorts were added and the treasure fleet began to take form. It remained only for regular schedules and naval commanders with staffs of officers to be added to complete the system. The beginnings of the armed escort lie in those early squadrons which were ordered to cruise off the coast of Spain and in the West Indies for the protection of the merchant fleet. As protection at each end of the route became inadequate it would naturally follow that protection would be given the fleet the entire way on both crossings.

The first squadron sent out to the Indies with the merchant fleet was that of Blasco Núñez Vela, which sailed in 1537. Three years later Cosmé Rodríguez Farfán commanded an armed escort to the trade and in 1542 a third sailed under the command of Martín Alonso de los Ríos. In 1543 a decree of the Crown established the sailing of armed fleets on a regular schedule probably as a result of the renewal of the war between Francis I of France and Charles V. This order provided that only ships of over 100 tons were to sail to the Indies in fleets of at least ten ships. It directed that the fleets sail for America in March and September and that each be protected by a man-of-war. Expenses of the system were to be met from the convoy tax. When the fleet entered the Caribbean, the warship was to leave it and sail to Havana, there to reprovision and sail against pirates infesting the waters of Cuba and Hispaniola. On the arrival of the merchantmen from Panama and Mexico the warship rejoined the fleet and escorted it back to Spain. As an exception to this order (there were exceptions to all Spanish orders), ships sailing from the windward ports on Hispaniola and Puerto Rico were permitted to leave without escort if they went in fleets of at least ten ships and chose the most heavily armed and lightly laden as the flagship.

No sooner had the first fleet sailed under the orders of 1543 when it was realized that the single warship offered inadequate protection to the convoy. The Casa therefore dispatched three additional warships with spare ordnance for the arming of two other ships in the Indies, thereby giving the returning fleet an escort of six warships instead of the single one first intended. In 1552 the fleet system was ordered abolished altogether along with the *avería*. In its place all merchant ships were to be armed sufficiently well to withstand attack by the average corsair. The owner was required to meet the expense of arming his ship. The Crown was to maintain two squadrons of armed ships, one off the Andalusian coast to cruise between Spain and the Azores, and another, stationed at Santo Domingo, to protect the West Indies. One last protected fleet was to sail, and did so escorted by four ships of 250 to 300 tons and two ships of 80 to 100 tons. The outbreak of a new war with France and her allies made a quick end to the plan to abolish the armed escort. The protected fleet system was quickly reestablished for the duration of the war. Ships were to sail in January and September with escorts of four warships each.

A royal cedula of July 20, 1554, prescribed sailings when eight or ten vessels were ready and armed according to the law. In August the number was reduced to six. Exceptions to the rule were so common as to become almost rules themselves. Single well-armed vessels, called "ships of register," undoubtedly continued to sail for America after clearance by the Casa, and probably did so until the end of Spanish rule in America.

From 1564 through 1566 there appeared new ordinances which gave to the American trade the character it was to retain until the beginning of the eighteenth century. The ordinances of 1564 provided for a separate fleet to sail to New Spain (Mexico) and Panama each year. The Mexican fleet was to sail in April (later changed to May) accompanied by ships for Honduras, Cuba and Hispaniola. The Panama fleet was to sail in August conveying ships for Cartagena and other ports on the Spanish Main. Both fleets were directed to winter in America, "the Panama ships leaving in January, those at Vera Cruz in February, so that distinction was made between the flotas for New Spain and Tierra Firme [mainland South America]; and although occasional circumstances made it necessary for the two fleets to sail together they always retained their separate character and organization. Each was conducted by its own convoy, each had its own general, and *almirante* or rear-admiral."[8] The next year decrees prescribed details for size and armament of the escorts. Until this year the "armada" had consisted of a few of the larger merchantmen armed just a little better than the others and carrying soldiers. The abuses of the merchants owning these ships had often rendered the escort partially or completely ineffective through so overloading the ships with goods that the guns could not be worked. The new regulations provided that the *Capitana* be of at least 300 tons "burthen," carry 8 large brass guns, 4 iron, 24 smaller pieces and swivels, and 200 men including crew and soldiers. The *Capitana* could not carry merchandise unless it had been rescued

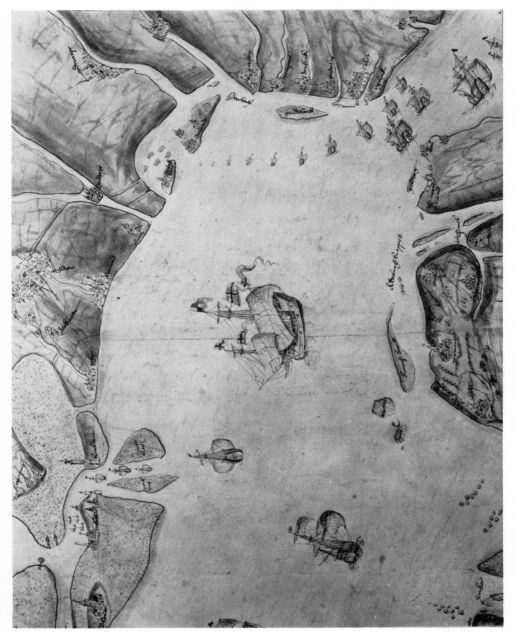

A Spanish treasure galleon. Pen drawing in the Cotton Manuscript (ca. 1550), British Museum

Brass naval gun on two-wheel carriage, ca. 1570. Photograph of a model in the Smithsonian Institution

from the sea or from wrecks. In 1566 the same rules were applied to the *Almiranta*. (The larger guns were carried on carriages on the weather deck and the deck below. Swivels were light guns carried on the rails of the poop and quarterdeck for close action.)

While the fleet system was developing, the two squadrons established earlier to protect the trade between the Canaries and Cape St. Vincent, and which occasionally sailed all the way to the Indies, continued in service. These, the Armadas de la Guardia de la Carrera de las Indias, began in the reign of Philip II to accompany the fleets all the way to America to protect the enormous treasure of silver which began to flow to Spain from the new mines of Potosí in Upper Peru. By the seventeenth century transatlantic guard duty had become a rule. The fleet going to Panama became known as the Galeones from the type of warship escorting it, while the Mexican fleet came to be known as the Flota and was defended by the *Capitana* and *Almiranta*, which had been prescribed by the laws of 1564 and 1566. Like any complex institution which exists over a long period of time, some changes in the treasure fleet occurred during its long life, but the essential character had been established by the reign of Philip II and during that reign, with the high tide of Spanish wealth and power, the treasure fleets reached their peak of development.

The chief officer of the fleet was the captain general of the Galeones. He was appointed directly by the Crown, sometimes for a single voyage, sometimes for life. This position was usually purchased, as were other positions in the fleet. When the Indies trade had fallen into decay during the reigns of Philip IV and Charles II, and the Crown was constantly in debt, candidates for the position of captain general would advance the Crown 100,000 pesos to be repaid them in the Indies with eight percent interest. Under the captain general the following officials carried on their duties:

almirante de Galeones: second-in-command of the Galeones
general de Flota: in command of the Flota to Vera Cruz
almirante de Flota: second-in-command of the Flota
capitanes: in command of individual vessels
veedor: a representative of the King who went along with the fleet to see that all the King's ordinances were observed; in the Galeones he had the title of *veedor general*
contador: the comptroller general of the armada
gobernador de tercio: commander of the regiment of infantry which was distributed among the Galeones
maestra de plata: official in charge of the treasure

And so on down the line to the doctors and surgeons who held the lowest rank.

The Spanish genius for overorganizing and formalizing everything is well demonstrated in the staffing of their fleets. In the middle of the seventeenth century over twenty-four types of officials accompanied the Galeones and the Flota. These ranged from general of the Galeones, the highest rank, with a salary of 8,000 ducats a year, to surgeon, the lowest in the hierarchy, at a salary of 300 ducats. This salary was not very good but neither was the surgery. The dispenser of rations made more than the surgeon. In the navies of today this would be equivalent to the storekeeper's outranking the ship's doctor. Surgery has come a long way since the seventeenth century and so have the surgeons.

The general of the Flota, who was appointed by the Casa and not directly by the King, was inferior in rank to his counterpart in the Galeones and received only half the salary.

Before the fleet system matured, small groups of ships might sail in company to the Indies. The "fleet" in which Don Alonzo Enríquez de Guzmán sailed to America in 1533 numbered only four ships.[9] In the reign of Philip II the armada which accompanied the Tierra Firme fleet to Cartagena usually numbered six to eight galleons and several dispatch boats. Under unusual conditions the number was increased. In 1595, while Drake and Hawkins were threatening the Indies on their last voyage, an armada of twenty ships was sent. In 1627 twelve galleons were sent, and in 1630, twenty. Additionally, in times of special danger, extra ships were mustered on the Spanish coast to reinforce the galleons when they reached the Azores on their return from the Indies.[10]

The number of merchantmen in the Indies fleets varied with the condition of the trade. The fleet of 1550 contained eleven or twelve. The 1552 fleet consisted of forty, twenty-four for the South American trade and sixteen for Vera Cruz. Of these, seven returned from Panama and five returned from Vera Cruz. The others were in such poor condition they were left in the Indies. The outgoing fleet of 1554 contained fifteen merchantmen, that of 1557, fourteen. In 1562 Pedro Menéndez de Avilés sailed for the Indies with forty-nine. Since the outbound cargoes were usually more bulky than the valuables returned to Spain, the returning fleets were generally smaller than the outgoing. This led to the practice of buying up old ships good for one more voyage and sending them to the Indies with a cargo. At their destinations they were scrapped and the hulks burned for the metal fittings.

In the latter 1500's the fleets numbered from thirty to ninety merchantmen. The number of merchant ships returning from Nombre de Dios in Panama during the late sixteenth century and first few years of the seventeenth indicates a prosperous trade but foreshadows the decline which set in during the reigns of the later Hapsburgs:

Year	Number of Merchantmen
1585	71
1587	85
1589	94
1592	72
1594	56
1596	69
1599	56
1601	32
1603	34

Before the perfection of the fleet system, the schedules on which the fleets sailed to and from the Indies were somewhat irregular. Despite royal orders circumstances would not permit prompt sailings, and delays of many months or even a year or more occurred. The return

Spanish galleon of the mid-sixteenth century. From the title page of a work on navigation of the period. Photograph from the Smithsonian Institution

Warship of forty guns. From an engraving by Théodore de Bry, late sixteenth century

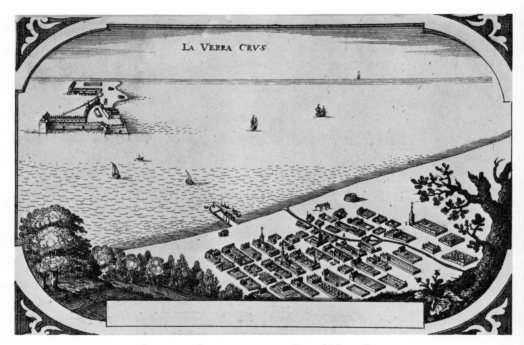

Seventeenth-century engraving of Vera Cruz

voyages were equally erratic. For example, ships bringing the royal treasure from the Indies in 1551 arrived in the following order: three in June from New Spain; one in July from New Spain; eleven all together in September and a straggler later in the month; two in October from Honduras; two in November from Hispaniola.

The pattern of sailings was pretty well established by the middle 1550's. Normally the fleets sailed in company until, entering the Caribbean, they split up for their various destinations. In the fleet in which Thomas Gage sailed for the Indies in 1625 from Cádiz, thirty-three ships formed the fleets for the Indies and eight galleons convoyed the ships beyond the Canaries: "To Porto Rico went that year two ships; to Santo Domingo three, to Jamaica two, to Margarita one, to Havana two, to Cartagena three, to Campeche two, to Honduras and Trujillo two, and to St. John de Ulhua, or Vera Cruz, sixteen."[11]

In returning, the ships attempted to meet at Havana and sail home in company. Circumstances sometimes delayed either the Galeones from Cartagena or the Flota from Vera Cruz and they frequently missed connections. This occurred in 1637, when Thomas Gage returned to Spain from Central America. He was a passenger on one of the ships escorted by the Galeones from Tierra Firme. The Flota from Vera Cruz was to have arrived in Havana to join the Galeones by September 8. Having delayed some days to wait for the Flota, the general of the Galeones sailed, only to have the Flota arrive that night. Fearing storms from the lateness of the season, he still went on ahead, not wishing to wait for the Flota to provision.

Even when the Indies fleet system had reached the peak of its development, regular sailings every year were not always accomplished. "Annual sailings, too, were not the rule, although they were the ideal striven after, and sometimes achieved. From 1580 onwards a year was frequently skipped, and toward the middle of the seventeenth century, as the monarchy declined, the sailings became more and more irregular. The incurable dilatoriness of the Spaniard also contributed to confuse the schedules of the American fleets. The Mexican Flota sometimes did not get away till the end of June or even August and that for Panama till October or November. There was always a plausible excuse for delay."[12] Contrary winds, poor roads which delayed the shipment of outgoing goods to Seville, lack of mariners, guns and the like were standard excuses. The true case probably lay in the absence of any means whereby the merchants could be compelled to observe punctual schedules in preparing for the fleets' departure.

The earliest ships in the Indies trade were exceedingly small by modern standards. Few displaced more than 200 tons. In 1522 an ordinance prohibited ships smaller than 80 tons to engage in the trade. A cedula dated 1609 set the minimum size at 200 tons. Larger vessels were common after the middle of the sixteenth century, but the bar at Sanlúcar limited the size of incoming ships and in 1557 a cedula set the maximum at 400 tons. In 1628 the upper limit was raised to 550 tons and by this time the galleons frequently displaced more, as much as 1,000 tons. The earliest ships were caravels, light-draft ships of about 100 to 200 tons usually lateen-rigged on at least one mast. Columbus's two smaller ships were of this type. In addition to the caravels, which were swift and smooth sailers, the comparatively clumsy nao, or merchant ship, was a favored cargo carrier in the early sixteenth century because of its capacity. The galleon, which appeared in the late sixteenth century as the warship carrying treasure and protecting the fleets, was a longer, swifter ship of two or even three decks; it was heavily armed and stoutly built. By this time the caravel had been replaced by sloops or frigates, which now accompanied the fleets of larger and slower ships as dispatch boats, sailing ahead of the main formation to warn of its arrival and to carry royal dispatches as well. At the same time, the nao had given place to the urca, a longer and less clumsy merchant ship with high poop and quarterdeck. The urca carried on the tradition of the slow vessel of great capacity which the nao had been. Very large carracks, broad-beamed cargo carriers, were used also in the trade and many types of smaller vessels of various rigs.

In the beginning of the American trade Spanish law had required that all ships sailing to and from America be Spanish-built. This ideal was pretty well realized in the golden period of the trade but with the decline of the monarchy the picture changed. By the eighteenth century Spanish ships became the exception, not the rule. In the fleet of merchantmen escorted by Admiral Don Rodrigo de Torres which sailed from Havana in July 1733, the following ships were included:

1 Genoese built ship 20 guns mounted about 400 tons.
1 La Vera Cruz built ship 30 guns mounted this ship had two teer of
   ports   800 tons
1 Dutch built frigate 24 guns mounted   500 tons
4 English built vessels each 24 guns   600 tons apiece
1 New England built ship of 3 decks had 36 guns mounted 2 teer of
   ports   900 tons
6 Old England built frigates of 4 and 500 tons apiece some 20 guns
   others 24 guns mounted
1 Old England built ship 30 guns mounted about 700 tons[13]

This evidence not only indicates the normal use of foreign-built ships in the period of the decline of the Spanish monarchy but also demonstrates the changes in individual ship size and armament which had occurred since the early seventeenth century. The merchant ships were very much larger and much better armed. The opening of Cádiz as the seat of the Casa de Contratación and port of entry permitted the use of larger ships in the American trade since Cádiz was on deep water.

To defend themselves against the enemies that swarmed along the treasure routes, the ships were required by law to carry a great diversity of weapons. Naval warfare in the days of sail involved two phases: the duel with heavy guns when the enemy was softened up, and the grappling alongside when the attacking crew attempted to board. The defensive weapons thus fall into two classes: the heavy guns, which defended the ship at a distance, and the small arms and swivels, which were designed to resist boarding.

The era of discovery coincided with a period of great change in ships' armament. Since the beginning of the fifteenth century ships had carried heavy ordnance to sea, but the latter part of that century saw the beginning of improvement in the broadside pieces, which con-

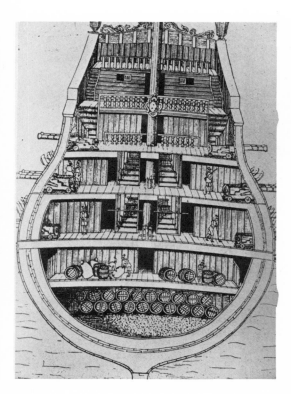

Cross section of a first rate of the mid-seventeenth century, from an old print. Stowage of cargo in larger merchant vessels and galleons was on the same plan. Photograph from the Smithsonian Institution

Ship construction, from a French engraving of the eighteenth century. Photograph from the Smithsonian Institution

tinued throughout the sixteenth century. At the time of Columbus's voyages the heavy gun of the armed ship was an iron piece built up of bars of iron surrounded by hoops of the same metal sweated on. It was a breechloader, the powder and ball being loaded into a chamber which was wedged into the breech. The piece was mounted on a solid timber which slid on the deck or rode on two wooden wheels just forward of the center so the mount would rest on the deck at the breech. At the turn of the sixteenth century founders had perfected their art to such an extent that fine new bronze guns were making their appearance. These muzzle-loading pieces began to replace the breech-loading built iron tubes which were of shorter range and uncertain performance, much trouble in gas leakage occurring at the breech. The iron tubes were not immediately supplanted, of course—they continued to be used on merchant ships and lesser warships—but the bronze pieces became the badge of the flagships. During the middle of the sixteenth century English gunfounders in the Weald perfected methods of casting muzzle-loaders in iron, and the wrought-iron tubes in the broadside pieces had largely disappeared by 1600.

A great variety of projectiles were available to throw at an attacker. The Spanish showed great ingenuity in developing, or adopting, projectiles designed to maim or kill the attacker and to cripple or burn his ship.

The plain ball came in many materials: stone·for the lighter *pedreros* (stone throwers), iron for the heavier pieces, and throughout the sixteenth century, lead and even brass ball were used. One interesting variation was a lead ball with bits of iron cast in it, a sort of early shrapnel, which was supposed to split on striking and to scatter iron fragments about.

Another projectile deadly to men as well as rigging was the bar shot. This shot, consisting of two ball, half ball or short cylinders, spun through the air as it left the gun and in striking would literally tear a man apart or rip lines and sails to shreds. A variation of this was the expanding bar shot in which the bar of two pieces, one sliding on the other, spread out to double its length as it spun through the air, covering a wider area in its flight and increasing the chance of a hit.

Fire, a thing most to be feared at sea, was another weapon which the Spanish could call upon in defense of their treasure. The incendiary shot, an iron ball with a serrated spike projecting from each side and wrapped in tar-soaked rope, left the piece flaming, and if the spike struck the enemy ship properly, it stuck there resisting attempts to remove it. The result could be a flaming death for the attacker.

If the attackers could weather the Spanish broadsides, they then faced the secondary defenses. Backing up the broadside pieces were the swivel guns, usually carried on the forecastle, poop and quarter-decks. These pieces were brought into play when an enemy approached in an effort to board, firing everything from pebbles and scrap iron to lead ball. Here the wrought-iron breechloader remained in use until the eighteenth century, especially with the stone throwers, since the lesser gas pressure caused little trouble in the breech. How disconcerting it must have been to the enemy who, sticking his head over the gunwale of his intended victim, got a handful of gravel or scrap iron fired into his face!

The third line of defense was the small arms wielded by the crew and by the military guard that many ships carried. These weapons were of the most diverse variety. Heavy muskets firing a lead ball of an ounce or two would literally dismember a victim, the smaller arquebus firing a lead ball of lesser weight, and lastly, the pistol firing an even smaller projectile. During the earliest period of the American trade these pieces were matchlocks, fired by lowering a slow-burning match into the flashpan. In the late sixteenth century the efficient but expensive wheel lock came into use among the officers, but the man in the ranks continued to use the matchlock until the middle of the seventeenth century, when the introduction of the flintlock spelled doom for both the matchlock and the wheel lock.

In addition to the small firearms, hand grenades were available from the late sixteenth century on. These were metal spheres loaded with gunpowder and ignited by a wooden tube charged with fine powder. Curiously, some of the earliest were made of brass with finely threaded fuses of metal, even though brass tended to split rather than shatter and was much more expensive than iron. Soon, however, the advantages of cast iron made that metal universal and the grenade thus produced changed very little until the end of Spanish rule in America.

If the enemy succeeded in boarding their victim, they were met with edge weapons as well as the pistol and shoulder arms. Here equally diverse types appeared. The soldiers aboard would wield the fine Spanish sword and dagger, the sailors could use the sword or cutlass. In addition, pole arms such as the halberd and ax would wreak havoc when wielded by a determined crew. Until the eighteenth century the soldiers wore breastplates and steel helmets.

From the very first voyages of Columbus the Spanish had learned that the sea and air currents of the Atlantic basin north of the equator could be utilized to carry them from Spain to the Indies and back again. Antonio Vázquez de Espinosa described the great Indies routes as they were in 1628:

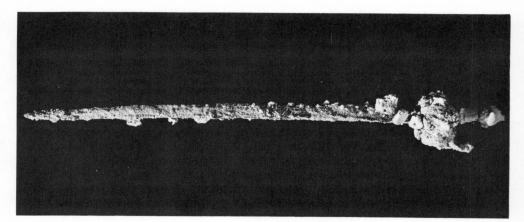

The feared Spanish rapier, a sand-encrusted example recovered from the Tucker treasure site (ca. 1595) off Bermuda. With a dagger in his left hand and a rapier in his right the Spanish soldier who defended the treasure ship from boarders was a formidable opponent. Photograph from the Smithsonian Institution

The galleons, fleets, and other ships which sail to the Indies of New Spain, the Spanish Main and other parts thereof, leave Sanlúcar de Barrameda or Cádiz, which are at 37 degrees N.; sailing from there, they round the island of Salmedina, which is half a league SE. of Sanlúcar; in summer they steer SW. and in winter SW.¼S to Cape Cantin, at 32 degrees, because of the breezes blowing from the Barbary coast; from there they steer SW. ¼W., to Point Anaga on the island of Tenerife in the Canaries, which is at 28 degrees and 250 leagues, sailors' reckoning, from Spain, and they usually pass within sight of those islands. Thence they sail through the Great Gulf WSW. to 20 degrees, and from that latitude they steer W.¼SW. to 15 degrees 30 minutes, from which point sailing W. they make the island of Deseada, and if they sail along 15 degrees, the island of Marigalante, which will be over 750 leagues from the Canaries, and 1000 from Spain. . . . From there the fleets for New Spain sail within sight of the islands of Puerto Rico and Santo Domingo [Hispaniola], to the S. of them some 500 leagues, to Cape San Antón, the westernmost point of the island of Cuba. From there they sail to the port of Vera Cruz; the due course and time for the voyage are known by the pilots, who take care to plot a good course.

. . . From the above-mentioned islands to Cartagena and Puerto Bello there is a direct E.–W. route, but for greater safety they pass between Domínica and Metarino and sail 50 leagues WSW. and then W.¼SW. to 12 degrees, sighting a headland on the Cape de la Vela; immediately upon recognizing the Sierra Nevada which lies above Santa Marta, they sail WNW. until they sight the light-colored water of the Río Grande [Magdalena], whereupon they steer SW., aiming at Morro Hermoso and the Point de la Canoa, up to Cartagena; from Cartagena they sail to Puerto Bello, a matter of 90 leagues.

. . . From Vera Cruz it is 300 leagues' sail to Havana; on leaving port they head NE. up to 25 degrees; from there they steer E. till they sound at the Tortugas, and from them they run to Havana. From Puerto Bello it is also 300 leagues' sail to Havana. On leaving the harbor they steer E. till they make a N.–S. line with Cativa Head; then ESE. to the island of San Bernardo, from which they sail E. to Cartagena. From there they steer NE. to 13 degrees; from 13 degrees to 16 degrees 30 minutes lie the shoals of Serrana, Serranilla, etc., where they navigate cautiously on account of the shoals; on the same course they sight the Isle of Pines, passing within view of it, and then Cape San Antón, to which they have to give head on account of shoals; right afterward they come to Havana harbor.

. . . From Havana the galleons and fleets leave by the Bahama Channel and once out, they steer NE. up to 32 degrees; thence E¼NE. to 38 degrees or 39 degrees; on this course they make the Terceras Islands; this is the summer route.

. . . On the winter route they steer from the Bahama Channel E. for the island of Bermuda, which lies at 32 degrees 30 minutes. Passing along its southern coast and following the route, they sail as far as 37 degrees, on which lies the island of Santa María; for the Island of Tercera, they sail to 38 degrees; for San Miguel, to 37 degrees; at these they take on necessary fresh provisions. From there it is 300 leagues to Spain; 40 or 50 of them are sailed E. and then they turn E.¼S.E. till they sight Cape St. Vincent; from the cape they sail an E.–W. course to Sanlúcar. That is the most usual and secure route set and followed by the galleons and fleets, to go to the Indies and return to Spain.[14]

Despite the great school for pilots which was established at Seville early in the sixteenth century, the pilots serving with the American fleets, by the seventeenth century at least, were frequently unable to calculate exact or approximate position during a voyage. When Thomas Gage came to the Indies in 1625, he witnessed an exchange between the pilots and the admiral that illustrates how far wrong a pilot could be:

The Admiral of our Fleet wondering much at our slow sailing, who from the second of July to the 19th. of August had seen nor discovered any land, save only the Canary Islands, the same day in the morning called to council all the pilots of the ships, to know their opinions concerning our present being, and the nearness of land. The ships

75

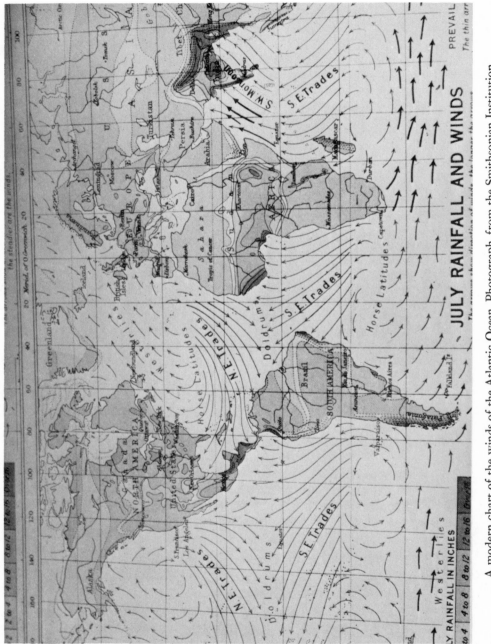

A modern chart of the winds of the Atlantic Ocean. Photograph from the Smithsonian Institution

therefore drew unto the Admiral one by one, that every pilot might deliver his opinion. Here was cause of laughter enough for the passengers to hear the wise pilots' skill; one saying we were three hundred miles, another two hundred, another one hundred, another fifty, another more, another less, all erring much from the truth (as afterward appeared) save only one old pilot of the smallest vessel of all, who affirmed resolutely that with the small gale wherewith we then sailed we should come to Guadeloupe the next morning. All the rest laughed at him, but he might well have laughed at them for the next morning by sun-rising we plainly discovered an island called Deseada by the Spaniards, or the Desired Land.[15]

Admiral Ybarra, commander of the fleet in which Gage returned to Spain in 1637, had hired pilots to carry them through the Bahama Channel but the quality of their pilotage again was poor. Gage remarks that "the best of the pilots not knowing where they were, had like to have betrayed us all to the rocks of Bermuda one night, had not the breaking of day given us a fair warning that we were running upon them."[16] As a last resort the pilot had a prayer ready. In one tight situation where the ship was in danger of running on the rocks, Gage quotes the pilot as crying, "Help us O most Holy Virgin, for if not, here we perish."[17]

Several lesser routes fanning out from the main course in the Caribbean basin served the American trade. Ships from the Greater Antilles would drop off at those ports as the Flota for Vera Cruz sailed by. Ships leaving from the Antilles for Spain were permitted to sail directly if organized into small fleets with one chosen as a leader, since beating back toward Havana would have entailed undue hardship and loss of time.

The Central American trade was served by the Guatemala and Honduras ships. Gage was able to observe the Guatemala trade while he was there in the 1630's: "The chief side of Guatemala is that on the east, which points out the way to the Gulf, or Golfo Dulce, or as others call it, St. Thomas de Castilla. . . . Besides the great trading, commerce and traffic which this city enjoyeth by that gulf from Spain hath made that road exceed all the rest. In July or at furtherest in the beginning of August come into that gulf three ships, or two, and frigates, and unlade what they have brought from Spain in *bedegas* or great lodges, built up on purpose to keep dry and from the weather the commodities. They presently make haste to lade again from Guatemala those merchants' commodities of return."[18] The Gulf of Honduras served both Honduras and Guatemala. Ships bound from the Golfo Dulce would proceed to Trujillo in Honduras and there take on the local products destined for the Spanish market.* "The city does a large business and has much commerce on account of the port and the ships running from Spain to Guatemala, which stop here going and coming, and ships and frigates ordinarily come here for cargoes of native products."[19]

In times of danger when "Hollanders" and other interlopers appeared off the Gulf of Honduras to threaten the trade there, the King's treasure from Guatemala, private goods and other cargo were shipped by the Lake of Nicaragua and the San Juan River to Cartagena, where it could be given the protection of the fleet escorted by the Galeones to Havana. Thomas Gage made this journey in 1637 and described the route:

> The merchants of Guatemala fearing to send all their goods by the Gulf of Honduras, for that they have been often taken by the Hollanders between that and Havana, think it safer to send them by the frigates to Cartagena, which passage hath not been so much stopped by the Hollanders as the other. So likewise many times the King's treasure, and revenues (when there is any report of ships at sea, or about the Cape of St. Anthony) are this way by the Lake of Grenada [Lake Nicaragua] passed to Cartagena.
>
> That year that I was there [1637] before I betook myself to an Indian town, in one day there entered six *requas* (which were at least three hundred mules) from St. Salvador and Comayagua only, laden with nothing else but indigo, cochineal and hides; and two days after from Guatemala came in three more, the one laden with silver (which was the King's tribute from that country), the other with sugar, and the other with indigo. . . . I heard much of the passage in the frigates to Cartagena, which did not a little dishearten and discourage me. For although, whilst they sail upon the lake they go securely and without trouble, yet when they fall from the lake to the river . . . to go out to sea, *hic labor, hoc opus est,* here is nothing but trouble, which sometimes makes that voyage to last two months; for such is the fall of the waters in many places amongst the rocks that many times they are forced to unlade the frigates, and lade them again with the help of mules which are there kept for that purpose by a few Indians that live

* "To the north of Comayagua some 14 leagues is the city of San Pedro, near Puerto Caballos [Puerto Cortés], where they used to unload the merchandise coming from Spain for Guatemala and all these provinces; it was dismantled in the year 1604 by order of the great Governor Dr. Alonso Criado de Castilla, President of the Circuit Court of Guatemala, and transferred to the port of Amatique, to which he gave the name Santo Tomás de Castilla; this is where the ships lie discharging their cargoes and loading native products, and where the garrison stays which the ships bring along, until they leave to take on what additional cargo there is at the port of Trujillo" (Vázquez de Espinosa, pp. 242–243).

Woodcut of a galleon in port. From the title page from an early English
book on navigation. Photograph from the Smithsonian Institution

about the river, and have care of the lodges made for to lay in the wares, whilst the frigates pass through those dangerous places to another lodge, whither the wares are brought by mules, and put again into the frigates. Besides this trouble . . . the abundance of gnats is such which maketh him to take no joy in his voyage, and the heat in some places so intolerable that many do die before they get out to sea.[20]

Alas, after such suffering to avoid the "Hollanders," Gage was captured after all and lost several thousand pieces of eight, barely getting back to the coast with his life and some coins sewn in his clothes.

In the Pacific two great routes fed the main route through the Caribbean. The first of these extended from Chile on the south to Panama City on the western coast of the Isthmus of Panama. Having received word of the impending arrival of the Galeones at Cartagena, the Viceroy of Peru would order the settlements in the south to forward the King's treasure to Callao. From there the Armada of the South Seas would then sail, taking the treasure of Peru and Chile and the merchants going to Porto Bello to trade. At Paita the armada would be joined by the Golden Ship carrying the treasure of the province of Quito and the country about. At Panama the merchants would load their money and products on mules to transport it to Porto Bello, the King's treasure going the same route.

An alternate route followed the trail to Venta Cruz, where the treasure or merchandise was transferred to boats and carried down the Chagres River to the sea and thence to Porto Bello. This route was used principally in winter and at other times for bulky merchandise. The land route via the Las Cruces Trail was the more secure, although more expensive, and treasure was invariably shipped that way when corsairs threatened the coast at the mouth of the Chagres.

Thomas Gage traveled the Chagres River route in 1637, having been foiled by "Hollanders" in his attempts to go via Lake Nicaragua. His description of the journey is one of the best surviving:

at midnight I set out from Panama to Venta de Cruces, which is ten or twelve leagues from it. The way is thither very plain for the most part, and pleasant in the morning and evening.

Before ten of the clock we got to Venta de Cruces, where none live but mulattoes and blackamoors, who belong unto the flat boats that carry the merchandise to Portobello. . . . after five days of my abode there, the boats set out, which were much stopped in their passage down the river; for in some places we found the water very low, so that the boats ran upon the gravel, from whence with poles and the strength of the blackamoors they were lifted off again; sometimes again we met with such streams that carried us with the swiftness of an arrow down under the trees and boughs by the river side, which sometimes also stopped us till we had cut down great branches of trees. . . . after twelve days we got to the sea, and at the point landed at the castle [San Lorenzo] to refresh ourselves for half a day. . . . The governor of the castle was a notable wine-bibber, who plied us with that liquor the time that we stayed there, and wanting a chaplain for himself and his soldiers, would fain have had me stayed with him; but greater matters called me further, and so I took my leave of him. . . . We got out to open sea, discovering first the Escuda de Veragua, and keeping somewhat close unto the land we went on rowing towards Portobello, till the evening which was Saturday night; then we cast anchor behind a little island, resolving in the morning to enter Portobello. The blackamoors all that night kept watch for fear of Hollanders, whom they said did often lie in wait thereabouts for the boats of Chagres; but we passed the night safely, and next morning got to Portobello.[21]

While in Porto Bello, Gage went about the town seeing the sights and watched the arrival of the packtrains from Panama: ". . . but what most I wondered at was to see the *requas* of mules which came thither from Panama, laden with wedges of silver; in one day I told [counted] two hundred mules laden with nothing else, which were unladen in the public market-place, so that there the heaps of silver wedges lay like heaps of stones in the street, without any fear or suspicion of being lost."

The other principal route in the Pacific was that of the Manila Galleon from the Philippines to Acapulco in New Spain. From the late sixteenth century to the end of the eighteenth this route carried the trade of the Far East to Mexico and Spain. The silks, dyestuffs, porcelains, gems and spices were loaded on mules at Acapulco and carried to Vera Cruz to be shipped to Spain in the ships of the Flota.

The prevailing winds of the Pacific basin governed the routes of the Manila Galleon just as the currents and winds of the Atlantic controlled the routes of the Indies fleets: "The eastward and westward paths of the galleons were separated by over twenty degrees of latitude. The westward route lay within the wide belt of the northeast trades, whose southern limit is close to the equator and whose northern limits lie under the thirtieth parallel. During most of the year these could be depended on to carry a ship across the Pacific speedily and steadily with all canvas filled. To the north the prevailing westerlies, blowing above latitude thirty, marked the natural path of the galleons on their eastward passage."[22]

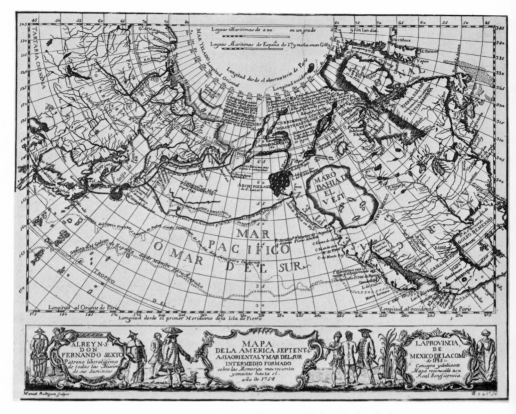

Route of the Manila Galleon. Chart published in Spain in 1754

The variable winds of the western Pacific, however, caused much difficulty in the Manila navigation. The long voyage to and from Manila in times of adverse weather could be calamitous. Padre Cásmiro Díaz described the return to Acapulco as "the longest, most tedious, and most dangerous voyage in all the seas."[23] Yet through all these difficulties and in spite of the great risk, the rewards of the trade were sufficient to support the Spanish trading community in Manila in opulence, and the Manila trade was the source of most of the Far Eastern goods reaching the Spanish-American colonies and the mother country.

The departure of a fleet for America was marked by much confusion, excitement and color. The citizens of the port of Seville or Cádiz would flock to the harbor to watch the proceedings and join others gathered to bid relatives and friends goodbye. There must have been great sadness among this group, for the length and dangers of the voyage and long residences in America assured that many would never see their loved ones again. Several accounts of the sailing of the fleet have come down to us. Again we can turn to Thomas Gage to get a characteristically graphic description of what he saw and heard. He sailed from Cádiz in 1625: "Upon the first day of July in the afternoon, Don Carlos Ybarra, Admiral of the Galleons that then lay in the Bay of Cádiz, gave order that a warning piece should be shot off to warn all passengers, soldiers, and mariners to betake themselves the next morning to their ships. Oh, what it was to see some of our apostolical company who had enjoyed much liberty for a month in Cádiz: now hang down their heads, and act with sad demure looks, loath to depart."[24] Gage was sailing with a company of his Dominican brothers and it must have been a sad time when the younger friars had to leave the pleasures of Cádiz and face the uncertain fate of a long voyage to America and more uncertain assignments among the Indians there.

Having taken aboard all the stores, cargo, passengers and crew, the fleet unfurled and set a course for the entrance of the bay to the shouted good wishes of the lucky ones on shore and the shouted good-byes of those on the ships: "Then went out the ships one by one crying *A dios, A dios*, and the town replying *Buen viaje, Buen viaje;* when all were out and no hopes of enjoying more Cádiz' pleasures and liberty, then began my young friars to wish themselves again aland: some began presently to feed the fishes with their nuns' sweet dainties; others to wonder at the number of stately ships, which with eight galleons that went to convoy us beyond the Canary Islands were forty-one in all."

Seasickness having overtaken the weaker, or perhaps the more "hung-over" passengers before leaving the bay, what must have been their feelings when the fleet entered the turbulent waters which lay off Cádiz: "Thus the convoy of eight galleons* for fear of Turks and Hollanders . . . set forward our fleet with a pleasant and prosperous gale, with a quiet and milken sea, until we came to the gulf called Golfo de Yeguas, or of Kicking Mares, whose waves and swelling surges did so kick our ship that we thought they would have kicked our St. Anthony's gilded image out of our ship . . . and that all our ship's galleries would have been torn from us with these spurnings and blows of that outrageous gulf."

The time having come for the galleons to return to Cádiz, goodbyes

---

* The additional armed escort which sometimes accompanied departing fleets through the dangerous waters off the Strait of Gibraltar.

were said with much ceremony and with visiting between the vessels and feasts among the officers: ". . . the eight galleons took their leave of us, and left our merchant ships now to shift for themselves. The departure of these galleons was most solemnly performed on each side, saluting each other with their ordnance, visiting each other with their cock-boats, the Admiral of the Fleet feasting with a stately dinner in his ship the Admiral of the Galleons; and the like performing most of the other ships."

Ninety years before Gage sailed from Cádiz, Don Alonzo Enríquez de Guzmán sailed for the Indies. In his journal written during the voyage, he describes his feelings and those of his fellow passengers: "It is now ten days since we have seen land, and we shall consider our-selves lucky if we see it in twenty days from this time. Fortunate are they who now sit down content before their fresh roast meat, espe-cially if a fountain of water flows near their doors. They have now begun to serve water to us by measure, and the people on board prefer drinking what is in the ship, to seeing that which is outside. I really believe that there are many here who would be glad to return to Spain and to have paid their passage without making the voyage."[25] These impressions were written ten days out from the Canaries. Fifteen days later Guzmán's ship arrived at the Virgin Islands, having "gone eight hundred leagues over the sea, suffering hunger and thirst, and seeing no land for twenty-five days."

In spite of hunger and thirst, life in the fleet on the long passage had some diversions to take the minds of the travelers from their stomachs. Saints' days were celebrated with plays and other divertissements. Gage describes such a day:

The last day of July (being according to the Jesuits' Order, and Rome's appointment, the day of Ignatius their patron and founder of their religion), the gallant ship called "Sta Gertrudis" (wherein went thirty Jesuits) for their and their saint's sake made to all the rest of the fleet a most gallant shew, she being trimmed round about with white linen, her flags and topgallants representing some of the Jesuits' arms, others the picture of Ignatius himself, and this from the evening before, shooting off that night at least fifty shot of ordnance, besides four or five hun-dred squibs (the weather being very calm) and all her masts and tack-lings hung with paper lanthorns having burning lights within them; the waits ceased not from sounding, nor the Spaniards from singing all night. The day's solemn sport was likewise great, the Jesuits increasing the Spaniards' joy with an open procession in the ship; singing their . . . hymns . . . all this seconded with roaring ordnance, no powder being spared for the completing of that day's joy and triumph. The fourth of August following, being the day which Rome doth dedicate to Dominic, the first founder of the Dominicans or Preachers' Order, the ship wherein I was named "St. Anthony" strived to exceed "Sta Gertrudis" by the assistance of the twenty-seven Dominicans that were in her. All was performed both by night and day as formerly in "Sta Gertrudis" both with powder, squibs, lights, waits, and music. And further did the Dominicans' joy and triumph exceed the Jesuits', in that they invited all the Jesuits, with Don John Nino de Toledo, the President of Manila, with the Captain of the ship "Sta Gertrudis" to a stately dinner both of fish and flesh; which dinner being ended, for the afternoon's sport they had prepared a comedy out of famous Lope de Vega, to be acted by some soldiers, passengers, and some of the younger sort of friars; which I confess was as stately acted and set forth both in shews and good apparel, in that narrow compass of our ship, as might have been upon the best stage in the Court of Madrid.[26]

Food in the fleets was the normal food carried to sea in the centuries before ice or mechanical refrigeration. If it could be dried, pickled, salted, preserved in sugar or honey, or carried on the hoof, then it could be taken to sea. In practice, the sailors, soldiers and poorer passengers would be restricted to a diet of salted meat, beans or peas, perhaps a little cheese and butter, hard biscuit with a little vinegar to use as a relish, and wine. The armada of Pedro de las Roelas, 1563–1564, carried hardtack, wine, beef, salt fish, salt pork, beans and peas, rice, oil, cheese, vinegar and garlic. The diet was augmented by fish caught on the voyage, which added a welcome fresh dish to the preserved food. Don Alonzo Enríquez de Guzmán describes a windfall which came to his ship in mid-Atlantic: "There are fish that they call flying fish, which fly for twenty paces, more or less, and sometimes fall on board the ship. I saw and ate some, which had a smoky taste: I do not know whether this was caused by the smoke in which they were roasted, or whether it was natural."[27]

When Gage's fleet arrived in the Gulf of Mexico it was becalmed, and while everyone sweltered in the heat, some fished with great success:

we came to what the Spaniards call *La Sonda*, or the Sound of Mexico; for here we often sounded the sea; which was so calm that a whole week we were stayed for want of wind, scarce stirring from the place where first we were caught by the calm. Here likewise we had great sport in fishing, filling again our bellies with *dorados* [dolphins], and saving that provision which we had brought from Spain. But the heat was so extraordinary that the day was no pleasure unto us; for the repercussion of the sun's heat upon the still water and pitch of our ships kindled

A bowl and pitcher of rough pottery from an unidentified wreck on the Bermuda reefs dating from about 1580, discovered by Donald Canton and Brian Malpus. Life in the treasure fleets was a rough one for the common seaman. He dined sitting on the deck with his messmates and ate with his sheath knife. Photograph from the Smithsonian Institution

Brass crucifix from Andalusia, recovered from the site of a large unidentified Spanish ship that sank on the western reefs of Bermuda about 1560. On the dangerous voyage to and from America passengers and crew took comfort from the assurances of their Catholic faith and many met death clutching their crucifixes. Photograph from the Smithsonian Institution

A pewter clyster pump from the Tucker treasure site (ca. 1595) off Bermuda. Passengers and crew had little opportunity for exercise and constipation was a common complaint. This pump in the hands of the ship's surgeon effectively corrected the condition. Photograph from the Smithsonian Institution

a scorching fire, which all the day distempered our bodies with a constant running sweat, forcing us to cast off most of our clothes. The evenings and nights were somewhat more comfortable, yet the heat which the sun had left in the pitched ribs and planks of the ship was such, that under deck and in our cabins we were not able to sleep, but in our shirts were forced to walk, sit, or lie upon the deck.[28]

In the calm water the mariners swam about the ship until one was attacked by a shark and killed while he was attempting to swim to another vessel to visit friends.

The diet on ships returning to Spain was a little different from that eaten on the trip out. The usual European foods were augmented with those of the New World. Gage mentions meal (probably maize), bacon, fowls, and honey. At Havana his fleet loaded tortoises:

> Now as hog's flesh there is held to be so nourishing, so likewise no other meat is more than it and tortoises, wherewith all the ships make their provision for Spain. The tortoises they cut in long slices, as I have noted before of the *tasajos* [jerked beef], and dry it in the wind after they have well salted it, and so it serveth the mariners in all their voyage to Spain, which they eat boiled with a little garlic, and I have heard them say that to them it tasted as well as any veal. They also take into their ships some fowls for the masters' and captains' tables, and live hogs, which would seem to be enough to breed some infection in the ship, had they not care to wash often the place where such unclean beasts lie. In the ship where I was passenger, was killed every week one for the masters', pilots', and passengers' table.[29]

Near the end of the voyage across the Atlantic, whether from or to Spain, the provisions would always be in poor condition, especially when bad weather prolonged the voyage. Gage thus describes the drinking water as the fleet approached the Azores: "[the water] we had taken in at Havana now began to stink, and look yellow, making us stop our noses whilst we opened our mouths."

The arrival at Vera Cruz was a joyous occasion and Gage describes the festivities:

> As soon as we came to shore we found very solemn preparations for entertainment, all the town being resorted to the seaside, all the priests and canons of the cathedral church, all the religious orders of the several convents (which were Dominicans, Franciscans, Mercenarians, and Jesuits) being in a readiness, with their crosses borne before them, to guide the new Viceroy of Mexico, in procession, to the chief cathedral church. . . . In the meantime all the cannon playing from ships

and castle, landed the Viceroy and his lady and all his train, accompanied with Don Martín de Carrillo the Visitor-General for the strife between the Count of Gelves, the last Viceroy, and the Archbishop of Mexico. The great Don and his lady being placed under a canopy of state, began the *Te Deum* to be sung with much variety of musical instruments, all marching in procession to the Cathedral, where were many lights of burning lamps, torches, and wax candles . . . a prayer of thanksgiving sung, holy water by a priest sprinkled upon all the people, and lastly a Mass with three priests solemnly celebrated.[30]

The Spanish fleet system has been likened to the ancient system of the caravan, and the method of trade at the destination was the same used at the terminus of the caravan route—the fair. In Spanish America fairs were held in several ports at which the Galeones, Flota and ships of register called. The greatest was that of Porto Bello, where the treasure routes from Peru and, on occasion, Guatemala, met the Galeones and merchantmen from Spain and in a space of a few weeks carried on the annual trade.

Next in importance was the fair of Vera Cruz, which was the terminus of the routes from the rich Mexican silver mines and the route to the Philippines and the Far East. Other lesser fairs were probably held when single ships would call at the Central American ports and when they reached Havana.

During fair time the ports, normally sleepy little villages, exploded with merchants, who poured in seeking lodging at any price. When Gage arrived at Porto Bello in 1637, the Galeones from Spain were expected daily. He had difficulty in getting a lodging and when he did, it cost outrageously and was only a "mouse hole."

> It was no bigger than would contain a bed, table, and a stool or two, with room enough besides to open and shut the door, and they demanded of me for it during the aforesaid time of the fleet, sixscore crowns, which commonly is a fortnight. For the town being little, and the soldiers that come with the galleons for their defence at least four or five thousand, besides merchants from Peru, from Spain, and many other places to buy and sell, is the cause that every room, though never so small, be dear; and sometimes all the lodgings in the town are few enough for so many people, which at that time do meet at Portobello. I knew a merchant who gave a thousand crowns for a shop of reasonable bigness to sell his wares and commodities that year that I was there, for fifteen days only, which the fleet continued to be in that haven.[31]

The prices of provisions were as outrageous as the rents, climbing as high as fifteen or twenty times their normal level:

Then began the price of all things to rise, a fowl to be worth twelve reals, which in the main land I had often bought for one; a pound of beef then was worth two reals, whereas I had in other places thirteen pound for half a real, and so of all other food and provision, which was so excessive dear that I knew not how to live but by fish and tortoises, which there are very many, and though somewhat dear, yet were the cheapest meat that I could eat. It was worth seeing how merchants sold their commodities, not by the ell or yard, but by the piece and weight, not paying in coined pieces of money, but in wedges which were weighed and taken for commodities. This lasted but fifteen days, whilst the galleons were lading with wedges of silver and nothing else; so that for those fifteen days, I dare boldly say and avouch, that in the world there is no greater fair than that of Portobello, between the Spanish merchants and those of Peru, Panama, and other parts thereabouts.

The press of strangers from Europe and America in the normally unhealthy climate of the coastal cities led to epidemics, and many who came to gain wealth in trade found only death. When Gage was at Porto Bello, disease racked the town:

Don Carlos de Ybarra, who was the Admiral of that fleet, made great haste to be gone; which made the merchants buy and sell apace, and lade the ships with silver wedges; whereof I was glad, for the more they laded, the less I unladed my purse with buying dear provision, and sooner I hoped to be out of that unhealthy place, which of itself is very hot, and subject to breed fevers, nay death, if the feet be not preserved from wetting when it raineth; but especially when the fleet is there, it is an open grave ready to swallow in part of that numerous people which at that time resort unto it, as was seen the year that I was there when about five hundred of the soldiers, merchants, and mariners, what with fevers, what with the flux caused by too much eating of fruit and drinking of water, what with other disorders lost their lives, finding it to be to them not *Portobello* but Porto malo.

Antonio de Alcedo, writing in the eighteenth century, described Porto Bello at fair time:

This city, which is but poorly inhabited, was, in the time of the galleons, one of the most populous in the world; for its situation upon an isthmus of the two seas, the N. and S., the goodness of its port, and its vicinity to Panama, gave it the preference of all the other settlements of America for the celebration of the richest fair in the Universe, and which was carried on nearly every year by the Spanish merchants of Spain and Peru.

Immediately on the arrival at Panama of the fleet of Peru with its

European goods exported to Spanish America during the colonial period. Brass spoons, bronze knee buckles, pewter knee buckles, paste gems and cheap costume jewelry—all from the wreck site of the *Matanceros,* sunk on the coast of Yucatan in 1741 and discovered and explored by Robert Marx and Pablo Bush Romero. The small glass tumbler and the brass coat and waistcoat buttons are from an unidentified wreck site of the mid-eighteenth century on Pedro Bank in the Caribbean. All manufactured goods were imported into colonial Spanish America, for the Spanish government suppressed manufacturing in the colonies. Photographs from the Smithsonian Institution

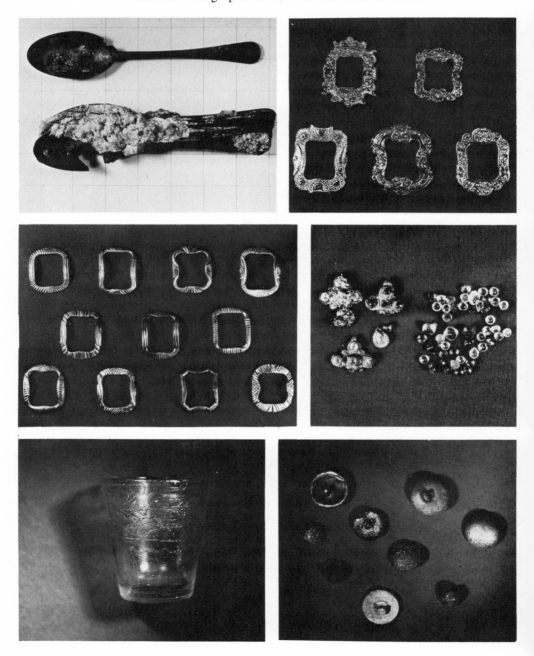

Religious medals and small crucifixes formed important parts of the cargoes of manufactured goods sent to America in the Spanish trade. These were recovered from shipwreck sites in the Caribbean and on the coast of Yucatan.
Photographs from the Smithsonian Institution

riches, the galleons of Cartagena dropped down to Portobello; not doing it sooner in order to avoid many inconveniences such as sickness and the exorbitant expences which arose from the vast concourse of people which used to assemble on the occasion; when a moderate sized parlour and bed would cost 1000 dollars [for sixty days], and the houses let for 5000 or 6000. Scarcely did the sailors bring their vessels to anchor, but they formed with sails a large booth in the square of the town where to disembark and lodge cargoes, each one recognizing his own effects by his mark, at the same time was to be seen the arrival of large mule-droves of 100 mules each, loaded with chests of gold and silver from Peru; some of these would lodge their valuable burdens in the custom house, others in the square; and it was, indeed, well worthy of admiration to see with what little disorder and confusion everything was conducted amongst so great a diversity of men and characters; robbery, murders, or any other less serious disturbances being entirely unknown on these occasions.

Again, the spectator who had just before been considering Portobello as a poor, unpeopled state, without a ship in its port, and breathing nothing but misery and wretchedness, would remain thunderstruck at beholding the strange alteration which takes place at the time of this fair. Now he would see the houses crowded with people, the square and the streets crammed with chests of gold and silver, and the port covered with vessels; some of these having been brought by the river Chagres from Panamá the effects of Peru, such as *cacao* bark, *vicuña* wool, Bezoar stone, and other productions of those provinces. He would see others bringing provisions from Cartagena; and he would reflect that however detestable might be its climate, this city was the emporium of the riches of the two worlds, and the most considerable commercial depot that was ever known.

Scarcely had the merchants of Spain disembarked their merchandise and those of Peru, attended by the president of Panamá, arrived with their riches, then the general of the galleons and the deputies of the two trading parties proceed to regulate the prices of all articles; and this being price published nothing will alter. Thus the sale and exchange used to be made in the course of 60 days, the time of the duration of the fair; during which period the vessels laden with the newly purchased Spanish goods would proceed up the river Chagres, the same kind of articles being carried by land to Panamá; and the European merchants would begin to put a-board the treasures of America; the city at the end of the aforesaid period remaining in the same deplorable state as before.[32]

The fairs concluded, the ships loaded and sought to get away for Spain as quickly as a good wind came. The admiral and captains wanted to stay in the ports of Porto Bello and Vera Cruz only long enough to finish their business. These fever-ridden places took a fear-ful toll of the officers, seamen and soldiers, and an early sailing was necessary to reduce the risk of epidemic illness. Also, the longer the treasure ships lay in American ports, the more danger was there of intelligence of their presence getting far abroad, bringing in additional enemies to join those already lying in wait along the route to Havana and Spain. The weather was also a very important factor in the sailing. The Spanish, through bitter experience, had learned of the hurricane season, and while they tended to "crowd" that season until fear of the weather had driven the corsairs from the lanes, they were not com-plete fools and had no intention of tangling head on with a hurricane if they could avoid it.

The first concern of the flag officers and captains as well as the civil royal officials with the fleet was the safe stowage of the King's gold and silver. They were also concerned in the stowage of the gold and silver on private accounts. After 1592 the direct responsibility for the safety of all the treasure, royal and private, rested with the *maestre de plata* (silver master), a carefully chosen official at first appointed by the captain general of the fleet but later appointed by the Crown. Not only was he chosen with great care but, as appointee, he was required to post 25,000 ducats in silver as bond with the officials of the Casa. His documents of identification included a certificate of this bond and all royal officials and private persons shipping treasure from American ports were warned by the Crown to check this identification and bond before turning over any treasure to him.

Several copies of the cargo manifest were prepared, two being for-warded in ships other than that which carried the treasure, one going with the treasure, and another remaining behind. All of these precau-tions were taken to facilitate accounting in the event of disaster to the ship or the entire fleet. In theory, every piece of gold and silver going aboard for Spain had to be posted on the manifest and had to be certified as tax-paid. In actuality, smuggling was practiced on such a scale that it must have had the connivance of many of the officials concerned. The laws against smuggling were increasingly severe, an admission by the Crown of the growing prevalence of the practice. The law of 1580 held that if any captain or officer carried any unregis-tered goods or bullion and it was confiscated, the captain or officer was liable in full to the owner. By the law of 1593 the offense was punished by loss of position for four years, and if the offender was an ordinary seaman, he was sent to the galleys for the same period of time. In that year it was also decreed that if the officials of the merchants' guild in Seville ordered the introduction of gold, silver or other commodities into Spain without registration, they would forfeit all their property to the Crown and would be banished from Spain and Spanish territory forever. Later punishments became even more severe.

Every piece of gold or silver going aboard ship for Spain was supposed to be in the form of coin or to bear stamps showing that the tax had been paid. Actually much of the bullion went home unmarked and undetected. The illegal trade at Seville alone was estimated at ten million pesos a year in the last half of the seventeenth century. The accounting problems arising from the control of the trade must have been enormous.

The shipments of bullion on private accounts were often very small individually. In *American Treasure and the Price Revolution in Spain*, Hamilton cites a caravel which came from the Indies in 1544. In it there were 154 different shipments of bullion. The first six were of 561, 578, 398, 245, 151 and 188 pesos of gold. In 1548 a treasure ship brought 324 shipments. The first six of these were 297, 329, 101, 64, 107 and 303 marks of silver. The very complexity of the bookkeeping made it quite impractical and much bullion and merchandise must have slipped by unrecorded.

The occasion of the arrival of the fleet from America was one for much rejoicing throughout Spain. With the arrival of the ships off the bar of Sanlúcar, word flashed to Seville and the city anticipated their coming. Sometimes the Sevillians had a long wait to endure, for the heavily laden ships had to remain off the bar until a high tide combined with a fair wind to carry them over the obstruction and into the Guadalquivir River. No one was permitted to leave the ships after arrival at Sanlúcar until each ship was inspected by an official of the Casa. This inspection had to be made within one day after the Casa was notified of the arrival of the ships at Sanlúcar.

When the vessels finally reached the quay in Seville, great must have been the excitement of the officials and merchants. No goods or bullion could be unloaded without the permission of the Casa, and all bullion, pearls, and other treasure had to be deposited in the Casa strongroom, which was built of heavy masonry with iron-barred windows. The treasure was kept in chests, and each chest was provided with three locks so that all three officials of the Casa, each with a key, had to be present when any of the chests was opened. When unusually large amounts of gold and silver were secured, there were special guards on duty around the clock. The silver master, who had accompanied the treasure from the New World, had yet to see to the distribution of the precious metals to the private owners or their agents in Seville. At the time of delivery the owner might again be required to prove that the metal was legally possessed and had been duly taxed. The law required that all the private silver and gold be delivered to the owners within four months of arrival in Seville unless there were special orders from the Crown to delay such delivery. In any case, the silver master could not embark on another voyage to America until the last shipment for which he was responsible had been distributed or otherwise accounted for.

The returning ships were often so stuffed with merchandise, much of it to the account of the ships' officers, that the guns could not be worked. On one occasion, this was a contributing cause to the loss of an entire fleet, an event we shall hear of later. Numerous ordinances were passed regulating the loading of private goods, but private enterprise would not be denied and the laws did little to correct the abuse.

The arrival of the fleet was eagerly awaited by all the Spanish, from the King down to the lowliest merchant. Philip II took an intense personal interest in the trade as he did in everything concerning his empire. Lively as his interest was, it did not exceed that of the Fuggers and other banking families of Europe, who almost always held a mortgage on the shipment. The constant drain on resources of the Spanish Crown in maintaining its far-flung lands both in Europe and the Americas caused the monarchs, from Charles I on, to fall into the hands of the international bankers. So close was the association and so close the interest of the Fuggers in Spain's finances that much of the news that got out of Spain came from the agents of that famous banking family. Their reports have been preserved and today form one of the most prolific sources of information on the fleets and on Spanish and Spanish-American affairs in general.

One such report written at Lyons on December 1, 1589, gives news of the Indies fleet and the anxiety of the Spanish court for the safety of unreported ships:

> From Madrid in Spain comes news . . . that twelve vessels from India [that is, the West Indies] have reached San Lúcar with general cargoes, but the big ships which are to bring some twelve millions worth have not yet arrived. They are supposed to have steered a different course for greater safety. There are still 25 English raiders at sea which are said to have attacked and pillaged Valenga and carried some vessels from Brazil and Porto Rico. But as the entire fleet of New Spain with its escort numbers over 80 vessels, it is hoped that it will be able to get past the English without damage. Others report that news has come in these letters from Spain that the fleet from New Spain had separated into two divisions. Twenty-eight of the largest ships with the bulk of the valuables have taken a different route, but of their whereabouts

nothing is known, whereas the majority of the fleet, that is 60 vessels with the less valuable cargo, came the most direct way and reached Seville on the 12th. Seven of them were damaged in a storm and a few sunk. However, most of the property on board was recovered. The Spanish Court awaits news of the 41 remaining ships with the utmost eagerness.[33]

In spite of the confused mass of regulations and exceptions to them, the diversion of fleets to other uses, the inconstancy of Spanish official-dom, the attacks by pirates and lawful enemies, natural disasters, cumbersome ships, and inefficient royal officials who had often purchased their offices, the commanders of the fleets were surprisingly successful in bringing home the treasure safely. They were eminently more successful in delivering the money than the King and his ministers were wise in spending it—often on ill-advised projects in Europe. This success, however, was as much testimony to the size of the North Atlantic and the difficulty of finding a fleet there as it was to the skill of the admirals.

Often, the treasure of private persons, having escaped shipwreck and capture at sea, fell victim to the agents of the King in Seville. Using his final prerogative the King, when in financial distress, sequestered gold and silver, giving in return long-term securities. In the winter of 1556–1557, the prize grab was perpetrated when Philip II, at the very beginning of his reign, sequestered all the private bullion in the Vera Cruz and Nombre de Dios ships. The gold and silver taken at this time amounted to 1,600,000 ducats.

And yet, against all these hazards, the trade with America continued. Goods went out and bullion and gems, dyestuffs and drugs, leather and rare woods came back, and the Spanish government continued as the great and reluctant supplier of gold and silver to the rest of Europe.

IV

The Poachers

These corsairs come fully supplied with all lines of merchandise, oils and wines and everything else which is lacking in the country. The colonists' needs are great and neither penalties nor punishments suffice to prevent them from buying secretly what they want. As a matter of fact, they make their purchases, but nothing can be learned of them, for they buy at night and cover each other, and no measures suffice to prevent it.
    —Letter from Diego Ruiz de Vallejo,
        royal official at New Segovia, Venezuela, to Philip II,
        April 21, 1568

 IN THE EARLIEST YEARS of the Spanish exploration and development of the Caribbean lands, the royal monopoly seemed to work quite well. The French and English had, of course, sent out Verrazano and Cabot, but these explorers had concerned themselves with the distant North, and their voyages were not followed up by their sponsors. A few pirates got into the area, but the Caribbean was, in effect, a locked box, with the Spanish Crown holding the key. The city of Santo Domingo remained the administrative center in the early years, when commercial activity centered around the plantations and mines of Hispaniola and Cuba. In the early and middle 1520's, the impact of the opening of Mexico had not yet been felt on the system. This serenity was soon to be broken.

On November 25, 1527, an unprecedented event occurred at Santo Domingo. A large three-masted vessel anchored off the city and sent a launch into the harbor, bearing the ship's master and a dozen or so seamen. Poachers had arrived. The men landed and informed the Spaniards who had come down to the shore that they were English and that they were sailing in the service of the King of England. They said that

this ship together with another, cleared perhaps nine months ago from England on order of their King, to make certain exploration toward the north, between Labrador and Newfoundland, in the belief that in that region there was a strait through which to pass to Tartary; and that

97

they sailed as far north as fifty and some degrees, where certain persons died of cold; the pilot had died; and one of the said vessels was lost.

For which reasons they came to this land to take in water and subsistance and other things which they needed.[1]

The English master asked for a safe conduct to enter the port. The Licentiates Cristóbal Lebrón and Alonso Zuazo, judges of the High Court of Justice and Equity, granted the request and sent Diego Méndez, the high sheriff, and two pilots to bring the ship in. The morning after its arrival off the port, it was anchored in the river mouth, from where it was to be warped into the harbor against a strong north wind. When the sheriff and pilots had gone aboard the Englishman, "the master received them well and gave them to eat and drink abundantly indeed and showed them certain linens, woolens and other merchandise which he carried for barter."[2] The sheriff observed that the ship "was well equipped for war, with much heavy brass artillery, in two tiers, that she was ready for action and clean, and that he . . . thought that all the vessels which were in [the] harbor were not sufficient to fetch her in by force."[3]

In his sworn testimony about the incident, the pilot Antonio Martín goes on to describe what occurred next: "Just as they had dropped anchor, and, the ship being anchored, all hands had begun to eat, with much pleasure and good humour, from the fortress of this city a lombard was fired, and the stone passed by the poop of the ship, very near to it; whereupon the ship's master turned colour, saying to witness and his companion that it was a plot to betray them."[4] Martín went on to say that he had tried to assure the master that he could enter the harbor safely, but the master could not accept the story that the live shot from the fort was merely a salute, and after putting the pilots and the sheriff ashore, he immediately set sail. As the small boat bringing the Spaniards ashore passed under the fort, Martín called to the warden of the fort and asked him if he considered his action in firing on the ship a wise one, since the ship had sailed because of it. The warden replied that the judges had told him nothing and therefore he had fired the lombard.

The action of the warden, from the point of view of the Spanish, was very unwise indeed. The ship had sailed with detailed information on the harbor and defenses of Santo Domingo and had not even been specifically identified by the Spanish. They only knew she was English. To this day the ship has not been identified—it was probably lost on the way to England. Our record of the event lies in the depositions taken before the judges of the High Court at Santo Domingo, whereby the officials sought to protect themselves from punishment by the Crown for their lack of wisdom, if not actual infraction of the Spanish law, which prohibited the ship's being there at all. The judges were very angry at the warden for having frightened away the ship with the cannon shot. The warden replied that the judges had not told him what was going on even though he had sent a man to find out, and he therefore did what his duty required.

From the point of view of the English, the shot was perhaps fortunate. For had they come ashore to trade or resupply, there is a good chance that they would have been betrayed by the townspeople, some of whom favored killing the English and stealing their ship—a much bigger and more powerful one than any the colony possessed. The next year, on March 27, 1528, the King signed a letter in Madrid expressing his concern over the visit of the English ship and its quick departure:

> I would have been much pleased had you taken and detained it, and had there not been such carelessness in this matter; for, as you will have learned, we are at war with the King of England,* and even were we not, it would have been well had you learned what voyage the ship was making and what she carried, and had not let the master and men of said ship go (as go they did), after they had landed and visited the city, and seen how it lies, and its harbour, inasmuch as they were from a foreign kingdom, and this was a thing not heretofor experienced in those parts. Nor can you exonerate yourselves in the matter, for there was great carelessness and negligence.[5]

We do not know the outcome of the affair, but the novelty of the event probably saved the officials from the royal punishment. Nothing like this had ever happened before, and the officers of the Crown were genuinely in doubt about what measures to take since there was no law specifically covering such a situation. Already the colonists of Hispaniola had grown rich from cattle and sugar exported both to Spain and to some of the other colonies in the Caribbean basin struggling to establish themselves. The new affluence had created a rich market thirsting for European goods, which the Spanish merchants could not supply because of the King's monopolistic control. This paradoxical situation—rich markets hungry for the luxury goods of Europe and a system of control that made supplying those markets a virtual impossibility—was to be the cause of the eventual disintegration of the system

* Charles was defending the rights of Catherine of Aragon against Henry VIII at this time, but no war had been declared and even the court in London could not tell the Spanish ambassador if war existed. The officials of Santo Domingo could not have been expected to know this.

Sir John Hawkins in 1576, at the age of forty-four. From a contemporary portrait

the Spanish Crown had so carefully designed to maintain control of the American trade. The first evidence of the breakup is seen in the interest the people of Santo Domingo displayed in the goods that the English master had shown them and in the eagerness of the townspeople to attempt to seize the ship as a means of getting their products to market. Over the next thirty years, as Mexico, Peru and the northern coast of South America were settled, the demand for European goods gradually extended through the entire Caribbean basin, and the need for Negro slaves to work in the mines and on the plantations (the Indians had been all but decimated) rapidly added another market that the Spanish merchants could not satisfy. Into this situation came another Englishman, the first of that nation to seriously challenge the Spanish commercial monopoly.

John Hawkins was the son of a distinguished seaman of the West Country, William Hawkins, who is credited with being the first Englishman to sail into the "Southern Seas." William had made several early voyages to Guinea to collect slaves, which he sold to the Portuguese colonists in Brazil. John followed the sea in the family ships and made several voyages to the Canary Islands. Here he had learned something of the state of things in the West Indies. He had heard of the great demand for slaves in the colonies and knew of the Portuguese traffic in them. He probably found out also that, despite the Spanish monopoly, colonial officials were conniving in the traffic to furnish the colonies with a labor supply, which was necessary to their economic survival. Backed by certain wealthy Londoners, Hawkins sailed in October of 1562 with three vessels—the flagship *Salomon* of 120 tons, the *Swallow* of 100 tons, and a bark, the *Jonas*, of 40 tons. Touching first at Tenerife in the Canaries, Hawkins watered and took on supplies. From here he went to Sierra Leone on the coast of Guinea, where by violence and trading, whichever was required, he secured three hundred or more Negroes. Resupplying his ships with water and provisions, he sailed to Hispaniola, capturing a caravel on the way. He arrived first at the town of Puerto de Plata, and sailed west to the port of Isabela on the north coast. Here, skillfully combining the use of force with offers of the much-needed slaves, Hawkins began his trading. Sailing back to Puerto de Plata, he disposed of a number of Negroes and then sailed westward to Monte Christi, where he emptied his ships. In return for the Negroes, Hawkins had obtained cargoes of hides, ginger, sugar, and a quantity of pearls.

The arrival of Hawkins had startled the Spanish but had probably pleased them as well. In these times, when the colonial officials were under royal orders to resist any incursions, commercial or otherwise,

Armed ship of the mid-sixteenth century. From an engraving of the period.
Photograph from the Smithsonian Institution

and were absolutely forbidden to traffic with foreigners, they were also under much pressure from their own slave-hungry landowners to permit such traffic. The situation was difficult for them, as they were caught in a cross fire. In this instance, Hawkins was well armed and there was always an implied threat of force if he were not permitted to trade; yet the officials could lose their heads if they were caught. The answer to the dilemma was an elaborate subterfuge. The officials constantly warned their subjects of the penalties for illegal trading, but the enforcement was only a pretense to protect them from the Crown. Under a threat of force by the trader, which the officials insisted on as window dressing, they would issue him a trading license and a warning at the same time, and the traffic would proceed.

On Hawkins's arrival off the northern coast of Hispaniola, the Licentiate Alonso Arias de Herrera, president of the Audiencia (court) at Santo Domingo, sent Licentiate Lorenzo Bernáldez to proceed "against" the English. The result was a license permitting Hawkins to trade in his slaves. The Spanish documents give us an interesting picture of the ritual followed in the matter. President Arias's report to the King tells of Hawkins's arrival and the efforts to resist him:

A Lutheran Englishman with a large ship and a shallop, both well supplied with artillery, and a caravel and a large bark, both handsome vessels, which they had taken from merchants as they left the Portuguese islands, arrived off the town of Puerto de Plata in this island. As soon as the captain and *alcaldes* of this town saw them, fearing lest they march inland to pillage the country, they entered into negotiations with them to the end of procuring their departure and inquired of them what they wanted. The English said they would go if they were shown a port where they could careen a caravel and shallop. In order to get rid of them they sent them to the port of La Isabela, which is twelve leagues from there.

The *alcalde* at once advised me of what was happening and immediately I sent a certain Licentiate Bernáldez, lawyer of this *Audiencia*, who is a diligent man and knows the country thoroughly. He was instructed to use all possible means to endeavour to arrest those Lutherans and seize their goods and not to allow a man to trade an article.

He went and in the adjacent settlements raised as many as seventy horsemen, who proceeded to a hut to which the English were accustomed to come. Advancing by night and endeavouring to discover and encounter them, they came upon three Englishmen, very well armed with arquebuses, who were spies and sentinels for the English, whom they seized. When the English became aware of their presence they retired and put to sea, believing this was a larger body of men than it was in fact, and sent to demand the prisoners of the said licentiate adding that they would conduct themselves courteously and give what might be desired.

Seeing how small a force he had compared with the Englishman's, the licentiate replied that he was agreeable. They then came up and the Englishman said that he would give one hundred and four head of slaves. In fine, they reached an agreement, but when it came to delivery the Englishman hung back a little in handing them over, demanding that the licentiate first give him written authorization to dispose by barter of thirty other pieces he had. The licentiate answered that he could not do so since his commission read quite to the contrary—that he could do no such thing. Nevertheless the Englishman again insisted that he give him this authorization as best he could, since it was nothing to him; wherefore, in order to get possession of his negroes, the licentiate gave it to him in so far as he was legally empowered to do so and no further. He obtained the slaves and turned them over to the treasurer of that town. Having consulted your majesty's royal officials, the *Audi-*

encia sent order to sell these slaves to the burghers of those places, who had had to do with the matter, because of their need of slaves.[6]

The president anticipated an adverse report to the King from another licentiate in Santo Domingo, whose report was in fact made, and added at the close of his letter: "I have reported this matter to your majesty at such length because I am aware that many persons intend to write to your majesty concerning it, and are writing, in sense quite contrary to this."

Hawkins had been in port over a month before the president reported the matter to the King. On April 19, Bernáldez came to the agreement referred to in the president's letter, a document which gave permission to Hawkins to trade his Negroes after "giving" one hundred and four slaves.

The slaves Hawkins presented to Bernáldez and which were subsequently sold to the planters of the north coast, presumably for the King's account, were supposed ransom for the captive Englishmen but were, in reality, a gentle bribe. Bernáldez' agreement with Hawkins is a masterpiece of evasion in that it gives Hawkins permission to trade against the law, requires him to pay duties imposed by the King on legal Spanish traders, and then threatens him with attack if he has not gone by a specified date, even though the weakness of the Spanish compared with the English was the official excuse Bernáldez and the president gave for permitting the English to trade in the first place. The profits must have been enormous if Hawkins could give away two thirds of his slaves and still lade three or four vessels with hides, gold and silver. The goods he had stolen in the caravel off Africa helped. The agreement read in part:

I, Licentiate Bernáldez, captain commissioned by his majesty against the English who are upon this coast of La Isabela, do hereby state that whereas according to the articles I have entered into with you, Captain John Hawkins, concerning the negroes and the caravel which you delivered to me for his majesty, it was agreed that you may sell the thirty-five negroes which remain to you, and are the fourth part of the hundred and forty you had aboard your ships when I reached this coast, provided that you or the purchaser of same pay to his majesty his license charges and customs duties;

To assure this payment I charge you and whosoever may purchase to satisfy Francisco de Cevallos, his majesty's treasurer, in the amount of the said license charges and customs duties;

And by these presents in so far as I am authorized and by law may do so, and no further, I grant you license to sell the said thirty-five negroes, with the proviso above set forth; provided further that you sell them within twenty days and within the said period furnish your ships and depart. Otherwise I may freely attack you.

Done on this coast on April 19, 1563.

The Licentiate Bernáldez.

By his order, Alvaro Ortiz, notary.[7]

On May 27, a week after the president had written the King, Licentiate Echegoyan, an official at Santo Domingo, either through pique for having been excluded from the deal or political enmity, wrote the Crown of the affair and the illegality of the proceedings. Two months later he again wrote:

One Licentiate Lorenzo Bernáldez (recently converted Christian, whose brother is son-in-law to Licentiate Angulo, former judge of this *Audiencia*) was given a commission to go out against the English. This was contrary to my opinion in the matter and I did not sign it.

He stated that he captured two Englishmen and to ransom them the English delivered to your majesty one hundred and five slaves, which are in the possession of your majesty's officials in those ports. He said the English repeatedly offered these slaves in exchange for a permit to trade and in the accompanying certificate it appears that they did deliver them in exchange for license to dispose of the cargoes. According to the permit, he authorized them to sell thirty-five negroes, and . . . thirty-five for one hundred and five. The said permit is tinted with deceit and the case involves more than I can here lay before your majesty.

Since the licentiate went out as captain against them, according to the text of said permit, why did he not arrest them? How does it happen that he entered into an arrangement with heretics, as the document states? How is it that the Englishman gave . . . slaves? The *Audiencia* is writing of the matter.

Further, all the merchandise the said English had was stolen goods, taken off the coast of Guinea from a man named Francisco Espíndola. In brief, this has been a very scandalous business. I conferred regarding it with Licentiate Valderrama, of your majesty's council, who was in this city, with whose opinion I agree that I should inform your majesty.[8]

Hawkins, having successfully traded his slaves and merchandise, made the blunder of sending the hides and other bulky cargo to an agent in Spain. Echegoyan's letter of May 27 had alerted the officials at home, and the goods were seized and the agents arrested. Bernáldez apparently went home to be questioned after having written the King a long letter in August. The last letter from Echegoyan is dated November 4:

> because the affair is being hushed up and it is my duty not to cover such matters, therefore do I write, much against my desire.
> The captain's brother is married to a daughter of Licentiate Angulo, and he is very rich. So, too, is Licentiate Angulo, whose wealth imposes quietude—not because he participated in the profits, for he is a well-intentioned, good person. The captain is a son and grandson of recent converts from Jewry. . . . To prove his services he relies on depositions made by persons under obligation to him and upon farcical witnesses.[9]

We don't know what happened to Bernáldez, but being rich and married to the daughter of an influential official, he probably bought his way out in good order.

As for Hawkins, undiscouraged by the loss of his bulky merchandise, he began another cruise to the West Indies in the fall of 1564. Again he raided the coast of Guinea for slaves, using deceit and the sword to secure hundreds of Negroes to sell into slavery in the West Indies. John Sparke the Younger, who accompanied the expedition, has left an account that is the only detailed source on the voyage.[10]

Hawkins sailed from Plymouth on October 18 with four ships: the *Jesus of Lubeck,** the flagship of 700 tons; the *Salomon* of 120 tons; the *Tiger* of 50 tons; and the *Swallow* of 30 tons.† One hundred and seventy men manned the ships, which were well armed and supplied for a voyage of long duration. Setting course for the Canary Islands, the squadron sailed on a fair wind until October 21, when a great storm arose and the ships were battered for one whole day, during which the *Swallow* disappeared in the driving rain. To the great relief of the company, the *Swallow* reappeared two days later. A southwest wind arose and the ships put in at the Spanish port of Ferrol in Galicia to await a favorable change in the weather. Here Hawkins issued detailed orders that if the ships became separated and could not find their consorts, they should make for Tenerife in the Canaries. He ended his orders with the admonition: "Serve God daily, love one another, preserve your victuals, beware of fire, and keep good company."

On November 8, Hawkins made the port of Adexe on Tenerife, where he intended to land, get provisions and water, and visit with the

---

* This ship had been purchased from Lubeck by Henry VIII for the Royal Navy.
† Another, smaller ship. The *Swallow* on the voyage of 1562 displaced 100 tons.

The *Jesus of Lubeck*, flagship of John Hawkins. Drawing in a sixteenth-century manuscript. Photograph from the Smithsonian Institution

governor, who was a friend. As he approached the shore in a small boat, he was startled to find the men of the town drawn up on the beach with muskets and small cannon. Hawkins stood off and described the purpose of his visit and his desire to see the governor. After some parleying, an agreement was reached for supplying the ships with fresh food and water, and a message was sent to the governor, who was visiting another town down the coast. While Hawkins waited for the governor to come back, the mainmast of the *Jesus*, which had been sprung in the storm, was repaired. On the governor's arrival, he gave Hawkins "as gentle entertainment as if he had been his own brother."

At this time, the Canaries were almost unknown to the English, and Sparke describes for his readers the wonders of the place, including camels, an animal utterly strange to the English; trees that "rained"; grapes as big as plums; wines and fruits in abundance; and cattle and fowl in great numbers. The English indeed found it a veritable paradise, and they filled their bellies, drank the wine, and absorbed the sunshine to the limit. After a week at Tenerife, the English sailed for the coast of Africa, where they captured some slaves and had several brushes with the natives.

On January 29, Hawkins departed for the West Indies. The voyage was a bad one. The ships were becalmed, then were beset by contrary winds, and made no headway for eighteen days. Having only a minimum of water aboard, the English feared the worst for themselves and the Negroes, but as Sparke says, "the Almightie God, who never suffereth his elect to perish, sent us the sixteenth of Februarie, the ordinary Brise, which is the Northwest winde, which never left us, till wee came to an Island of the Canybals, called Dominica, where wee arrived the ninth of March, upon a Saturday": a remarkable commentary on the attitudes of that day toward religion and the despicable slave trade. At Dominica, the English went ashore for water but found nothing but rain water in puddles. No Caribs were to be seen—they had been driven from that part of the island by the drought. If the Indians had been there, the English would have had to fight for every drop of water they got. The Caribs' reputation was well known to the English, Sparke remarking that they "are the most desperate warriers that are in the Indies, by Spaniardes report, who are never able to conquer them, and they are molested by them not a little, when they are driven to water there in any of those Islands: of very late, not two monethes past, in the said Island, a Caravel being driven to water, was in the night sette upon by the inhabitants, who cutte their cable in the halser, whereby they were driven a shore, and so taken by them, and eaten."

On the sixteenth of March, the English arrived at Margarita, where they were entertained by the *alcalde*, but the governor of the island refused them both a license to trade and a pilot to take them to the mainland, and sent word by caravel to Santo Domingo of their arrival in the Indies. This was to prove troublesome to Hawkins in his later efforts at trading, for the viceroy at the capital sent word of the impending arrival of the English to all the settlements in Hawkins's path along the Spanish Main. Not being able to trade at Margarita, Hawkins sailed four days later and on March 22 arrived at Cumaná on the mainland. Here the English met a party of Spanish soldiers who were not able to buy anything but directed Hawkins to a watering place at Santa Fe six miles away, where a freshwater river rushed into the sea with such force that the English were able to water the ships while lying well offshore. The day after the arrival at Santa Fe, the local Indians came down to the shore to trade, and the English were able to get corn, chickens, potatoes and pineapples, for which they gave pewter whistles, mirrors, knives and glass beads. These Indians were "surely gentle and tractable, and such as desire to live peaceably" according to Sparke, who observes that otherwise it would have been impossible for the Spanish to have conquered them and to have lived

A mid-sixteenth century galleon and galley. After a contemporary engraving

among them in peace. On the twenty-eighth of March, Hawkins sailed, and the next day passed the island of Tortuga;* then he continued along the coast of the mainland until April 1, when he took the pinnace of the *Jesus* and went inshore to "discerne the coast." Here the English saw Indians ashore and in canoes, who showed them gold and urged them to come ashore to trade. The English refused and this saved their lives, for these apparently peaceful natives were Caribs, who would have killed and eaten them. A few days later, at Borburata, the English learned of their close brush with death when they were told the story of a Spanish caravel which Sparke relates:

> These were no such kinde of people as wee tooke them to bee, but more devilish a thousand partes and are eaters and devourers of any man they can catch, as it was afterwards declared unto us at Burboroata, by a Caravel comming out of Spaine with certaine souldiers, and a Captaine generall sent by the king for those Eastward parts of the Indians, who sayling along in his pinnesse, as our Captaine did to descry the coast, was by the Caribes called a shoore with sundry tokens made to him of friendshippe, and golde shewed as though they desired trafficke, with the which the Spaniard being mooved, suspecting no deceite at all, went ashore amongst them: who was no sooner ashore, but with foure or five more was taken, the rest of his company being invaded by them, saved themselves by flight, but they that were taken, paied their ransome with their lives, and were presently eaten.

Hawkins had arrived at Borburata on the third of April, and the squadron anchored while he went ashore to make arrangements to trade. He carried with him a letter from the Licentiate Lorenzo Bernáldez of Santo Domingo, who had issued him the license to trade on the northern coast of Hispaniola on his last voyage. The letter was addressed to Lorenzo's nephew Alonzo Bernáldez, governor of Venezuela, who was resident at Coro some miles inland. Hawkins went through his usual act of proclaiming himself a servant of Elizabeth and saying he came in peace to trade but threatening force if refused. His arrival was reported to Governor Bernáldez by Antonio de Barrios, his deputy at Borburata, who urged the governor to come to the town or at least issue a license to Hawkins to trade:

> Tuesday, there appeared off this town seven sails, one of which vessels is very powerful. The fleet is English and so rich in slaves and merchandise that they affirm it to be worth more than 100,000 *pesos*. The commander is an Englishman who time past came to Santo Domingo.

* Not to be confused with the island of Tortuga off the coast of Hispaniola.

He advertises that he is a great servitor of [your honour]. His intention is to sell with authorization and unless this license is given him he threatens with great oaths to do what harm and damage he may be able.

Your honour is already aware of the necessity existing in all the province and of the serious illnesses all the province is suffering because of its penury. I entreat your honour to deign to come to apply the remedy, for the best good of all. . . . The royal revenues would be augmented and the country benefitted. . . .

There is nothing more to write, except to entreat your honour to come. Greater evil is ahead of us, for if the town is burned it will mean its abandonment, in addition to which we will be turned into the woods in weather bad enough to kill us even were we strong, as we are not, but very sickly.[11]

Hawkins gave the governor ten days from April 5 to answer Bernáldez' request. He agreed to pay the royal duties into the colonial treasury.

On receiving Barrios's letter the governor came to Borburata, arriving on the fourteenth, but affected to disapprove issuing a license and reminded the people of the royal prohibition. Thereupon the people elected a citizen, Alonso de Valenzuela, procurator. He gathered together witnesses to support their case for the issuance of a trading license by the governor and cited the dire consequences of not doing so. One witness, Juan Pacheco, stated in his deposition:

Deponent believes it would be a great service to God and to his royal majesty to give to him, although he is a foreigner and of a nationality with which his majesty has prohibited trade. For if it not be given him . . . he would now do more damage than he first threatened . . . from here down the whole coast he would leave not a thing standing upright. . . .

Many would die of sickness occasioned by the rainy season, and if scattered in the woods their lives would be endangered, especially since in these regions there are very many Indians and they have killed many Spaniards. . . . Deponent believes that were Borburata abandoned the inhabitants of Valencia would also be in great danger from the Indians, and he considers that God, Our Lord, and his royal majesty will be better served by granting the said license than by ruining the people of this city and Valencia and risking the safety of the whole province and the entire coast [by refusing to grant it].[12]

On the same day depositions of the citizens were being taken, Hawkins petitioned the governor:

Very magnificent sir: I, John Hawkins, captain general of my fleet, in the person of Cristóbal de Llerena, my procurator, appear before your honour in the manner most advantageous to my interests, and state that:

Whereas by order of Elizabeth, queen of England, my mistress, whose fleet this is, I cleared on a certain voyage, and was by contrary weather driven to these coasts where, since I have found a convenient harbour, it behoves me to repair and refurnish my ships to continue said voyage;

And whereas to do this I have need to sell the slaves and merchandise I carry;

And whereas I am a great servitor of the majesty of King Philip, whom I served when he was king of England;

I therefore petition your honour to grant me license to sell my cargo. I stand ready to pay his majesty the duties usual in this land and to sell the said merchandise at acceptable prices.[13]

With the depositions of the citizens and Hawkins's petition in hand, the governor issued a license for the sale of the Negroes. Hawkins was then informed that the duty on each Negro was thirty ducats, a sum that would more than eat up all the profit at prices the Spanish were willing to pay. The time had come for Hawkins to use force. On the afternoon of the sixteenth, after failing to persuade the Spanish governor to lower the duty, Hawkins armed a hundred men with bows, arrows, arquebuses and pikes, and led them toward the town. The governor sent messengers to learn of Hawkins's intentions. The Englishman declared again his intention to trade and offered to pay a duty of 7½ percent, but not the thirty ducats on each Negro. To this the governor agreed.

So it was that the elaborate farce had been acted out: the arrival with offers of much-needed slaves at reasonable prices, the excuse that the English needed to repair their ships and resupply them, the threat of force to enable the local officials to approach the governor for permission to trade, the governor's notifying the people that such trade was illegal and his receiving the depositions of the people of the town in favor of the license, Hawkins's petition, the governor's granting the license but requiring the usual thirty ducats' duty on each slave, Hawkins's arming and marching on the town, at which time the governor agreed to lower the duty to 7½ percent. In this manner, the governor prevented trouble with his superiors at Santo Domingo, the people were able to trade for the slaves, and Hawkins made his profit. The governor probably also received a bribe, but this, of course, does not appear in the documents.

In receiving the license to trade, Hawkins had yet to bargain with his shrewd Spanish customers. The first Negroes sold were those who were sickly from the voyage and who required immediate care. These were purchased at reduced prices by the poorer Spanish. Only the wealthy landowners could afford to pay the higher prices Hawkins asked for the Negroes in better health, but they held back, hoping that Hawkins would reduce the price as his expenses in maintaining them and his fleet mounted. The English, answering guile with guile, made preparations to sail on the twenty-eighth of April. This had its intended effect on the planters, and they flocked to the harbor to buy the slaves they needed. While this trade was going on, a French ship arrived in the harbor short of supplies and water, with some merchandise to trade.

The French had lost a captain and several men on the coast of Africa and were no threat either to the English or the Spanish. Hawkins remained at Borburata until May 4, when he sailed leaving the Frenchmen in the harbor. The night before sailing, two hundred Caribs from down the coast approached the town in canoes hoping to burn and loot the place, but the presence of the English and French had caused the Spanish to be more alert than usual and the Caribs were driven off. The guide of the Caribs was caught and impaled on a sharp stake, "thrust through his fundament, and so out his neck."[14]

Arriving at Curaçao on May 6, the English traded for hides and fresh meat while riding at anchor at sea, since they could find no suitable protected ground. Sparke remarks that the increase of the cattle on the island was so prodigious that only the hides were sold. The meat not required by the local population was given away or left to rot in the fields. In one field he saw a hundred oxen lying "all whole, saving the skinne and tongue taken away." For nine days Hawkins remained at Curaçao and loaded with hides, fresh meat, and supplies.

On May 15 the English set a course for Río de la Hacha on the mainland past Cape de la Vela in the viceroyalty of New Granada. On their arrival four days later, Hawkins visited the royal treasurer resident there, showing him a certificate the governor of Borburata had given him. The warning that had been sent out from Santo Domingo had reached the town, and Hawkins was informed that the Spanish had been directed not to trade but to resist the English with all force. According to Sparke, the treasurer, Miguel de Castellanos, further said that "they durst not traffie . . . in no case, alleaging that if they did, they should lose all that they did trafique for, besides their bodies at the magistrates commaundment." Hawkins replied that he was in a fleet of the Queen of England, driven to that coast by contrary winds, and knowing of no enmity between the King of Spain and Queen of England could not see why they should not trade in friendship. The Spanish then decided to grant a license on condition Hawkins would sell his slaves at half the price obtained at Borburata. Now the pageant began.

Hawkins countered that his goods were as reasonable as any others and in any case no one else was there to sell to them. During the night a party of about one hundred men were armed and prepared to land in the morning. When day broke the English approached the shore in pinnaces armed with great guns. The Spanish made a brave show of force, lining the beaches with their foot soldiers and sending horsemen coursing up and down armed with lances and white leather shields. But the brave show ended when the heavy guns of the pinnace were fired over the beach. Taken by surprise at the heavy artillery they didn't expect in small ships, the Spanish withdrew. Hawkins landed and marched toward the town. On the way the English were met by a messenger sent by the local officials praying Hawkins to stop and wait for the treasurer, who was coming out to parley. Shortly afterward, that worthy official arrived and negotiated.

Hawkins got his license that day, signed by Castellanos, by the accountant Hernando Costilla, the *alcalde*, and by other officials. The terms allowed him to sell slaves, cloth, linen, wine, arms and any other commodities he had to the townspeople. The usual customs duty of 7 ½ percent was to apply. While trade was proceeding quietly, the Spanish moved some cannon into position, thinking they might have the slaves and their money back as well. But the English were on the alert and nothing came of the scheme. When Hawkins sailed on May 31, he took with him Spanish money and goods, and a certificate of good conduct as well, signed by Hernando de Heredia, notary public and clerk of the council:

> To all whom it may concern that from Saturday, in the morning, which was the nineteenth day of the present month of May, when the very magnificent John Hawkins, captain general of the English fleet, entered with said fleet into the harbour of this city, up to to-day, Wednesday, at about four o'clock in the afternoon, when he got under weigh with said fleet, the said captain and the men of his fleet have traded and transacted business with all the people of this town in the slaves and merchandise which their vessels brought, maintaining the peace and without disturbing it, and working no harm to any person whatsoever of any quality or condition.[15]

Hawkins set a course for the western end of Hispaniola but was swept far beyond it by the current and made a landfall at the center of the south coast of Jamaica. He had on board a Spanish merchant from Jamaica whom he had rescued from the Negroes of Guinea. The Spaniard failed to recognize the coast of his home island and convinced Hawkins that they were sailing along the southern coast of Hispaniola. Accordingly Hawkins set his course for the west. Not only did they reach Cuba by mistake, but they were delayed by storms and contrary winds, and the water supply got dangerously low. Now off the southern coast of Cuba they faced death from thirst. Here Hawkins went in a pinnace to scout the coast for fresh water. He ran among the islands of the "Gardens of the Queen" but found no water until he had reached the Isle of Pines to the westward. The water was standing in pools and was brackish, but the English filled their casks since there was no other to be had. By trusting to his Spanish passenger, Hawkins had lost several thousand pounds in trade and a chance to supply the ships with good water and fresh provisions, but worst of all, he had been carried so far westward that he now had to round Cape San Antonio and beat his way eastward. He followed the Spanish practice and sailed up into the Gulf of Mexico to catch the northwest winds and the Florida Current. By June 29, they were off the western coast of Florida and on July 5, the Dry Tortugas. Here in just six hours, they took many tortoises and carried them live in the holds to supply themselves with fresh meat on the long voyage home. The next day they sighted the coast of Cuba. Here again an error of navigation brought great trouble to Hawkins. This time a Frenchman on board misled him and he was persuaded to sail westward along the coast of Cuba, thinking Havana to be in that direction. When the error was realized, the English had to beat back eastward against the wind. The water was again running out, only one day's supply remaining in the casks, and Hawkins was determined to go inshore and look for a river, but at that moment, Sparke says,

> almighty God our guide, who would not suffer us to run into any further danger, which we had bene like to have incurred, if we had ranged the coast of Florida along as we did before, which is so dangerous (by reports) that no ship escapeth which commeth thither, (as the Spanyards have very wel proved the same) sent us the eight day at night a faire Westerly winde, whereupon the captaine and company consulted, determining not to refuse Gods gift, but every man was contented to pinch his own bellie, whatsoever had happened; and taking the sayd winde, the ninth day of July got to the Table.

The Table was a low flat hill west of Havana which navigators looked for when approaching Cuba from the Dry Tortugas. Hawkins had seen it but had been persuaded by the Frenchman that it was another landmark. Sailing on the west wind, the English squadron overran Havana in the night and rather than sail west again and then beat eastward, determined to reach for the Florida Straits. Here off the Florida Keys, the pinnace of the *Jesus* and the boat of the *Salomon* were sent ashore with twenty-one men to search for water. At the time the boats set out, the ships were not in the Florida Current but they were soon caught by it and swept to the northeast. The boats were signaled to come off but went on, not knowing what was happening to the ships and hoping to find water near, which they soon did. The job of filling the casks took longer than expected and night fell. The ships tried to remain off the point where the boats were ashore, but they weren't able to sail against the current and Hawkins sent the two smaller ships near shore where the rush of the water was not so great. Here they remained all night, showing lights and firing off guns. The next morning the boats were still out of sight, and it was determined if they did not appear by noon, the squadron would have to sail without them. At the last minute, the boats sighted the masts of the small ships and coming to them were taken up. Two days later, on July 14, the rescue ships joined the *Jesus* and the *Salomon* to the great joy of the whole company.

The English sailed slowly up the coast of Florida, exploring every creek and keeping their water casks full. Hawkins may have had some ulterior purpose in mind. Even though the French had established themselves to the north, he may have thought that Florida might be a good prospect for further English exploration and possible settlement. But he may have only been satisfying his curiosity. (The French experiment was to end just a few months later, when a relief fleet under Jean Ribaut was wrecked and all the French were massacred by the Spanish admiral Menéndez.)

While the English sailed up the coast, they observed the plants and animals of the country. Sparke in his narrative has left descriptions of what they saw, some of the best of the land and the Florida Indians:

> In ranging this coast along, the captaine found it to be all an Island, and therefore it is all lowe land, and very scant of fresh water, but the countrey was marvellously sweet, with both marish [marsh] and medow ground, and goodly woods among. There they found sorell to grow as abundantly as grasse, and where their houses were, great store of maiz and mill, and grapes of great bignesse, but of taste much like

our English grapes. Also Deere great plentie, which came upon the sands before them. Their houses are not many together, for in one house an hundred of them do lodge; they being made much like a great barne, and in strength not inferiour to ours, for they have stanchions and rafters of whole trees, and are covered with palmito-leaves, having no place divided, but one small roome for their king and queene. In the middest of this house is a hearth, where they make great fires all night, and they sleepe upon certeine pieces of wood hewen in for the bowing of their backs, and another place made high for their heads, which they put one by another all along the walles on both sides. In their houses they remaine onely in the nights, and in the day they desire the fields, where they dresse their meat, and make provision for victuals, which they provide onely for a meale from hand to mouth. . . .

In their apparell the men onely use deere skinnes, wherewith some onely cover their privy members, othersome use the same as garments to cover them before and behind; which skinnes are painted, some yellow and red, some blacke & russet, and every man according to his owne fancy. They do not omit to paint their bodies also with curious knots, or antike worke, as every man in his owne fancy deviseth, which painting, to make it continue the better, they use with a thorne to pricke their flesh, and dent in the same, whereby the painting may have better hold. In their warres they use a sleighter colour of painting their faces, thereby to make themselves shew the more fierce; which after their warres ended, they wash away againe. In their warres they use bowes and arrowes, whereof their bowes are made of a kind of Yew, but blacker then ours, and for the most part passing the strength of the Negros or Indians, for it is not greatly inferior to ours: their arrowes are also of a great length, but yet of reeds like other Indians, but varying in two points, both in length and also for nocks and feathers, which the other lacke, whereby they shoot very stedy: the heads of the same are vipers teeth, bones of fishes, flint stones, piked points of knives, which they having gotten of the French men, broke the same, & put the points of them in their arrowes head: some of them have their heads of silver, othersome that have want of these, put in a kinde of hard wood, notched, which pierceth as farre as any of the rest. In their fight, being in the woods, they use a marvellous pollicie for their owne safegard, which is by clasping a tree in their armes, and yet shooting notwithstanding: this policy they used with the French men in their fight, whereby it appeareth that they are people of some policy: and although they are called by the Spanyards Gente triste, that is to say, Bad people, meaning thereby, that they are not men of capacity: yet have the French men found them so witty in their answers, that by the captaines owne report, a counseller with us could not give a more profound reason.

The women also for their apparell use painted skinnes, but most of them gownes of mosse, somewhat longer than our mosse, which they sowe together artificially, and make the same surplesse wise, wearing their haire downe to their shoulders.

Arriving at the River of May (St. Johns River), the English found a French ship of 80 tons and two pinnaces of 15 tons each. Here they were informed that the French settlement, Fort Caroline, lay up the river six miles away. Hawkins asked for a watering place and the Frenchmen furnished a pilot to guide one of the English barks eight miles upriver where the water was fresh. Hawkins went with the bark and small boats, which anchored off the fort while he went ashore to call on the French commander, Captain René de Laudonnière. Here he was "very gently entertained" and learned that the French had settled the place fourteen months before with two hundred men. The French had brought little food with them, hoping to live off the land, but the soldiers would not cultivate the soil or fish, and very soon they had eaten the supply of corn the Indians had sold them. Because the natives lived from hand to mouth, as was their custom, and never laid in large reserves of food, the French were faced with starvation—they still refused to work for their food. Eighty of the soldiers rebelled and, stealing a bark and pinnace, which they stocked with what little food remained, went cruising to Hispaniola and Jamaica, where they captured two caravels. But they were in turn captured at Port Royal by Spanish warships sent out from Santo Domingo. Some were hanged, some escaped back to Florida, and others were transported to Spain. The leaders who returned to Fort Caroline were hanged. Laudonnière thus lost sixty men of the garrison. The remainder were reduced to eating acorns and stealing what they could from the Indians. This led to constant fights with the natives, in which Frenchmen were killed and wounded, thereby further reducing their ability to defend themselves against the hundreds of Indian warriors who lived in the area. By the time the English arrived, the French had been reduced to forty effective soldiers, and just ten days of provisions were left. Laudonnière and his companions viewed the arrival of the English as nothing less than providential. Hawkins, before leaving, provided the French with twenty barrels of meal, four barrels of beans, and other provisions and supplies, as well as one of the barks of 50 tons, for the French were determined to abandon the fort as quickly as possible and return to France. These plans were never followed, for Jean Ribaut had sailed from Havre-de-Grâce (now Le Havre) and arrived at Fort Caroline on August 28 before Laudonnière and his company left.

Hawkins sailed from the River of May on July 28 and was immediately beset by bad weather, which prolonged the voyage. Food and water ran so short that the English feared they would never reach England. When the situation was really desperate, a fair wind arrived and Hawkins sailed to the banks of Newfoundland, where he found two French fishing vessels and was able to buy sufficient fish to provide for the rest of the voyage. From here the fleet caught a good westerly wind, and on September 20 they arrived on the southwestern coast of England. Sparke expresses the joy of arriving safely home at Padstow in Cornwall, loaded with treasure and other valuable goods which brought great profit to Hawkins and his backers.

With gold in his pocket and those of his backers, Hawkins soon began planning another assault on the West Indies market. This voyage was to end in disaster for the English, but was to spawn a dragon and a generation of trouble for the Spanish.

V

The Dragon

Drake is a man of medium stature, blond, rather heavy than
slender, merry, careful. He commands and governs imperiously.
He is feared and obeyed by his men. He punishes resolutely.
Sharp, restless, well-spoken, inclined to liberality and to ambition, vainglorious, boastful, not very cruel. These are the qualities I noted in him during my negotiation with him.
          —Letter of García Fernández de Torrequemada,
          royal factor at Hispaniola, to King Philip II,
          February 1, 1587

THE DESCRIPTION ABOVE is hardly one's idea of a dragon, but
this able, firm, and merry Englishman was to become a
scourge to the Spanish. His reputation for efficient destruction and
looting was one of his greatest weapons, for having been nurtured on
stories of his exploits, which were invariably exaggerated, most of the
Spanish colonials had no stomach to stand up to him and his men.

Drake had come by his hatred of the Spanish honestly. It all began
on the third voyage of John Hawkins to the West Indies. Hawkins
sailed from Plymouth on October 2, 1567, with the flagship *Jesus of
Lubeck,* the *Minion,* and four other ships, which included the *Judith,* a
bark of 50 tons commanded by Drake. A cousin of Hawkins's, Drake
had been reared and educated under the protection of the older man.
At twenty, he had gone on a voyage to Guinea after gaining experience on coasting ships and was with John Lovell in 1566, when the
English had attempted to trade at Río de la Hacha. Lovell was en-
deavoring to deliver slaves contracted for with Hawkins the year before but was forced to leave ninety-two Negroes described as "old,
and very sick and thin."[1] The Río de la Hacha officials at that time
were under investigation by the Audiencia of Santo Domingo for having traded with Hawkins in the first place and they successfully resisted the English. Hawkins blamed the failure of the venture on the
inexperience of Lovell and Drake. Lovell and Drake arrived back in
England only a month before Hawkins sailed.

For a week after leaving Plymouth, the ships had reasonable

Francis Drake. From a contemporary miniature

weather, but on the eighth day of the voyage a violent storm struck 120 miles north of Cape Finisterre. For four days they were battered. The ships' boats were swept away, and the *Jesus* was so badly damaged Hawkins resolved to return home. When the storm passed, however, a fair wind sprang up, and the English determined to go on to the Canary Islands, where they met at the island of Gomera. Sailing from the Canaries on November 4, the squadron arrived at Cape Verde two weeks later. Here they landed men to take Negroes. Hawkins describes the hardships they suffered at the hands of the natives, including a description of tetanus contracted by the wounded from poisoned arrows:

> we landed 150 men, hoping to obtaine some Negros, where we got but fewe, and those with great hurt and damage to our men, which chiefly proceeded of their envenomed arrowes: and although in the beginning they seemed to be but small hurts, yet there hardly escaped any that had blood drawen of them, but died in strange sort, with their mouthes shut some tenne dayes before they died, and after their wounds were whole; where I my selfe had one of the greatest woundes, yet thankes be to God, escaped.[2]

Until January 12, the English remained on this coast hunting Negroes but captured fewer than 150, far less than necessary to continue the voyage profitably. As they were about to sail for another region, a local chief visited Hawkins and proposed an alliance to attack a rival tribe, promising Hawkins his choice of the captives for his help. Hawkins describes the action and the subsequent deception by his new ally:

> we concluded to give aide, and sent 120 of our men, which the 15 of Januarie, assaulted a towne of the Negros of our Allies adversaries, which had in it 8000 Inhabitants, being very strongly impaled and fenced after their manner, but it was so well defended, that our men prevailed not, but lost sixe men and fortie hurt: so that our men sent forthwith to me for more helpe: whereupon considering that the good successe of this enterprise might highly further the commoditie of our voyage, I went my selfe, and with the helpe of the king of our side, assaulted the towne, both by land and sea, and very hardly with fire (their houses being covered with dry Palme leaves) obtained the towne, put the Inhabitants to flight, where we tooke 250 persons, men, women, & children, and by our friend the king of our side, there were taken 600 prisoners, whereof we hoped to have had our choise: but the Negro (in which nation is seldome or never found truth) meant nothing lesse: for

that night he remooved his campe and prisoners, so that we were faine to content us with those few which we had gotten our selves.

The English had now gotten together about 450 Negroes, and though they were not able to get the youngest and strongest because of the chief's deception, they resolved to continue to the West Indies and sailed from the coast of Africa on February 3. While on the coast of Guinea, Hawkins had received into his company the Frenchman Captain Bland (Paul Blonden), with his *Grace à Dieu*. After a troublesome voyage lasting longer than usual, Dominica was sighted on March 27. At the island of Margarita, Hawkins had "reasonable trade" and secured meat, corn and water for linens, cloth and iron. Sailing to the mainland, he arrived at Borburata on April 14, where he learned that a French trading fleet under Beautemps and an English squadron under Drake's old companion John Lovell had preceded him with slaves from Africa and manufactured goods from France and England.* At Río de la Hacha, where Hawkins had traded two years before, the treasurer resisted him with a hundred arquebuses on the defenses. Hawkins attacked with two hundred men and took the town with the loss of two "and no hurt done to the Spaniards because after their voley of shot discharged, they all fled." When the royal factor of the town, Lázaro de Vallejo, and the royal accountant, Hernando Costilla, wrote the King in September of the attack by Hawkins, they stated that Hawkins had attacked with six hundred men and had lost over thirty men to the Spanish troops commanded by the treasurer of the town, Miguel de Castellanos, adding that the treasurer "had rendered such signal service that all were astonished at his great valour (both his adversaries and also the residents), for certainly it was a business that to-day, on looking back at it, fills with fright those who were present and those who hear it related."[3] The Spanish were not too terrified to trade with Hawkins, for after the skirmish, they flocked to the English after dark to buy slaves, linens and cloth with gold, pearls and some silver. Hawkins claimed that the favor of the treasurer assured the success of the trading, and that "in all other places where we traded the Spaniards inhabitants were glad of us and traded willingly."

Hawkins in his account makes no mention of Francis Drake during this part of the cruise, but we can assume that the young master was enlarging his experience in trading, which had begun on the voyages with Lovell, was closely watching and analyzing his Spanish customers,

---

* Illicit trade with the goods-hungry Spanish colonials was multiplying at a great rate. One colonial official at New Segovia reported that five fleets had called at the port of Borburata in 1567.

and was laying in his mind details of the coast and waters of the area for future use. Whether he was convinced at this point that trade with the Spanish was preferable to looting we cannot say, but by the time the English were in the Florida Straits, Drake certainly had made up his mind about his future course. For a month after their arrival at Río de la Hacha, Hawkins sailed at a leisurely pace along the mainland, arriving off Cartagena on July 12. Here the English were resisted by the local officials with armed companies, while the inhabitants of the city fled inland with their goods. Hawkins was surprised at the honesty of the local officials and decided to sail on: "At Cartagena the last towne we thought to have seene on the coast, we could by no meanes obtaine to deale with any Spaniard, the governour was so straight, and because our trade was so neere finished we thought not good either to adventure any landing, or to detract further time, but in peace departed from thence the 24 of July."

The futile delay of twelve days in Cartagena harbor was later to bring the English to disaster, for the hurricane season now approaching was a real threat as they attempted to get clear of the Caribbean and the Gulf of Mexico on their way to the Florida Straits. On August 12, nineteen days after sailing from Cartagena, while the fleet was passing Cape San Antonio at the western end of Cuba, they were struck by "an extreme storme which continued by the space of foure dayes, which so beat the Jesus, that we cut downe all her higher buildings, her rudder also was sore shaken, and withall was in so extreme a leake that we were rather upon the point to leave her then to keepe her any longer, yet hoping to bring all to good passe, we sought the coast of Florida, where we found no place nor Haven for our ships, because of the shalownesse of the coast."*

While hunting a safe anchorage in which to repair the ships, the English were struck by a second storm, which lasted three days and further damaged the already suffering fleet. At this, Hawkins had no choice but to find refuge in the only harbor in that area, San Juan de Ulúa (Vera Cruz). On the way there, the English captured three ships with one hundred passengers which Hawkins planned to hold as hostages, "the better to obtaine victuals for our money, & a quiet place for the repairing of our fleet." When the English entered the port on September 16, the Spaniards thought the ships to be the Flota from Spain which was daily expected. When the chief officials of the port boarded the *Jesus,* they were astonished and terrified, but Hawkins

---

* At the time Hawkins wrote, Florida was a term applied to all of North America north of Mexico, so Hawkins could here be referring to the Gulf coast west of the present limits of Florida.

A carrack of the mid-sixteenth century. From a contemporary engraving

assured them he was there only to repair his ships and to obtain supplies. In the port, Hawkins says, were "twelve ships which had in them by report two hundred thousand pound in gold & silver." These were awaiting the Flota to accompany it back to Spain.

Hawkins set the captured passengers free and took two local officials hostage to assure his safety while in port. The English had occupied the low flat stone-encompassed island that formed the breakwater of the port and had moored their ships to it, immediately beginning repairs and negotiations for supplies of the badly needed food and water they were unable to obtain at Cartagena. Hawkins also sent a messenger to Mexico City the night of his arrival to inform the officials there that he had called out of the necessity to repair and resupply, and to reach an agreement with them before the arrival of the Flota "for the better maintenance of amitie." Before a reply could be had, the Flota arrived, and the morning after, the English looked out and there were "open of the Haven thirteene great shippes . . . the fleete of Spain." The English were in a terrible dilemma. If the fleet were allowed to enter, the badly outnumbered English could be attacked and destroyed in port. Without the island in their hands, the English would have been at the mercy of the Spanish—the cables of the English ships could have been cut at the first north wind, allowing them to be swept ashore. If the Spanish fleet were kept out, this being the season of storms and no other anchorage available, it would have almost certainly been wrecked on the shallow sandy coast near the port. The latter alternative was something Hawkins knew Queen Elizabeth would never countenance, since she was at peace with the Spanish. Making the best of a very bad situation, Hawkins sent a message to the captain general of the Flota on Saturday morning, September 18,

> doing him to understand, that before I would suffer them to enter the Port, there should some order of conditions passe betweene us for our safe being there, and maintenance of peace. . . . I beganne to bewaile that which after followed, for now, said I, I am in two dangers, and forced to receive the one of them. That was, either I must have kept out the fleete from entring the Port, the which with Gods helpe I was very well able to doe, or else suffer them to enter in with their accustomed treason, which they never fails to execute, where they may have opportunitie, to compasse it by any meanes: if I had kept them out, then had there bene present shipwracke of all the fleete which amounted in value to sixe Millions, which was in value of our money 1800000. li. which I considered I was not able to answere, fearing the Queenes Majesties indignation in so waightie a matter. Thus with my selfe revolving the doubts, I thought rather better to abide the Jutt of the uncertainty, then the certaintie. The uncertaine doubt I account was their treason which by good policie I hoped might be prevented, and therfore as chusing the least mischiefe I proceeded to conditions.

Hawkins's suspicion of the Spanish later saved the English from complete disaster. His conditions for the entry of the Flota were the possession of the low island-breakwater, to which the English were moored, and the exchange of ten prominent men of each fleet as hostages. As it happened, the new viceroy of Mexico was aboard the Spanish flagship, and his reply, an obvious dissimulation, came back to Hawkins the next morning:

I well believe that your honour's arrival in that port was forced by the great need your honour had of subsistence and other things, as your honour writes me. So also I am certain that, as your honour says, your honour has not mistreated any vassal of his majesty's, nor done any damage with your fleet in those ports and parts where it has called, but that your honour has engaged solely in bartering slaves and other merchandise carried, paying in same for the subsistence taken, at its just value; and further that your honour has paid the dues payable to his majesty's royal revenues.

Wherefore I am content to accept the proposal which your honour makes in your letter, asking me to deliver hostages and to enter the port in peace, although I was determined to the contrary. Therefore I send ten principal persons and rely upon what your honour states, that those your honour sends me are similar persons. I well believe that although the people of this fleet enter without arms into the island, they will not be prevented from going about their affairs, nor harassed in any fashion. And I am very confident that when we meet, friendship will augment between these fleets, since both are so well disciplined.[4]

On Monday, September 20, the Spanish fleet entered the port, and for two days the Spanish and English worked at "placing the English ships by themselves & the Spanish ships by themselves, the captaines of ech part & inferiour men of their parts promising great amity of al sides." But the Spanish had no intention whatsoever of letting the English escape. Hawkins and his companions were violating Spanish law by even being in the Indies; they had carried on illicit trade on two previous voyages and this one. Before, Hawkins had always been dealing with Spanish colonial officials whose interests were not entirely different from his own, that is, in trade which, even though illegal, was clearly to the advantage of both. Now Hawkins was up against high-ranking officials, fresh from the Spanish court, whose interests, or even very lives, depended on resisting him with all the force they had. How it must have rankled their proud Castilian hearts to have this English commoner, and a heretic at that, sit in the King's port and dictate the terms by which they might enter with the King's own fleet! In his account, Hawkins charges the Spanish with treachery, and Drake was marked for life by the events that occurred, but the Spanish from their point of view could not have acted in any other way than they did.

As soon as they had entered port, the viceroy held a council to determine the best means by which to attack and destroy the English:

Wherefore in order in council to determine ways and means to seize and punish him and eject him from the island, his lordship again sum-

moned the said general and admiral and the other captains and masters
and asked their views and took measures to drive the enemy from the
harbour and to make the necessary attacks and assaults, which persons
expressed their opinion and his illustrious lordship determined that the
following Thursday, which was the twenty-third of the said month of
September, at about eleven o'clock in the morning, the attack should be
made.[5]

The plan was to load a hulk with 150 soldiers armed with arquebuses,
shields, and swords to attack the English ships while another party
from the town would attack the island-breakwater where the English
controlled a battery of artillery. The hulk was to be used since the
flagship of the fleet lay too far away from the English to make the
attack if the wind was adverse.

For their part, Hawkins and his companions were becoming more and
more suspicious of the Spanish intentions. As Hawkins describes it:

> The same Thursday in the morning the treason being at hand, some
> appearance shewed, as shifting of weapon from ship to ship, planting
> and bending of ordnance from the ships to the Iland where our men
> warded, passing too and fro of companies of men more then required
> for their necessary busines, & many other ill likelihoods, which caused
> us to have a vehement suspition, and therewithall sent to the Viceroy to
> enquire what was ment by it, which sent immediatly straight com-
> mandement to unplant all things suspicious, and also sent word that he
> in the faith of a Viceroy would be our defence from all villanies.

While the viceroy was attempting to reassure Hawkins, the plan the
Spanish had hatched in their council of war was being carried out. The
hulk (which Hawkins estimated at 900 tons) loaded with Spanish soldiers had been moved next to the *Minion*. Hawkins suspected that
soldiers were aboard and about to attack, and so he sent the master of
the *Jesus*, Robert Barrett, who could speak Spanish, to the viceroy to
inquire further about the hulk and the intentions of the Spanish. During the half hour preceding the attack, Hawkins also had the crews of
the *Minion* and *Jesus* set about preparing their ships for a quick escape
if one became necessary. The viceroy and the captain general of the
fleet, knowing there was no way to deceive the English further, seized
Barrett and blew the trumpet signaling the attack. Hawkins describes
the confusion and carnage that followed: "Our men which warded
[camped] a shore being stricken with sudden feare, gave place, fled,
and sought to recover succour of the ships; the Spainardes being before provided for the purpose landed in all places in multitudes from

The *Minion,* commanded by Francis Drake. Drawing in a sixteenth-century manuscript. Photograph from the Smithsonian Institution

their ships which they might easily doe without boates, and slewe all our men a shore without mercie, a fewe of them escaped aboord the Jesus. The great ship which had by the estimation three hundred men placed in her secretly, immediatly fell aboord the Minion." Fortunately for the English, the Spanish admiral had given the signal prematurely, before the hulk loaded with soldiers was alongside the *Jesus.* This and the suspicions of the English saved them from complete destruction.

The *Minion* successfully fought off the attack by the Spanish soldiers in the hulk and managed to slip her moorings and escape from the harbor. The Spanish now turned to the *Jesus* and boarded her. Here the English in fierce hand-to-hand fighting were able to repel the enemy but lost many of their men. At the same time, two other Spanish ships assaulted the *Jesus,* and only with great difficulty was she able to slip her moorings and pass out of the harbor. The bark *Judith,* under the command of Francis Drake, also escaped, but the other English ships were left behind. The town did not escape looting either, for the townspeople, in hastily moving their goods to safety, were robbed by the poorer Spanish who had pitched in to help them.

After passing out of the harbor, the English were in little better position. The artillery on the island was now turned on them, and the *Jesus'* spars and rigging were shot to pieces. Hawkins, knowing she could not be saved, moved her between the Spanish guns and the *Minion* to act as a shield. The Spanish now sent two fireships against the English. At this, the crew of the *Minion* set their sails without orders and left the *Jesus*. Hawkins and a few men were able to board the *Minion*, and later a few escaped in the only small boat remaining, but some were left behind to be captured by the Spanish. Darkness fell and stopped the fighting. The *Minion* lay all night a few hundred yards off the harbor entrance. By morning, she was alone. The *Judith*, under the command of Francis Drake, had left in the night. Hawkins in his account never mentions his nephew by name, but says only "so with the *Minion* only and *Judith* (a small barke of 50 tunne) we escaped, which barke the same night forsokke us in our great miserie." Captain Bland and some of his men escaped with Hawkins, but he lost the *Grace à Dieu*.

When morning came, Hawkins found himself with one damaged ship and three hundred men, very little water and food, a strong enemy just a few hundred yards away, and no anchorage that would be safe from a north wind, which could have come at any time. In this desperate situation, the English sailed to a small island a mile away, and here the north wind arrived. Fortunately, the Spanish did not attack. With only two anchors and two cables left, the *Minion* was able to ride out the two-day storm. Now followed two weeks of sailing about to find a watering place and food.

Back in port, the Spanish were busy with their own troubles. Great damage had been done to their ships by the artillery duel, two ships had been sacrificed as fireships, and many men had been killed and wounded. The Spanish, thus occupied, made no effort to pursue the *Minion*, which could have been captured without doubt.

The English were really desperate. Anything that could be chewed was being eaten, and water was short. Hawkins describes their despair:

> having a great number of men and little victuals our hope of life waxed lesse and lesse: some desired to yeeld to the Spaniards, some rather desired to obtaine a place where they might give themselves to the Infidels, and some had rather abide with a little pittance the mercie of God at Sea: so thus with many sorrowful hearts we wandred in an unknowen Sea by the space of 14 dayes, till hunger inforced us to seek the land, for hides were thought very good meat, rats, cats, mice and dogs, none escaped that might be gotten, parrats and monkeyes that were had in great price, were thought there very profitable if they served the turne one dinner: thus in the end the 8 day of October we

came to the land in the botome of the same bay of Mexico in 23 degrees and a halfe, where we hoped to have found inhabitants of the Spaniards, reliefe of victuals, and place for the repaire of our ship, which was so sore beaten with shot from our enemies and brused with shooting off our owne ordinance, that our wearie and weake armes were scarce able to defende and keepe out water.

The English found only one place where, with some danger, they might land a boat. Here, half of the men asked to be put ashore to take their chances with the Indians and the Spanish. This was done and water was taken aboard. With little to eat in the hold, Hawkins and the remaining 150 men set sail for the Florida Straits, which they cleared November 16. As the *Minion* crossed the Atlantic, winds for England were found to be adverse, and Hawkins determined to go to the Spanish coast for water and food. The hardships of the voyage almost did them in: "growing neere to the colde countrey, our men being oppressed with famine, died continually, and they that were left, grew into such weakenesse that we were scantly able to manage our shippe, and the winde being alwayes ill for us to recover England, we determined to goe with Galicia in Spaine, with intent there to relieve our companie."

Having reached a port near Vigo on the Spanish coast, on December 31, the English found that their troubles were not over: with plenty of food now at hand, the starving men overate and many died from the effects. Hawkins remained on the Spanish coast for three weeks. The men did not go ashore but were supplied by Spanish vendors who came to the ships: the English were wary lest word had arrived from America and an attempt be made on them, since their weak condition was apparent. Hawkins says that the Spanish constantly sought to betray them, but the English were able to survive, and the remnants of the party finally sailed on January 20 and reached Mounts Bay in Cornwall five days later. Hawkins ends his narrative with a lament which expresses the desperation they felt: "If all the miseries and troublesome affaires of this sorowfull voyage should be perfectly and throughly written, there should neede a painefull man with his pen, and as great a time as he had that wrote the lives and deathes of the Martyrs."

Drake had arrived home intact the day Hawkins had sailed from the coast of Spain. Later, Drake's action was to be defended by his admirers. When he had become a great hero to the English, having distinguished himself in action against the hated enemy, his action at San Juan de Ulúa was explained away as the result of the confusion of the moment and poor communication with the *Minion*, but he had really no excuse for abandoning his comrades. The public likes their heroes untarnished. Perhaps the chagrin he must have felt intensified the violent hatred he forever afterward had for the Spanish. In the confusion, suffering, sorrow, and shame that came out of the battle at San Juan de Ulúa, a dragon was spawned. And this dragon was destined to do more damage to Spanish wealth and ego than any other enemy they faced in the three centuries of Spanish rule in America.

Drake's action at San Juan de Ulúa had not deterred Hawkins from working with Drake to revenge their loss, for on his arrival in England, he immediately sent Drake to London to request letters of reprisal against the Spanish from Lord Burghley. Their immediate rage at their treatment on the coast of Mexico and their desire for revenge overcame any immediate distaste Hawkins felt for his nephew. Drake had the personality to present the case to Burghley with eloquence and passion, and Hawkins knew him to be the best one for the task. The request for a commission was denied. The Queen was not yet ready for open violence against the Spanish.

Drake would have his revenge whether under commission or not, and he set about laying his plans. It would be three years before he would attack the Spanish directly with a force under his command, but during the interval he made two, and possibly three, more voyages to the Caribbean.

The year following the return of Hawkins from the disaster at San Juan de Ulúa, 1569, marked the beginning of a new phase in foreign incursions into Spanish America. Until then, voyages by the English and French had been trading ventures, even though some force had been applied here and there, largely to give the Spanish colonials the means to acquiesce without getting into trouble with the Spanish Crown. Two important events had changed this comparatively peaceful activity to outright military assault with cruelty and violence. In 1562, a few months after Hawkins had visited Fort Caroline in Florida while returning to England, the French colonists had been slaughtered almost to a man by Admiral Pedro Menéndez, thereby winning for the Spanish the undying hatred of the French. The other was the treatment of Hawkins and Drake at San Juan de Ulúa six years later.

To the credit of the English, and especially Drake, they did not practice the monstrous cruelties the French inflicted on the dons. Drake was always to maintain a balance in his conduct and the conduct of his men which prevented any large-scale atrocities—a fact recognized by the Spanish themselves when they describe him as "not very cruel." Thus, while Drake enthusiastically destroyed Spanish property

ELIZABETHA REGINA

Diua potens velis, populóque potentior, aequat
Ingenio Reges, et pietate Deos

Queen Elizabeth I. An engraved portrait of the early seventeenth century

and spared no efforts to wipe out the Spanish military when they resisted him, he did so without excessive damage to noncombatants. Some of the French, by contrast, were inhumanly cruel. In one instance a Norman captain captured a Spanish vessel off Santa Marta in a fleet under the command of Pedro Menéndez. On the ship were a Spanish lady, her two children, other women, fifty-eight friars and monks, and many other passengers and seamen—in all 265 persons. The French threw them all overboard to their deaths and made off with the ship, which was valued at 100,000 ducats.

Smarting over the treatment he and Hawkins had received at San Juan de Ulúa, Drake prepared to sail again to the West Indies. It is possible, though we cannot be certain, that he returned as early as the spring of 1569. There is some evidence to indicate this. Neither can we be certain that he got to the Indies in 1570. Even though it is clearly stated in *Sir Francis Drake Revived* that he sailed that year in two vessels, the *Dragon* and the *Swan*, the Spanish sources indicate that no depredations occurred in the Indies in 1570, and there was no mainland fleet that year. Drake at this time was still dependent on Hawkins, being neither rich enough nor experienced enough to exercise independent command. It is quite possible he had been sent on yet another trading venture by Hawkins, one that was never recorded. The Hawkins family for all of their rage at the events of the voyage of 1568 are known to have kept on with their trading, even though irregular warfare with the Spanish had begun, with the French doing most of the damage.

In any case, Drake appeared on the coast of Panama in February 1571, in the *Swan*. The French were there also, possibly under Captain Bland, who had lost his ship with Hawkins at San Juan de Ulúa when Drake had escaped with the *Judith*. Drake anchored the *Swan* at Cativas Headland and did his work in a pinnace, a technique he was to use to good advantage in the future. The French corsairs, with whom Drake possibly joined, sailed up the Chagres River, capturing a richly laden bark belonging to Baltazar Melo. The prize was loaded with velvets, taffetas, and other sumptuous goods that had just come from the Spanish fleet of Diego Flores de Valdés, which was at Nombre de Dios. The cargo was so rich and the capture so audacious that it created great alarm among the Spanish, who called it "a thing not ventured until this time present."[6] Two years before, Diego Flores had been humiliated when corsairs captured prizes right under his nose as he lay in port with his galleons. Now, in an effort to retaliate, he sailed for the mouth of the Chagres River with the two most powerful ships of his fleet, only to see the corsairs escape again in their light-oared pinnaces, which the Spanish could not pursue in shoal water. The French, with the goods from Melo's bark, escaped to sea and sailed north. Drake remained behind with his pinnace, eluding the Spanish in the shallows along the coast. Seeing the impossibility of capturing the enemy with his large warships, Flores now sent out small frigates to give chase, but the English outsailed, outrowed, and outsmarted them.

Drake continued to plunder and may even have sailed all the way up the Chagres River to the wharf at Cruces, a transshipping point, and robbed the place. After the Melo capture, he hovered about the mouth of the Chagres and here captured some small barks going from the fair at Nombre de Dios to Cruces with goods for Panama and Peru. The English "took twelve or thirteen Chagres River barks laden with clothing and merchandise, to an approximate value of 150,000 pesos; and, finding themselves in possession of so great a number, they selected two of these barks, loaded them with bales of clothing and boxes and carried them off."[7] The loot was taken to the *Swan* at Cativas Headland. Drake remained on the coast until May, making several more captures and then cleared for home with a wealth of booty in the hold of the *Swan* and a head full of information on the geography of the Chagres River and the Panama coast, information which was to serve him well in the future.

New dangers were shaping up for the Spanish in another quarter. In the jungles of Panama, communities of escaped slaves were growing in numbers and audacity, and these blacks, called Cimarrons, were now raiding the Spanish muletrains carrying goods and bullion across the isthmus. This state of affairs was reported to the Crown by Licentiate Carasa, a judge of the high court in Panama, in a letter dated March 27, 1570: "The matter which, in this kingdom, most urgently demands remedial action is the problem of dispersing the *cimarrones,* black outlaws in rebellion in the mountainous, unpopulated interior. They are numerous and (such is their daring and audacity) they come forth upon the roads leading from this city to that of Nombre de Dios, kill travellers, and steal what these have with them, if it be clothing and wine. So far they have not taken money."[8] The blacks took no money for the obvious reason that it was useless in the jungle. This delinquency on the part of the Cimarrons was soon to be remedied: on Drake's return to Panama, he was to work with them against the Spanish muletrains and demonstrate the very great interest the English had in the gold and silver the blacks disdained.

After some nine months of preparation, Drake sailed from Plymouth on May 24, 1572. The *Pasha* of 70 tons was the flagship, and the *Swan* sailed under the command of his brother John, who was vice admiral.

View of Plymouth, Devonshire, from a seventeenth-century engraving. The town appeared much the same when Hawkins and Drake sailed from here on their voyages to America

View of Nombre de Dios. A seventeenth-century engraving

Equipment and supplies were carefully chosen, and the men were all volunteers, "of which the eldest was fifty, all the rest under thirty: so divided that there were forty seaven in one ship, and twenty six in the other: both richly furnished, with victualles and apparell for a whole yeare: and no lesse heedfully provided of all manner of munition, Artillery, Artificers, stuffe and tooles, that were requisite for such a Man of warre in such an attempt, but especially having three dainty Pinnaces, made in *Plimouth*, taken a sunder all in peeces and stowed aboard, to be set up as occasion served."[9]

Drake's plan was to sail directly to Nombre de Dios and sack it. The little squadron sailed on a "prosperous and favorable" wind and raised the Canary Islands in twelve days, and on June 28, without ever anchoring or even striking sail, the English sighted Guadeloupe and landed on the south coast of Dominica to take on water and fish, and to refresh the men. Fortunately, the Caribs were not at home. Sailing again on July 1, Drake and his men reached "Port Phesant" on the coast of Panama, so named by Drake from a previous visit, when he had seen large numbers of the birds there. The ships were anchored in a small protected bay. Here Drake found a message from John Garret, an English corsair, chiseled on a plate nailed to a large tree:

> Captain Drake, if you fortune to come to this Port, mak hast away, for the Spaniards which you had with you here the last yeer have bewrayed [discovered] this place, and taken away all that you left here. I departed from hence, this present 7. of July, 1572
>
> Your verie loving friend
JOHN GARRET

As before, Drake had selected this place as a base, and despite the warning, he was determined to set up his "three dainty pinnaces" here. Preparing for a possible attack, Drake began fortifying a point on the beach where the ships were to be assembled and the English were to camp. A great pentagon-shaped palisade of tree trunks thirty feet high was built around a plot three quarters of an acre in extent. One side faced on the beach where the pinnaces were to be launched. Here the work proceeded, and the pinnaces were set up and ready to sail in just seven days. The day after Drake arrived, he was joined by Captain James Ranse of the Isle of Wight with thirty men and a captured caravel of Seville in tow. Hearing of Drake's plans, Ranse and his men joined the company "upon conditions agreed on between them." On July 20, the reinforced company sailed for Nombre de Dios. At the

Isle of Pines,* about one hundred miles east of the city, Drake found two Spanish ships manned with Negroes loading planks and timber. From the Negroes he learned that numbers of Spanish soldiers were expected in the city to protect it from a threatened attack by the Cimarrons. This report proved to be an exaggeration. The Isle of Pines was to be the base from which Drake would take his pinnaces to attack the city.

At the anchorage, called Port of Plenty by the English, Drake left the large ships under the charge of Captain Ranse. Taking his three pinnaces and a shallop of Ranse's, he sailed with seventy-three men, armed with pikes, firepikes, muskets and bows, on to the island of Cativas, some twenty-five miles from his objective. Here he landed the men, drilled them in the use of their arms, and explained the plan of attack: "And exhorting them, after his manner, he declared the greatnesse of the hope of good things that was there, the weaknesse of the towne, being unwalled, and the hope he had of prevailing to recompense his wrongs, especially now that he should come with such a crew, who were like minded with himselfe, and at such a time, as he should be utterly undiscovered." Sailing in the afternoon, the English reached the Francisco River and here turned inshore and anchored until dark to escape detection as they approached the city. The plan had been to attack at dawn, but as the men lay in the pinnaces waiting, the talk of the city and the Negroes' reports of numbers of Spanish soldiers there began to depress them. Drake, sensing this, resolved to attack at night by moonlight. In the harbor of Nombre de Dios, the English found a small ship which had just arrived from Spain. The Spanish crew tried to send the ship's boat to warn the town, but this was cut off, and the English landed without being detected. The beach defenses were a platform with "six great pieces of brasse Ordnance, mounted upon their Carriages, some Demy, some whole Culvering."† Leaving twelve men in the pinnace, the English landed. The lone gunner on the platform escaped and gave the alarm. The guns on the platform were dismounted. A bell in the church rang out, and the roll of drums was heard as Drake and his men entered the town. Drake divided his men into two parties: one under John Drake and John Oxenham would attack the marketplace from the east; the other under Drake himself would attack from the west. The English advanced with firepikes flaming, a trumpet sounding, and drums rolling. These firepikes "served no lesse for fright of the enemy than light of our men,

---

* Not to be confused with the Isle of Pines off the southwestern coast of Cuba.
† That is, half and whole culverins, which were long guns firing balls weighing from ten to sixteen pounds.

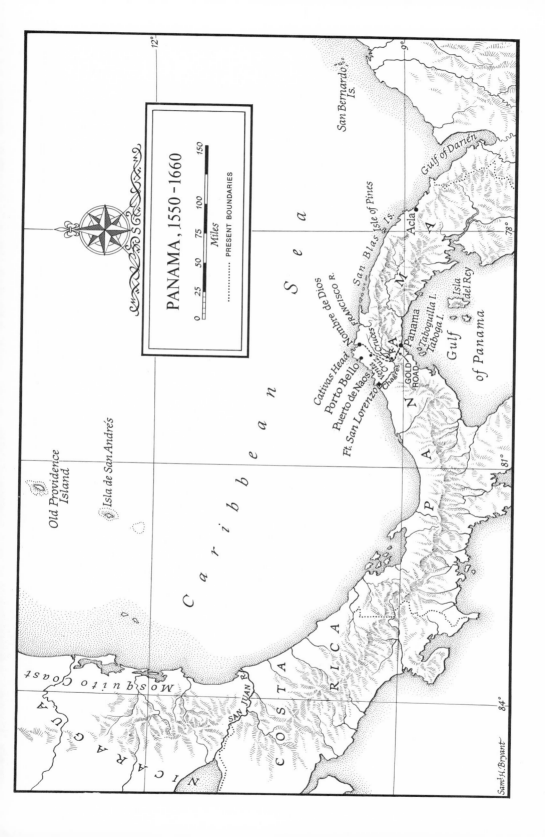

PANAMA, 1550–1660

Miles

.... PRESENT BOUNDARIES

0 25 50 75 100 150

Old Providence Island

Isla de San Andrés

Mosquito Coast

NICARAGUA

COSTA RICA

SAN JUAN R.

Caribbean Sea

San Bernardo Is.

Gulf of Darién

Isle of Pines

San Blas Is.

Acla

PANAMA

Cativas Head

Nombre de Dios

Porto Bello

Puerto de Naos

Ft. San Lorenzo

Chagres

Venta Cruces

FRANCISCO R.

GOLD ROAD

Panama

Taboga I.

Taboguilla I.

Isla del Rey

Gulf of Panama

12°

9°

78°

81°

84°

Sam'l H. Bryant

who by this means might discerne everie place verie well, as if it were near day, whereas the inhabitants stood amazed at so strange a sight, marvelling what the matter might be and imagining, by reason of our Drums and Trumpets sounding in so sundry places, that we had beens a farre greater number than we were." With surprise on their side, Drake's party entered the marketplace. The defenders, who were the armed civilians of the town, met them with "a jolly hot volley of shot" from their muskets. Drake's account mentions soldiers but none were there when the English attacked. The volley wounded some of the English and killed the trumpeter, but Drake and his men answered with a shower of arrows and drove forward with their pikes, which the Spanish resisted by using the butts of their muskets as clubs. At this moment, the other party of English entered the eastern side of the square, and the Spanish broke, fleeing out of the town into the jungle. From a prisoner, Drake learned the location of the governor's house. Here, by the light of candles, the English discovered "a huge heap of silver . . . being a pile of barres of silver, of (as neere as we could gusse) seventie foote in length, of ten foot in breadth, and twelve foot in hight, piled up against the wall. Each barre was between thirty five and forty pound in weight." Drake commanded his men not to touch the silver but to stay with their arms, since the town was full of defenders and could attack again at any time. He encouraged them by saying that "there was in the Kings-treasure house neere the waters side, more gold and jewels then all our foure pinnaces would carrie."* At this moment, a message arrived from the pinnaces that they were in danger of being captured, and a sudden rainstorm struck, wetting the matches of the muskets. The men became alarmed and clamored to retreat to the pinnaces, but Drake addressed them and "told them that he had brought them to the mouth of the treasure of the world, if they should want it," and as soon as the storm passed, he stepped forward, directing his brother John and Oxenham to break open the King's treasure house.

> But as hee stept forward, his strength and sight and speech failed him, and hee began to faint for want of bloud, which as then we perceived, had, in greate quantitie, issued upon the sand, out of a wound received in his legge in the first incounter, whereby though he felt some paine,

---

* This report is hardly credible. The Spanish never brought such treasure to Nombre de Dios until the armed fleet was there to receive it. Some silver was probably there, accumulating for the sailing of the next fleet, which was not due until early the next year. The fleet of 1572 had sailed several weeks before Drake's attack.

yet . . . would he not have it known to any, till this his fainting, against his will bewrayed [revealed] it; the bloud having first filled the verie prints which our foot-steps made, to the great dismay of all our Companie, who thought it not credible that one man should be able to spare so much bloud and live.

Knowing full well that if they lost their captain their chances of surviving and reaching England were very remote, the men, over Drake's protests, retreated to the pinnaces carrying their captain. Embarking just at dawn, the English went to an island lying some three miles from the town, taking along the Spanish ship, which proved to be loaded with Canary wines "for the more comfort of our companie."

The English had failed in the attack on Nombre de Dios and now lay close to the enemy with many men wounded. For two days Drake and his men stayed on the island, called by the Spanish "Bastimientes" but named by the English "The Isle of Victuales" by reason of the gardens of fruits and vegetables and the poultry they found there. Here the surgeon treated the wounded and they quickly revived. On the first day, the governor of the town sent a gentleman messenger to the English to inquire if the arrows which had wounded many of the townsmen had been poisoned and if the Spanish could furnish any supplies the English required. Drake received the messenger with courtesy and informed him that Englishmen never used poisoned arrows and that the island was sufficiently stocked to supply their needs, advising "the Governor to hold open his eyes, for before hee departed, if God lent him life and leave, hee meant to reape some of their Harvest, which they get out of the Earth." The Spanish had been relieved to find that their attackers were English and not French, the messenger saying "that at first they feared that we had beene French, at whose hands they knew they should find no mercie, but after they perceived by our Arrowes that wee were Englishmen their fears were lesse, for that they knew that though wee tooke the Treasure of the place yet wee would not use cruelties towards their persons." After the messenger was entertained at dinner and presented with suitable gifts, he was sent back to the town. Thus, the English and Spanish tempered their actions with a code of chivalry that is a curiosity in the twentieth century. Now that the country was alerted by his abortive attack, Drake knew that further action at Nombre de Dios must wait for the future, and they set sail for their ships at the Isle of Pines, arriving on August 1. Hearing of the failure, Captain Ranse asked to be released from·his agreement with Drake, who consented, and Ranse sailed north with his ship and bark. While the pinnaces had been lying off Nombre de Dios during the attack, a Negro named Diego had come to them and was taken aboard. He appeared to have useful information for the English, and when Drake sailed back to the Isle of Pines, Diego came along. He was to remain with his new friends during their entire stay on the coast and was to be a major agent in their eventual success.

For six days the English remained at the Isle of Pines preparing their vessels for an attack on Cartagena, for Drake was determined to go there. Sailing with the two ships and three pinnaces, the English spent another six days reaching port because of calms. At Cartagena, Drake was again frustrated, the town having been alerted. The English contented themselves with taking a ship and several frigates which were released. Drake now withdrew to the islands of San Bernardo, lying about fifty miles southwest of Cartagena, and here he decided to destroy the *Swan* because he did not have men enough to provide proper crews for the two ships and three pinnaces. He swore the carpenter of the *Swan* to secrecy and had him bore holes in the bottom of the ship by the keel. This handsome ship had served Drake on two voyages to the Indies and was held in great affection by Drake's brother John, her captain, and her crew. Drake knew they would never have consented to scuttle her. In fact, if they knew "he thought verily they would kill him." The scheme succeeded, the ship settled, and the crew, though working valiantly at the pumps, were unable to save her. Drake then had the pinnaces come alongside the *Swan*, and his men were permitted to take anything they wanted from the ship. Then she was burned. He then placed his brother in command of the *Pasha* until such time as he could capture him a frigate, and he took command of the pinnaces which now were well manned for the work ahead. Sailing to the Gulf of Darién, Drake now established a base where the *Pasha* could be anchored as a storeship, resolving to do his work with the pinnaces alone. Here Diego and other Negroes who had befriended the English used their skills to help build houses for the lodging of the men and even a meeting house. Drake, good leader that he was, did not let his men remain idle but kept them busy trimming and overhauling the pinnaces and, when not working, saw that they had time for archery and playing at bowling, quoits and skittles. By turns, he allowed half the crew time off.

In two weeks, the base was in order, and Drake, taking two pinnaces, sailed eastward to explore the mainland coast and the Magdalena River. Passing by Cartagena, out of sight of the city, they landed on September 8 a few miles west of the mouth of the river, where they found many cattle and friendly Indians who traded them beef for trinkets. That afternoon about three o'clock, the English entered the river.

By dark, they had made only a few miles when they tied the pinnaces to trees for the night. Here they were drenched by a violent thunder-shower, and after the storm had passed, they were attacked by myriads of mosquitoes. Nothing would avail against the insects but lemon juice, which they found acted as a repellent. The next day, in a wide and very deep part of the river, they saw houses on the shore and a smoke signal. The Spaniard in charge of the houses which were full of provisions had mistaken the English for Spanish vessels which came to get provisions for the fleet. As the English approached the shore, the Spaniard, seeing his mistake, fled, and Drake and his men sacked the houses at their leisure, taking aboard the pinnaces "white rusk, dried bacon, that Country Cheese (like Holland Cheese in fashon, but farre more delicate in taste, of which they send into *Spaine* as speciall Presents), many sorts of sweet meats and Conserves, with great store of sugar, being provided to serve the Fleet returning to *Spaine*." Knowing the alarm was spreading, Drake and his men now started back downstream, arriving at the mouth of the river the next day. As they sailed westward toward their base, they captured five or six frigates between Cartagena and Tolú, loaded with live hogs, hens and maize. Two of the best were taken along to the base on the Gulf of Darién, and the rest were released without harm. Arriving at their base, Drake and his men now had provisions enough for a company many times the size of theirs. Later, storehouses were built at intervals along the coast and stocked with the food to provide for the future needs of the company. In this work, the Negroes who had joined the English demonstrated their "speciall skill in the speedy erection of such houses."

While Drake had been on his journey to the Magdalena River, his brother John had been looking out for Cimarrons with Diego. A meeting was arranged and the Cimarrons agreed to ally themselves with the English. Drake and his party would have their gold and silver, while the Negroes would have useful goods and revenge on the hated enemy. From the Cimarrons Drake had learned that the Spanish did not send treasure over the trail from Panama City during the rainy season, which was now upon them, and the months which they had before them required a secure place to pass the time. A base was established on a small island fifteen miles from Cativas Headland and perhaps fifty miles east of Nombre de Dios in waters thick with shoals. The ship was moored behind the thickly wooded island out of sight, and the ordnance was moved into the trees ashore to fortify the place. The English now had a strong, well-camouflaged base which could be easily defended if necessary.

Drake's ignorance of the customs and methods of the Spanish is surprising. That he was ignorant is perfectly clear from both his and the Spanish accounts. He had attacked Nombre de Dios after the fleet had been there to remove most of the treasure. He evidently had no clear notion of the schedules followed by the Spanish in sending the loot over the isthmus from Panama City. The amount of silver the English reported seeing in the governor's house during the raid on Nombre de Dios was probably an exaggeration, although some could have been there awaiting the next fleet. The report of gold and jewels in the royal storehouses there was probably false, since the treasure would have been on its way to Spain by the time Drake and his men arrived. But now the English were getting the cold facts from the Cimarrons who were well acquainted with the Spanish system. Treasure did not even leave Peru in great quantities until advice arrived in fast dispatch boats from Spain and Panama that the fleet had cleared from Spanish waters. The treasure was then sent to the isthmus and held there until other dispatch boats arrived at Nombre de Dios with the news that the fleet was arriving at Cartagena. The treasure was then sent by muletrain across the isthmus to Nombre de Dios and stored in guarded strongrooms until the ships arrived from Cartagena. Here the fair was held, with South American merchants trading for the goods in the fleet, the King's treasure was shipped as was private gold and silver, and in a month the whole business was concluded and the fleet sailed for Spain.

By the last of September, the fort was finished and houses had been built for the men. Drake now sailed, with the three pinnaces, to Cartagena "to learne true intelligences of the state of the Countrey and of the Fleets." He left his brother John in command of the fort, which was being completed, while he remained near Cartagena capturing ships and gathering supplies, provisions and intelligence on the state of things. On November 22 he sailed for his base, arriving there November 27. He found to his great sorrow that his brother John had been killed in an ill-advised attack on a Spanish vessel off the coast. Drake now resolved, very wisely "to keep himself close, without being descried, untill hee might heare of the comming of the Spanish Fleet, and therefore set no more to Sea." The wants of the English were well supplied from the warehouses and from the liberal bounty of the surrounding forest. In his Cimarron allies, Drake had an excellent intelligence service and waited securely and comfortably for the time to attack. But an invisible enemy now struck the English. Early in January, yellow fever broke out among the men, ten falling ill at once and most dying within two or three days. In this epidemic, Drake lost another brother, Joseph, who died in his arms. In an effort to identify the mysterious disease, Drake directed the surgeon to perform an autopsy on his brother's body. The surgeon "found his liver swolen, his heart as it were sodden, and his guts all faire." The narrator in *Drake Revived* goes on to say, "This was the first and last experiment that our Captain made of Anatomy in this voyage." Within four days, the surgeon who had performed the autopsy killed himself with an over-dose of a powerful laxative of his own invention.

Amidst all this grief and sorrow, Drake awaited word of the arrival of the fleet from the Cimarrons who were ranging up and down the isthmus. He had not long to wait, for less than two weeks after he buried his brother, Drake heard from the Negroes that the fleet had come to Nombre de Dios. A pinnace was sent to look in on the port, and her men returned to say that the fleet was indeed there. The time had come to attack the treasure trail. Here again the Cimarrons proved invaluable, for they were able to advise Drake on the supplies and provisions needed, including many extra pairs of shoes because of the rocky trails and stream beds the English would encounter. Leaving Ellis Hixom in charge of the base, Drake set out across country with eighteen Englishmen and thirty Cimarrons. Each man carried as many provisions as he could in addition to his arms, and the Cimarrons promised to supply what else was needed from the jungle.

The men marched along jungle trails in early morning and after-noon, with a long rest in between, and when stopping for the night, used houses the Cimarrons had previously erected or which they threw up in a matter of a few minutes from branches and leaves. The third day of the march brought the party to a Cimarron village, the organization and cleanliness of which impressed the English who had ex-pected much less:

> a Towne of their own, seated near a fair river, on the side of a hill, environed with a dike of eight foot broad and a thicke mud wall of ten foot high, sufficient to stop a sudden surprizer. It had one long and broad street lying East and West, and two other crosse streets of lesse bredth and length. There were in it some five or six and fiftie house-holds, which were kept so cleane and sweet that not only the houses but the verie streets were verie pleasant to behold. In this Towne we saw they lived very civilly and cleanely, for as soone as wee came thither, they washed themselves in the river, and changed their apparel, which was verie fine and fitly made (as also their women doe weare) some-what after the Spanish fashon, though nothing so costly.

Contrast this town with any English counterpart of the time, where the chamberpots were still emptied from the bedroom windows into the streets to the hazard of those walking below. No wonder the English were impressed.

The Cimarrons urged Drake and his men to stay with them for several days but the captain politely declined, feeling the urgency of getting on with the raid before the Spanish heard of his activity. The order of march was well thought out, with four Cimarrons going ahead as scouts, a dozen going as a vanguard to the English, and the same number bringing up the rear. "The way was thorow woods very coole and pleasant, by reason of those goodly and high Trees that grow there so thicke that it is cooler travelling there under them in that hot region, then it is the most parts of England in the Summer time." Soon after the English arrived near the highest point on their jungle trail, they were intrigued by the Cimarrons' description of a certain great tree, from the top of which one could see the Pacific Ocean. And indeed Drake and John Oxenham climbed the tree to see the South Sea, beseeching "Almightie God of his goodnesse to give him life and leave to sayle once in an English Ship in that sea." This ambition was to lead Drake to a glorious voyage around the world and knighthood, while the same pretensions were to lead John Oxenham to his death on a gallows in Lima.

Two more days of marching through the jungle brought the party to the grassy savannah which extended from Panama City to Venta Cruz. Here the country was open rolling hills, covered with tall grass, but the English and the Cimarrons marched with great caution. They stayed well away from the main road connecting Panama City and Nombre de Dios, and were not discovered. The last three days of march, before they reached a certain grove of trees near the road three miles from Panama, the party caught glimpses of the city in the distance, and on the last day could see ships riding in the harbor there. Having reached the grove, the men hid themselves while Drake sent a Cimarron spy dressed in the proper clothing into the city to gain intelligence on any muletrains leaving for Venta Cruz. These trains would travel the eighteen miles from Panama to Venta Cruz at night to avoid the heat in the grasslands, while the journey from Venta Cruz to Nombre de Dios through the jungle was made during the day in the shade of the trees. The spy, having gone into the city an hour before dark, returned in a short time with news that electrified the raiders. That very night the treasurer of Lima was to leave with his family for Nombre de Dios, where he intended to ship on the dispatch boat for Spain. With him were to be fourteen mules, eight of which would be laden with gold and one with jewels. There were to be two other muletrains laden with American goods and some silver which were also leaving that night. With this news, Drake and his party left immediately for a point twelve miles east, toward Venta Cruz, where they intended to attack the trains. Moving double-time along the deserted road, with the thoughts of the great treasure running through their heads, they reached their destination quickly and took cover. One party, under John Oxenham, lay 150 feet off the road in the grass. Another, under Drake, took up a similar position further down the road where they could take the lead mules while Oxenham's party could cut off any means of retreat back to Panama. As the party had marched back toward Venta Cruz, the Cimarron scouts out in front had captured an armed Spanish soldier they had found asleep by the road. The scent of the burning match of his musket had given him away,* and he was captured while still asleep. Taken to Drake, the soldier had confirmed the facts reported by the spy and said he was placed there to help guard the trail for the treasurer's passage.

Within an hour of hiding in the grass, the bells of approaching mules were heard in the still night air. Mules were approaching from both directions, one group coming from Venta Cruz loaded with merchandise, the other farther off coming from Panama. The account in *Drake Revived* describes what happened as the train from Venta Cruz approached the raiders:

> Now though there was great charge given as might be that none of our men should show or stirre themselves, but let all that came from *Venta Cruz* to passe quietly, yea their *Recos* [muletrains] also, because we knew they brought nothing but Merchandise from thence, yet one of our men called *Robert Pike*, having drunken too much *Aqua Vitae* without water, forgat himselfe, and entising a *Symeron* [Cimarron] forth with him, was gone hard to the way, with intent to have shewne his forwardnesse on the forward Moyles [mules]. And when a Cavalier from *Venta Cruz*, well mounted with his page running at his stirrop, past by, unadvisedly he rose up to see what he was; but the *Symeron* (of better discretion) puld him downe, and lay upon him, that he might not discover them any more. Yet by this the Gentleman had taken notice by seeing one all in white (for that we had all put our shirts over our other apparell, that we might be sure to know our owne men in the pell mell in the night). By meanes of this sight, the Cavalier (putting spurs to his horse), rode a fast gallop, as desirous not onely himselfe to be free of this doubt, which he imagined, but also to give advertisement to others that they might avoid it.

---

* At this period the military musket was fired by a slowly smoldering inflammable cord called a match. Sentries kept their matches lit for obvious reasons.

Being thus warned, the trains of merchandise coming from Panama were sent ahead, while the train of the treasurer with the gold and jewels took up the rear; and finding the report true when the raiders attacked the lead trains, the treasurer and his party turned and hastened back to Panama saving themselves and the treasure. The loss of the treasure after so much effort was a great blow to the morale of the English, who had marched and suffered so much to reach this point on the trail. But Drake, ever the leader, "knowing it bootlesse to grieve at things past, and having learned by experience that all safetie in extreamites consisteth in taking of time . . . resolved, considering the long and wearie marches that we had taken, and chiefly that last evening and day before, to take now the shortest and readiest way." He resolved to march down the road through Venta Cruz. The hungry men were allowed to refresh themselves from the supplies on the muletrain, and the raiders then started off, some riding the captured mules. Within a mile of the town, the party dismounted and prepared to fight their way through the streets where Spanish soldiers were sometimes stationed. (Drake was working off the frustration of his men on the Spanish.) In the woods just outside the town, Drake and his men met a party of friars and soldiers going to Panama and, being challenged, identified themselves as English. At this, the Spanish soldiers fired a volley which mortally wounded one of the English. Replying with a shower of arrows and lead, the English charged with their Cimarron allies. The Spanish were scattered and fled, leaving six dead on the field, including one Dominican friar. One Cimarrron who had been run through by a pike summoned enough strength to kill the Spanish pikeman before he died. The way was now clear to the town and the raiders swept through it. They found no treasure, but the Cimarrons found goods, which they valued above money. Leaving Venta Cruz on January 29, the raiders now faced a three-week march back through the jungle to their base on the coast. Disappointed, their clothing in shreds, all of the shoes they had, including the spares, worn out, and their stomachs empty, they struggled back through the woods. On February 22, they reached the coast and found their pinnaces waiting for them.

The raid had caused consternation among the Spanish. This new threat to the most vital link of the treasure trail from Panama, which carried all of the rich trade from Peru, opened up the wealth of Peru to direct attack and menaced the whole Spanish system. With the Cimarrons as allies and guides, the enemy could go anywhere on the isthmus and strike where they would. Alarmed reports flowed back to the Crown from the officials at Panama and Nombre de Dios, one stating that "since they have done these things at this time, it is to be presumed that they will venture to do worse."[10] Pedro de Ortega Valencia, the royal factor at Nombre de Dios, who wrote this, was predicting exactly what Drake and his men were to do along the trail.

Drake, a great psychologist, as every great leader must be, knew he must restore the confidence of his men, their failure having borne heavily on the minds of them all. But Drake, showing his usual cheerful nature, encouraged the men to think of the success he said would soon be theirs. The hungry and tired men quickly regained their strength, while the enthusiasm of the men who had remained behind at the base on the coast was raised by the accounts of the near-miss on a treasure muletrain and the assurances of Drake that he meant to keep trying until they had all captured some of the treasure they knew was coming down the trail for the fleet at Nombre de Dios. Knowing "that no sickness was more noysome to impeach any enterprise then delay and idlenesse," Drake kept his men busy working on the pinnaces, maintaining their arms, practicing their archery, and raiding along the coast. The captain general of the fleet at Nombre de Dios, Diego Flores de Valdés, knew the English were based at Acla inlet but did not attempt to attack them there. On March 21, one of the frigates raiding along the coast met with a French corsair who had been hunting the English for five weeks. He was Captain Testu of Havre-de-Grâce and he brought news of the terrible St. Bartholomew's Day massacre of French Protestants in Paris on August 24 of the year before. Admiral Coligny of France and almost seventy thousand persons had been killed in one night. This news did not increase the love the English felt for the Spanish Catholics who had celebrated the massacre and congratulated the French Catholics on the slaughter.* Testu and twenty men agreed to serve with Drake for shares. And the Cimarrons, many of whom had returned to their villages after the abortive raid, were sent for to join the English and the French.

A month had passed since the exhausted English and the Cimarrons had returned to the coast from their disappointing failure on the treasure trail. Now they were again marching through the woods from the mouth of the Francisco River, fifteen miles from Nombre de Dios, where the pinnaces had landed them and where the ships were to await their return. As before, the English and the Cimarrons marched in silence, the French quickly learning the routine. This time, they had determined to attack the trains near Nombre de Dios to avoid the

---

* Pope Gregory XIII caused public celebrations to be held and had a medal struck commemorating the massacre.

exhausting long march through the forest and the danger of being cut off by forces now guarding the trail. The raiders came within a mile of the trail and settled down for the night to eat and sleep in silence until morning. They were so near the port they could hear the Spanish working on the ships at night, which they did to avoid the heat of the day. The next morning, mule bells were heard and the men knew the time to attack had come. The account in *Drake Revived* describes the capture:

> there came three Recoes, one of fifty Moyles, the other two of seaventy each, every of which caryed 300. pound weight of silver, which in all amounted to neere thirty Tun. We putting our selves in readinesse, went down neer the way to heare the Bels, where we stayed not long, but we saw of what metall they were made, and took such hold on the heads of the foremost and hindmost Moyles that all the rest stayed and lay downe, as their maner is. These three Recoes were guarded with fortie five Souldiers or there abouts, fifteene to each Reco, which caused some exchange of Bullets and Arrowes for a time, in which conflict the French Captaine was sore wounded with hayle-shot in the belly, and one *Symeron* slaine. But in the end these Souldiers thought it best way to leave their Moyles with us, and to seeke for more helpe abroad, in which meane time we tooke some paine to ease some of the Moyles, which were heaviest loaden, of their cariages. And being wearie, wee were contented with a few bars and quoits of gold,* as we could well cary, burying about fifteen Tun of silver, partly in the boroughs which the great Landcrabs had made in the earth, and partly under old trees which are fallen thereabout, and partly in the sand and gravell of a River, not very deepe of water.

The whole operation had taken two hours, and now the raiders heard the Spanish approaching on the road. The French captain had been badly wounded by a Spanish Negro muskateer and had to be left behind with a friend as the party fled toward the coast. Another Frenchman, drunk on captured wine and weighted down with gold, had started back early but lost himself in the woods. Drake and his party had either planned well or were lucky, for they had struck the muletrains when they were nearing Nombre de Dios and felt that they were out of danger of attack. One Spanish account says that "being near the city, where they thought there was no danger, they were travelling in some disorder."[11]

When news of the attack reached Nombre de Dios, the *alcalde mayor* had a drum beaten to summon the townspeople and issued a

* Quoits were round ingots weighing some 20 to 30 ounces each.

proclamation "bidding all to follow him on penalty of being adjudged traitors."[12] When this party arrived at the place of the attack, they found some gold and silver scattered about the road and the captured French captain lying wounded in the woods. He was killed by the aroused townspeople, a very unwise action since he could have given them information about where the loot that was left behind had been buried. Later, a French gentleman who had remained with the captain was captured and tortured until he revealed the hiding place, after which he was torn apart by horses, a form of execution in which a horse is tied to each arm and leg and driven in different directions. The captain general of the fleet, on hearing of the raid, sent out ten pinnaces filled with armed men under the command of Captain Cristóbal Monte. These pinnaces headed for the Francisco River, where the boats of the raiders were to have waited for the return of Drake and his men to the coast. A storm drove the Spanish boats off their post for one day, and Drake's boats arrived at the rendezvous late. This saved the raiders, for if the Spanish had met with Drake's pinnaces, they would surely have captured them, and the raiders would have been marooned. As it was, the sight of the Spanish pinnaces off the coast threw the raiding party into fear and confusion as they marched off for the Francisco River, for they thought their boats had been captured. Again, in this moment of distress and danger, it was Drake who took things in hand. To speed up his journey to the mouth of the river, he had a raft built and sailed down the stream constantly drenched by the rushing water. He arrived on the coast near his pinnaces and brought them to the beach to pick up the returning men.

At last, Drake had made his voyage. After almost a year of struggle against the Spanish, disease, storms and discouragement, Drake had led his men to the "mouth of the treasure of the world" and had captured a good portion of it, although he had to abandon much of the silver. Spanish accounts describe the treasure at 150,000 to 200,000 pesos, of which some 20,000 pesos in gold represented taxes going from Popayán in New Granada to the King. When the party returned to their ships, Drake divided the loot equally between the English and the French, who then disposed of it among themselves according to their agreement. Drake, determined to get the treasure they had left behind, sent John Oxenham and Thomas Sherwell with a party of men in a pinnace to recover what they could. When they arrived at the spot, they found the earth dug up in all directions as if everyone in Nombre de Dios had been out looking for the loot. But the Spanish had missed some of the treasure, and the party was able to recover thirteen bars of silver and a few quoits of gold, as well as another French gentleman who had remained behind with his captain and had escaped into the woods when the Spanish approached.

With the treasure secure, it was now time to prepare for the voyage home. Drake sailed eastward past Cartagena, looking for frigates loaded with supplies for the Spanish fleet lying in the harbor. A frigate of twenty-five tons, loaded with corn, hogs, hens and honey was captured, and the English returned to the coast of Panama to prepare their ships. Here the pinnaces were dismantled and the hulls were burned to give the Cimarrons the ironwork. Then the ships were tallowed and loaded with the captured provisions. Before taking leave of their Cimarron friends, Drake presented them with many gifts of cloth and other goods, and "thus with good love and liking . . . tooke . . . leave of that people." Setting sail for Cape San Antonio at the western end of Cuba, the English reached it without incident. Here, they landed, captured 250 turtles, and found great numbers of turtle eggs. They salted and dried many of the turtles—another mistake of inexperience: the turtles could have been laid on their backs in the hold, where they could have lived for weeks, furnishing fresh meat all the way home. Fair winds carried the ships from the debouchment of the Florida Straits to the Scilly Isles in just twenty-three days. During the voyage, plenty of rain provided the water the men needed, and on August 9, 1573, the small fleet arrived in Plymouth harbor.

Drake and his men had been gone a year and three months. The voyage had cost the lives of many of his companions, including his two brothers, the life of Captain Testu and some of his companions, the lives of several of the brave Cimarron allies without whom he could not have succeeded. It cost the Spanish colonials many killed and wounded and incalculable damage to their shipping, and it cost them a fortune in treasure and costly goods. Drake and his small but determined party had succeeded in stealing Spanish treasure right out from under the noses of the Spanish commanders, including the captain general of the powerful annual fleet to Cartagena and Nombre de Dios. To a great extent, the success of the attack was due to the leadership qualities Drake displayed. He insisted on firm discipline and on maintaining the ships and weapons at top efficiency; yet he had real compassion for his men in an age when cruelty was the rule. In a crisis, Drake always stepped forward and did what he would not ask his men to do; and he understood the mood of his men and their need for rest, recreation, and encouragement when things went badly. This man, a scourge to the Spanish, now became, with his triumphant return, a hero to his English compatriots as word of his exploits swept the kingdom. Drake had sailed away as just another English captain bent on a raid to the

West Indies. He had returned wealthy, with a head full of information about the geography of the Caribbean and the customs of the Spanish in handling their treasure and with a dream to sail on that great South Sea he had seen from a tree on the heights of Isthmus of Panama. Drake had pointed the way, and soon other English captains were to appear in Panama, among them John Oxenham who had viewed the Pacific with Drake.

Drake's raid had caused consternation among the Spanish. Never before had the enemy penetrated the very pipeline through which the treasure of South America flowed to the fleets in the Caribbean. In a letter to the Spanish Crown, dated May 9, 1573, the royal officials of Panama reported the depredations of Drake and his party and concluded with gloomy prediction of what they expected would follow:

> We remark this that your majesty may comprehend the shamelessness of these persons, and realize to what affliction and oppression this realme has been brought by the calamities it anticipates, arising out of this alliance.* It entails such detriment to traders and merchants that only with the very greatest danger can they get their merchandise over. They endeavour to send it under guard of forces sufficient for defense, out of which arise heavy costs and expenses.
>
> It is expected that, encouraged by the very valuable booty they have secured, these corsairs will return to this realm in very much greater strength, and by means of their federation with the negros so situate themselves as to succeed in any venture they may undertake.[13]

The officials at Panama were correct in their predictions. When news of Drake's return, with the treasure, swept the ports of southern England, other, lesser captains began plans to emulate him. The raids on the Spanish Main and the coast of Panama, which had been sporadic, were now intensified. But these captains were not Drake and would not succeed as brilliantly as he. Drake's old companion in arms, John Oxenham, penetrated all the way to the Pacific with a party of English, and realizing his ambition ahead of Drake, he sailed on the ocean as he had promised he would when he and Drake viewed it. Using canoes constructed with the aid of the Cimarrons, the English terrorized the Spanish there, but after initial successes, many of Oxenham's men were killed or captured, and Oxenham himself with several companions was taken and sent a prisoner to Lima.

Drake, now wealthy, busied himself with affairs at home, at one time fitting out at his own expense two warships for the Queen's service in

* The English alliance with the Cimarrons.

the Irish Rebellion. This loyalty did not tarnish his image in the eyes of Elizabeth, who was hearing more and more of this able young captain. Not until 1577 did Drake sail again to the West, and this voyage was to win him greater wealth and fame, the increasing attention of Elizabeth and her court, and a knighthood at the hands of that admiring monarch.

Drake sailed on his epic voyage around the world on November 15, 1577. After a tedious ten months, which were marred by an incipient mutiny, the execution of a gentleman, and the abandonment of two of the five ships, the English entered the Pacific Ocean by way of the Strait of Magellan on September 6, 1578. Then a storm struck. One ship was lost and another became separated from Drake in the *Golden Hind*. Undaunted, Drake sailed north alone. The Spanish, never dreaming an enemy would penetrate the Pacific in a large warship, were taken completely by surprise, and for months Drake sailed up and down the coast pillaging and capturing the treasure that flowed from the mines of Peru to Panama. Armed ships were sent against him but without success, and finally he sailed north until the cold drove him back. On a spot near San Francisco Bay in what is now California, Drake nailed a brass plate to a tree and claimed the area for Elizabeth. That he was deadly serious about this is proved when he later added to a chart, submitted for his approval, the royal arms of England and the name New Albion. When he was on the coast of Peru, Drake had heard that Oxenham and several companions were languishing in prison in Lima. Characteristically, Drake attempted to help them by cutting out some ships in Callao to hold in ransom for the prisoners. The scheme failed when the current and winds grounded the Spanish ships and the English could not take them off. Several months after Drake sailed from the west coast, John Oxenham went to the gallows, perhaps after another look at that ocean which irresistibly lured him and had brought him to his death at the hands of a Spanish hangman.

Drake sailed westward across the Pacific to England and the fame that awaited him. He arrived home on November 3, three years after his departure. His initial reception by the Queen was not cordial. The word of his depredations on the west coast of the Americas had preceded him, and the Spanish government was protesting violently to the English Crown. Elizabeth, in these circumstances, could not immediately give Drake the hero's welcome the adoring people wanted, but after a suitable interval and after she had been regaled with treasure from the voyage, Elizabeth went to Drake's ship and there on board knighted him. Drake had reached the top. When he next sailed against the Spanish in America, he was to go as the captain of a powerful fleet, supported directly by the Queen.

Relations between Spain and England had been steadily deteriorating through the years of unofficial warfare. Finally, Philip II saw all his intrigues with the English Catholics fail, and Elizabeth realized that her political and diplomatic dexterity could not suffice forever. The pressures developed by Drake's raids into Spanish territory and the increasing insistence of the more hawkish of her subjects were driving her toward open hostilities. Yet, it is difficult to say just when warfare began. Drake's great raid of 1585 is usually given as the starting point, but this raid was just a larger, more elaborate, and better-organized operation of the type he had started thirteen years before, with his raid on the Isthmus of Panama. Julian Corbett points out: "It is a conspicuous feature of the great Elizabethan war, that there is no moment when it can be said to have begun, no place where a line can be clearly drawn between the period of reprisal and the period of formal hostility."[14] Hostilities were almost inevitable. England was exploding onto the seas of the world. An insular people bursting with the new energy which the age of exploration had engendered, prospering under the wise rule of the great Elizabeth, and feeling the early effects of the Renaissance, the restless English had nowhere to go but to the seas. The boom in English shipbuilding and mercantile activity alarmed the Spanish ambassadors there, who rightly saw that this island nation would be a challenge to the might of Spain. Hawkins's early trading voyages, Drake's raids, and the efforts of Sir Humphry Gilbert to plant colonies in territory Spain claimed in the New World were symptoms of this bursting energy, which the Spanish would not be able to contain. Philip refused to recognize the futility of his stubborn ambition to conquer and convert the Protestant island, which had escaped him in the death of his wife Mary and the failure of his suit for the hand of Elizabeth. His own captain, the Duke of Alba, recognized the illogical nature of his King's direction and had remarked, "The King of Spain could make war with any prince in the world he would, so long as he had peace with the Kingdom of England."[15] And so hostilities began, with the first blows falling on the West Indies, the very center of the Spanish commercial empire, where Drake had twice before generously sampled the treasure which was the lifeblood sustaining Spain as the leading military power of Europe.

Drake sailed from Plymouth on September 14, 1585, with a fleet of twenty ships and pinnaces manned with twenty-three hundred sailors and soldiers. Christopher Carlisle went as his lieutenant general in com-

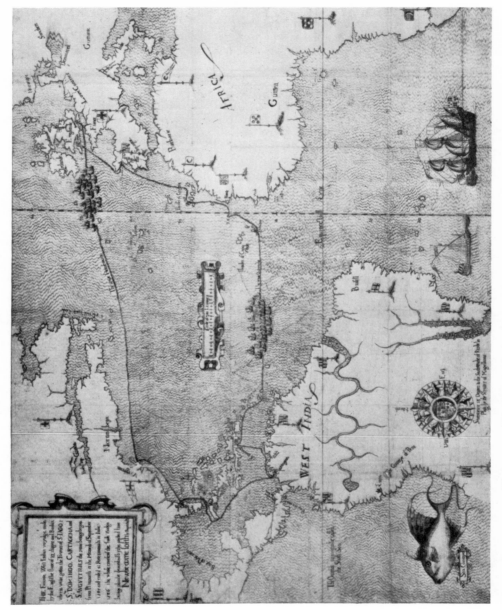

The route of Drake's raid of 1585–1586, a contemporary map by Boazio

mand of the land forces. Martin Frobisher sailed as vice admiral. After touching the coast of Spain and making some captures there, including "the principal churchstuffe of the high Church of Vigo, where also was their great crosse of silver, of very faire embossed worke, and double gilt all over,"[16] the fleet sailed to Santiago in the Cape Verde Islands. Arriving there November 16, Drake set ashore a thousand men under General Carlisle, who assembled in the dark on a plain two miles from the city. With daylight, the forces entered the city without resistance. Here the English remained "the space of 14. dayes, taking such spoiles as the place yeelded, which were for the most part, wine, oyle, meale, and some such like things for victuall, as vinegar, olives, and some such other trash, as merchandise for their Indians trades. But there was not found any treasure at all, or any thing else of worth besides." While there, many of the English saw their first coconuts, and the account published by Thomas Cates, from which we quote, describes this fruit in the natural state, which few men in England had ever seen:

> the saide cochos hath a hard shell and a greene huske over it, as hath our walnut, but it farre exceedeth in greatnesse, for this cochos in his greene huske is bigger than any mans two fistes: of the hard shell many drinking cups are made here in England, and set in silver as I have often seene.
>
> Next within this hard shell is a white rine resembling in shewe very much even as any thing may do, to the white of an egge when it is hard boyled. And within this white of the nut lyeth a water, which is whitish and very cleere, to the quantitie of halfe a pynt or thereaboutes, which water and white rine before spoken of, are both of a very coole fresh tast, and as pleasing as any thing may be. I have heard some hold opinion, that it is very restorative.

On November 26, Drake embarked with his men. During their stay, no local leader had come forward to speak with the English, and the principal persons of the city remained hidden with their leaders in the hills. Before the English rear guard left the town near sunset, the place was set ablaze and the whole town consumed. Cates's account attributes this rough handling of the place to the fact that the locals some years before had murdered several Englishmen in a party of traders that had landed there. A few days after sailing, an epidemic struck the fleet, which Cates's account describes:

> Wee were not many dayes at Sea, but there beganne among our people such mortalitie, as in fewe dayes there were dead above two or three

Christopher Carlyle. From a contemporary engraved portrait. Photograph from the Smithsonian Institution

hundred men. And until some seven or eight dayes after our comming from S. Iago, there had not died any one man of sicknesse in all the fleete: the sicknesse shewed not his infection wherewith so many were stroken, untill we were departed thence, and then seazed our people with extreme hot burning and continuall agues, whereof very fewe escaped with life, and yet those for the most part not without great alteration and decay of their wittes and strength for a long time after. In some that died were plainely shewed the small spots, which are often found upon those that be infected with the plague.

With a tenth of his men lost to the disease, Drake pushed on, making a remarkable passage of only eighteen days from Santiago to Dominica. Here the English filled their water casks, the local Caribs helping them without hostility. The numbers of the English, no doubt, discouraged an attack by these voracious cannibals. With them, the Caribs had two Spanish downcast captives, downcast no doubt because they knew they would soon be eaten. From Dominica, the fleet sailed to St. Christopher (now St. Kitts) to rest the sick men and to clean the bottoms of the ships and air them. Here they celebrated Christmas, and at a council of war, Drake and his commanders decided to attack Santo Domingo, still the administrative capital of the Caribbean.

The ships' bottoms clean and the hulls aired and rigging tight, the refreshed armada sailed for Santo Domingo. On the way, a Spanish frigate was captured. One of the Spanish captains, when questioned, informed Drake and Carlisle that the harbor of Santo Domingo was a "barren Haven" and would not provide an anchorage for the fleet and that the castle and landing places near the city were well provided with artillery. The captive agreed to take the English to a landing place some ten miles to the west of the harbor where small boats could land on a beach. The plan was now to land a thousand men under Carlisle in boats and pinnaces and attack the city by land from the west. On New Year's Day, 1586,* the boats put off from the ships lying offshore, Drake going with them, and as Cates remarks, "having scene us landed in safetie, returned to his Fleete, bequeathing us to God, and the good conduct of Master Carliell our Lieutenant Generall." The landing was completed by eight o'clock, and by noon the small army had reached the outskirts of the town. The Spanish had been warned by Don Diego Osorio, captain of a royal galley which had sighted the English fleet while on patrol off the city. As the English approached the defenses of the city, a party of Spanish gentlemen "and those of the better sort" approached on horseback. The English greeted them with a shower of

* The Spanish dated the landing January 10 by their calendar.

musket shot, and they withdrew after riding around the English and looking them over. Carlisle had his men marching in close order, protected by the pikemen, and it was evident to the Spanish they could not attack without committing suicide. Carlisle now divided his forces into two groups with which to attack two gates of the city on the water side. He commanded one of the parties and Captain Powell the other. Powell was to meet Carlisle in the great square of the city after taking the gate assigned to him. The first volley of Spanish small arms and light artillery fire wounded and killed a few of the English, but with their officers leading the charge, they advanced to the gates at a run and captured them. The Spanish, after the first shots, abandoned their posts and escaped through the city to the countryside. By mid-afternoon, the English were in the square fortifying it against a counterattack. Drake came into the harbor with his ships, and the next day the English spread out through the town, finding suitable quarters near the square that could be defended.

Having secured his position, Drake now demanded of the Spanish a ransom of one million ducats, a figure ridiculously high. The Spanish pleaded that they could not raise such an enormous sum, which, indeed, represented many years of income for the island. Drake then lowered the amount by degrees to a hundred thousand, which was equally impossible for the townspeople to raise. To give the Spanish more incentive, Drake now began to fire the city, and two hundred sailors were employed every morning during the cool hours at this task, but so large was the town and so well built of stone that the English were not able to "consume so much as one third part of [it]." All during the occupation, the Spanish were constantly treating with the English to save their dwindling city, and finally, as Cates discloses, "wearied with firing, and what happened by some other respects, wee were contented to accept five and twenty thousands Ducats of five shillings sixe pence the peece, for the ransome of the rest of the towne."

When Drake first began to treat with the Spanish, he had sent out a flag of truce with a small Negro boy, one of his favorite servants. As the lad approached a party of Spanish lancers, one of the horsemen rode him down and mortally wounded him with his lance. The boy staggered back to Drake and died in front of his captain. In a fury, Drake sent two captured Dominican friars, guarded by a company of soldiers, to the spot where the boy had been wounded and here the clergymen were hanged, the Spanish watching from a distance. He then sent a message to the enemy telling them he would hang two captives every day until the Spaniard who had done the deed was delivered to him. The next day, the man was brought in by some of his companions. Drake forced them to string him up to a nearby tree.

Spanish accounts of the raid mention other treasure captured from the royal coffers, but the English were disappointed in the little gold and silver afforded by the old and supposedly rich town. At this time, the wealth of the place came from farming, not mining, and the populace lived comfortably, though not on the lavish scale of the richer towns to the south on the Spanish Main. The English left Santo Domingo in wretched condition. They had not spared much in their fury at finding so little treasure. The place, in one Spanish account, is described as having "its temples burned and profaned, its monasteries demolished, its altars, images and holy places destroyed, and most of its residences burned."[17] To raise the ransom, even some of the cathedral plate was turned over to the raiders. All the ships in the harbor, including the royal galley, were burned, except five which Drake took with him when he sailed. The occupation had lasted thirty days.

The English fleet, now resupplied with food and water, with some loot and the ransom, sailed for Cartagena. They also carried another more sinister cargo—yellow fever, which many of the men, especially those standing watch at night, had contracted. A large percentage of them died.

According to Spanish accounts, the English entered Cartagena harbor at three or four o'clock on the afternoon of February 19. The outer harbor mouth lay about three miles west of the town, with a low wooded spit extending toward the settlement. Having heard of the capture of Santo Domingo soon after it happened, the people of Cartagena immediately began preparations for defense. A wall that reached almost across the spit on the approaches to the town was extended to the water by earthworks and barrels of earth. Six culverins and demi-culverins were emplaced on a platform to command the narrow approaches, and two royal galleys were placed with their bows to shore so that their heavy guns and musketeers could rake the approaches to the defenses across the spit. The inner harbor, which was entered by a narrow passage from the outer, was defended by a strong stone castle with heavy guns. As word of the approach of the English reached the Spanish, a large harbor-defense chain secured to barges was extended across the inner-harbor mouth. The chain being too short to reach the entire distance, the defenders extended it with some heavy chain from the local jail. Meanwhile, the townspeople were busy moving themselves and their valuables to the countryside. The Spanish raised in the streets defenses the English later described as "very fine Barracados of earth-workes, with trenches without them, as well made as ever we

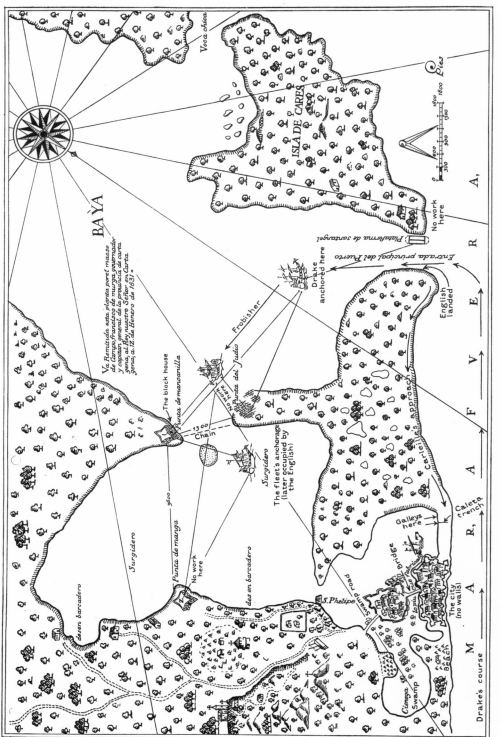

Chart of Drake's attack on Cartagena. From Irene A. Wright's *Further English Voyages to Spanish America, 1583–1594*

HONI SOIT QVI MAL Y PENCE
·THE·SVRGEONES·
CHEST

A military surgeon's medicine chest of the late sixteenth century. From a contemporary woodcut

saw any worke done." Although the defense works were good, the defenders in the ensuing action were unable to hold them against the raiders. At about ten o'clock that night, six hours after the English fleet had entered the outer harbor, Lieutenant General Carlisle began landing the one thousand troops who were to attack. Drake prepared the pinnaces that were to enter the inner harbor and land men in the town proper. By midnight, the troops were assembled and commenced marching up the beach by the water's edge. This was to save the lives of many of the English, for Indian allies of the Spanish had studded the spit with sharp-pointed, poisoned sticks. Even so, many English later died in agony from the effects of wounds received from stakes planted near the beach. Spanish horsemen had been sent out to watch for the English, and word was soon brought to the defenders that the enemy had landed. The governor of Cartagena, Pedro Fernández de Busto, led 220 men at the Caleta, the defense position across the spit. The English struck at two o'clock, four hours after the landing began. Cates's account says that the Spanish "in this their full readinesse to receive us, spared not their shot both great and small." Carlisle, taking advantage of the dark, sent his men along the water side attacking the weakest point in the defenses where they had been extended by barrels filled with earth. The Spanish behind the wall and barrels had the advantage of cover, but the darkness served the English, and the Spanish fire had no major effect. The account of the Spanish governor says, "It was the blackest night I have ever seen in my life."[18] 'And while artillery and musket fire was directed against the enemy, "the night was so dark, we could not see what we were doing."

After the third Spanish volley, the English charged the defenses at a run and overwhelmed them. Most of the Spanish turned tail and ran. In the confusion, a voice had been heard saying in perfect Spanish, "Retire, gentlemen for we are lost."[19] This led to the first break in the Spanish line. The governor, sword in hand, attempted to stop the retreat, saying, "Do not retreat, brothers, but fight," but he was unable to stay the fleeing townspeople and most of the soldiers. He remained on the beach with a few of the men, but the fire was so heavy they finally had to withdraw. In the disorder and darkness, the governor stumbled into a trench full of men which he thought were Spanish and urged them to continue the fight, only to discover he was in a hole with fifteen or so aroused Englishmen. Before the surprised English could seize him, he got away in the darkness. The voice in the night that had urged the Spanish to retreat was an Englishman speaking the language of the enemy, an example of psychological warfare at its best.

View of Cartagena. From a seventeenth-century engraving

By morning the town had been occupied, and the retreating Spanish soldiers and armed citizens had joined their women and children in the countryside. The two royal galleys were burned by their crews in the inner harbor to prevent capture, but Drake managed to salvage some brass artillery from them. With the battle over, the city was systematically sacked, but the Spanish had removed most of their valuables and only ordinary goods were found in any quantity. Drake now began negotiations for the ransom of the city, and these were carried on between Drake and his officers and the Spanish governor and his aides in a most polite and refined manner. The governor called on Drake to discuss the ransom. Drake at first demanded 400,000 ducats. Cates describes the way in which the negotiations were conducted: "During our abode in this place, as also at S. Domingo, there passed divers courtesies betweene us and the Spaniards, as feasting, and using them with all kindnesse and favour; so as amongst others there came to see the Generall, the Governour of Cartagena, with the Bishop of the same, and divers other Gentlemen of the better sort." Finally, after much feasting and passing of compliments, Drake was convinced that the Spanish simply could not pay the amount he demanded. He settled for 100,000 ducats and agreed never to attack Cartagena again as long as he commanded English forces. As it was, Drake was only able to extract this amount by getting out large brass bombs and other explosive devices and preparing to blow up the town. His officers had recommended that he accept the 100,000 ducats, in a remarkable document which pointed out the deplorable state of the men in the ranks.

While the negotiations were going on, yellow fever continued to infect the English ranks and lasted for the six weeks they occupied the town. Cates mentions the effects the illness had on the strength of the English forces:

> The sicknesse with mortalitie before spoken of still continued among us, though not with the same furie as at the first: and such as were touched with the sayde sicknesse, escaping death, very few or almost none could recover their strength: yea, many of them were much decayed in their memorie, insomuch that it was growen an ordinarie judgement, when one was heard to speake foolishly, to say he had bene sicke of the Calentura, which is the Spanish name of their burning Ague: for as I tolde you before, it is a very burning and pestilent ague. The originall cause thereof, is imputed to the Evening or first night ayre, which they tearme La serena, wherein they say and hold very firme opinion, that who so is then abroad in the open ayre, shall certainly be infected to the death, not being of the Indian or naturall race of those countrey people: by holding their watch, our men were thus subjected to the infectious ayre, which at S. Iago was most dangerous and deadly of all other places.*

Drake had originally intended to attack Panama overland as he had attacked Venta Cruz in 1573, but now his forces had been severely reduced by the fever, and intelligence reached him that the Cimarrons had made peace with the Spanish and could not be counted on as allies. Carlisle and several captains presented a document to Drake in which they declared that the men were exhausted, ragged, and sickly. These facts, along with the news of the Cimarrons' new attitude, led Drake to abandon his Panama project and depart for the Florida Straits by Cape San Antonio.

After one false start, when the fleet had to return to unload a large prize ship loaded with loot which had sprung a leak, the fleet got away from Cartagena and reached Cape San Antonio on April 27, 1586. Here, finding no suitable water, Drake decided to reach for Matanzas

* Cates is referring to Santiago in the Cape Verde Islands.

Bay to the eastward of Havana, but after fourteen days of fighting headwinds, the English found themselves back at Cape San Antonio. In desperate need of water now, the English dug holes in the soggy soil and watered the ships from these. Here Drake worked with the men to encourage them in their task. Three days were spent in taking on water, and the fleet sailed a second time from the cape on May 13. Now following the Spanish custom, the English sailed up into the Gulf of Mexico to avoid the headwinds which had driven them westward, and without touching land, they rounded the Florida Keys and set a course up the Straits of Florida, speeded along by the Gulf Stream. Fifteen days after leaving Cape San Antonio, the fleet arrived off St. Augustine. The English quickly reduced the fort and captured the town, along with fourteen brass cannon and the royal money chest containing £2,000 sterling.

From here Drake was determined to call at the English colony that had been established on the coast of Virginia by Sir Walter Raleigh and soon found a party of Englishmen who had built a great fire ashore to attract the fleet. Ralph Lane, the governor, came to the beach, and the desperate condition of the English settlement was discussed. It was at first decided that Drake would leave a ship and provisions and that the colony would hang on for another year, but a severe storm scattered the fleet and swept the ship to be given Lane to sea without her anchors, which were lost when her cables broke. At this, it was decided to embark the English and return them to England. The ship which Lane was to have had was not seen again until the fleet returned to England. The fact that Drake had ravaged three Spanish towns to the south may have had a bearing on the ultimate decision to abandon the Virginia settlement, since the Spanish could be expected to retaliate against the colony. On June 18, the fleet sailed from Virginia with the 103 colonists aboard. One month and ten days later, on July 28, 1586, it arrived at Portsmouth.

The expedition had done severe damage to Spanish settlements in the Cape Verde Islands and the Caribbean, and had brought home loot valued at £60,000, probably equivalent to $3 million in modern money. The share of each man was £6 or the modern equivalent of $300, hardly good pay for the sickness and danger through which they had suffered. Seven hundred fifty men had died on the voyage or the shares would have been even less. Two thirds of the loot, from which the expenses of the expedition had to be paid, went to Drake, his captains and the Queen. In addition to the booty in goods and treasure, two hundred brass and forty iron cannon had been captured, a great prize in itself.

Drake and his men looting a Spanish settlement. From an eighteenth-century engraving

Drake, John Hawkins, and the other naval leaders of England now devoted their time to preparations to meet the growing threat of attack by Spain. War was inevitable, and the great Armada was forming in the ports of Spain and Portugal. Drake again distinguished himself in his attack on Cádiz, when he destroyed many Spanish ships on April 19, 1587. This was the incident later referred to as "Singeing the King's beard." When the actual attack by the Armada came, Drake, as vice admiral of the English forces, made his contribution to the repulse of the Spanish fleet, which was largely finished off by storms around the coasts of Scotland and Ireland as the Spanish sought to return to Spain. The year after the defeat of the Armada, Drake led a fleet which sought to restore Don Antonio to the throne of Portugal, an expedition that failed.

Hostilities with Spain continued, and in 1594, Drake sailed with a combined fleet, jointly commanded by his cousin John Hawkins, to attack the Spanish settlements in the Caribbean. The now aging commanders could not agree on a plan of operations, and nothing came of their early efforts against Puerto Rico. Both John Hawkins and Drake died of fever on that expedition. It is believed that the great disappointment of the expedition's failures contributed to Drake's death, which occurred on January 28, 1595, off the coast of Panama. He was buried at sea in a lead coffin. Today that coffin lies somewhere in the shallow waters off Nombre de Dios, a fitting burial place for this great captain who, as a young man, first won fame in his attacks on the Spanish treasure trail.

The great Drake was gone. No longer would the Dragon capture, pillage and destroy. But the Spanish were to have no respite. While other English captains were to follow, though with less success than their predecessor, it was to be the Dutch, in their bitter hatred of the Spanish for the cruelties practiced in the Lowlands, who were to become the scourge of the dons on the great treasure routes of America.

VI

Lutheran Infection and
Catholic Cure

I was their enemy, and was waging a war of fire and blood
against them because they were Lutherans, and had come to
spread their evil sect in these Your Majesty's dominions, and
instruct the Indians therein.
—Admiral Pedro Menéndez to King Philip II,
October 15, 1565

THE EARLIEST INTERLOPERS in the treasure seas of Spanish
America came as explorers or pirates. They were enemies of
the Spanish monopoly but they were Catholics. Lutheranism had not
yet spread in Europe dividing the continent into opposing philosophies.
As the new religion took root and grew over large areas of Germany,
France, Switzerland, and Scotland, and after Henry VIII broke with
the Church of Rome, the new element of religious differences brought
even more bitterness into the struggle between Spain and her enemies.
In France, the Huguenots grew to be a formidable segment of the
population. To the Spanish Crown, this was nothing less than an infection, a deadly disease threatening the "true" religion; and Charles V and
his son Philip II watched with increasing dismay as Protestantism continued to spread over Europe, thereby adding a new concern to their
overpowering economic and political burdens. The heresy must be
stopped at all costs and the Catholic Kings became the champions leading the counterattack. Now the lands in America had to be defended
against this heresy as well as against illegal traders and pirates.

The French had shown much more vigor than the English in con-
testing the claims of Spain in America. Sharing a common border, and
conflicting ambitions in Italy, France and Spain were frequently at
war, and these hostilities spilled onto the sea and influenced French
attitudes toward the monopolistic Spanish claims in the Western
Hemisphere. The English government had shown an early interest in
the new lands by sending John Cabot on his voyage of discovery, but

the English Crown had not followed this up—leaving any exploration to private subjects on private voyages—and had not pressed any claims in America. Breton fishermen had fished the Newfoundland Banks from a very early period, probably even before the voyages of Columbus, and this fact gave the French a foundation for later claims in America.

French corsairs had attacked Spanish shipping as early as the last voyage of Columbus, and they became a real threat to returning Spanish treasure ships in the first two decades of the sixteenth century. Some French may have even sailed to the West Indies in search of loot. In 1522 ships belonging to Jean Ango, a powerful merchant of Dieppe, returned to port with gold, silver, pearls, jewels, and strange feather-work which was displayed to the wondering citizens of Dieppe. One captured galleon had yielded several hundred pounds of gold dust, gold ingots, and pearls. These riches whetted the appetites of the Norman merchants, and attacks on Spanish shipping continued. When the arrogant and ambitious Francis I succeeded to the French throne in 1515, he took a new and bellicose attitude toward the Spanish claims in America. He did not recognize the exclusive rights of Spain and Portugal in America and early in his reign directly challenged them by sending a Florentine pilot of Dieppe, Giovanni da Verrazano, on a voyage of discovery to America. At first exploring to the north for a passage to China in 1523, Verrazano was driven back to Brittany by storms. The next year he sailed again, raising the coast of Florida at about 34° north latitude (on the present North Carolina coast) and then sailing northward to 50° in the Gulf of St. Lawrence. The expedition returned to France in July 1524, and Verrazano reported his findings to Francis, referring to his discovery as Gallia Nova, and in his report he mentioned that his four ships had been ordered by the Crown to carry out the explorations. This was the first official challenge by another government of the arrangements made by Spain and Portugal to divide up the New World.

A decade after Verrazano's voyage, Jacques Cartier of St.-Malo was commissioned by Francis to look for the Northwest Passage, and he sailed on April 20, 1534, with two ships and sixty-one men. Arriving on the coast of Newfoundland, he planted a cross and claimed the country for France. In August, he touched the coast of the mainland opposite Anticosti Island. Wishing to make known his discovery to Francis, Cartier returned to St.-Malo, arriving September 5. The next May, he set out on a second voyage of discovery with three ships, again on orders from Francis, touching the coast of Newfoundland early in July. The squadron discovered and explored the St. Lawrence River, reaching the present site of Quebec. Later, Cartier pushed up the river to where Montreal is now, finishing the last difficult part of the voyage with boats when the river could not be navigated with his larger vessels. From the top of Mount Royal, he viewed the lands to the west. On rejoining his companions downstream, he claimed the country for France a second time. Here at the mouth of the present St. Charles River, he built a fort in which to spend the winter. In the following five cold months, twenty-five of Cartier's men died of disease and exposure. Early in May 1536, Cartier raised another cross with the arms of France attached and again asserted claim to the new lands in the name of Francis I. With this, he returned to France, reaching St.-Malo on July 16. Cartier was now honored for his discovery, and Francis determined to follow it up with an effort at settlement, but new hostilities with Spain broke out soon after Cartier's return and occupied the French King until June 18, 1538, when the Treaty of Nice was concluded. With the arrival of peace, preparations began for Cartier's third voyage. This time, five ships were fitted out at St.-Malo on royal orders and with royal money.

The voyages of Cartier were watched by the Spanish with great concern. Charles V of Spain had made diplomatic efforts at getting France to recognize the papal Line of Demarcation and the Treaty of Tordesillas, but Francis consistently refused to do so. The Treaty of Nice was ambiguous about the question of French claims in America and guaranteed freedom of navigation to both parties. To the French, this meant they were free to pursue their project in Canada. The Spanish interpreted the treaty in quite the opposite way and held that it recognized the Line of Demarcation and forbade French navigation west of the line. Thus the treaty settled nothing. In an effort to dissuade the French from the Canada project, Charles related the question of the future of the duchy of Milan with the French colonization project, intimating that he would approve the succession of a French prince to the duchy if Francis would give up his claims in Canada. Not wanting to endanger the negotiations over Milan, Francis held up Cartier's departure until 1540. During this period, Charles had been urging the Council of the Indies to fit out a squadron to intercept Cartier and destroy him. The council had replied that there was no money in the treasury to finance the squadron, and the plan was abandoned. Spanish spies at the French court and at St.-Malo kept Charles well informed of the French activities, but he was not able to prevent Cartier's departure. On October 11, 1540, Charles gave the duchy of Milan to his son Philip and, having no further reason to delay, Francis gave Cartier his commission to sail. The following months were spent in preparations for the voyage.

Charles violently protested the commissioning of Cartier through his ambassador at the French court, but Francis replied that the French claims to Canada were based on a discovery by Bretons as early as 1462 and that the lands he sought to settle had never been occupied or even seen by the Spanish. At an interview with the Spanish ambassador, Francis is supposed to have said that he would like to have seen the testament of Adam and how he had partitioned the world. A few months after commissioning Cartier, Francis conferred the title of lieutenant general on Jean-François de la Roque, sieur de Roberval, and commissioned him to occupy Canada, develop the land, and Christianize the Indians. It specifically forbade Roberval's occupying any land belonging to Spain or Portugal. Charles continued his efforts to counter Francis's moves diplomatically, but without success. Having been disappointed over the loss of Milan and being interested in founding an overseas empire, Francis was willing to risk war rather than give up his American project.

On May 23, 1541, Cartier sailed on his third voyage to Canada, leaving Roberval to follow. The ships were buffeted all across the North Atlantic by storms but finally arrived at the Bay of St. Croix in the St. Lawrence River on August 23. On the St. Lawrence, Cartier established a fort, naming it Charlesbourg Royal. At first the Indians were friendly, but things soon turned sour, and the ensuing winter the French suffered from the weather and Indian hostility. When Cartier had sailed in May, Roberval was still in the midst of preparing his fleet and took a leisurely pace. When some of his ships were ready, Roberval went cruising off the coast of France, preying on the merchantmen there. The temptation to enrich himself with his new fleet was more than he could resist. His piracy caused a furor at court when the ambassadors of the nations whose merchants had been wronged began protesting. Francis was thoroughly enraged at his general, but Roberval was able to complete his preparations and get away from France in the spring of 1542 before the King could remove him from his command. Roberval's squadron reached America just as Cartier had decided to return to France with a report on his two winters there and some shiny stones which the French thought were diamonds. Cartier's squadron met by chance that of Roberval on the coast of Newfoundland, and the general ordered Cartier to return to the settlement with him. Not relishing another severe winter in Canada and anxious to tell the King of his discovery of precious stones, Cartier slipped away with his squadron in the dark and sailed off. When it was discovered that Cartier's "diamonds" were merely quartz crystals, his disappointment and the disappointment of the court knew no bounds. And the expression "false as a Canadian diamond" entered the French language.

Roberval continued to the St. Lawrence despite Cartier's desertion and reached Charlesbourg Royal, which he renamed France-Roy. The following winter was long and severe, and some fifty of the French died of scurvy. When the ice broke up in April 1543, Roberval prepared to explore the upper reaches of the St. Lawrence. Early in June, he sailed upriver, losing a bark and eight men on the trip. He claimed for France all of the land he visited. Increasingly discouraged at his failure to find precious metals or gems and encountering hostile natives, Roberval decided to abandon the colony despite new supplies which the King had sent out. By September 1543, he was back in France. The terrible climate, lack of natural treasures, hostile natives, and war with Spain had defeated the first efforts of the French to establish an American empire.

While French colonizing efforts were going on, a new ingredient was being added to the French social and political scene. The Protestant sect was growing in spite of rigorous persecution by the Church and the French government. The Protestant church of Paris was founded in 1556, and three years later the Synod of Paris met to unite the Protestants for protection. By 1561 there were over two thousand Protestant churches. In the face of such numbers, the government of France was powerless. Thousands were leaving the Catholic Church to join the Protestants, among them men of rank and power, including Admiral Gaspard de Coligny. Much of Coligny's efforts were directed at protecting his fellow Protestants from persecution. For one solution to the problem, Coligny looked to the New World as a place where the Protestants, by now known as Huguenots, could find a refuge from the intolerance and fury of the Catholic French. In 1555 Coligny had sent an expedition to Brazil to establish a colony in direct challenge to Portuguese claims. The colony was destroyed in 1560 by a powerful Portuguese expedition.

A year following the return of Roberval from Canada, the Treaty of Crépy-en-Laonnois, signed on September 18, 1544, temporarily ended hostilities between France and Spain. In the treaty, Francis agreed that the lands to the west belonged to Spain and Portugal and gave up any further attempts at colonization. Francis's death (on March 31, 1547) ended his dreams of a French empire in America but not those of his successors. The French corsairs, not recognizing any treaty or law, continued their depredations in the Indies, and French and Spanish fishermen fought on the Newfoundland Banks.

Formal hostilities again broke out between France and Spain, and another treaty, that of Vaucelles, signed on February 5, 1556, patched things up for the time being. In the treaty, Henry II of France agreed that no French subjects were to go to America (that is, across the Line of Demarcation) without the specific permission of the Spanish Crown. The Spanish were to be permitted to use force against any French found beyond the line, the one exception to the five-year truce established by the treaty. Unfortunately, the French considered the truce to apply to America for five years only, while the Spanish interpreted the treaty as prohibiting incursions into America indefinitely. Soon after the truce was signed, Henry II resumed hostilities with Spain without provocation at the urging of Guises. The war, while gaining Calais from the English, plus Luxembourg and several other small territories, put an end to French ambitions in Italy and lost Savoy. In the Treaty of Cateau-Cambrésis signed in August 1559, France would not give up her claims to freedom of the seas, and Spain would not relinquish pretensions to her monopoly in America. Neither power wished for further hostilities, however, and the result was an agreement to a principle which stated that hostilities beyond the Line of Demarcation would not be reflected in the relations between the two powers in Europe. West of the line, French ships went at their own risk, and the Spanish reserved the right to attack and destroy them on sight. The French did not specifically renounce any further claims to any American territory not already occupied by the Spanish. Thus was established the concept of "no peace beyond the line," which remained active until the eighteenth century.

In France the time for a showdown between the Catholic party and the Protestants was approaching, and the next decade and more was to see the cruelest of wars between the two factions. Protestants had been persecuted under Francis I after an initial period when they were granted tolerance. Henry II, a Catholic fanatic, attempted to suppress the Lutherans but was defied by their increasing numbers and their increasing political and economic power. His death in a jousting accident in 1559 saved the Protestants. Under his successor, the sickly young Francis II, the Catholic Guises were entrusted with governing France, but Francis died the year following his accession. During the reign of the next king, Francis's brother Charles IX, who was a minor, the real power of the Crown was wielded by their mother, Catherine de' Medici. This accomplished woman saw the danger to the Crown inherent in a religious struggle between the two factions. The Catholics were led by the duke de Montmorency, the duke de Guise, and the marshal de Saint-André, while the Protestants followed the prince de Condé and Admiral Coligny. Catherine attempted a policy of toleration and conciliation, and the Protestants were granted liberty of conscience. In January 1561, they demanded liberty of worship as well, but events had gone too far, and Catherine's policy of toleration was to have no chance in France.

Having failed in the cold north and tropical Brazil, the French were now to attempt settlement in the temperate zone in an area not settled by the Spanish on the North American coast. The reasonableness of this idea was apparent to Admiral Coligny, who saw the colonization idea as a means by which the Protestants of France could find a refuge from the increasing intolerance of the Catholics. A small party sailed in two ships from Havre-de-Grâce on February 18, 1562, under the command of Jean Ribaut of Dieppe and René de Laudonnière with a Spanish pilot named Bartolomé. After a storm, which sent them into port again, and a reasonably quick passage of ten weeks, the French sighted the coast of Florida on April 30. The next day they entered a river, which they named the River of May in honor of May Day (the present St. Johns River). Ribaut and his followers were entranced by the beauty and fertility of the country: ". . . with wynd at will we sailed and veered the coast all along with inspeakeable pleasure of thoderiferous smell and bewtye of the same . . . we did behold to and fro the goodly order of the woodes wherewith God hathe decked everywhere the said lande. . . . It is a place wonderfull fertill, and of strong scituation, the ground fat so that it is lekely that it would bring fourthe wheate and all other corn twise a year."[1] Here they saw numbers of Indians along the shore who greeted the visitors without "feare or doubte." The natives showed Ribaut the best landing place and an Indian was sent into the water to guide the boats ashore. As Ribaut and his men landed, one who was evidently a chief came forward to greet them in a gentle and friendly manner, his warriors following "with great silence and modestie." Small gifts were exchanged and the French fell on their knees to thank God for their safe arrival. Ribaut describes the reaction of the Indians: "While we were thus praying, they sitting upon the ground, which was dressed and strewed with baye bowes, behelde and herkened unto us very attentively, withowt eyther speaking or moving. And as I made a sygne unto there king, lifting up myne arme and stretching owt one fynger, only to make them loke up to heavenward, he likewise lifting up his arms towardes heven, put fourthe two fyngers wherby it semed that

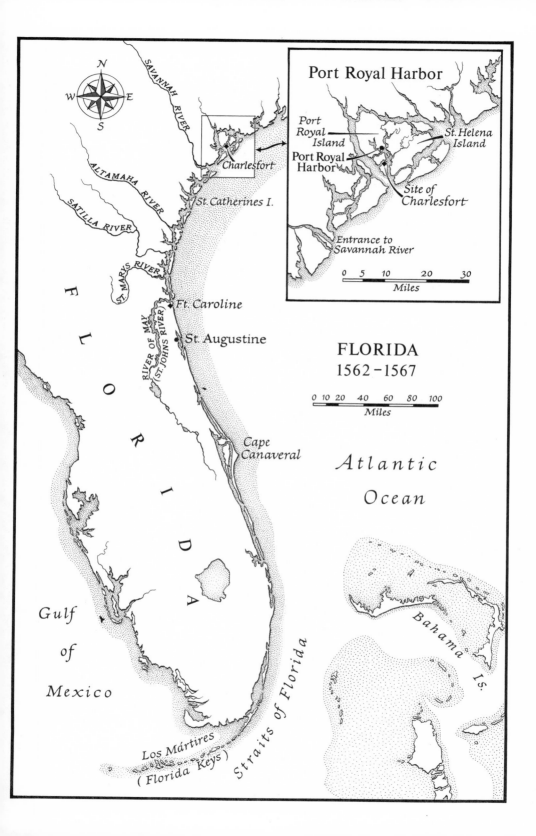

Port Royal Harbor

Port Royal Island

St. Helena Island

Port Royal Harbor

Site of Charlesfort

Entrance to Savannah River

0   5   10   20   30
Miles

N
W   E
S

SAVANNAH RIVER

Charlesfort

ALTAMAHA RIVER

SATILLA RIVER

ST. MARYS RIVER

St. Catherines I.

RIVER OF MAY (ST. JOHNS RIVER)

Ft. Caroline

St. Augustine

FLORIDA
1562–1567

0 10 20   40   60   80 100
Miles

F L O R I D A

Cape Canaveral

Atlantic

Ocean

Gulf

of

Mexico

Los Mártires
(Florida Keys)

Straits of Florida

Bahama Is.

he would make us tunderstand that thwy worshipped the sonne and mone for Godes, as afterward we understode yt so." Ribaut observed the great obedience which the Indians showed their king, chiefs, and elders. He was impressed by their fine physique and natural clothing:

> They be all naked and of a goodly stature, mighty, faire and aswell shapen and proportioned of bodye as any people in all the worlde, very gentill, curtious and of a good nature.
>
> The most parte of them cover their raynes and pryvie partes with faire hartes skins, paynted cunyngly with sondry collours, and the fore parte of there bodye and armes paynted with pretye devised workes of azure, redd, and black, so well and so properly don as the best paynter of Europe could not amend yt. The wemen have there bodies covered with a certen herbe like unto moste, whereof the cedertrees and all other trees be alwaies covered. The men for pleasure do allwayes tryme themselves therwith, after sundry fasshions. They be of tawny collour, hawke nosed and of a pleasaunt countenaunce. The women be well favored and modest and will not suffer that one approche them to nere.

Having spent several hours on the north side of the river, Ribaut pledged peace and friendship to the Indians and presented them with gifts of blue cloth decorated with yellow flowers. Then he set out for the south shore. Some of the Indians entered the water up to their necks to move the boat into the stream, while others dashed to nearby fish traps and brought back fish which they threw into the boat as a gift of friendship.

On the south shore Ribaut again met a large party of warriors armed with bows and accompanied by their king and chiefs. And again, the French and the Indians pledged their friendship. Ribaut presented his hosts with "gifts of haberdasherye wares, cutting hooks and hatchettes, and clothed the king and his brethern with like robes we had given to them on the other side." After this, the French, accompanied by the chief and his warriors, walked into the country which Ribaut found to be "the fairest, frutefullest and plesantest of all the worlde, habonding in honney, veneson, wildfoule, forrestes, woodes of all sortes, palme trees, cipers, ceders, bayes, the hiest, greatest and fairest vynes in all the wourld with grapes accordingly, which naturally and withowt mans helpe and tryming growe to the top of okes and other trees that be of a wonderfull greatnes and height."

Then the French visited one of the Indian villages and observed the gardens of maize and vegetables, which the Indians cultivated with wooden tools tipped with stone or seashells. The villages were thick with walnut and hazelnut trees, and fruits and herbs abounded. The great lesson to be learned here apparently escaped most of the French, for later they would prove unable or unwilling to support themselves on the land. The rest of the first day ashore was spent talking to the Indians by sign language about the mines of the legendary Cibola, which was supposed to lie north of Mexico. The Indians indicated that the country could be reached in a twenty-day boat trip. The fact that some of the Indians wore gold and silver ornaments and pearls seemed to indicate to the French that the country abounded in wealth. In actuality, the gold and silver probably came from shipwrecks on the Florida coast through trade with the Florida Indians, although some gold was found in the mountains to the west. The pearls, the French soon learned, came from oysters and freshwater mussels, which abounded in the streams and inlets of the coast. After their first intoxicating day ashore, the French returned to their ships, lying eighteen miles down the river and off the bar. As they left, they promised the Indians to return the next day.

The following morning, Ribaut and a party of soldiers returned, taking with them one of five stone markers brought from France. On the south side of the River of May, with the Indians looking on, they set up the column on "a littell hill compassed with cipers, bayes, palmes, and other trees, and swete pleasant smelling shrubbes." This marker was to be the southern limit of the land which they claimed for the French King. This done, the French went to the north side of the river where were assembled the Indians they had seen the evening before. When those natives on the south shore saw the French cross the river and stay sometime with the Indians there, they ran to look at the column Ribaut had set up, "which they vewed a gret while withowt touching yt any waye, or abasshing, or ever speaking unto us therof at any tyme after."

Ribaut noted "some ennemytie" between the peoples of the south bank and the north, a fact that became more apparent when the French established a settlement on the River of May. Ribaut and his men were received with enthusiasm and friendliness by their Indian friends on the north bank, who brought presents of "harte skins, paynted and unpaynted, meale, little cakes, freshe watter, rootes like unto rubarbe . . . littel bagges of redd coullours and some small peces like unto oore [ore]." The Indians also told the French of gold, silver, and copper, lead, turquoises, and pearls which were found in their land. They were at great pains to try to please the French and encourage them to stay, sensing that the visitors would be powerful allies against their enemies on the south bank. But Ribaut, not wishing to neglect the other Indians who waited for them, crossed to the south shore with some grief at leaving "the comodyties and great ryches which we understode and sawe might be gotten there." Ribaut describes the reception they received from the south-bank Indians:

> We founde them tarring [sic] for us quietly and in good order, trymed with newe pictures upon there faces, and fethers upon ther heddes, their king with his bowes and arrowes lieing by him, sett on the ground, strewed with baye bowes, bitwen his two brethern [whiche were] goodly men [&] well shapen and of wonderfull shewe of activetie, having about there heddes and heare, which was trussed up of a height, a kinde of heare of some wilde beast died redd, gatherd and wrought together with great cunyng, and wrethed and facioned after the forme of a diedeme. One of them had hanging at his necke a littell round plate of redd copper well pollished, with an other lesser of silver in the myddst of yt (as ye shall se) and at his care a littell plate of copper wherewithe they use to scrape and rake awaye the sweat from their bodies. They shewed unto us that there was grett store of this mettall within the cuntry, abowt five or six jurnaies from thence, bothe on the southe and nourthe side of the same river [the St. Marys River].

The Indians displayed their boats, with which they navigated the river for great distances. These were large dugouts which could carry fifteen to twenty persons. Since night was falling, Ribaut, with real regret, left to return to the ships lying off the bar at the mouth of the river.

If the French had dared to cross the bar in their vessels, Ribaut would probably have picked the River of May as the location of his first settlement just as René de Laudonnière did later, for the place seemed ideal and the friendship of at least one group of Indians could be counted on. But without wishing to risk his ships, Ribaut felt it necessary to find a protected harbor where they could ride out a blow in safety, and therefore set sail for the north on the morning of May 3. As the French coasted the new land, they were entranced by the numbers of beautiful rivers they found and the pleasant meadows and woodlands that lay along the shores. About twenty-one miles north of the River of May, Ribaut found another river mouth and entered it in a boat. It proved to be "almost like unto that of the River of Maye, and within the same as great a depthe and as large, dividing yt self into many sea armes." The French sailed up the river about nine miles, where they again found friendly natives, although the Indians sent their women and children and some goods into the woods as the French approached. The visitors were allowed to come into the houses and look at the gardens. It was here that the French first saw one of the great longhouses that were the center of tribal life: "But there was one [house] amonges the rest verry great, long and broode, with settelles round abowte made of reedes, tremly couched together, which serve them bothe for beddes and seates; they be of hight two fote from the ground, sett upon great round pillers paynted with redd, yellowe and blewe, well and [trimly] pullished."

When the Indians, who had hung back cautiously watching, saw that the French were not harming their property, they approached in a friendly manner and conversed with the visitors in sign language. The French were struck by the quality of the buildings and the well-groomed fertile gardens. In going back to the ships, they missed the high tide over the bar and spent the night in their boats. They named the river the Seine, and this precedent they followed as they sailed up the coast naming each river after one in their beloved homeland.

Sailing the next morning, Ribaut found another broad bay and river some twenty miles to the north, which they did not enter but named the Somme. The French were ravished by the beauty of the land and the numerous islands and channels which formed fingers of the sea. They described the Somme as "deviding yt self into many great rivers, that sever the cuntry into many faire and great ilandes and smale goodly medowe ground and pastures, and every where suche aboundaunce of fishe as is increadeble." Another great river, perhaps the Satilla, was discovered coming from the mountainous country to the west: "And on the west northwest side there is a great river that comithe from the highe country, of a great leage [length] over, and on the other on the northest side which retourn into the sea. So that (my lorde) yt is a country full of havens, rivers and islandes of suche frutefullnes as cannot with tonge be expressed, and where in shorte tyme great and precyous comodyties might be founde."

For all of the beauty of the place, Ribaut could find no entrance deep enough to accommodate his ships, and he pushed on up the coast still seeking a harbor and a place to plant his colony. On Sunday May 17, 1562, the French entered a great harbor which they named Port Royal, and it was here that Ribaut decided to build his fort. He described the bay as "one of the greatest and fayrest havens of the worlde." No Indians were found near the harbor but were discovered some thirty miles inland. The area abounded in great trees and numbers of birds of all descriptions.

Soon after landing, Ribaut and his men discovered the local Indians at their inland villages and found them to be more timorous than those to the south, but after the French had presented gifts and indicated by signs that they came in peace, the Indians became less fearful. On May 22, Ribaut planted a second column bearing the arms of the King of France on the shores of Port Royal and claimed the land for Charles IX. On the shores of Port Royal, Ribaut erected a small fort which he named Charlesfort in honor of his King. He then decided to return to France to secure more men and supplies, and called his party together to ask for volunteers to hold the fort until his return. Almost to a man the French asked to be left behind, but Ribaut selected "to the number of XXX in all, of gentilmen, souldiers, and merryners" to man the fort until his return. To command them he appointed Albert de la Pierria as captain. Ribaut sailed from Charlesfort early on June 11 and reached France on July 20, to find the country in the agony of civil war between the Protestant and Catholic parties. Ribaut joined his fellow Protestants at Dieppe in their revolt against the Catholic government party. Even though aided by the English, Dieppe fell to the Catholic forces and Ribaut fled to England. He had promised to return to his colony in six months, but was not to return to Florida for three years.

Back in Florida, Captain Albert and his men prospered at first, having ample supplies which had been left with them. They explored some of the coast, probably near the Savannah River, and obtained samples of crystal and silver ore from the Indians. The Frenchmen continued to be enchanted by the beauty and apparent abundance of the country, but this state of affairs was not to last. Expecting Ribaut to return within four months with supplies and more men, the little French party denied themselves nothing from the provisions left for their use, and the food was soon at the point of exhaustion. As the food dwindled, the French looked to their Indian neighbors to supply their needs, and they were soon on bad terms with the Indians who had been their friends. The Indians were alarmed by the constant demands on their food, which was just enough for their own use. In this worsening condition, Captain Albert became more and more tyrannical. Some difficulty involving a drummer occurred, and Albert hanged the poor man. The French then determined to rid themselves of their leader, and Albert was murdered. In his place they elected one Nicolas Barre their captain. Forsaken by Ribaut, the Indians now hostile and their supplies gone, the French determined to return to France and set about building a small boat. In this the Indians gave all the help they could, wanting to speed the departure of their unwelcome neighbors. A small bark was constructed of local, poorly aged timber. Their caulking was the moss which hung from the oaks and their sails were pieced together from shirts and other linen. The cordage was made from palmetto fibers. With some provisions gotten from the Indians, the desperate French set sail in their pitifully inadequate vessel, and in a short time were in a hopeless condition. The vessel made very little headway drifting on the Florida Current for the North Atlantic, and soon the inadequate provisions gave out. At this the men consumed their sword belts, shoes, and anything else they could chew. Finally, when it was evident they would all die unless one was sacrificed to save the rest, they drew lots to see which one would be killed to furnish food. This dubious honor fell to one Leclerc, who was quickly dispatched by his fellows and eaten. Soon after, the little boat fell in with an English ship and the survivors were rescued.

While Ribaut was in Florida, the Spanish government had learned of the voyage and were alarmed at the prospects of a French incursion into their seas. Ribaut's enterprise had been called a private venture in order not to provoke the Spanish, but there is ample evidence that the French government backed Admiral Coligny, who was behind Ribaut. Charles IX and his mother, Catherine de' Medici, both viewed the Florida enterprise as a possible solution to the growing problem of the Huguenots. Soon after Ribaut sailed, the Spanish ambassador at the French court requested assurances that Ribaut would not attack Spanish shipping in America and later warned the French government that Spain would not permit the French to settle in America. After Ribaut's return to France, Philip II himself was told of the French settlement, and Admiral Pedro Menéndez de Avilés warned him of the dangers to the Spanish treasure route if the French should build a fort on the coast of Florida and keep a fleet there. Determined to destroy the French settlement and remove the two columns, Philip commissioned Hernando Manrique de Rojas to perform the task. When Manrique sailed for Florida in May 1564, the French at Port Royal had long since abandoned the settlement. Manrique made his way up the Florida coast looking into every estuary just as Ribaut had done before him, but he missed the River of May and did not find the column erected there. Finally having reached the area of Port Royal, he learned from the Indians of a young Frenchman, seventeen years old, who had remained behind when his fellows abandoned the colony and had set out on their perilous journey. He was Guillaume Rouffi, who had chosen to stay with the Indians rather than attempt crossing the Atlantic in the ridiculous craft his fellows had built. Rouffi had learned the language of his Indian hosts and had adjusted well to native life. On hearing of the presence of the Frenchman on June 11, Manrique had immediately sent two Indian messengers inland to the village where Rouffi was living. The Indians carried with them a small piece of wood with a Christian cross carved on it which Manrique had furnished them as proof to Rouffi that Christians were on the coast. The next day Rouffi, dressed in the manner of the Indians, appeared before Manrique. Through one of his sailors who spoke French, Manrique learned the details of Ribaut's enterprise and the location of the abandoned fort and column. Rouffi led the Spanish to the fort, which they burned, and to the column, which they loaded into their boat and took to the frigate. On June 15, Manrique set sail for Havana, taking the column and Rouffi with him. At midnight on July 9, he entered the harbor of Havana and reported the destruction of the French fort and the removal of the column, saying "that as it appeared evident that the French had not made any settlement beyond this harbor and had gone back to France, it was advisable to render to His Majesty prompt account of what has been found on this coast."[2]

In England, Ribaut sat out the Protestant revolt, which ended with the Edict of Amboise in 1563. While there, he got involved in a scheme to help lead an English expedition to Florida. Having second thoughts, he tried to escape to France but was caught and imprisoned. With the return of peace to France, Admiral Coligny determined to send a strong, well-equipped expedition to Florida in another attempt at a Huguenot settlement. Since Ribaut was in prison in England, Coligny appointed René de Laudonnière leader. Laudonnière had been second in command when Ribaut first went to Florida, and he was known for his strong religious leanings, bravery, intelligence, and prudence. Coligny made a large sum of money available to Laudonnière to outfit the expedition. Catherine de' Medici and the Crown backed the project. Catherine herself wrote orders for the expedition and warned in them that Laudonnière was not to provoke the Spanish. During March and April, Laudonnière outfitted three ships furnished by the Crown with all the weapons and supplies necessary to establish a fortified settlement. Some three hundred persons were selected to go with the expedition. Most of the party were Huguenots but some were of other faiths. The company included distinguished persons as well as riffraff from the French Channel ports. On April 22, the expedition sailed from Havre-de-Grâce on the southern route by way of the Canaries and Lesser Antilles. Sailing up the chain of islands, they passed between Anguilla and Anegada and on June 22 arrived on the Florida coast. Two days later, they entered the River of May, where they found the column left by Ribaut intact and now an object of worship by the Indians. At this same moment, Manrique de Rojas was sailing through the Bahamas en route from Port Royal to Havana. He never sighted the French expedition and knew nothing of their presence on the Florida coast.

Charles IX, King of France, 1560–1574.
From a contemporary engraved portrait

Catherine de'Medici, who ruled France
as regent to her son Charles IX. From a
contemporary engraving

René Goulaine de Laudonnière, a contemporary engraved portrait. Photograph from the Smithsonian Institution

Laudonnière busied himself and his followers in unloading supplies and weapons, and a fort was begun. The site selected was near St. Johns Bluff on the River of May. The place was near navigable water, was easily defended, and the natives, with pleasant memories of Ribaut's brief visit two years before, were friendly and had plentiful supplies of food. The fort, a triangle of high timber walls, was armed with platforms for the artillery. Houses were constructed both inside and outside the walls. The high bluff nearby was manned by sentinels to watch for the approach of any hostile Spaniards or Indians. Within a few weeks, Laudonnière sent the two larger ships of his squadron back to France for supplies. In the early weeks, the colonists, busy with getting their houses furnished and with plenty of food in the storehouses, were happy enough. The promise of wealth in the strange new land lent enthusiasm to the work. By the end of summer, however, things were not so well with them. The area had produced no great wealth in gold and silver, but only a few trinkets which had been obtained from the Indians by barter. The settlers, expecting food to be sent from France, did not cultivate the fertile soil but lived on their supplies, which should have been kept as reserves. The game around the settlement proved to be scarce, and the Indians became reluctant to give up their own limited reserves of food.

Laudonnière was able with some success to remain aloof from the wars being fought between the rival tribes of the area, although these efforts irritated some of the Indians who sought help against their enemies. Several parties were sent into the interior to explore for the mines of gold and silver they believed to be there, and some of these soldiers became involved in local warfare between the Indians, but on the whole, Laudonnière was able to preserve good relations with the Indians and to prevent major warfare near the fort. On one occasion, he forced King Satouriaua to give up some prisoners which the French commander wished to return to their king, Olata Ouae Utina, as a means of preventing a major intertribal war. The chief reluctantly gave up the prisoners when the French commander threatened to use his well-armed soldiers. The captured men were sent back to their king who rejoiced in their return and in the friendship of the French. Satouriaua, quite the contrary, sulked in his lodge while his hatred of the French increased. At this point, a great lightening storm swept the area and set fire to the woods and fields near the village of Satouriaua. The king was struck with terror, thinking that Laudonnière had discharged his great ordnance against him. Laudonnière's own words describe the event which he turned to his advantage:

Thus things passed on this maner, and the hatred of Paracoussy Satourioua against mee did still continue, until that on the nine and twentieth of August a lightning from heaven fell within halfe a league of our Fort, more worthy I beleeve to be wondered at, and to bee put in writing, then all the strange signes which have bene seene in times past, and whereof the histories have never written. For although the medowes were at that season all greene, and halfe covered over with water, neverthelesse the lightning in one instant consumed above five hundred acres therewith, and burned with the ardent heate thereof all the foules which tooke their pastime in the medowes, which thing continued for three dayes space.[3]

At first, the French had thought the Indians had burned their village and were moving away. But soon Indians appeared in camp to plead with Laudonnière not to discharge his great guns again or the tribe would be forced to abandon their homes and move to another country. Laudonnière wisely saw an opportunity to turn the event to his advantage, telling the Indians he had fired his guns to warn them of his displeasure at the sulking of the chief. He pointed out that he could easily have reached the chief's own house several miles from where the lightning struck and that the chief would do well to have the French, who possessed such great power, as his protectors. With this, the chief apparently recovered his good nature.

The French did not find the wealth they dreamed of in the interior, and their food supplies decreased as the Indians became more cool toward them and their strange concept of friendship between traditional enemies. Laudonnière's followers became restive in their idleness as they saw their rations reduced daily and none of the wealth they dreamed of coming into the fort. As the discontent increased in direct proportion to the decrease of food and other supplies, some of the French hatched a plot and mutinied in December 1564. Before this, thirteen men had stolen a boat and had sailed to Cuba where they plundered the coast but were captured almost at once. Now, however, the plot was a major one, with sixty-six men involved. They seized Laudonnière as he lay sick in his quarters, took two barks lying in the river, and forced their captain to agree to their going to the West Indies on a voyage of adventure. Laudonnière describes the incident:

Hereupon the five chiefe authours of the sedition armed with Corslets, their Pistolles in their handes already bent, prest into my chamber, saying unto mee, that they would goe to New Spaine to seeke their adventure. Then I warned them to bee well advised what they meant to doe: but they foorthwith replyed, that they were full advised already, and that I must graunt them this request [and] deliver them the armour which I had in my custodie, for feare least I might use them to their disadvantage (being so villanously abused by them:) wherein notwithstanding I would not yeeld unto them. But they tooke all by force, and caried it out of my house, yea and after they had hurt a Gentleman in my chamber, which spake against their doings, they layd hands on mee, and caried mee very sicke, as I was, prisoner into a shippe which rode at ancker in the middest of the River, wherein I was the space of fifteene dayes. . . . And they sent mee a passeport to signe, telling me plainly after I had denied them, that if I made any difficulty, they would all come and cut my throat in the shippe. Thus was I constrained to signe their Passe-port, and forthwith to grant them certaine mariners, with Trenchant an honest and skilfull Pilot.

The mutineers sailed December 8, 1564, but before reaching the sea, they fell out among themselves and separated at the mouth of the River of May, going their separate ways. One group sailed to Cuba, while the other sailed through the Bahamas. They did not meet again for six weeks. The bark which had gone to the coast of Cuba with d'Orange in command and Trenchant for pilot captured a brigantine loaded with cassava. Transferring to the brigantine, they apparently rejoined their companions and captured a Spanish vessel sailing from Santo Domingo to Santiago, Cuba. On board the Spanish ship was one Francisco Ruiz Manso, who later gave a deposition in Seville, which describes the incident:

Some time in the month of February of this year witness sailed from Santo Domingo as pilot on a vessel bound for Santiago de Cuba on board of which there was a Judge of Commissions who had been appointed by the Royal Audiencia of Santo Domingo and sent to the Island of Cuba; that the total number of persons on board were twelve including passengers and crew; that while on their voyage on the sixteenth day of the said month of February, while close to Tiburon on a dark night about eleven o'clock more or less, a small dispatch boat manned by oars came alongside of their vessel, while a large ship appeared close by, both vessels being French. As soon as they discovered the vessels were French they tried to escape, but the dispatch boat caught up with them and they commenced fighting and defending themselves. The French killed the Judge of Commissions and a slave belonging to him and wounded witness and four or five others. They then entered our vessel and plundered her of everything she carried; wines, sugar, clothing and slaves; taking the witness and the other men as prisoners. They then transferred them to the large ship where they were placed under decks and where they remained for eight days.[4]

The Spanish were finally released from the hold of the ship, and in conversing with his captors, Ruiz Manso learned of the fort in Florida, the starving condition of the colony, and the fact that the ship had provisions for only two days. The French asked Ruiz if food were available in Jamaica, and the Spaniard saw his chance to secure freedom for himself and his companions because he knew the forces on that island were strong enough to take the French pirates. At this the French sailed for the island.

On arriving in Jamaica, the French sent Ruiz and two others with a message to the governor demanding food. The three returned with cassava, beef, and other provisions. Meanwhile, the governor prepared to capture the pirates, and three days later attacked them, with the result which Ruiz describes:

> About dawn the Governor of the Island, having previously armed and equipped two ships and a frigate, came down on the French ship and commenced firing shot into her. From the first shot they killed two Frenchmen, and in view of this the dispatch boat ran off. The Governor then tried to board the French ship with his frigate, but the French cut the cables and also ran off. But the wind blowing from the sea and the Governor's frigate having oars, she soon caught up with her. . . . They then surrendered and delivered their arms to witness, and when the Governor came on board he took possession of the ship and arms. After that the Governor held a conference with the officers of his council, to decide what should be done with the French prisoners, and it was decided that they should be kept under arrest and sent to Spain. In this situation witness left them, but as to the dispatch boat (which escaped) witness does not know what became of her.

The ship that escaped the captured brigantine was piloted by Trenchant, who had been forced to sail with the mutineers. They resolved to return to Fort Caroline and managed to bring this ship around Cape San Antonio, along the coast of Cuba and up the Florida Straits to the fort without harm from the aroused Spanish. On March 25, they arrived near Fort Caroline, where their sail was seen by an Indian chief friendly to Laudonnière. At first the French thought the ship part of the supply fleet they had awaited so long, but the identity was soon established, and the French commander sent a boatload of armed men to bring the mutineers to the port. Here Laudonnière tried the four remaining leaders and sentenced them to death by hanging. They begged of him to have them shot like soldiers and Laudonnière agreed, the sentence being carried out immediately. The rest of the mutineers and the mariners were released. The incursion of the mutineers into

Florida Indian man and woman. From a drawing by John White, late sixteenth century

the Caribbean had not only aroused the Spanish to the south but had also given them additional information about the French settlement and the intentions of the intruders. The occurrences in France during preparations for the Laudonnière expedition were well known to the Crown of Spain as were the preparations for a relief expedition under Ribaut, through spies who were constantly at work among the French, but the information given the Spanish by the captive mutineers furnished the Spanish new and definite knowledge of the actual situation at Fort Caroline. The Spanish bureaucratic mill began to grind out plans to eliminate the heretics from Florida.

Laudonnière's chief concerns at Fort Caroline after the departure of the mutineers were the reestablishment of his authority and the continuing struggle against starvation. The Indians still furnished the fort some provisions but these were never enough. Fishing helped, but the Frenchmen were either unable or unwilling to make a serious effort at supplying themselves, looking every day for the relief ships from France. During the months of January through March, the Indians were accustomed to leave their villages and go on long hunts in the woods, living in temporary shelters at a distance from the fort. During this period, it was impossible for the French to get food from them. By May 1565, the food had been virtually exhausted. Laudonnière describes the ensuing period of near-starvation:

> The moneth of May approching and no manner of succour come out of France, we fell into extreme want of victuals, constrained to eate the rootes of the earth and certaine sorrell which we found in the fields. For although the Savages were returned by this time unto their villages, yet they succoured us with nothing but certaine fish, without which assuredly wee had perished with famine. Besides they had given us before the greatest part of their maiz and of their beanes for our merchandise. This famine held us from the beginning of May untill the middest of June. During which time the poore souldiers and handicraftsmen became as feeble as might be, and being not able to worke did nothing but goe one after another in Centinel unto the clift of an hill, situate very neere unto the Fort, to see if they might discover any French ship.

In their hunger and discouragement, the French pleaded with Laudonnière to evacuate the fort and return to France. Laudonnière finally consented. It was decided to finish a galiote* which Laudonnière had begun and to enlarge the brigantine which the mutinous soldiers had

---

* A small open vessel with sail and oars.

brought back, thereby enabling the entire company to make the attempt. The French set to work as if their lives depended on it, for indeed they did. They could not have survived another winter at Fort Caroline. As the ships neared completion, Laudonnière had to face the problem of provisioning them for the long voyage across the Atlantic. With a company of soldiers he took the bark and sailed some 150 miles in search of food, but without success. When he returned to the fort, he found "the souldiers beginning to be wearie of working, because of the extreme famine which did consume them." In this situation, the soldiers petitioned Laudonnière to capture an Indian chief and hold him for a ransom of food, since they were planning to abandon the country and the political consequences of such an outrage could hardly concern them. Laudonnière, statesman that he was, refused this tactic and renewed his efforts at getting food from the Indians by trading for it every expendable thing the fort contained. The Indians, sensing the desperate situation of the French, traded at exorbitant rates, and the French leader had his hands full to prevent his soldiers from attacking the Indians. Conditions got progressively worse as the starving Frenchmen became more desperate. Open warfare with some of the Indians broke out. Yet Laudonnière was able to preserve friendship with eight of the leading chiefs in the surrounding region. These chiefs helped the French as much as they could with their meager food reserves. The famine slowed down the construction of the remaining ship, and the desperate French spent most of their time grubbing for roots or sitting weakly on a cliff looking for the relief ships from France. Laudonnière describes the frantic hunger of his men and the bizarre methods with which they attempted to alleviate it:

> In the end we were constrained to induce extreme famine, which continued among us all the moneth of May: for in this latter season, neither Maiz nor Beanes, nor Mast was to be found in the villages, because they had employed all for to sowe their fields, insomuch that we were constrayned to eate rootes, which the most part of our men punned in the morters which I had brought with me to beate gunnepowder in, and the graine which came to us from other places: some tooke the wood of Esquine, beate it, and made meale thereof, which they boyled with water, and eate it: others went with their harquebusies to seeke to kill some foule. Yea this miserie was so great, that one was found that gathered up among the filth of my house, all the fish bones that he could finde, which he dried and beate into powder to make bread thereof. The effects of this hideous famine appeared incontinently among us, for our bones eftsoones beganne to cleave so neere unto the skinne, that the most part of the souldiers had their skinnes peirced

thorow with them in many partes of their bodies: in such sort that my greatest feare was, least the Indians would rise up against us, considering that it would have bene very hard for us to have defended our selves in such extreme decay of all our forces, besides the scarsitie of all victuals, which fayled us all at once.

In his desperation, Laudonnière was now forced to capture the chief Utina, a former ally, and ransom him for food, a measure that had been urged weeks before. By this means the French were again saved, but at the price of war with the chief's men. During this time Utina behaved himself with superb nobility. He urged his people to give the French food and even warned his captors when his men hatched a plot to fell trees into the stream where the ships were building to prevent their departure. Hostilities culminated in pitched battles between hundreds of Indians and companies of arquebusiers, in which the French barely escaped with their lives. In this critical situation, the French were overjoyed to see four sails on the horizon. Succor had arrived, but not the sort they had expected.

The sails were sighted on August 4, 1565, and the French immediately concluded that it was the relief fleet from France they had so long expected. Then a messenger arrived, one Martin Atinas of Dieppe, to announce that he came from the fleet of John Hawkins, which was on the way to England from the West Indies and was short of water. Hawkins had been led to the French fort by Atinas, who had been in the service of Laudonnière in 1562 and knew the location of the French settlement. Hawkins asked permission to come up the river to water at the fort and sent a gift of two flagons of wine and wheat bread to Laudonnière. Permission was quickly given, and Hawkins, perceiving the plight of the French and learning of their resolve to abandon the fort and return to France, offered to take them home. Laudonnière refused, not knowing whether France and England were at peace and in doubt of the motives of the Englishman. While Laudonnière did not accept the offer to go with the English, he worked out a trade with Hawkins, giving brass artillery from the fort soon to be abandoned for a small vessel. The generous Hawkins gave, as well, food sufficient to see the French home, and seeing the French soldiers barefoot, gave them forty pairs of shoes. As a matter of form, Laudonnière gave Hawkins a bill for his indebtedness, but this was never paid. Before he departed, Hawkins gave Laudonnière more presents of food and gave all the officers presents "according to their qualityes." Of Hawkins, Laudonnière later said: "We received as many courtesies of the Generall, as it was possible to receive of any man living. Wherein doubtlesse he hath wonne the reputation of a good and charitable man, deserving to be esteemed asmuch of us all as if he had saved all our lives."

After Hawkins's departure, Laudonnière speeded preparations for his departure from the fort. Hawkins's arrival had impressed the Indians, and the French now had a period of peace in which to prepare the vessels for their escape. As it turned out, they were not to leave as planned: beginning in the spring events had been proceeding in Europe which would lead most of them to their deaths.

Early in 1565 Ribaut, having been freed from prison in England, returned to France, and Admiral Coligny went ahead with his preparations of a relief fleet for Florida to be commanded by the newly arrived officer. The fleet was to be a powerful one. Ribaut had as his flagship the *Trinity*, of thirty-two guns, purchased especially for the Florida enterprise by King Charles. A royal ship, the *Emérillon*, of twenty-nine guns, was commanded by Vice Admiral Nicolas d'Ornano of Corsica, who was known to his companions as "Corsette." The rest of the fleet consisted of the *Pearl*, of ten guns, commanded by Ribaut's son Jacques, three transports chartered in Dieppe—the *Levière*, the *Shoulder of Mutton*, and a second *Emérillon*—and a seventh vessel, possibly the *Trout*. About one thousand French men, women, and children, including royal troops, sailed with the ships. Ribaut took his fleet out of Havre-de-Grâce on May 10, 1565, but delays caused by foul weather and supplies late in arriving delayed the sailing until May 26. After clearing the coast of France, Ribaut was further delayed two weeks at the Isle of Wight waiting for a fair wind. He finally got away around June 10, while Laudonnière and his men were struggling with famine at Fort Caroline.

At the time Laudonnière's colony was being established at Fort Caroline, Philip II decided to send an expedition to settle Florida to protect the territory from further incursions which were such a direct threat to the treasure route. Philip appointed Pedro Menéndez de Avilés *adelantado** of Florida. Since the royal funds were especially short at this time, Menéndez was to make the effort at his own expense, for which he was granted broad rights in the new lands. A formal agreement between the Crown and Menéndez was reached on March 20, 1565. At almost the same time, news came from the Indies of the new French settlement and the raids of the mutineers in the Antilles on the ship from Cuba. Documents containing the interrogations of cap-

---

* Lord lieutenant or governor.

A Spanish galleon of the mid-sixteenth century after a contemporary engraving. Ships of this type formed the backbone of the squadrons commanded by Pedro Menéndez de Avilés

tured raiders were sent, and three of the captives arrived with them. The Spanish ambassador at Paris sent a number of reports from France that gave additional information on French activities and intentions. From all this intelligence, Philip realized the seriousness of the French enterprise and determined to eliminate at any cost and by any means this colony of heretics which threatened the economic lifeline of his kingdom and the "infection" of the Indians with the Lutheranism he so despised. Details of Fort Caroline, which the captives had supplied, were furnished Menéndez, along with Spanish troops, arms, and supplies at the expense of the Crown. Menéndez' forces were now larger and more powerful than those of the French. The urgency of the situation inspired the Spanish to unusual speed, and Menéndez' fleet, though battered and damaged by storms, reached Puerto Rico on August 8, six days before Ribaut reached the Florida coast south of Fort Caroline.

At the time Ribaut arrived in Florida, he knew nothing of the presence of the Menéndez fleet in the Caribbean fleet and the imminent threat of attack. Had he known, he would have sailed directly to Fort Caroline and prepared his defenses. As it was, he took a leisurely course up the Florida coast, looking into each river and exploring the shores. He was still the lover in love with the new land. Ribaut did not reach the mouth of the River of May until August 28. Here he took the three smallest vessels over the bar and left the four largest outside at anchor with a skeleton crew aboard each. The joy at the arrival of the relief fleet was unbounded. Laudonnière describes the reception he and his men gave the arriving Frenchmen:

> Being therfore advertised that it was Captaine Ribault, I went foorth of the Fort to goe to meete him, and to do him all the honour I could by any meanes, I caused him to be welcomed with the artillery, and a gentle volley of my shot, whereunto he answered with his. Afterward being come on shore and received honourably with joy, I brought him to my lodging, rejoycing not a little because that in this company I knew a good number of my friends, which I intreated in the best sorte that I was able, and such victuals as I could get in the countrey, and that small store which I had left me, with that which I had of the English General.

Laudonnière and his men, on the verge of returning to France, had taken down part of the timber parapets of the fort and had loaded their little ships to leave. Ribaut's arrival changed all this, and the French prepared to refurbish the fort and unload the supplies which Laudonnière and his starved companions had so long awaited. But first the feasts and celebrations had to be held.

The joy of the French was to be very short indeed. Three days before Ribaut had reached Fort Caroline, Menèndez had sighted Cape Canaveral and was coming up the coast with a battered but still powerful fleet. Six days after Ribaut's arrival, on September 4, 1565, Menéndez sailed up between the four French ships and the shore off the River of May and challenged them. In a letter to his sovereign, Menéndez describes the event:

> Sailing thence on our search on the 4th of September . . . the same day at two in the afternoon we discovered it, and four ships anchored there, showing the flags of Captain and Admiral. Being thus certain that the succor had come to them, and that by falling suddenly on these four ships we should be able to take them, I decided to attack, and being yet half a league away from them, there came up great thunder and lightning and rain, and then the wind left us becalmed. But about ten at night, it came on to blow again, and, it appearing to me that, in the morning, the ships that might be in the harbor would come out with

reinforcements for these four, I resolved to anchor alongside of them, with the intention of attacking them at daybreak. So, I anchored between the Captain and Admiral with my flag ship, and having spoken them, asking, what they were doing there? And who was their Captain? They answered that they had Juan Ribas [Jean Ribaut] for Captain General, and that they had come to this country by command of the King of France, and asked what ships were ours, and who was our General? I answered them, that I, Pero Menéndez, by command of Your Majesty, had come to this coast to burn and hang the French Lutherans whom I should find there, and that, in the morning I should board their vessels to see if any of that people were on them, and that, if there were any, I should not fail to execute upon them the justice that Your Majesty commanded. They answered that it was no use, and that I might come on and not wait till morning. As it appeared to me that this opportunity was not to be lost, although it was night, turning my ship from stem to stern, I ordered cable to be paid out, so as to come alongside of her, but they cut their cables, and hoisted their sails, and all four of them took to flight.[5]

While the French fleet fully manned could easily have defended themselves or even have defeated Menéndez, with only a few men to serve the sixty-one guns aboard their ships, they had no choice but to slip their cables and flee. The Spanish gave chase, but the fleeter French ships soon outdistanced the Spanish and escaped. With this, Menéndez turned south and sailed to the site of what was to be the first permanent European settlement in what is now the United States. One of the French ships shadowed the Spanish and later reported Menéndez' landing to their commander. Ribaut, with most of his forces at the fort, wanted to go to the rescue of his ships offshore, but the action was over before he could move. While he waited ashore, the suspense must have been agonizing for him. His ships had disappeared over the horizon with the Spanish in pursuit, and he had no way of knowing the outcome of the encounter.

Two days later two of the French ships returned, and Ribaut immediately went out to them for an account of what had happened. Later, when he learned of the landing of the Spanish south of Fort Caroline, he was aroused to fury and immediately resolved to attack Menéndez before he could fortify himself. Laudonnière was ill with a fever at the time and his fear of seeing his superior sail away leaving the fort practically unprotected was great indeed. Laudonnière describes the meeting of Ribaut with his captains:

After he understood these newes hee returned to the fortresse, and came to my chamber where I was sick, and there in the presence of the

A French raid on a Spanish-American town, from a sixteenth-century engraving. The cruelty of the French toward the Spanish increased markedly after news of the massacre of the French Protestants in Florida reached France

captaines, La Grange, S. Marie, Ottigny, Visty, Yonville, and other gentlemen, he propounded, that it was necessary for the kings service, to embarke himselfe with all his forces, and with the three ships that were in the rode to seeke the Spanish fleete, whereupon he asked our advise. I first replyed, and shewed unto him the consequence of such an enterprise, advertising him among other things of the perilous flawes of windes that rise on this coast, and that if it chanced that hee were driven from the shore, it would be very hard for him to recover it againe, that in the meane while they which should stay in the Forte should be in feare and danger. The Captaines, Saint Marie, and La Grange declared unto him farther, that they thought it not good to put any such enterprise in execution, that it was farre better to keepe the land, & do their best indevour to fortifie themselves.

Ribaut disregarded the advice of his commanders and resolved to go south and attack Menéndez. He asked Laudonnière to lend him some of his best soldiers and his ensigns but Laudonnière refused. Ribaut then told Laudonnière that Admiral Coligny had written him of Menéndez' expedition. Laudonnire's own words describe the conversation:

> He came into my chamber, and prayed me to lend him my Lieutenant, mine ensigne, and my sergeant, and to let all my good souldiers, which I had, goe with him, which I denied him, because my selfe being sicke, there was no man to stay in the fort. Thereupon he answered me that I needed not to doubt at all, and that he would returne the morrow after, that in the meane space Monsieur de Lys should stay behind to looke to all things. Then I shewed unto him that he was chiefe in this Countrey, and that I for my part had no further authoritie: that therefore hee would take good advisement what hee did, for feare least some inconvenience might ensue. Then he tolde me that he could doe no lesse, then to continue this enterprise, and that in the letter which he had received from my Lord Admirall, there was a postscript, which hee shewed mee written in these wordes: Captaine John Ribault, as I was enclosing up this letter, I received a certaine advice, that Don Pedro Melendes departeth from Spaine to goe to the coast of Newe France: see you that you suffer him not to encroch upon you, no more then he would that you should encroch upon him. You see (quoth he) the charge that I have, and I leave it unto your selfe to judge, if you could do any lesse in this case, considering the certaine advertisement that we have, that they are already on lande, and will invade us. This stopped my mouth. Thus therefore confirmed or rather obstinate in this enterprise, and having regard rather unto his particular opinion then unto the advertisments which I had given him, and the inconveniences of the time whereof I had forewarned him, he embarked himselfe the eight of September, and tooke mine ensigne and eight and thirtie of my men away with him.

The *Trinity* and one other ship had now returned, and Ribaut had his fleet at full strength as he sailed south to attack Menéndez at St. Augustine. With him, he had small rowing craft to effect a landing.

Laudonnière was left with few effective troops. In his account, he describes the pitiable condition of the garrison faced with the possibility of overland attack from the Spanish:

> Wee beganne therefore to fortifie our selves and to repaire that which was broken downe, principally toward the water side, where I caused

threescore foote of trees to be planted, to repaire the Palissado with the plankes which I caused to bee taken of the Shippe which I had builded. Neverthelesse notwithstanding all our diligence and travaile, wee were never able fully to repaire it by reason of the stormes, which commonly did us so great annoy, that wee, could not finish our inclosure. Perceiving my selfe in such extremitie I tooke a muster of the men, which captaine Ribault had left me, to see if there were any that wanted weapon: I found nine or ten of them whereof not past two or three had ever drawen sword out of a scabbard. . . . Of the nine there were foure but yong striplings, which served Captaine Ribault and kept his dogs, the fift was a cooke . . . there was a Carpenter of threescore yeeres olde, one a Beere-brewer, one olde Crosse-bow maker, two Shoomakers, and foure or five men that had their wives, a player on the Virginals . . . about fourescore and five or sixe in all, counting aswel Lackeys as women and children. . . . Those that were left me of mine owne company were about sixteene or seventeene that coulde beare armes, and all of them poore and leane: the reste were sicke and maymed in the conflict which my Lieutenant had against Utina. This view being thus taken, wee set our watches. . . . I ceased not, for all the foule weather nor my sicknesse which I had, to oversee the Corps de garde.

Ribaut caught Menéndez outside the bar, an event which Menéndez describes in a letter to Philip II:

I being on the bar, in a shallop, with two boats loaded with artillery and ammunition, the four French galleons which we had put to flight, came down on us, together with two or three pinnaces astern, in order to prevent us from landing here, and to capture our artillery and stores. Although the weather was bad for the bar, I was obliged to attempt it. . . . Our Lord was pleased to deliver us miraculously at this low tide, for there was only a scant fathom and a half of water on the bar, and the ship required a full fathom and a half.[6]

Soon after his escape, some Indians came to Menéndez and told him that Fort Caroline could be reached overland in two days. Concluding that Ribaut must have borrowed troops from Fort Caroline to reinforce his fleet, Menéndez decided to march on the fort, using Indian guides to lead his forces through the woods and swamps. In his letter of October 15 just quoted, Menéndez told Philip of the march and the successful attack:

I immediately ordered 500 men to be got ready, 300 of them arquebusiers, and the remainder armed with pikes and bucklers (although few of these), and we packed our knapsacks so that every man carried six pounds of biscuit on his back, with his canteen of a measure and a half or two of wine, together with his arms, which every captain and soldier and I myself among the first for example's sake, carried with this provision and drink, on my shoulder. As we did not know the way, we thought that we should arrive in two days and that it was only six or eight leagues distant, for so the Indians who went with us had indicated to us. So we left this fort of St. Augustine in this manner and with this intention. On the 18th of September we found the rivers greatly swollen with the much rain that had fallen, so that we advanced but little until the 19th at night, when we came to sleep a league more or less from the Fort; then for more than 15 leagues, through morasses and desert paths never yet trod, so as to be able to get round the streams, and on the 20th, on the eve of the day of the Blessed Apostle and Evangelist St. Matthew, in the morning when it began to dawn, having prayed to God Our Lord and to his Blessed Mother that they would give us the victory over these Lutherans, for we had already determined to attack it openly with twenty scaling ladders that we had brought with us, and the Divine Majesty showed us such favor and so directed us that, without losing a man killed, nor wounded, save one, who is well already, we gained the fort and all that it contained. One hundred and thirty men were put to death, and the next day, ten more, who were taken in the mountain, among them many gentlemen; and he who had been Governor and Alcayde, who called himself Monsieur Ludunier [Laudonnière] a relative of the Admiral of France, who had been his Major domo, fled to the woods, and a soldier pursuing him gave him a blow with a pike. We could not see what became of him. About 50 or 60 persons escaped by swimming to the mountain, and also in two boats from the three ships that they had in front of the fort.

Laudonnière's account gives pretty much the same dismal story of the attack, with additional details of his escape that Menéndez could not have known. How bitter must have been his thoughts of Ribaut's gross error of judgment which brought this disaster on the French. "The night betweene the nineteenth and twentieth of September La Vigne kept watch with his company, wherein he used all endevour, although it rayned without ceasing. When the day was therefore come, and that hee saw that it rayned still worse then it did before, hee pitied the Centinels so too moyled and wette: and thinking the Spanyardes woulde not have come in such a strange time, hee let them depart."

In the early dawn the Spaniards attacked. Two of Laudonnière's men who were working outside the fort saw the enemy and aroused the garrison with cries and a trumpet. The hopelessly outnumbered Frenchmen fought as best they could. As the vanguard of the Spanish

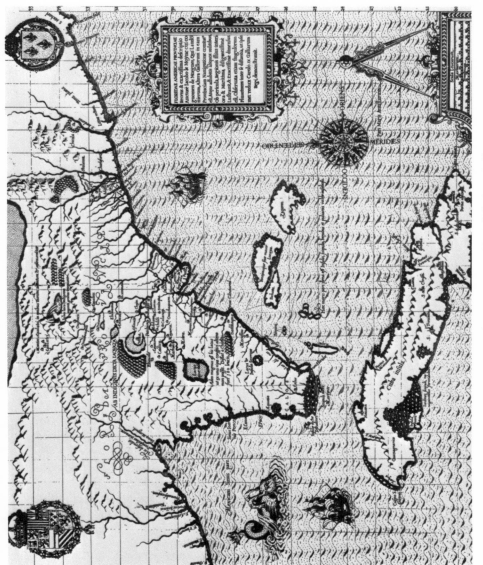

Map of Florida by Le Moyne, engraved by Théodore de Bry, 1591

came through a breach in the wall the few professional soldiers left in the fort rushed in and engaged them. All were quickly slain. Laudonnière, hearing the alarm, rushed out of his quarters with a sword and target to a breach in the southwest side but seeing large numbers of Spanish entering he dashed back toward his quarters and escaped through a small breach into the woods. As he fled a Spaniard struck at him with a pike (as Menéndez' account states) but it struck his target and he was uninjured.

Jacques Le Moyne de Morgues, who escaped the Spanish at the same time as Laudonnière, described the attack and slaughter in a narrative published years after the events:

> When the day broke, nobody being seen about the fort, M. de la Vigne, who was the officer of the guard, pitying the drenched and exhausted condition of the men, who were worn out with long watching, permitted them to take a little rest; but they had scarcely had time to go to their quarters, and lay aside their arms, when the Spaniards, guided by a Frenchman named François Jean, who had seduced some of his messmates along with him, attacked the fort at the double quick in three places at once, penetrated the works without resistance, and, getting possession of the place of arms, drew up their force there. Then parties searched the soldiers' quarters, killing all whom they found, so that awful outcries and groans arose from those who were being slaughtered.[7]

Seeing that the fort was lost, Le Moyne escaped through a breach into the woods as his leader had done. There he found four of his companions. After discussing what should be done, they decided that the four should go to the Indians while Le Moyne headed for the seashore to find the French vessels there. He was accompanied by yet another Frenchman, Grandchemin, who had joined him. Together they straggled toward the coast through swamps and thick brush and woods. Finally, Grandchemin, discouraged by the difficulty, decided to go back to the fort and surrender. He urged Le Moyne to do likewise. He pointed out that they were both artificers* and the Spanish would spare their lives because they were needed. Unable to dissuade him, Le Moyne agreed to return to the fort but not to surrender. His account continues:

> We therefore made our way back through the woods, and were even in sight of the fort, when I heard the uproar and rejoicing which the Spaniards were making, and was deeply moved by it, and said to the

* Craftsmen, including armorers.

Stone column erected by the French at the River of May. Engraving by
Théodore de Bry after a drawing by Le Moyne

soldier, "Friend and companion, I pray you, let us not go thither: let us
stay away yet a little while; God will open some way of safety to us,
for he has many of which we know nothing, and will save us out of all
these dangers." But he embraced me, saying, "I will go: so farewell." In
order to see what should happen to him, I got up to a height near by,
and watched. As he came down from the high ground, the Spaniards
saw him, and sent out a party. As they came up to him, he fell on his
knees to beg for his life. They, however, in a fury cut him to pieces,
and carried off the dismembered fragments of his body on the points of
their spears and pikes.

Making his way back toward the sea Le Moyne was joined by three
others, including Laudonnière's maid. "We made our way towards the
open meadows along the seashore; but, before getting through the
woods, we found M. de Laudonnière himself, and another man named
Bartholomew, who had received a deep sword-cut in the neck; and
after a time we picked up others, until there were fourteen or fifteen of
us in all." Though Laudonnière was suffering from fever, he and the
others struggled through the swamps and woods to the French vessels

anchored in the river below the fort, reaching them the morning after the attack. Le Moyne was able to save his drawings, the best source we have on the French expedition and the early Florida Indians.

One of the French ships near the fort was sunk by Spanish gunfire, but three, including the *Pearl*, commanded by Ribaut's son Jacques, and the *Levrière*, lying down the river, were untouched. To these, some thirty-five French fugitives including Laudonnière, Le Moyne, and the carpenter Le Challeux, made their way through swamps and woods, luckily eluding Spanish search parties. When all the survivors that could be found were aboard, the *Pearl* and the *Levrière* sailed for France. The other vessels and the boats, including the ship Laudonnière had purchased from Hawkins, were scuttled to prevent capture by Menéndez.

The disaster suffered by the French at Fort Caroline was complete. All the men captured ashore were killed. Women, infants, and boys of fifteen years or less were spared, but even this act of mercy rankled in the breast of Menéndez, for he feared to have them with his men "by reason of their wicked sect."[8] Even those French who returned to the fort and surrendered after the battle were immediately cut to pieces by the Spanish.

It is puzzling why Jacques Ribaut abandoned Florida while his father and the rest of the French fleet were unheard from. At the very least, he should have gone south in search of him, as Laudonnière had suggested. But Jacques had refused. If he had gone, the whole course of events that followed might have been changed, for just before Menéndez' attack on Fort Caroline, a severe storm of hurricane force caught the elder Ribaut's ships south of St. Augustine and wrecked them on the sandy coast. Not a single vessel escaped.

On September 22, while Menéndez was at Fort Caroline, some men from St. Augustine found a Frenchman on the beach south of the settlement. He had come from a small vessel sent to spy on the Spanish while they landed and had been stranded by the same storm that had driven the other French vessels ashore. Menéndez' brother Bartolomé took a party to the spot and refloated the French ship. Six days later, after his return from Fort Caroline, Menéndez heard from Indians of a large party of Frenchmen on the beach, some eighteen miles south of St. Augustine. He immediately took fifty soldiers in a barge and sailed down the river, reaching the inlet next morning. Keeping his soldiers concealed and taking only one companion, Menéndez walked to the northern side of the inlet, where he hailed the French, telling them he was Spanish. They identified themselves and asked him to come over to talk to them. Menéndez refused, but asked them to send a messenger

French ships off the Florida coast. Engraving by Théodore de Bry

Fort Caroline by Théodore de Bry, in Jacques Le Moyne's *Brevis Narratio*
(1591)

instead. From this man, Menéndez learned that Ribaut's fleet had been dispersed and driven ashore by the storm about sixty miles below the inlet, that some of the French had been drowned and others captured by the Indians. The messenger stated that Ribaut's ship, the *Trinity*, was ashore with her masts cut away, fifteen miles further south from the other wrecked ships. With this information, Menéndez knew he had the French in his power if he handled the situation with guile. In his account to Philip II, Menéndez tells how he persuaded the French to surrender when the first messenger returned to his companions:

> He begged me that he might go back with this message, and said that he would return at night, by swimming, and prayed that I would grant him his life. Which I did, seeing that he was dealing truly with me, and that he was able to inform me concerning many things. And, as soon as he was returned to his companions, there came across to this side, a gentleman, the Lieutenant of Monsieur Ludunier, very crafty, to tempt me; who having discussed some time with me, offered that they would lay down their arms and give themselves up if I would spare their lives. I answered that they might give up their arms and place themselves at my mercy; that I should deal with them as Our Lord should command me, and that he had not moved me from this nor could move me, unless God Our Lord should inspire in me something different. And so he departed with this reply, and they came over and laid down their arms.

Apparently the Lord commanded Menéndez to murder, for having bound the Frenchmen, he had them slaughtered: "I caused their hands to be tied behind them, and put them to the knife. Only 16 were left, of whom 12 were Breton seamen whom they had kidnapped, the other 4 being carpenters and caulkers of whom I had great need. It seemed to me that to chastise them in this way would serve God Our Lord, as well as Your Majesty, and that we should thus be left more free from this wicked sect to plant the Gospel in these parts and to enlighten the natives, and bring them to allegiance to Your Majesty."

Menéndez claimed in his letter to Philip of October 15, 1565, to have warned the first French messenger that he would "pursue them by sea and land, until I had their lives." But it is inconceivable that the French would have surrendered if they had known of their certain slaughter. The party was armed, and although on a hostile coast without water or food, would certainly have chosen to take their chances in the woods with the Indians rather than give up their lives so easily. There can be no doubt that the French believed they would be spared by their captors.

While Menéndez was writing the letter in which he reported the slaughter of the French, word reached him, on October 10, of a fire that had destroyed the remains of Fort Caroline and all the arms and provisions the Spanish had captured with it. Menéndez set out at once to go to the fort, but within an hour news of Ribaut arrived. The French leader was on the coast south of the inlet, where his luckless companions had crossed to their deaths eleven days before. Immediately Menéndez marched south. When he returned to St. Augustine and continued his letter to Philip, Menéndez tells of how he dealt with Ribaut and his followers:

I immediately went with 150 soldiers to seek him, and the next day at dawn, on the eleventh of this month, I came up to him, there being a river between us which he could not pass, save by swimming. We made on both sides a demonstration of our force with two colors displayed, and with our drums and fifes, and, on assurance of safety, he sent across his Sergeant-major to speak with me, who delivered me a message from Juan Rivao that I should allow his whole force safe passage to their fort. I answered, as I had to the others, that I was his enemy and waged war against them with fire and blood, for that they were Lutherans, and because they had come to plant in these lands of Your Majesty their evil sect, and to instruct the Indians in it; that he might undeceive himself as to his fort, for that we had taken it; that they might surrender their flags and arms to me, and place themselves at my mercy, that I might do with their persons as I should please, and that they could not do or agree otherwise with me. And the sergeant-major having gone back with this message, the same day in the evening, under assurance of safety, Juan Rivao came over to speak with me and to treat with me, of some course more safe for him; but, as I was not willing to accede to it, he said that the next morning he would return with his reply, and so he did, with about 70 companions, many principal men among them, three or four captains, among them Captain Cerceto, who was a long time captain of arquebusiers in Lombardy; Captain Lagrange, who was a captain of land infantry, was already dead. There also came with Juan Rivao among these men, four others, Germans and relatives of the Prince de Porance, great Lutherans. I wished to make sure whether there were any Catholic among them, but found none. I spared the lives of two young gentlemen of about 18 years old, and three others, drummer, fifer and trumpeter, but Juan Rivao and all the others I caused to be put to the knife, understanding this to be necessary for the service of God Our Lord, and of Your Majesty.

There is no doubt that Ribaut and his followers thought their lives were to be spared, as had their unfortunate countrymen who were

slaughtered eleven days before. Le Moyne in his narrative quotes a
French sailor who miraculously escaped the slaughter and described
the events to him later in France. Le Moyne mistakenly assumed that
the slaughter took place at Fort Caroline, not on the inlet south of St.
Augustine, and also described the slaughter of September 29 and that
of October 12 as one and the same, but his account gives us a Frenchman's point of view of the events:

> They went in a canoe with five or six soldiers, and, according to orders,
> showed themselves at a good distance off. The Spaniards, on seeing
> them, came in a boat to the other bank of the river, and held a parley
> with our men. The French asked what had become of the men left in
> the fort. The Spaniards replied that their commander, who was a hu-
> mane and clement person, had sent them all to France in a large ship
> abundantly supplied, and that they might say to Ribaud that he and his
> men should be used equally well. The French returned with this mes-
> sage. Ribaud, on hearing it, believed too hastily this story about his men
> having been sent back to France, and summoned another council. Here
> most of the soldiers began at once to cry out, "Let us go, let us go!
> What is to hinder our going over to them at once? Even if they should
> put us to death, is it not better to die outright than to endure so many
> miseries? There is not one of us who has not experienced a hundred
> deaths while we have been making this journey!" Others, more pru-
> dent, said they could never put faith in Spaniards; for, they urged, if
> there were no other reason than the hatred which they bear to us on
> account of our religion, they assuredly will not spare us.
>
> Ribaud, however, perceiving that most were of his mind, that it was
> best to surrender to the Spaniards, decided to send La Caille in to the
> Spanish commander, with orders, if the latter should seem inclined to
> clemency, to ask, in the name of the lieutenant of the king of France,
> for a safe-conduct, and to announce, that, if the Spanish leader would
> make oath to spare all of their lives, they would come in, and throw
> themselves at his feet. The greater part of the company assented to this,
> and La Caille was accordingly sent; who, coming to the fort, was taken
> before the commander, and throwing himself at his feet, delivered his
> message. Having heard La Caille through, he not only pledged his faith
> to La Caille in the terms suggested, and confirmed the pledge with
> many signs of the cross, and by kissing the Evangelists, but made oath
> in the presence of all his men, and drew up a writing sealed with his
> seal, repeating the oath, and promising that he would without fraud,
> faithfully, and like a gentleman and a man of honesty, preserve the lives
> of Ribaud and his men. All this was handsomely written out, and given
> to La Caille; but this fine paper promise was worth just as much as the
> blank paper. La Caille, however, took back this elegant document with

him; which was joyfully received by some, while others did not entertain any great expectations from it.

Ribaud, however, having made an excellent speech to his people, and all having joined in offering prayer to God, gave orders to proceed, and with all his company came down to the bank of the river near the fort. Upon being seen by the Spanish sentinels, they were taken over in boats. Ribaud himself, and D'Ottigny, Laudonnière's lieutenant,* were first led into the fort by themselves; the rest were halted about a bowshot from the fort, and were all tied up in fours, back to back; from which, and other indications, they quickly perceived that their lives were lost. Ribaud asked to see the governor, to remind him of his promise; but he spoke to deaf ears. D'Ottigny, hearing the despairing cries of his men, appealed to the oath which had been taken, but they laughed at him. As Ribaud insisted on his application, a Spanish soldier finally came in, and asked in French if he were the commander, "Ribaut." The answer was, "Yes." The man asked again, if Ribaud did not expect, when he gave an order to his soldiers, that they would obey; to which he said again, "Yes."—"I propose to obey the orders of my commander also," replied the Spaniard; "I am ordered to kill you;" and with that he thrust a dagger into his breast; and he killed D'Ottigny in the same way. When this was done, men were detailed to kill all the rest who had been tied up, by knocking them in the head with clubs and axes; which they proceeded to do without delay, calling them meanwhile Lutherans, and enemies to God and to the Virgin Mary. In this manner they were all most cruelly murdered in violation of an oath, except a drummer from Dieppe named Dronet, a fifer, and another man from Dieppe, a fiddler named Masselin, who were kept alive to play for dancing.[9]

The story of the sailor who brought the account of the massacre of Ribaut and his men to Le Moyne later in France is an incredible tale of suffering and miraculous escape:

He was among those who were pinioned for slaughter, and was knocked in the head with the rest, but, instead of being killed, was only stunned; and, the three others with whom he was tied falling above him, he was left for dead along with them. The Spaniards got together a great pile of wood to burn the corpses; but, as it grew late, they put it off until the next day. The sailor, coming to his senses among the dead bodies in the night, bethought himself of a knife which he wore in a wooden sheath, and contrived to work himself about until little by little he got the knife out, and cut the ropes that bound him. He then rose

* D'Ottigny had been leader of the first group killed September 29.

up, and silently departed, journeying all the rest of the night. When the day broke, he laid his course by the sun to get as far away from the fort as possible (for those of maritime occupations acquire the ability to judge which way they are going from observing where the sun is); and, after travelling for three days without stopping, he came to a certain Indian chief, who lived forty miles from the fort.

Here the sailor remained in comparative comfort and safety for eight months. The Spanish had heard that certain escaped Frenchmen were living with the Indians and sent word to the chiefs that all the refugees must be surrendered. The Indians, fearing reprisals from the Spanish unless they complied, forced the sailor to leave their village and go to surrender himself at Fort San Mateo.* No other Indians would give him refuge, and the sailor set out to give himself up. Near the fort his resolution failed him:

> Not knowing what to do, he set out for the fort; but, having come within two miles of it, he could not resolve to go any farther, but stopped and exhausted with sorrow, anxiety, and despair, gave himself over to die, and remained for three or four days in that miserable state. At the end of that time three Spaniards came out hunting, one of whom discovered him, and, at the sight of what was more like a dead corpse than a live man, felt (what is hardly to be found in one out of a thousand Spaniards) a sensation of pity upon beholding the sailor at his feet, and begging for mercy. Being asked by the Spaniard how he came to be there, he told him his story; upon which the Spaniard, who was affected by it, agreed that he would not take him at once to the fort, for fear of his being killed on the spot, but would see the governor first, and try if some indulgence could not be had from him; and that, after ascertaining about this, he would come back. Leaving him, therefore, the soldier went to the governor, and managed to get him to promise that the sailor need not be killed, but should only be made a slave. Next day he accordingly returned to the miserable Frenchman, and carried him to the fort, where he served as a slave for a year.

After this he was sent to Havana where he was bonded to another Frenchman, a gentleman named de Pompierre. Finally, after a period of captivity, the two were sold together and put on a ship bound for Portugal. On the voyage, the ship fell in with a French vessel commanded by one Bontemps and after a sharp battle the French took the prize. The sailor and de Pompierre were found in chains in the hold and were freed.

* After capture by the Spanish, Fort Caroline had been renamed San Mateo.

For years, French captives who had escaped the slaughter were picked up by the Spanish or surrendered themselves. As late as 1571 prisoners were being held in Spain in jail or as galley slaves.

Laudonnière and Jacques Ribaut had sailed from the River of May on September 25, 1565. A day out Jacques Ribaut deserted his companions, and having the faster ship sailed on ahead. He had refused Laudonnière a pilot, certain equipment, and supplies of which he had plenty. He had left Florida without knowing the fate of his father. When we compare his manifestly defective character to that of his father, we can only wonder at the strange working of the laws of heredity. Compare his actions with those of his father when the elder Ribaut knew he was going to die under the knife of a Spanish soldier. Jeanette T. Conner, in her classic introduction to Ribaut's account of his discovery of Florida, tells of his last minutes, as based on Spanish sources:

> Ribault seems to have had a ray of hope—but once they were behind a sand dune, once he had heard that because of their number their hands must be bound, for they could not be trusted to march to camp unbound, once the terrifying question was asked: "Are you Catholics or Lutherans, and are there any who wish to confess?" the scales fell from Ribault's eyes. In that foreshortening of life's events, that lightening flash of retrospect and understanding which sometimes comes to those who are about to die, the noble Ribault must have realized the mistakes of those last two months. And then appeared in him the simple, solemn grandeur peculiarly characteristic of his coreligionists in times of trial. He answered that he and all the rest were of the new Lutheran religion. He began to sing a psalm . . . and repeated the words "From earth we come, and unto earth must we return." He said "that twenty years more or less were of little account"; Menéndez was to do with them as he wished.[10]

Captain San Vincente then stabbed him in the stomach with a dagger, Gonzalo de Solís thrust a pike in his chest, and then they cut off his head. After the slaughter, Menéndez returned to St. Augustine and finished the interrupted letter of October 15, 1565, to his king. In it, he penned the greatest epitaph that could have been written for his dead rival: "I hold it our chief good fortune that he is dead, for with him the King of France could do more with 500 ducats, than with any others with 5,000, and he would do more in one year than any other in ten, for he was the most skillful sailor and corsair that was known, very experienced in this navigation of the Indies and of the coast of Florida."[11]

Laudonnière had arrived in the Azores on October 28 and later, to his surprise, in Swansea Bay, Glamorganshire, South Wales, about November 12. In a hurry to get to France, he left his ship and proceeded overland to the English Channel, which he crossed to Calais. Shortly after, he arrived in Paris. Laudonnière, of course, did not know the fate of Ribaut and his squadron, only that of his garrison, and could not report the massacres south of St. Augustine. Jacques Ribaut could report nothing more either. Menéndez' letter of October 15 had been delayed by a fateful accident. The letter had been entrusted to Captain Diego Flores de Valdés, but his ship had been wrecked in the Azores, and it did not arrive at the Spanish court until February 13, 1566. Meanwhile both the court of Spain and that of France were anxiously awaiting word from Florida. When it finally arrived, Philip immediately cautioned Alba, his ambassador in Paris, to be ready for a great outcry when news of the massacre reached the French court. At the same time, he decreed that the surviving French prisoners be put in the galleys as slaves. Ambassador Alba, in an audience with Catherine de' Medici on March 16, told her of the massacre. The Queen Mother almost in a rage voiced the disgust and outrage of the French people. The French ambassador to Spain, Fourquevaux, was instructed to enter the strongest protests with Philip, which he did in an audience on April 1. Fourquevaux also busied himself at finding out the location of the captives, which included the many women and children Menéndez had spared at Fort Caroline. This task was to take years to complete and many of the captives never lived to return to France. In further communications between the French and Spanish courts, Philip refused to pay any compensation to the families of those slaughtered in Florida or any reparations to the French government. Satisfaction for the outrage was not to be had through any official channels. The dishonor that had fallen on the French was to be avenged by a hero in the classical sense of the word. One man was to take it upon himself to wipe the stain from the French escutcheon. This man was Dominique de Gourgues.

De Gourgues was born about the year 1530 in Mont-de-Marsan, Gascony. He and his family were Catholics of gentle birth. In the warfare of the mid-sixteenth century between France and Spain, de Gourgues fought with his countrymen in Italy. Here, he and twenty men held off an entire Spanish company during a siege. After a brilliant defense, de Gourgues was captured and his companions were slaughtered. He was sentenced to life in the galleys and spent some time at the oar. His ship was later taken by the Turks, and de Gourgues continued as a slave until the vessel was captured in turn by a French commander. On gaining his freedom, de Gourgues went on several voyages to the coast of Africa and to the Indies, and eventually served in France with the Catholic forces under the Guises. As a galley slave under the Spanish lash, chained to his oar, de Gourgues had learned the cruelty of the Spaniards and had developed a deep and permanent hatred for them. When word arrived in France of the massacre of the French Huguenots, the anger de Gourgues felt knew no bounds. When it became evident that King Charles IX and his ministers were too afraid of war with Spain and the influence of the Spanish (Catholic) party in France to avenge the dishonor done his nation, de Gourgues determined to seek revenge himself. During the winter of 1566–1567, with money obtained by mortgaging his estate and borrowing from his brother, de Gourgues prepared his expedition. The principal source for his voyage is found in *L'Histoire notable de la Floride,* published in Paris in 1586 by M. M. Basanier. In it he describes the disgust and anger felt by the French nation at the slaughter of Ribaut and the other Huguenots in Florida:

> The news of this cruel massacre having been brought to France, the French people were wonderfully incensed at such cowardly treachery and detestable cruelty; and particularly so when they heard that the traitors and murderers, instead of being blamed and punished in Spain, were praised there, and rewarded by receiving the greatest estates and honors. All Frenchmen expected that such a wrong done to the King and the whole French nation would be soon avenged by public authority, but as they were disappointed in that expectation for the space of three years, they hoped that some private citizen might be found who would undertake to perform an act so glorious in itself and so necessary to the honor and reputation of France.[12]

De Gourgues worked through the first half of 1567 at getting his vessels ready and recruiting the necessary soldiers and sailors. He equipped two ships of light draft which could be propelled by oars as well as by sail and assembled his men: "There were one hundred arquebusiers, many of whom were gentlemen, all having arquebuses of the regulation calibre, with morions on their heads; and eighty sailors who, if need be, knew well how to perform the duty of soldiers. He had suitable arms for them, such as crossbows, pikes, and all kinds of long, wooden-handled weapons." He then secured permission to sail from France with a false declaration. He gave his destination as Benin in West Africa and received approval for the voyage from Monsieur de Montluc, the King's lieutenant for Guyenne. About the eleventh of August, 1567, he sailed from Royan. After being driven back to the coast by a storm which had held him there for eight days, he finally got away on August 22. The voyage was to be a hard one. Contrary winds and high seas battered the tiny ships as they reached for the southern latitudes:

> With great difficulty he reached the Cape of Finibus-Terrae [Cape Finisterre], where he was once more assailed by the west wind, which blew for the space of eight days, during which he was in great danger of shipwreck. He had great trouble with his men, who prayed to him earnestly to return. The vessel which had his lieutenant on board strayed away, and for fifteen days it could not be known whether she was safe or lost. She finally reached the meeting-place, which was at the Lor River in Africa, where Captain Gourgues was awaiting her. Here he allowed his men to rest and refresh themselves. They were so weary and overworked that they were worn out.

De Gourgues then stopped at Cape Blanco to accustom the men to the climate. Here they were twiced attacked by Negroes but easily drove them off. After some days, the two vessels made Cape Verde and set out on the trade winds for the Antilles. Touching at Dominica, they lingered eight days, resting and watering the ships, and then made a course up the islands for Florida. On one island they found the prickly pear and were urged to eat it by a trumpeter who had been in Florida and had come along to serve as an interpreter. Basanier's history describes the amusing results:

> They found a kind of fig, very large and long, which grows on bushes. It is green and prickly outside and red as scarlet inside. . . . The figs are a little bitter, yet have a very good taste, and greatly satisfy thirst. But when one has eaten half a dozen, they make one urinate freely, and render the water as red as the color of their insides. Our men thought they were passing blood and dying, and cried out against the trumpeter who laughed at them. When they were about to rush upon him, he assured them that there was no danger, and that it was the nature of this fruit so to color urine without doing any harm.

At Mona Island, the native chief presented the French with much fresh fruit after de Gourgues had given him a linen shirt as a sign of friendship. Here the wondering Frenchmen discovered the banana and the potato. Off Santo Domingo, they encountered contrary winds and were driven back to Hispaniola. Here de Gourgues was in danger of attack from shore but had to lie in a harbor to avoid the storm. The French did not land even though they needed water. When the storm had cleared, they reached for Cape St. Nicholas, and here they careened the ships and recaulked them, as the storm had loosened the planks and flooded the holds. Some supplies were lost to the water, among them much bread. This was a great loss, for the men had to go on half rations. The most dangerous part of the voyage now lay ahead as they passed Cuba to round Cape San Antonio and reach for the Florida Straits. Here they were exposed to a hostile land, where the Spanish would have attacked them had they been driven ashore by storm or thirst. Until this time, the Frenchmen in the ranks did not know of their destination. In the neighborhood of Cape San Antonio, de Gourgues landed at an uninhabited spot:

Here . . . having assembled all his men, [he] declared to them what he had hitherto kept from them: How he had undertaken this voyage to go to Florida to avenge on the Spaniards the insult they had done the King and all France. He excused himself for not having communicated to them sooner the plan of his enterprise, showed them the means by which he hoped to succeed in his design, and prayed and exhorted them to follow up those means with as much heart as he had hoped from them, when he chose them from among many as the most fit for the execution of such a purpose. He lay before them the treachery and cruelty of those who had massacred the French, and the shame there was in having left so long unpunished such a wicked and unfortunate act. He showed them the honor which would redound to them for such a fine deed. In brief, he animated them so well that, although at the beginning they thought the thing well might be impossible (because of their small numbers and of that coast being one of the most dangerous in all the Indies), they promised nevertheless not to forsake him, and to die with him. The soldiers even became so ardent that they could hardly wait for the full moon to light their way through the Bahama Channel, which is very dangerous. The pilots and sailors who were cool at the beginning were soon warmed by that ardor of the soldiers. The moon therefore being full, they entered the Bahama Channel, and soon afterwards they discovered Florida.

When the French passed St. Augustine in full daylight, the Spanish, thinking the ships their own, saluted with two cannon shot. De Gourgues replied in the same manner and maintained his course. After nightfall, he turned back and anchored off St. Marys River. As daylight came, the French saw the shores lined with armed Indians, who had mistaken the visitors for Spaniards. When the French trumpeter went forward to talk to them in their own language, the Indians recognized him and began to dance for joy at the return of their friends. The trumpeter told them that the French had returned to renew their friendship and bring them the gifts they so enjoyed. King Saturiba, hearing of the return of his late allies, sent a roebuck as a gift and inquired why the French had returned. De Gourgues answered they had come to renew old friendships and bring gifts. The Frenchman was too cunning to show his hand before he knew how the Indians were faring with their new Spanish neighbors. The Indians replied that they were going to inform their king of what de Gourgues had said and left. The French captain had his pilots sound the river mouth and found they could take their ships up the river for better cover and to be nearer the Indians.

The day after the first meeting with the Indians, Saturiba himself came to the shore with other kings, all relatives. What he told the French gladdened their hearts:

> Captain Gourgues had his men lay down their arquebuses and retain their swords, and thus he went to find King Saturiba, who came to meet him, and make him sit on his right hand on a wooden seat covered with moss, which he had ordered made similar to his own. When they two were seated, two of the most aged among them came to pull up the brambles and grass which were in front of them, and they all sat down on the ground in a circle.
>
> As Captain Gourgues was about to speak, King Saturiba, who is not accustomed to the European customs, cut him off, telling him that since the Spaniards had captured the fort built by the French, Florida had never had one good day, that the Spaniards had continually made war upon them, had driven them from their houses, cut their maize, ravished their wives, carried away their daughters, and killed their little children; and although he and the other Kings had suffered all these ills on account of the friendship they had entered into with the French, by whom the land had first been inhabited, yet they had never ceased to love the French because of the good treatment they had received from them when they commanded there.

De Gourgues was to have his allies. According to Basanier's history, Saturiba and his chiefs were overjoyed when they heard that the French had come to make war on the Spaniards. De Gourgues answered with a speech designed to identify the cause of the Indians with that of the French:

> "And what do you think about it?" said Captain Gourgues, concealing his plan in order to bring it into play with proper effect. "It is time right now to avenge the insult they have done our nation; but for the present I had only intended to renew our friendship with you and to see how things are going in order afterwards to return at once against them, with such forces as I should see would be needed; yet when I

hear of the great wrongs they have done and are doing you every day, I feel compassion for you, and a longing to fall upon them without any more waiting, to deliver you from their oppression today rather than tomorrow."

They resolved to attack the Spanish as early as possible, and Saturiba promised to have his forces ready in three days. At this, de Gourgues had presents distributed to his new allies:

knives, daggers, hatchets, scissors, bodkins, needles, purses, mirrors, bells, rosaries of glass beads, and other similar things. And after having divided them among them all, according to the rank of each, as far as he could judge, he said to King Saturiba and the other Kings: "Think if there is anything else that you would like to have; do not be sparing."

They, although they were more than pleased with what they already had, yet seeing the good will of Captain Gourgues, answered that they would each very much like to have one of his shirts, for which they asked not to be clothed in them—unless it were sometimes on some notable occasion—but to have them buried with them after their death, as they do likewise with the most beautiful things they have been able to collect during their lives. Captain Gourgues immediately gave one to each of the Kings, adding to them besides all that was at hand that he thought could be agreeable to them. Then King Saturiba, who had two strands of silver beads around his neck, gave one to Captain Gourgues. The other Kings gave him deerskins dressed according to the fashion of the country.

In their innocence and trust of the French, Saturiba and his chiefs had traded their allegiance to an ally who was to be with them only long enough to destroy the Spanish garrison and then would leave Florida forever. The Indians were not to discover this alarming fact until the French sailed away leaving their future in the hands of the infuriated Spanish.

From a young Frenchman who had survived the massacres and had stayed with Saturiba, de Gourgues learned that the Spanish garrison might number as many as four hundred soldiers. He also learned that the Spanish had not only rebuilt the main fort but also had erected two smaller forts near the mouth of the river to defend the estuary. This young Frenchman, sixteen years of age, was Pierre de Bré of Havre-de-Grâce and after the attack on the Spanish was to return to his joyful parents with de Gourgues. During the three days Saturiba was assembling his warriors, de Gourgues sent parties to reconnoiter the forts with Saturiba's own nephew, Olotoraca, as guide. He charged Captain

François of his ship to see that both vessels were recaulked and prepared for a speedy departure once the soldiers returned. In a scene
which touched the hearts of the soldiers and seamen alike, de Gourgues
left the keys of his chests with his captain and friend, saying if it were
God's will that he should die in the battle ahead, François should have
all of his goods and was to see to the safe return of his soldiers to
France. The voyage to Africa and on to America had taken the months
of the fall of 1567, and spring had arrived before the French reached
Florida. Now Easter week had passed and they were ready for the
attack. The Indians joined them as promised.

The first target was one of the forts on the river below San Mateo.
Basanier's history describes the approach of the French and the complete surprise of the Spanish:

> The Spaniards had just dined and were still picking their teeth when
> our men, with their heads down, taking great strides, were seen at two
> hundred paces from the fort, from a terrace by the gunner who had
> just mounted to that terrace, who at once began to cry out in Spanish:
> "To arms! To arms! Here are Frenchmen! Here are Frenchmen!" And
> immediately he discharged a big culverin which was on the terrace, and
> fired it twice. As he was about to load it a third time, Olotoraca, who
> had not been taught to keep his place in the ranks and was more swift
> in the running than any other, sprang forward and mounted the ter-
> race, which was not very high, and transfixed him right through with
> his pike. The Spaniards, having rushed to arms at the cry of the gunner,
> sallied forth from the fort either to fight or to retire towards their
> comrades, according to what they should see when they were outside.
> Captain Gourgues, at their coming out, had arrived just in time at the
> foot of the platform, his lieutenant being near the door. As he was
> mounting the platform, his lieutenant called out that the Spaniards were
> escaping, and then Captain Gourgues, returning quickly toward the
> door, shut them in between his lieutenant and himself, so that out of
> sixty there not one escaped death. By order of Captain Gourgues they
> took as many alive as they could to do to them what they had done to
> the French.

The first fort was no sooner captured and the Spanish slain or taken
than the French attacked the other:

> Captain Gourgues with eighty arquebusiers quickly crossed the river in
> the boat that had been brought there just in time.
> He landed between the fort and a wood there was very near it,
> suspecting what would happen, that the Spaniards would flee into the
> woods to retreat afterwards into the large fort, which was one league

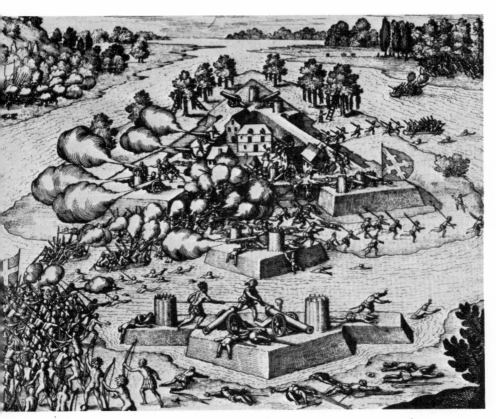

St. Bartolemew's Massacre, Paris, 1572. From a contemporary woodcut

from there. Captain Gourgues was hardly across the river when the savages, who could not wait for the boat to be returned for them, leaped into the water, and swimming with one arm and holding their bows aloft with the other, they covered all the river from bank to bank.

The Spaniards to the number of sixty, seeing such a great and resolute multitude, and not distinguishing between the French and the savages because of the surprise that seized them, and thinking they could escape into the woods, precipitated themselves among the Frenchmen there who discharged their arms on them so thick and fast that most of them fell dead, stretched out on the spot. The others, wishing to turn back, found themselves surrounded by the savages. Thus, not being able either to fight or to flee, they threw down their arms and begged for life, which was taken from them as they pled for it.

De Gourgues succeeded with the greatest of difficulty in saving fifteen Spaniards from his soldiers and the Indians. These were to be hanged later. The Monday and Tuesday following the capture of the two smaller forts, de Gourgues rested his men and had eight ladders made for the coming attack on San Mateo. He had information on the height of the fort from one of the captive Spanish. Later, a spy from San Mateo disguised as an Indian was taken, and de Gourgues learned that the garrison of the main fort numbered only 260 men. On Wednesday morning, he marched to a high spot overlooking the fort, and unseen by the doomed Spanish, inspected it from the cover of the trees there. The French leader had intended to attack the next morning, but an unexpected sally by sixty arquebusiers who came out to look over the French forces forced the battle. The Spanish were trapped outside the walls and were killed to a man. The rest of the garrison panicked:

> Those within, seeing in a moment that they had lost all the best and finest of their men, and thinking that they who had caused that defeat were only a small part of a greater number, despaired of being able to hold out. Besides, they had no hope for any settlement with those whom they had so outrageously wronged, so they abandoned the fort, and fled into the woods which were on the other side of the fort. There Captain Gourgues had stationed a great multitude of savages who shot their arrows at the Spaniards. Among others, there was one who at one shot pierced the shield of a Spanish captain, and the arrow entered far into his body through the left nipple and knocked him down dead. Captain Gourgues, who had seen the Spaniards issuing forth, and had come running after them, stopped them between the woods and the fort as they were fleeing from the arrows of the savages, and there they were killed and cut to pieces, except those whom with great difficulty he was able to reserve for a robber's death.

As the French looked over the trophies of their victories in the fort, they found five double culverins, four minions, and several small iron swivel guns, along with eighteen large barrels of gunpowder. The small arms included arquebuses, corselets, shields, and pikes. The next day, the cannon were loaded on the ships, but before the French could secure the small arms, the powder magazine blew up destroying the magazine, the weapons, and all the houses of the fort. Before the final Spanish defeat, they had laid a powder train to the magazine and, being unnoticed by the French, an Indian set fire to it accidentally while cooking fish for his lunch. No one was injured, for all the men were in the woods or outside when the accident occurred, but de Gourgues was cheated of the remainder of the booty.

The time had now come for the captured Spanish soldiers to be hanged. The prisoners were taken to a spot near the fort where Menéndez was thought to have hanged French captives in 1565. Here ropes were strung over the branches of trees, and the Spanish prepared to die. Not the least of the punishment they had to endure was a long impassioned speech by de Gourgues:

[He] pointed out to them the injury they had done the King, massacring his subjects, robbing him of the land his Majesty had conquered and of the fort he had had erected, he said that they must have realized that such a cowardly treachery, such a detestable cruelty, exercised against a King so powerful and a nation so generous, would not remain unpunished. He said further that he, who was one of the least of the gentlemen the King had in his kingdom, had taken upon himself the avenging at his own cost and expense; and that if the most Christian and Catholic Kings had been enemies and at mortal war with each other, they could not, even so, have justified themselves for the treachery and extreme cruelty that had occurred. He reasoned that since their Majesties were friends and so closely allied, the Spaniards' deed could not but be considered abominable, and still less could a penalty be found corresponding to the deed.

"Although you cannot suffer the penalty you have deserved," said he, "it is necessary that you should endure that which the enemy can give you honestly, in order that others through your example may learn to keep the peace and alliance which you have so wickedly violated."

The unfortunate captives were then hanged.

When word of Menéndez' capture of Fort Caroline had reached France with Laudonnière and Jacques Ribaut, a rumor was widely circulated that Menéndez had hanged certain of the Huguenots and had placed a sign by them reading, "I do this not as to Frenchmen but as to Lutherans." This was probably a fiction. None of the accounts of the Spanish eyewitnesses mention it and the story was probably the product of someone's imagination. Nevertheless, it was believed, and de Gourgues had a sign burned into a pine board with a hot iron: "I do this not as to Spaniards, nor as to Marannos but as to traitors, robbers, and murderers."

The ceremonies concluded, de Gourgues now ordered the forts destroyed. When this was done, the French marched back to their ships with their admiring allies. The Indian men and women lined the way cheering the destruction of the hated Spanish. The ships had been prepared for the voyage home while the battles were being fought. When de Gourgues took leave of his allies, he thanked them for their friendship and announced he would return in twelve moons with more gifts for them—another stratagem to lessen the sorrow of the Indians. On May 3, 1567, the French sailed with their captured trophies and the satisfaction of having avenged the deaths of their countrymen with a remarkable victory over a superior force well entrenched and armed. The passage was quick—only thirty-four days—but it was marred by a disaster which took much of the joy from it: one patache was lost with several gentlemen friends of de Gourgues's. And another ship went astray near Bermuda and arrived in France a month later. Such was the uncertain navigation of the day.

The people of France received the news of de Gourgues's revenge with joy. At court, however, it was a different story. The Catholic party was in the ascendant, and the King and Catherine de' Medici feared the reaction of the Spanish King. This was not long in coming. When news reached Philip of the destruction of his garrison, he was furious. Now with the shoe on the other foot, he demanded the extreme punishment for de Gourgues and the other leaders of the expedition. De Gourgues had to go into hiding in a house in Paris called the Court of Rouen near St.-Germain-des-Prés. Here he remained for a year while the diplomatic exchanges between Philip and Charles went on. Charles secretly relished the new role he played, remembering how his protests against the slaughter of Ribaut had been rebuffed by his brother-in-law. Both Catherine and Charles could in honesty deny they had any knowledge of de Gourgues's destination when he sailed, as he had cleverly covered up his intentions. Like the protests of the French over the slaughter of Ribaut, those of the Spanish led to nothing and de Gourgues was finally able to come out of hiding and continue a distinguished career in the service of the French Crown.

Only five years after his return to France, de Gourgues was to serve in the siege of La Rochelle with the Catholic forces against the Huguenots and witness the horrible events of the night of St. Bartholomew, August 24, 1572, when throughout France over fifty thousand Huguenots were slaughtered by the Catholics. In the carnage, Admiral Coligny and most of the other Protestant leaders lost their lives. Laudonnière, having escaped the disaster at Fort Caroline, escaped death a second time. When the massacre occurred, he was in the West Indies on board his ship the *Countess Testu*, alternating trading with and attacking his old enemies the Spanish. Later he returned to France and was in the King's service.

The capture of San Mateo by de Gourgues in 1568. From an old engraving

After de Gourgues's attack, the Spanish continued to fear further incursions by the French. These never came, for the Spanish had won. In the next century, with Spanish power declining, the French were to establish their culture in Canada, where it remains strong today. In the West Indies, they seized and settled islands that became a deadly threat to the Spanish: the bases of the first of the buccaneers, who swept through the Caribbean like a scourge in the next century.

VII

Great Storms and Shipwrecks

... and all day from the sad dawn, dark and fearful, full of confusion, the sky overcast and the clouds in it sad and troubled with the changing winds, which seemed to cry and lament our trouble and the poor ships with their crews, set upon by mountains of water, which surrounded them and battled them, without being able to escape.

—Antonio Vázquez de Espinosa,
The True Story of the Voyage ... of 1622

 SHIPWRECK WAS a constant and terrifying threat to all vessels using the Florida Straits. From the earliest period, when navigators returning to Spain began to sail through the waterway, the bones of ships and their victims piled up on the beaches of the islands and coasts flanking it. As early as 1578, the governor of Cuba, Don Francisco Carreño, had written the Crown of the treacherous nature of the passage, describing the beaches of Florida as littered with treasure as well as the bones of shipwreck victims: "In another letter I informed Your Majesty of the great amount of gold and silver said to be lost in the islands and keys of this channel of Bahama. Many rumors are current here of men who have escaped on rafts and logs and got to Florida where they were seized by the Indians. Some inhabitants of this region talked with them before they died and affirmed this matter saying that there were many lost ships and many bones on the shore of people who died for lack of water and had taken their gold and silver to the land where it was lost."[1]

In many ways, the Straits of Florida represented a gamble with nature. When one considers the hazards besetting the navigator of these waters, it is not surprising that the course often led not to Spain but to speedy entrance into the afterworld. Even in fair weather, the powerful Florida Current (the Gulf Stream) and the sometimes erratic disturbances set up by this great river in the sea could bring ships to disaster, sweeping them onto a bar or reef. In times of foul weather with adverse winds blowing, as they frequently do, toward the Florida

Keys and the coast of the peninsula, only consummate seamanship and plain luck could save a vessel from bilging on the sharp reefs, stranding on the sandbars, or simply foundering in deeper water. And once having escaped the sharp grasping fingers of coral that jut out from the westward flank of the lower Straits, the treacherous sands of Cape Canaveral awaited victims.

With these manifest dangers facing them, why did the Spanish then use this course in leaving the western Caribbean and the Gulf of Mexico for Spain? The answer is simply that, for all of its dangers, the Florida Straits were still the best means of getting clear of the Greater Antilles and Mexico and catching the prevailing westerly winds which carried them home across the stormy Atlantic. The alternative was beating down the Old Bahama Channel, which lies between the northern coast of Hispaniola and the southernmost islands of the Bahama Archipelago, with no current to help them along and headwinds all too frequently blowing. It was simply a matter of risk versus convenience, with the latter winning. Thus, while ships clearing from Puerto Rico and the outer islands to the east might sail directly for Spain, ships and fleets coming from the treasure ports of Cartagena and Vera Cruz took their chances in the Florida Straits.

Andrés González de Barcia, under the year 1545 of his *Chronological History of the Continent of Florida*, states: "A ship on its way from New Spain was wrecked on the Florida coast. The people were saved, but were made prisoners of the Indians, who appropriated the merchandise and silver. Twenty years later one of the castaways gained his freedom and sought refuge with Jean Ribaut.* The Adelantado Pedro Menéndez de Avilés freed others from slavery soon afterward. The rest—as many as two hundred people—were sacrificed by the Indians to the Devil."[2] Again, under the year 1553, Barcia mentions the loss of ships, in this case a large part of the fleet of New Spain sent out by the viceroy, Don Luis de Velasco. In this disaster, all the ships but three or four were destroyed:

> The fleet reached Havana with a fair wind, and was held in that port only long enough to put aboard certain articles before it again set sail with everyone in the best of spirits. They had not even lost sight of land when the currents of the Bahama Channel pulled the fleet off its course and a furious wind swept the ships onto the coast of Florida. Neither human ability nor experience were enough to keep them from striking the rocks, where they were so badly shattered that, according to some reports, only one small ship was saved, and this brought the

* The castaway may have been the Fontaneda mentioned below.

tragic news to Vera Cruz. Others say that although the ship was damaged, it reached Spain almost miraculously. However, it is certain that three reached Seville, among them a small privateer. . . . Of the thousand people aboard the wrecked vessels, more than three hundred came ashore clinging to ships' planks or boxes of merchandise. For six days they subsisted at the seashore on ships' provisions cast up by the sea, each lending aid to the other in this great calamity.[3]*

Of this group, only two survived to carry the tale of suffering back to Mexico. Savage attacks by the Indians and thirst and hunger had accounted for the rest. And so the dismal chronicle went on year after year: dozens of ships wrecked, and hundreds of victims sacrificed to the elements or the savages ashore.

One of the earliest personal accounts of shipwreck in Florida to come down to us is the memoir of Hernando d'Escalente Fontaneda, written, it is believed, in 1575. It describes his shipwreck some twenty years before and his subsequent life among the Indians of Florida:

The King of Ais and the King of Jeaga are poor Indians, as respects the land; for there are no mines of silver or of gold where they are; and, in short, they are rich only by the sea, from the many vessels that have been lost well laden with these metals, as was the case with the transport in which Farfan and the mulatto owner were; with the vessel of the Vizcaíno, in which came Antón Granado, who was a passenger, and was captured; and with the vessel of which Juan Christóval was master and captain, lost in the year '51, when the Indians murdered Don Martín de Guzmán, the Captain Hernando de Andino, Procurador of the Province of Popayán, and Juan Ortiz de Zárate, Distributor of Santa Martha: and there came in her also two sons of Alonzo de Mena, with an uncle, all of them rich. He that brought least was I, but with all I brought twenty-five thousand dollars† in pure gold; for my father and mother remained in Carthagena, where they were *comenderos*, and served His Majesty in those parts of Peru, and afterwards in the city of Carthagena, where they settled, and I and a brother were born. Thence they sent us to Spain to be educated; when we were wrecked on Florida, as I have stated.

Other vessels have been lost, among them the armada of New Spain, of which it was said the son of Pedro Meléndez was General, for the Indians took a Spaniard that reached the shore whom they found starving. And I saw him alive and talked with him and one Juan Rodríguez, a native of Nicaragua. He told us that they came from New Spain, and

---

* Barcia has probably mixed two events in one account. This passage refers primarily to the fleet that was wrecked on the coast of what is now Texas. At that time "Florida" referred to any land north of New Spain (Mexico).
† The translator is referring to the Spanish pieces of eight.

were going to Castile; that the General was a son of Pedro Meléndez, the Asturian; that he came as a sailor in another vessel; and that the people of neither knew anything of what had befallen the other, until the Indians armed themselves to go to the coast of Ais, when he saw them go and return with great wealth, in bars of silver and gold, and bags of reals, and much clothing.[4]*

Fontaneda made certain recommendations concerning Florida to secure that coast for the safety of shipwreck victims:

> With this I will end, and say no more; for, if the conquest of that country were about to be undertaken, I would give no further account of it than I have rendered. Its subjugation is befitting His Majesty, for the security of his armadas that go to Peru, New Spain, and other parts of the Indies, which pass, of necessity, along that shore and channel of the Bahama, where many vessels are wrecked, and many persons die; for the Indians are powerful archers, and oppose them: and because of this, I say, it is well to have a small fort for the protection of that channel, with some income for its repair, and the maintenance of soldiers as a garrison in it, which income might be drawn from Mexico, Peru, and Island of Cuba, and all the rest of the Indies. Thus much should be done; and another thing also—to go in search of pearls, for there is no other wealth in that country. So, I conclude, and as this account may become important, I sign it.[5]†

When John Hawkins stopped at the French settlement in Florida in 1565, he and his men heard tales of Indians' using silver arrow heads and saw gold and silver which the French had procured from the Indians. The source of this was surmised to have been the shipwrecks of the Spanish that had occurred along the coast. A member of the Hawkins company, John Sparke the Younger, mentions this in his account of the voyage:

> . . . and how they came by this golde and silver the French men know not as yet, but by gesse, who having travelled to the Southwest of the cape, having found the same dangerous, by means of sundry banks, as we also have found the same: and there finding masts which were wracks of Spaniards comming from Mexico, judged that they had gotten treasure by them. For it is most true that divers wracks have been made of Spaniards, having much treasure: for the Frenchmen having

---

* Fontaneda is mentioning here several wrecks that occurred over a period of time, not all in 1551.

† By the time this was written, the fort at St. Augustine had already been established, but Fontaneda was probably referring to the area further south, which was left largely unprotected throughout the Spanish occupation.

travelled to the capeward an hundred and fiftie miles, did finde two Spanyards with the Floridians, which they brought afterward to their fort, whereof one was in a caravel comming from the Indies, which was cast away fourteene yeeres ago, and the other twelve yeeres; of whose fellowes some escaped, othersome were slain by the inhabitants.[6]*

The literature is filled with references to ship disasters in the Florida Straits and the seas around them, but one of the most graphic accounts to come down to us is the description of a series of great storms in 1622, which battered the fleets of Honduras and New Spain between Florida, Bermuda, and the Spanish coast. This account, written by Friar Antonio Vázquez de Espinosa, from whose *Compendium and Description of the West Indies*, we have quoted in an earlier chapter, tells the story of the destruction of the fleets in which he was returning to Spain.† The combined fleets, numbering over twenty ships, included the following:

FLEET OF HONDURAS
San Francisco de Campeche (flagship)
Nuestra Señora de la Candelaria (on which Vázquez sailed)
Nuestra Señora de la Concepción

FLEET OF NEW SPAIN
San Agustín (flagship)
Santa Ana María
Santa Catalina
Nuestra Señora del Rosario
San Ignacio
Perlita
San Juan

An omen of the terrible voyage to come was read in the strange events that accompanied the departure of the fleet of New Spain from Vera Cruz on June 27, 1622. It was customary for an image of the Virgin to be placed on a point near the fortress, to be saluted as the ships departed for Havana and Spain. At this sailing, however, the image was not there, the commander of the fortress having refused permission to place it there. This was the result of a feud between the

---

* One of the survivors was probably the Spaniard mentioned by Barcia under the year 1545.
† This account concerns itself with the fleets of Honduras and New Spain only. The fleet of Tierra Firme, sailing behind, was also caught and destroyed off the southwesternmost Florida Keys.

captain general of the fleet, Fernando de Sosa, and the commander—one of those rivalries which may have had its roots in some old family quarrel or may have resulted from the duel nature of the command, which complicated matters when the general of a fleet was present in the harbor. Then as the general fired a shot to signal the departure and the fleet passed slowly out of the port past the fortress, three shots were fired from the castle as a customary salute to the departing fleet. One of them entered a merchantman that was sailing by the flagship and took off the arm of a young man of eighteen; he soon died of the wound. But the tragicomedy was not yet over. One of the ships, *Santa Catalina*, under the command of Captain Lázaro Sánchez "paused for a devotional five-gun salute to the Virgin and one of [the guns] recoiled and wounded five men and women so badly that three died and one had a crippled arm for life."[7] Soon after this, the mast of the pinnace broke and had to be jury-rigged. Thus, the fleet of New Spain departed for Havana with the minds of commander and sailor alike oppressed by the unfortunate events that had occurred.

Three days after the fleet of New Spain left Vera Cruz, the fleet of Honduras weighed anchor in the port of Trujillo and set out for Havana to join the fleet of New Spain for the voyage to Spain. Friar Antonio sailed on one of the ships of this fleet, *Nuestra Señora de la Candelaria*. On his way to the port of Trujillo, the good friar had paused at a shrine of Our Lady of the Conception and had celebrated a sung mass with sermon. After this, he proceeded on his journey "confident and certain of divine mercy." Only one slight mishap marred the departure of the Honduras fleet, the anchor of *La Candelaria* stuck fast and could not be freed even though the pull of the cable on the capstan caused the bow to go down. Finally after a delay of some hours, the line was cut, leaving fifteen fathoms of cable and the anchor on the bottom. The fleet found good winds and sped along, making Cape San Antonio in eight days and Havana in thirteen.

At Havana, while transferring cases of dyestuffs, Friar Antonio's ship was found to be infested with rats. They had already eaten much of the flour, hardtack, chickpeas, beans, and meat that were to sustain the crew and passengers on the long voyage home. Over a thousand rats were killed on *La Candelaria* alone. While the ships were cleaning and stowing fresh provisions, the fleet of New Spain was proceeding painfully toward Havana through stormy weather. Many ships had spars broken, and then, almost in sight of Havana, several of the ships were stranded near Pan de Cabañas and remained aground for four days before being freed. The largest ship of the fleet, the *San Ignacio* of 900 tons, lost her main-topmast and other spars. On August 4, after

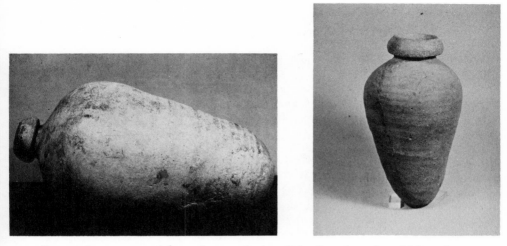

Pottery jars recovered from the wreck site of the *San Antonio*, which sank on the Bermuda reefs in 1621 and was discovered by Teddy Tucker. The jars were the standard containers for shipping many products to Spain and for carrying food for the voyage: the large jar, for shipping dyestuffs, gums, cotton fiber, and even treasure; both the small and large, for carrying food for the voyage. Antonio Vázquez de Espinosa describes how the rats gnawed through such jars and spoiled the food. Photograph from the Smithsonian Institution

thirty-one days from Vera Cruz, the fleet struggled into Havana harbor.

Ten days were required to refit the damaged ships, and after suitable masses and confessions, the combined fleets set sail from Havana on Sunday, August 14, in the very midst of the hurricane season. The fleet for Spain consisted of twenty-five ships, including patches* and small frigates. Three ships bound for St. Augustine in Florida sailed with them. For some ten days, the fleet sailed along on the Florida Current to the mouth of the Florida Straits, being followed by bad weather. A day after the northern end of the Straits was cleared, the bad weather caught the fleet:

> the Northeasterly failed, giving place to the Southeast wind, so that the haughty and horrible storm held us for more than 36 hours, from Thursday midnight to Saturday noon, though it reached its peak and did the most harm to us on Friday, from eight to five, and all day from the sad dawn, dark and fearful, full of confusion, the sky overcast and

* Small open boats used for communication between ships of the fleet.

the clouds in it sad and troubled with the changing winds, which seemed to cry and lament our trouble and the poor ships with their sad crews, set upon by mountains of water, which surrounded them and battled them, without being able to escape the force of the terrible storm because, as I have said, the sea, waves, and wind were contrary. Some with jibs rigged on the foreyard tried to outrun it, had their rigs carried away. Few escaped this trouble. The ships were scattered one from the other by the gale, and because of the darkness and mist, could not see one another. And on this sad, terrible, fearsome day the main-mast of our ship broke.[8]

To save the ship, spars were rigged to reinforce the broken mast, and men went aloft to cut away the wreckage: "Three of the most coura-geous seamen climbed up, with the wind and sea raging when the rocking of the ship dipped the ends of the yardarms in the ocean, with axes to take off the apparatus, and to cut the lanyards. . . . God was served and we were saved from the great danger in which we were. The toil ended and they were lowered down free." All through the storm, most of the passengers and crew were seasick, and the rats coming out of the timbers of the ship for food attacked the sick as they lay on the decks.

Hardly had the ships repaired the damage from the first storm when, near Bermuda, "the wind arose and blew out of the East-Northeast . . . and the sea grew rough and the waves swelled, the wind shifted Northeast and grew stronger . . . with whitecaps and contrary winds: and at eight it came from due North, and the storm increased in fury, so it seemed it might swallow us up and end us." The rocking of the ship shifted jars of water, vinegar, and oil in the stores and broke them, but Vázquez' ship, being one of the largest in the fleet, was damaged slightly compared to the smaller vessels. During the height of the blow, Vázquez says, "I spent the rest of the day stowed on the port side, along the poop walk, with a stole and a devout image of the Virgin around my neck, asking God our Lord for mercy by the inter-cession of his Sainted Mother, exorcising the stormy sea, the wind and waves, many blows, I say, splashed us and drenched me."

That same day, the *Santa Ana María*, a large ship on its maiden voyage, was so buffeted by the sea that her seams began to open. In this extremity, the crew threw "ropes, hawsers and cables" around the ship to brace her hull, and she was saved from sinking. One can only imagine the terror that must have gripped the passengers and crew of the stricken vessel as they felt the hull working and apparently break-ing up under them.

Vázquez, being a clergyman in an age when science was in its in-

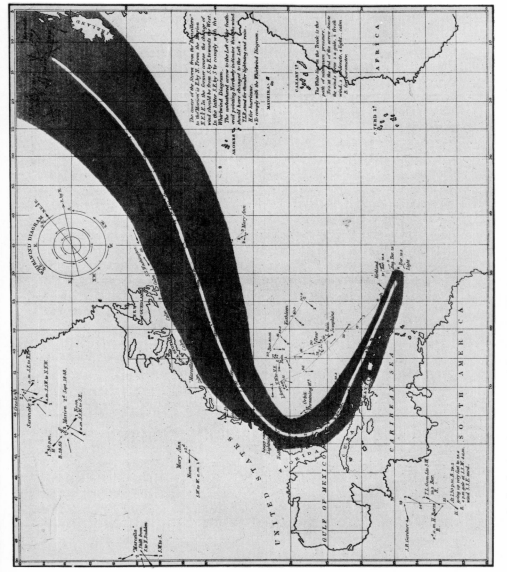

Path of a hurricane. From Matthew F. Maury's *Physical Geography of the Sea* (1855)

fancy, saw the Divine Hand in every natural incident and read allegorical meaning into every event. His description of the storms that tossed the ships are poetic and beautiful, but he was no seaman and could not describe in technical terms what was happening to a ship as it broke up at sea. For obvious reasons, not many accurate accounts of such events have come down to us. Those few seamen who witnessed such an event and lived to tell about it had to be content largely with recounting their stories orally, since for the most part they were illiterate or almost so. However, one account has come down to us from half a century after Vázquez' voyage, and while it describes the breaking up of an English ship of the 1680's, it also describes what happened to those unfortunate vessels of the fleet of 1622. The ship concerned was the *Terra Nova*, which sailed from Jamaica on December 24, 1688, under the command of Peter Daniel. Charles May, mate, was the unusually literate and articulate seaman who described the trials of the vessel when it fought for life in a terrible North Atlantic storm.

The duke of Albemarle, governor of Jamaica, died while the *Terra Nova* was at Port Royal, and the duchess arranged with Captain Daniel passage for fifteen of the duke's manservants and much of his household goods, including a chest "so heavy, that five or six men could but just draw it along the deck, full of pigs of silver, bags of pieces of eight, and some gold."[9]* This treasure almost proved their undoing, for as the ship left Port Royal and set a course for Cape San Antonio on the western end of Cuba, a pirate ship attempted to close with them, calling to Captain Daniel that they had a message for him. The captain wisely decided to remain uninformed instead of taking a chance of having his throat cut, and kept on his course. He succeeded in outrunning the predator. The voyage proceeded smoothly enough, Cape San Antonio and the Florida Straits being passed without incident. At the beginning of February, some five weeks after they had left Port Royal, the ship was in latitude 45° north and heading northeast toward home. The winds picked up from the southeast and then settled down again in four days. The ship was now in the North Atlantic and the weather closed in again. From the southeast, the wind began to blow with increasing fury until the ship was running under only one mizzen sail. On the ninth of February, while May was on watch near the tiller, a great sea swept over the ship tearing loose the yawl, which was stowed in the longboat on deck, and washing it

---

* This was probably part of the treasure William Phipps had salvaged from Silver Shoal north of Santo Domingo. The Duke had been one of the backers of the Phipps expedition and had gotten himself appointed governor of Jamaica in order to be near the port to which the treasure was being brought.

overboard. This incident was the first indication of the terrible days the crew and passengers were to live through as the ship was battered to pieces beneath their feet. Next, heavy seas breaking over the ship carried away her bower anchors and washed the sheet anchor overboard and then back against the ship, where it stuck in the channels and was later saved. Several sails had now been carried away and the seas and winds were still mounting. As May stood looking out of the steerage door,

on a sudden a prodigious wave broke to the windward of our ship. and fell with such violence upon us, that it set us all a-swimming, scarce knowing whether we were within or without the ship, but that on me roul'd the men, chests, handspikes shot, and whatever lay to windward. The same sea broke away our starboard gallery, in which were all our compasses but two that stood in the bittacle in the steerage, and staved in all the great cabin windows, so that it was like the rest, full of water; and the chest of drawers, cabbin table, charts, and whatever else lay to windward, fell upon the captain, keeping him striving for life under water. The passengers fared no better, for being in close low cabbins, they were almost smothered before they could get out. The violence of this sea had quite overset our ship, so that the coamings of the main-hatches lay under water, and a man might have walked upon her starboard side withoutboard, as he could upon the main deck. We could have not lain long in this condition without perishing, and therefore it pleased God, that the same sea which overset us, raking us along our weather quarter with so much violence, hove our ship quite round against the sea, so that tho' thus overset, being so violently tossed around, she brought the sea under our lee bow, and that side of the ship which before was the weather side, became the lee side. Having now the sea under our larboard bow it gave her such a second toss as set her upright again; and being at a stand, the water soon fell from off the deck.

Tho' this disaster all together was not the work of a minute, yet the damage our ship sustained by it was incredible. It carried away our head and cutwater, broke the bowsprit within a foot and a half of the stem, bore away the foremast close by the forecastle, the main mast within five foot and a half of the deck, and the mizzen mast which was stepped in the gun-room close to the quarter deck. It washed away chicken coops plated fast to the deck . . . staved the longboat in her lashings all to bits, and in her drowned and washed overboard six hogs, as many sheep, and some goats. Besides, six hencoops full of hens it carried away and in one hencoop left on the quarter deck, with about two dozen of hens, there was not one alive. Thirteen turkies were drowned in the forecastle standing on the guns, two tier of water casks washed off the main deck and a spare topmast which was broke in three

A hurricane. From a late-sixteenth-century engraving by Théodore de Bry

pieces, two minion guns, carriages and all, were lost from off the main deck, on each side of the steerage, tho' well lashed with new britchings and tackles; two falconets* and a paterero† were taken off the quarter-deck, and both the bulkheads of the steerage and the great cabin staved to bits. . . . But the worst of all was, that it carried away our starboard-side, fore and aft, from the steerage to the cookroom, as if it had been sawed close by the deck, and at the same time staved our bittacle to mash, with one of the compasses that were in it.[10]

When the captain, the mate, and all the company had recovered their feet and at least some of their composure, they set about as quickly as possible repairing the damage. May found the steering gear smashed and went into the gunroom to inspect the tiller. Water was deep on the gunroom deck, "which, with the beating of the ship,

---

* Small cannon.   † Very small cannon carried on the ship rails for close action.

washed from side to side in such a manner, that I had much ado to scramble in to feel for the tiller. Having at length waded thro', I found the tiller lying in the gun-room on the deck, broke off short at the rudder-head. Whilst I was groveling in the dark, I felt my body all over covered with rats, as thick as they could stand upon me, on my coat, arms, neck, and my very head, so that I was forced to make my escape into the light to get rid of those vermin."

On deck again, an inspection of the rudder proved it to be broken from the rudder post and hanging precariously by the upper gudgin and floating in the sea across the stern. Shortly after, it broke away and was lost. Now the situation of the stricken vessel appeared very bad indeed. With the starboard open to the sea and no means of steering, it would be only a matter of time before the ship would fill and sink.

All this while our gunnel lay open the water continually pouring down into the hold, and we could not tell which way to remedy it to prevent foundering. Our masts and yards lay still under our lee; and the ship driving in the trough of the sea upon them, it was hard to get rid of them, and it was altogether impossible to save any, because of the violence of the wind and sea, and the rouling of the ship. All our main chain-plates, both of shrouds and back-stays, both to leeward and windward, broke off short as if they had been glass, and not one of them held; so did all the chain-plates before, excepting the two aftermost plates of our larboard shrouds, which alone held and kept the wreck under our lee, till at last our boatswain cut them away with a hatchet.*

The mizzenmast chain plates on the lee side had held when the waves hit and, with these and the mizzen shrouds, May and the crew were later able to erect a jury mast from some of the small spars that were saved. But before this could be done, the next order of business was seeing to the pumps, which proved to be undamaged, and closing off the open hole on the broken side through which the sea was breaking. After rigging lifelines, May and the boatswain were able to close the hole with Holland duck nailed down on the deck and gunwale. They accomplished this while being tied around their waists to long ropes, with the sea continually beating over them as they nailed the canvas down. With the pumps going continually, the crew was able to lower the water in the hold, but the ship still leaked badly, and another day was required to get the hull reasonably tight.

As the storm continued, food and water supplies were examined, and the desperate plight of the passengers and crew was apparent. The live

---

* By "wreck" May means the wrecked masts that were floating beside the ship.

animals had all been killed by the sea, and some meat was recovered from the turkeys that were drowned but not washed overboard. But the supply would last only a day. Much of the bread and biscuit had been ruined by water, and the water supplies were largely lost when the extra water casks stowed on deck were washed over the side. All useless cargo, including the duke's rich furnishings, was thrown overboard to lighten the ship and permit examination of the hold for leaks. Needless to say, the treasure was not jettisoned. All the company was placed on strict rations, which were steadily reduced as the days passed, until they were eating corn that had been laid in to feed the sheep. This had been spoiled by seawater, but it was beaten between canvas and reduced to a smelly mush and eaten. Rainwater was their only drink. The storm lasted a full twenty days, during which time the ship drove sideways into the sea but steadily toward England. After the storm, a ship drew near, proving to be a Portuguese, but when the English would not go aboard, the captain refused any help and sailed away. As the fair weather continued, the jury rigging of the ship was improved somewhat and she was able to make a steady knot and a half. With a contrived steering apparatus, they at last reached home waters, where they fell in with a British squadron of warships. One can only imagine the amazement of the English when they saw this strange apparition drifting toward them. Here, a warship took the wreck in tow, and they reached Plymouth on April 11, 1689, where they finally ran the ship aground to save the hull. The voyage had lasted 109 days, over half of them in the wrecked ship. The damage was so great and the escape so miraculous, people came from miles around Plymouth to see the wreck sitting on the mud flats in the harbor.

When May wrote of guns being lost overboard, he matter-of-factly stated that they were washed from the ship by the force of the sea. Not so with Father Vázquez. *Nuestra Señora de la Concepción,* a ship of 250 tons in the company of *La Candelaria,* was damaged in the hull and water began to come in near the keel until it was four feet deep in the hold. At the same time the mainmast broke and went overboard. At a critical moment, a heavy cable and two guns were washed over the side and lightened the ship. As Vázquez tells it, "A wave came with great violence which almost foundered her, if the Virgin Mary had not lightened the ship by a cable and two cannon."[11]

Five distinct storms were to batter the fleet before the survivors reached Spain. Vázquez' account is of one disaster after another, as seamen struggled to save their ships, and passengers manned the pumps or huddled in terror in the hold. All the while, the Fathers said their beads and held masses when they could, which strengthened the stricken people and prepared them for the death which all felt was certain.

Early on September 10, four days less than a month of their departure from Havana, the galleon *San Agustín* was taking on water faster than the crew could pump. They fought to stay afloat, but at daylight the ship had to be abandoned, the survivors making their way to the *San Ignacio*. The *San Agustín* "in sight of all . . . sank at 9 in the morning, which was a fearful pity, taking with her much treasure, 80,000 ducats in silk, 7,000 pelts, anil [indigo], sugar, lumber, etc., and all cannon."

Now the *San Ignacio*, of 900 tons and the largest ship in the fleet, crowded with the survivors of the *San Agustín*, was in serious trouble. Her seams had opened and the oakum caulking had been battered loose by the force of the sea. Water was gaining in the hold faster than the crew could pump. A cannon was fired to signal for help from the other vessels. Launches fought their way through the boiling seas to the stricken vessel, but nothing could be done to save her. In abandoning her, many of the crew and passengers died in the sea. She remained afloat until the morning of September 12, when the "sea swallowed her in sight of all; she carried 300,000 ducats of merchandise, silk, cochineal, sugar, anil, lumber and more than 14,000 pelts and other goods, with all the artillery."

Five days after the loss of the *San Ignacio*, the storm abated, and the crews on the surviving ships set about repairing the extensive damage. Most of the ships had lost masts and rudders and were drifting helplessly. One small vessel, apparently with all aboard dead, sank within sight of Vázquez' ship. After some days, during which the ships were repaired sufficiently to continue with jury-rigged rudders and shortened rigging, the remains of the fleet continued the voyage in bad weather. Near Bermuda, the captain general called a meeting of the pilots, who advised tacking where possible rather than maintaining a direct course eastward. Masses were said, and all prayed for a steady wind from the west. For a while their prayers were answered and the fleet made some progress to the east, but another storm struck soon and another ship, one of 300 tons, her hull breaking up, had to be cleared of her crew and passengers. She sank shortly afterwards with all her cargo.

On Vázquez' ship, *La Señora de la Candelaria*, a new and terrible danger arose. The rats returned. Those that had survived the slaughter in Havana had increased during the two months to enormous numbers, and the ship was again infested from stem to stern. They threatened to destroy all the food and water stores:

to drink water from the jars, they gnawed the tops and stoppers off. And when they finished, they fell in and drowned and we found them when we went for water. Some chewed their way in from the bottom and we found the jars empty. And so they did us great harm by destroying our provisions. And to see such a multitude of rats frightened everyone, for they were all over the ship in great numbers, doing harm everywhere: on deck, in the hold, in rooms, in the pilots chair, and although we watched for them, they ate the boxes [sea chests] of the soldiers and sailors and everything in them. The many drowned made no difference. They chewed off the tops of the jars [containing the dry provisions], entered and ate, and died because they couldn't escape. In the hold they ate 12 quintals [about 1,500 pounds] of hard tack and cassava bread without leaving crumbs.[12]

Eight boxes of hardtack weighing over a thousand pounds were brought from the flagship in the Honduras fleet, the *San Francisco de Campeche,* and placed in the wardroom, and even here, with Vázquez sleeping on a cot to guard the boxes, the rats, made bold by their number, gnawed through the boxes and ate the bread. With this, the crew packed the remaining hardtack in iron-hooped casks and placed them on the wardroom deck, where they were guarded night and day, but the rats still came boldly out on deck, even in daylight, and attempted to gnaw into them. "The other cask which was still full we kept in the wardroom, guarded day and night, which wasn't enough because the hungry rats overran us, and chewed our hands . . . and many went into parrots cages and fought with them until they killed and ate them. And this happened many times." The rats entered and killed chickens in their pens and gnawed hams and bacon stored over the poop roundhouse. They even attacked the ship's cats and forced them to retreat, completely dominating the ship.

A counterattack was mounted by the crew, passengers, and soldiers aboard. Literally thousands of rats were killed. They had destroyed so many provisions and fouled so much water that everyone was placed on short rations of half a pound of hardtack a day, with the working sailors getting a little more. Water became so scarce the people were reduced to getting less than a pint a day and finally a half pint, "filthy from rats drowned in it." When this ran out, no water was to be had for several days until a providential rainstorm swept the fleet and saved the people. Even altar cloths were pressed into service along with spare sails and awnings to catch the precious liquid.

By October 19, the ration of hardtack had been reduced to six ounces, with two ounces of rotten crumbs. Three days later, only crumbs were left, and finally the people went for twenty-four hours without water or bread. A resupply from the flagship of the Honduras fleet again saved them, but the morale of the crew and passengers had sunk to zero. At this point, Vázquez held Divine Service, which lifted spirits but did little to allay hunger and thirst. The smaller ships in the fleet fared even worse than *La Candelaria*. These were the ships that had rescued the survivors of those ships that had sunk, and over-crowded as they were with extra people, their rations of bread and water were quickly reduced to a critical point. "The ship *San Miguel* . . . was really in extreme trouble also for carrying extra people. The little ship of Captain Fermen de Noriza ran on a half pint of water, a handful of hardtack or crumbs and a dozen beans (per person), people were dying of thirst, not only on this ship but on others, drinking sea water, they sickened and died. This was general throughout the fleet." By October 24, Vázquez' ship had only "2 half jugs of rat-spoiled water for rations for 90 people." Again the launch was sent to other ships to beg bread and water.

At this critical time, on the morning of October 25, with all hope fading, the island of Flores in the Azores was sighted. The crew lost no time in making for land.

> With the view of the Island of Flores, which seemed to us . . . like fragrant roses all the sadness and hunger of the people turned into joy. Our ship, being such a good sailer, after having told the good news to all the fleet with the cannon, putting on all sail we went on ahead, and arriving at the island, leaving all the fleet behind, desirous of tasting clean water . . . having finished that day the two half jugs of water containing dead rats, we lowered our small boat to look for the water and the ship approached the shore when we saw coming out from a point a barentine of Island Portuguese* greedy and churlish, they brought some bread, biscuits, hens, water and a sheep to sell us, and if they came greedy and churlish knaves we were more so for their food and refreshment. . . . They came with some distrust, afraid we were enemies, making in their little boat great ceremony and submissions, saluting our Captain and crew. And we desirous of their arrival, their ceremonies just aggravated our hunger, we told them we were friends . . . come from the Indies. Finally they came along side and we bought everything at whatever they asked, hunger doesn't haggle.[13]

Later, the captain went ashore and bought more provisions, which included beans, sheep, hens, two cows, hogs, and fresh produce.

The rest of the fleet arrived one after the other, and resupplied and

---

* Then as now the Azores were Portuguese territory. At this time, both Portugal and Spain were under the rule of Philip IV.

repaired while the winds were calm. Two days after the last ship limped in, the wind picked up from the east. If this wind had blown up while the fleet was approaching Flores, all would have been doomed. The arrival had come not a day too soon to save the people.

Having made necessary repairs and taken on water and provisions to get them to Spain, the fleet tacked out of the harbor the afternoon of October 29. Four days later, the islands of Faial, Pico, and São Jorge were sighted, and the next day Terceira came into view. Here Vázquez went ashore and celebrated mass on Sunday, November 6, after which the fleet sailed again, led by the flagship. Now the effects of the long deprivation of decent food and water became apparent: many died from the effects of overeating. In Vázquez' ship, a cabin boy died and was buried at sea. As the fleet passed the island of São Miguel, the winds began picking up and on Sunday, November 13, *La Candelaria* sprang a leak. This was successfully repaired, but just two days later a strong norther caught the ships. They were again battered by fierce winds and heavy seas. Some lost spars and were almost capsized by the force of the storm. Vázquez' ship lost her top masts, and listed so that her lower yardarms touched the water. A cabin boy of twenty was washed overboard and was swept away before help could be given him, "which broke our hearts seeing him on the waves asking help we couldn't give. We threw ropes he couldn't reach even though we turned the ship because of the cold sea and ice. And so crying we separated from him until we could no longer hear him and he gave his soul to his creator. . . . We all prayed for him and I gave last rites."[14] Vázquez attributed the storm to the fact that someone had robbed the alms box on the ship.

The next day, the storm broke and the ships were becalmed, but two days later, a good breeze sprang up and the ships began to make headway. At this time, the rats again became active, but Vázquez remarks that everyone was pleased that the rats ate only 250 pounds of hardtack, although much bread was lost. At 35° north, the fleet searched for sight of the Spanish coast, but on November 23 another storm struck. Again Vázquez sought the explanation for it in the conduct of the crew: "this was sent us for the little preparation or none, that being Christians we make at embarcation, embarking without law or fear of God, like barbarians, not content with sinning in port, they bring their women along at sea and others sail only to find the ones they left. And even robbing at sea during the God sent storms, when faced with death. The sea is reaping its harvest of sinners swearing and blasphemous aboard ship, thoughtless of God's vengence."[15] The battered ships, already in wretched condition and again running out of

Ship in a storm. From a late-sixteenth-century engraving by Théodore de Bry

food and water, faced the fifth storm of the voyage: "the sea was rising and the winds furious, felling all the topmasts, which caused us great concern because we were in search of land and in heavy overcast. The sea continued to rise. Night fell with mists and clouds. The sails were reefed and the pumps manned. . . . The fleet hove to at night, being close to land and not knowing exactly where it was because of the weather. Everyone [that is, each ship] was taking water, and pumping and praying all night, and asking God to pardon our sins, on our ship all praying remorsefully and crying to God." The storm continued with "the wind raising the waves to the sky and breaking over the face they turned to white spray making the sea look like snowy hills."

At four in the afternoon of November 25, the weather cleared and the desperate condition of the ships became apparent. The *Santa Catalina*, of 400 tons, one of the largest in the fleet, weathered the storm but "just as the sea began to calm, she opened, a total wreck topside, with nothing left to throw overboard, she began firing pieces for help to come." A launch from the patrol boat was sent but turned over in the heavy seas and all aboard were lost. Those aboard the *Santa Catalina* struggled to get their launch overboard, but the tackles slipped and the launch crashed to the deck. Again the crew and male passengers struggled to lift the four-ton launch, and their desperation gave them the strength to get it in the sea. Fifty-eight people and three Dominicans got into the launch and were saved by one of the vessels nearby. "The other 22 people were still aboard the sinking ship awaiting the help they didn't get until the sea opened its cruel mouth and swallowed the ship in the middle of their prayers, and they went to their creator, their bodies eaten by fierce fish. . . . And some of those who were drowned had already survived two other sinkings, from the lost *San Agustín* and *San Ignacio*."

Two days later, land was sighted: "Sunday morning, with 106 days gone by, November 27, we sighted the Isle of Cádiz and we thanked God for this view of our native soil, Spain." Vázquez' ship and seven others reached the bar of Sanlúcar at dark and took on bar pilots. The ships lay to that night, expecting to cross the bar the next morning and make their way up the Guadalquiver River to Seville. Five of the seven vessels that had separated from the fleet in the latest storm limped in after the loss of the *Santa Catalina*, but being deep with water in their holds and in too poor condition to keep afloat off the bar of Sanlúcar, entered Cádiz to repair and await a favorable wind. However, they were ordered to cross the bar of Sanlúcar in bad weather. The *Santa Ana* was thrown back and failed to cross, but after sailing all the way to Cape St. Vincent and back she got in.

As for the fate of some of the other ships, the *Almiranta*, which had disappeared off Bermuda, made it alone to Madeira, where she was beached and the cargo saved. One small ship, having survived the storms and severe damage, was captured by Dutch pirates off the coast of Spain, the survivors on the ship being sent ashore in a Dutch prize. One other vessel made it back to Santo Domingo and several others later struggled into Spanish ports. The final irony was furnished by the patrol vessel of the flagship. In attempting to cross the bar of Sanlúcar, this gallant little vessel, which had been picking up survivors from sinking ships all the way across the Atlantic, herself became a wreck. Some of the survivors had lived through three other sinkings, and finally arrived in Spain on a fifth vessel, having had four ships—*San Agustín*, *San Ignacio*, *Santa Catalina*, and the patrol ship—go down under them. Over a fourth of the fleet had been lost, with many lives and much treasure. Many of the survivors were made bankrupt by the loss of their goods, and some of those who had endured so much and who were able to arrive in Seville with some of their wealth intact saw it sequestered by the King's agents as a forced loan to the Crown. Against such odds did those in the American trade struggle with a courage, faith, and doggedness which astonishes modern man. While this voyage was of exceptional misfortune, it was still not the worst. The disaster of 1553 had all but wiped out an entire fleet and everyone in it, and two whole fleets were to be lost a century after the incredible voyage of the fleet of 1622.

VIII

Dutch Treat

Piet Heyn, Piet Heyn, Piet Heyn,
His name is small,
His deeds are great, his deeds are great.
He has won the Silver Fleet.
Hurrah, hurrah, hurrah,
He has won the Silver Fleet.
                                    —Old Dutch song

AFTER WINNING de facto independence from the Spanish and
having it recognized in the Twelve Years Truce of 1609, the
Dutch states leaped into a vigorous adolescence. Their merchant fleet
was expanded, trading companies were organized, and very soon the
Dutch were a sea power to be reckoned with. On the expiration of the
truce in 1621, the Dutch West India Company was formed and put to
sea a semimilitary navy. With memories of Spanish cruelty rankling,
it was natural enough that the Dutch should view the Spanish as their
mortal enemies. The fact that the Spanish were also immensely rich did
not seem to lessen the Dutch fury.

Even before the truce of 1609, Dutch traders had been penetrating
the West Indies and selling to the Spanish colonials a multitude of
manufactured necessities, such as cutlery, wines, cheese, butter, and
Negro slaves, both in the islands and along the coasts of the Caribbean.
They returned to the Netherlands with the natural products of the
area—hides, tobacco, dyestuffs, and sugar. As early as 1606, three years
before the truce, a proposal to establish a West Indies company in
concert with the French had been put forward. The promise of a
negotiated peace with the Spanish had caused this plan to be post-
poned. The Dutch who traded in the Indies in private ventures were
looked on there as pirates by the colonial officials, at least by those who
were not illegally trading with them, and the interlopers went prepared for any eventuality. The natural result of these trading voyages
was private war and privateering.

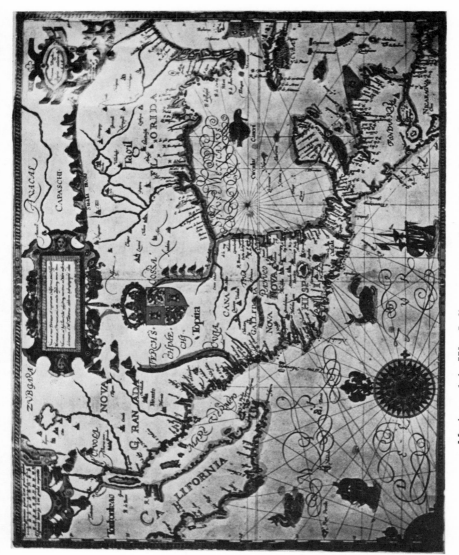

Mexico and the West Indies, an engraved map dating from 1600

So audacious and so persistent were the Dutch in their pursuit of Spanish ships, even in the Caribbean and the Gulf of Mexico, that the name "Hollander" became synonymous with "corsair" and "pirate."* Thomas Gage on his homeward voyage described the Spaniards' fear of the Dutch and English, and his own concern as well (as we have seen, he was himself captured off the coast of Central America while trying to get to Cartagena). No spot of the inner seas was safe from the marauders. On Gage's voyage from Porto Bello the Dutch struck again:

> The ships being laden, we set forth towards Cartagena; and the second day of our sailing we discovered four ships which made the merchant ships afraid, and to keep close to the galleons, trusting to their strength more than their own. The ship I was in was swift and nimble under sail, and kept still under the wings of either of the Admiral [admiral's ship] or of some other of the best galleons; but all the other merchant ships were not so, but some slowly came on behind, whereof two were carried away by the Hollanders in the night, before ever we could get to Cartagena.
>
> The greatest fear that I perceived possessed the Spaniards in this voyage was about the Island of Providence, called by them Sta Catalina, or St. Catherine, from whence they feared lest some English ships should come out against them with great strength. They cursed the English in it, and called the island the den of thieves and pirates, wishing that their King of Spain would take some course with it. . . .
>
> Thus with bitter invectives against the English and the Island of Providence, we sailed on to Cartagena, where again we met the four ships which before had followed us and had taken away two of our ships, and now at entering into that port threatened to carry away more of our company.[1]

The guns of the forts frightened away the pirates and no more losses were suffered.

At Cartagena fear again swept the Galeones and the ships accompanying them as reports of a large force of Hollanders off the coast circulated about the port, but Don Carlos de Ybarra, general of the Galeones, determined to sail for Havana anyway and the voyage was made in eight days without incident, the report about the pirates proving false.

The Galeones and the fleet of merchantmen left Havana on a Sunday, having given up waiting for the Flota because of the lateness of

---

* A corsair was a private man-of-war under commission; a pirate was a sea robber and outlaw.

Dutch warship of the early seventeenth century. From a painting of the period

the season. Twenty-seven ships in all stood off the port waiting for a favorable wind and the pilot, "which was not yet come out of Havana to guide us through the Gulf of Bahama." The first night out many strange ships arrived among the fleet and the Spaniards, thinking the strangers to be Hollanders, prepared for war. "A council of war was called, and all that night watch was kept, the guns prepared, red cloths hung round the ships, orders sent about both to the galleons and to the merchants' ships what posture and place to be in." The fears of the Spanish turned to joy the next morning when it was discovered that the strangers were the belated Flota from Vera Cruz: twenty-two ships whose officers and crews had been just as apprehensive and had likewise prepared to fight. "But when the day cleared our doubts, fears, and jealousies, then began the martial colours to be taken down;

the joyful sound of trumpets with the help of Neptune's kingdoms echoed from ship to ship, the boats carried welcoming messages from one to another, the Spanish *brindis* [toast] with *Buen viaje, Buen pasaje* [good voyage, good passage], was generally cried out, the whole morning was spent in friendly acclamations and salutations from ship to ship."[2]

The joyful morning was turned to sadness. While all the celebrations were going on, two strange vessels entered the fleet of fifty-two ships unnoticed, and getting the wind, cut out two merchant ships. The nationality of the interlopers was not discovered but it was assumed that one was English and the other a Hollander. One of the Spanish ships taken had a cargo worth 80,000 crowns.

> The whole business lasted not above half an hour; but presently she was carried away from under our noses; the Spaniards changed their merry tunes into *Voto a Dios* and *Voto a Cristo*, in raging, cursing, and swearing, some reviling at the captain of the ship which was taken, and saying that he was false and yielded on purpose without fighting because he was forced to come on that voyage; others cursing those that took her, and calling them *hijos de puta, borrachos, infames ladrones* [bastards, drunkards, infamous thieves] and pirates; some taking their swords in their hands, as if they would cut them to pieces, some laying hold of their muskets as if they would shoot at them, others stamping like madmen, and running about the ship as if they would leap overboard, and make haste after them.[3]

Orders were given for the vice admiral and two more galleons to chase the pirates but the wind was against them. "Laughing and rejoicing as much as the Spaniards cursed and raged, [the interlopers] sailed *con viento en popa* [with full sail] gallantly boasting with so rich a prize taken away from two and fifty ships, or (as I may say) from the chiefest, and greatest strength of Spain."

Well might the Spanish general and admiral and Gage and his shipmates sweat with fear at the thought of Hollanders off Havana, for nine years before, in these very waters, the Dutch had scored with their greatest capture by taking a whole treasure fleet. The perpetrator of this most audacious act against His Catholic Majesty was one of the most colorful naval commanders who ever sailed the seas. Piet Pieterzoon Heyn was born in 1578 in Delfshaven, a small port on the Meuse River near Rotterdam. His father was a fisherman of little means, but by following the secondary occupations of privateering and trade, he was able to keep his family in fair circumstances and even give Piet a good basic education. From his earliest years Piet was exposed to the lure of the sea, and no doubt he accompanied his father on many a voyage when he was old enough to be an asset aboard and when the voyage would not interfere with his schooling. The fishing boats of that period were small but went armed with two or three cannon and sailed in fleets for mutual protection against the Spanish and French corsairs. Combining a bit of trading, perhaps smuggling, and a little privateering with the basic job of fishing for herring in the North Sea gave the men of these fleets an ideal basic course in seamanship, fighting, and evading more powerful enemies.

This was a time of constant struggle as the United Provinces* fought the Spanish to maintain their independence. The Dutch were Protestant, the Spanish were Catholic; the Dutch had been cruelly oppressed by the Spanish and had replied with cruelty themselves. Every young Dutch boy grew to hate the Spanish as naturally as he learned to walk and talk. The Spaniard was the inveterate enemy of the Dutch and the highest calling a young man could follow was fighting the Spanish in war, in trade or in the profession of part-time fisherman and part-time corsair.

Very little is known of Heyn's early life, but we can surmise that twenty years of it went into the herring fishing and pirate fighting which was characteristic of the Channel at that period. Indeed, it could be said that Piet attended a leading graduate school in maritime mayhem.

Two years after hostilities began again between the Netherlands and Spain, Piet Heyn, whose reputation as a sea captain was by now very great, was offered the post of vice admiral of a fleet being sent against the Spanish American possessions by the Dutch West India Company. Composed of twenty-six ships with five hundred guns, sixteen hundred seamen, and seventeen hundred soldiers, the fleet sailed from the Texel under Admiral Willekens on December 21, 1623. The admiral carried sealed orders, which he was to open after reaching American waters. In April off the island of St. Vincent, he called a council of war and the orders were opened. They directed that the fleet sail straight for São Salvador (Bahia) on the coast of Brazil and capture it at any cost.† The town being secured, a garrison was to be left behind. In addition, the fleet was to sail against Spanish shipping in the area and inflict as much damage as possible on it.

São Salvador, the first capital of Brazil, had been founded in 1549

* The Protestant states of the lowlands.
† At this time Portugal, and thus Brazil, was under the Spanish Crown. The Dutch were attacking their hated enemies here in order to get a base for further operations against the Spanish Main and shipping in the Caribbean.

Brass naval gun, ca. 1620, the standard heavy broadside piece of the period.
Photograph of a model in the Smithsonian Institution

and through the years had been strongly fortified. The upper city, built on a high hill above the bay, was walled and defended by three fortresses, which commanded the harbor as well. The lower city, the commercial section, lay around the shores of the bay at the foot of the hill. The lower town was defended by redoubts at either end of the quay and a battery atop a precipitous rock in front of the quay.

On the morning of May 5 the Dutch attacked. Heyn led the column into the harbor and found the rock fort surrounded by a fleet of fifteen large Spanish vessels, which added greatly to the firepower of the emplacement. Heyn's ship, the *Gelderland*, was met by a shower of iron shot from the ships and fort but, sailing doggedly on, he attacked the position that could do him the most damage—the fort atop the rock and the ships around it. Coming up to the Spanish vessels, with the *Groningen* and *Nassau* close behind, Heyn fought a three-hour artillery duel with the enemy. To his great disgust and ire the rest of the Dutch fleet held back and the three ships bore the brunt of the attack under very hot fire. The decks of the Dutch ships were littered with wounded and dead sailors. Blood ran in the scuppers, and splinters from the ships' gunwales and masts became deadly missiles as they whizzed about after every hit. The captain of the *Nassau* signaled that his ship had been hulled. The critical position of Heyn and his companions must have been apparent to the rest of the Dutch lying off the shore from whence they were directing an ineffective fire against the hill forts. Still they did not come to Heyn's aid.

At this juncture, Heyn displayed that audacity which is ever the quality of the great commander. He called his captains together and ordered boats manned for an attempt at boarding the Spanish ships. Then full of rage, not a little of which was mentally directed against his timorous companions who had failed him, Heyn led the boats against the enemy. The first Spanish ship was taken as the Dutch sailors swarmed up the sides and rigging sword and pistol in hand. The Spanish crew, discovering urgent business ashore, abandoned ship. Quickly Heyn reboarded his boat and led it against the second Spanish vessel.

The Dutch were, it seemed, under a spell and a charm. Against the stiffest fire they rowed on and captured the second ship. At this, panic swept through the Spanish fleet and the water was full of Spaniards abandoning ship and making for the shore. Seven of the Spanish captains had the presence of mind to burn their vessels but eight fell into Heyn's hands. The entire boarding operation had taken thirty minutes and had been performed by fewer than one hundred inspired Dutchmen.

This sudden disaster to the Spanish fleet, which took place before the very eyes of the Spanish garrisons ashore, threw those worthy fighters into a fit of anger. All they could do was shoot since no ships remained with which to attack the Dutch, even if they had had the courage for it. In their fury they seized every firearm and heavy gun they had and rained projectiles of all sizes and shapes onto the Dutch below them in the harbor.

The position of Heyn and his small group of fighters was becoming untenable and Heyn's anger at his shirking comrades was becoming white-hot when voices of reinforcements approaching in small boats were heard through the smoke. Soon fourteen boats from the other ships appeared and Heyn quickly organized the men for an assault on the rock fortress. With his own party of battered troops and the reinforcements Heyn attacked the rock, which was manned by some six hundred men. For the Dutch it was literally do or die—if the assault failed they would be decimated.

It was low tide and around the base of the nine-foot walls was a slippery ledge only two or three feet wide. Onto this ledge sprang the Dutch almost to a man; some crouched so that others could stand on their backs and vault to the top of the wall. We are told that a trumpeter was first, and Piet Heyn, sword waving, was second, to reach the top of the battlements.

As the Dutch swept over the wall, those Spanish who had not already taken to boats in a panic, threw down their arms, and jumping to shallow water on a tongue of rock that was almost exposed at low tide, escaped to shore. The rock fort had fallen in minutes and by 8 P.M., with darkness closing in, the place was secured. Realizing he would be very foolish to remain on the rock through the night, Heyn had the guns spiked and the magazines blown up. Then, taking what loot they could, the Dutch withdrew to their ships lying in the harbor.

An anxious night was spent by the Dutch aboard their vessels only yards from the enemy on shore, but no harm came to them. Adding to Heyn's concern was the fact that the rest of the ships under Admiral Willekens still lay at the mouth of the bay without sending any word. The next morning, to his great surprise and relief, Heyn found the Dutch had stealthily occupied the lower town during the night. The quiet that pervaded the upper town led the Dutch to hope that the Spanish had evacuated it, as they had the lower town, and walking up to the gates they saw a lone man with a white flag. The bridge was lowered, the gates opened and the Dutch were politely invited to come in. The entire Spanish garrison had scurried into the surrounding woods leaving the civilians quivering with terror in their houses.

The Dutch soldiers and sailors, bursting into the city, could not be restrained by their officers, if indeed they tried to restrain them, and the pillage which ensued was not a credit to the Dutch character. We must remember that the Dutch had suffered the same treatment from the Spanish many times during the cruel wars in the Lowlands, and judged in the light of the times, such wholesale thievery was an accepted aspect of warfare. Every house, every shop, all the churches and public buildings were stripped. The inhabitants saved nothing except the little which had been spirited out of the town during the attack and the night before the occupation. Tradition tells us that Piet Heyn himself was strongly opposed to the looting and would have nothing to do with robbing private citizens, but his attitude toward the property of the King of Spain was quite different, as we shall see.

After securing the town with a garrison, the Dutch squadron set sail for home with eight prizes deeply laden with sugar, wines, oils, and spices. Word of the victory flashed across the Continent—the Dutch, with a small fleet manned by a thousand seamen and soldiers, had taken a larger Spanish fleet and had captured a Spanish stronghold with a garrison of twice as many Spaniards. The reception the fleet received on returning home was affectionate and joyful.

The personal reaction of Philip IV of Spain must be imagined. The official reaction of the Spanish government was forceful indeed. Within two years, the Spanish recaptured São Salvador and jailed the remains of the Dutch garrison.

After returning to the Netherlands from his startling victory at São Salvador, Heyn had been promoted to admiral and had been sent out with a fleet of nine men-of-war and five yachts.* With these he cruised against Spanish shipping and inflicted great losses. In 1626 his squadron was ordered to join Admiral Boudewyn in the West Indies to attack the Spanish plate fleet.† Unknown to Heyn, Admiral Boudewyn had died, and while Heyn was hunting for him, Boudewyn's squadron was on the way home. Heyn then went cruising for the enemy and on September 6 did sight a Spanish treasure fleet of forty ships. But Heyn, hot for attacking at once, was outvoted by his more cautious captains and had to suffer the sight of the loot disappearing over the horizon. The rest of the year he spent cruising without result and the following March found him again approaching São Salvador determined to attack the place. On learning that a large Spanish fleet lay in the harbor, Heyn decided to sail in at once and all the arguments of his captains could not dissuade him. As usual, Heyn led the way. It was low tide and the channel very narrow permitting only one ship at a time to enter. In this comparatively defenseless position Heyn sailed on against a fleet of superior numbers and force. As the Dutch came within range of the Spanish guns, shot rained upon the attackers. The bay held thirty large well-armed ships and the forts of the city had been reinforced since the disastrous defeat by the Dutch four years before. Heyn sailed straight for the Spanish fleet and came to anchor between the admiral and vice admiral. Then all the guns of Piet's ship thundered, and broadside after broadside poured into the Spanish hulls.

As in the attack of 1623, Heyn was supported by two other ships, which followed closely behind him, and all three anchored among the enemy at point-blank range. Soon heavy smoke filled the bay, and the Dutch could not see that their shot were grievously wounding the Spanish ships. In the midst of the carnage the Spanish had hauled down their ensigns in surrender but the thick smoke prevented Heyn from seeing this and the attack continued. Pulling closer to the vice admiral Heyn fired a full broadside at the waterline almost severing the hull. She sank so quickly that almost all of her crew that had survived the bombardment were drowned.

* A. lightly built and lightly armed sailing vessel used for communication and scouting.
† Treasure fleet.

By this time the other Dutch ships had joined battle and Heyn decided to attack the Spanish with boarding parties. As in the previous attack, the Dutch armed with cutlass, pistol and musket poured into the boats and set out for the *Almiranta*. The clambered up the sides and within minutes the flag of the United Provinces flew where the Lions and Castles had been. The same routine, for such it had become, was followed with the other Spanish ships, and as quickly as the Dutch boarded, the Spanish went over the side, swimming, paddling, and floating toward shore. In three hours the harbor was secured.

Heyn's ship was a demasted wreck, full of shot holes at the water-line. While trying to save her after the worst of the battle was over, he was struck by two musket shot fired from shore. At the same time another Dutch ship received a Spanish ball in the main magazine and blew sky high. In these straits Heyn made a wise but uncharacteristic decision. He decided to settle for the captured fleet and not to attack the shore defenses. He transferred his flag to another ship, saved all the equipment and supplies worth taking, and then sailed out of the harbor to the shouted curses of the Spanish whose courage mounted as the Dutch got farther and farther away.

With the Dutch sailed twenty-two prizes, all of the remaining Spanish fleet that was seaworthy. Well away from São Salvador, Heyn gathered all the best cargo into four of the prizes and burned the others. Again the Dutch received Heyn with great joy, and why shouldn't they? Here they had an audacious, able, and completely fearless commander who seemed to lead a charmed life and always brought home the loot. Heyn as usual seemed a little disgusted with the enthusiasm his countrymen displayed for the material results of his forays rather than the military accomplishments which called forth the best instincts of the fighting man. But the Dutch West India Company was not in the business of making heroes, just money, and Piet, the romantic and fighter, was lost among the merchants.

Piet's last great feat was distinguished mostly for material gain and hardly at all for bravery and military prowess. In fact, it saved the almost bankrupt Dutch government from financial collapse.

The ambition of every sea commander, great and small, of this period was to capture an entire Spanish treasure fleet. Up to then, only single ships had been taken. Like all of his fellows on the Protestant and anti-Spanish side of the fence, Heyn had long dreamed of such a capture. As we have seen, he had missed one only because he had permitted his more cautious captains to dissuade him from attacking.

Upon returning from his second successful attack on São Salvador, Piet had refitted and had sailed out again in May 1628. The country was in very bad financial condition. Public debts were unpaid and the government was straining its credit to survive; the navy was mutinous and seamen were demonstrating before the Dutch parliament; the admiralty board was attacked by a mob of sailors, their families, and probably the sailors' creditors. The central government was having trouble collecting taxes from some of the provinces and was borrowing money at eighteen percent interest. By November things were in a most critical state and the States-General was sitting at The Hague.

On the evening of May 18 a messenger arrived in the city and brought news which was so astonishing that the members of the parliament could hardly believe their ears. One of Heyn's fast yachts had just arrived at Rotterdam with the news that the squadron had captured an entire Spanish treasure fleet with loot valued at 12 million dollars. Some 140 miles west of Bermuda, on his way home with the loot, Heyn had sat down in his cabin on the *Amsterdam* and dictated to a clerk the letter which had just arrived in Rotterdam. This letter, which has come down to us in a unique pamphlet, is the only existing account of the capture in Heyn's own words:

Honorable, learned, wise, cautious, very discreet Gentlemen:
Since 21 June last, when the ship *Orange-boom* of Dordrecht with destination on the coast of Guinea, left us near the island of Palma, we have not had the opportunity to inform you of what happened to us on our voyage, as we have not met with other ships since. It would have been unwise to send you an express or advice boat before the accomplishment of something worthwhile, the more so as we hoped each day to find something good in view of the fact that we arrived at our destination, Cape S. Antonio, in the best time of the season, namely the 4th of August. We hoped to accomplish something worthwhile, since our fleet had not been discovered by the enemy until the 23rd of August, when we were seen by the Spaniards of Havana when we stayed near there a few days to look for the fleet of Mexico with their silver ships. The same day we were discovered, the governor of Havana, Don Lorenzo de Cabrera, sent out some advice boats to inform the aforesaid treasure fleets of our presence before Havana with 25 ships. It proves to have been God's will that these advice boats [had] missed the others and that one of them fell into our hands so that we could obtain all necessary information from it; through it I came to know that no ships had yet arrived in Havana, and that they were awaited there with anxiety. Also, that we were discovered by the Spaniards in Havana, as told above. Consequently, we went to Havana to see whether in the meantime, after the departure of the advice boats, some ships had entered Havana.
We came within shot of the harbour so that we could see everything

clearly. We found that there were no ships except for a galleon which had been built there and two other small ships, which checked very well with what the captured Spaniards had told us; this encouraged us and we hoped to achieve something good.

We decided to stay about two or three miles W. of Havana as the Spaniards who want to go to Havana ordinarily keep to the land. The third September the wind was from the south with a fresh breeze, which kept up for three or four days and caused us to drift away from Havana in a N.E. direction since the current was E. In the morning of the 7th September Vice Admiral Banckerts joined us with the ships *Neptune, Goude Zon, Munnekendan, Dolfijn,* the ship *Gouden Leeuw* and the yacht *Postpaard,* which ships now joined us for the first time. They intended to stay near the Cabeça dos Martires in accordance with your instructions, but I made them join us till we had more news about the Spanish ships.

On the 8th of September, at sunrise, we saw 12 sails to the N. of us. We did our best to get at them, presuming them to be the fleet from Mexico; we got nine of their ships, both small and large. We saw eight other ships most of them against the wind from us, viz., in the S.E., at such a distance that they could be seen from the topmast. We went at them after the capture of the said nine ships. But some of our ships which were in the wind from us got there before we did, as I had first to deal with our prizes, which is too complicated to tell here. But we followed immediately and did our best to block their way to Havana. Notwithstanding this, three of the enemy ships passed in front of us and we chased them. When I saw that we got to the leeward, I ordered three of our ships and one yacht to get at them, with the result that two of the enemy ships were chased aground. I did everything possible to sail to the Spanish ships that were to the windward of us, presuming them to be galleons as we had not found such ships among the prizes that we took. The aforesaid enemy ships sailed before the wind in the direction of the port of Matanzas. The Spanish admiral's ship and the vice admiral's carried even topgallant sails on the topmast on which ordinarily the flag is flown, which shows that they did everything possible to reach the aforesaid harbor or port of Matanzas in a hurry; they arrived there between light and dark, but we followed them close at their heels.

The foremost of our pursuing ships were the following: the ships *Vergulde Valk, Hollandia, Dolfijn,* and the yacht *Tijger.* These ships, when arriving at the entrance of Matanzas Bay, brailed their sails, waiting for my orders. In the meantime, Vice Admiral Banckerts arrived near these foremost of our ships and entered the bay. The ships, seeing this, followed him. When I arrived at the entrance of Matanzas Bay, I fired a gun and made two fires to signal the foremost ships to wait and the ships behind us to go in the direction of the firing and the

Capture of the Honduras Squadron by Piet Heyn in Matanzas Bay, Cuba.
From a Dutch engraving of the period

fires. When I came near the enemy ships, most of our foremost ships
had already anchored and three or four were put aground on a sandbank in the middle of the bay. I passed this bank, on which were our
grounded and anchored ships, with full sail until I came at about half a
musket-shot distance from the enemy ships. Here I dropped the anchor,
but we touched ground; we then fired some shots at the enemy ships. In
the meantime the boat of the ship *Hollandse Tuijn* came to our ship as
also the boat of the *Utrecht* and of the *Haarlem* fully manned with
musketeers and others; I manned the boat of the *Roode Leeuw* with
crew from my own ship. I went myself in the boat of the *Hollandse
Tuijn* and together with the other boats we proceeded to the enemy
ships to see what could be done there. In the other boats were the
following captains or skippers, viz., Rear Admiral Kornelis Klaasz, Captain Aalbert Hendriksz of the *Roode Leeuw*, Captain Frans Klaasz of
the *Haarlem*, and also some commissioners and officers.

We came first to the ship of the Spanish vice admiral in which there
still was a good number of Spaniards, who at first tried to defend her.
We attacked with a musket charge and boarded her, calling to them:
"*Buena guerra*,"* which caused the Spaniards to put down their muskets and go below deck. As soon as I had put things in order there, I

---

* "Good war"; in other words, "Let us have a good one." Presumably the enthusiasm of the Dutch demoralized the Spanish.

went with the other boats to the Spanish admiral's ship, the rear admiral's and another big ship, which had partly been boarded by the other boats. When we came to the admiral's ship, I opened a charge of musket fire and boarded her, calling "*Buena guerra*"; the Spaniards laid their weapons down and went below deck. In the meantime, a Spaniard jumped overboard with the intention to swim ashore but we took him in our boat. Then and there I asked him how many Spaniards were still aboard; he said that there were about 150, at which I told him to go back to the ship and to tell the Spaniards that I promised them quarter and that I would put them immediately ashore. The said Spaniard asked me what kind of person I was; I said to him that I was the general of the whole fleet, at which he asked me to let one of our men accompany him so that in coming aboard he would not be killed by our people, in which I consented. The Spaniard, coming aboard his ship, told the Spaniards below deck that the general was aboard and promised them quarter and that they would be put ashore immediately. At which all the Spaniards came up on deck and I had them be put ashore immediately because I feared some confusion between them and our people and consequently some arson because it was night and our people could not be kept in strict order because of the large amount of plunder present.

As soon as the Spaniards were ashore I made order in all the captured ships, which numbered six; no boats or barges were allowed to go to these ships or to leave them. Then I went to my own ship and thanked God Almighty for the good victory he had given us. The other day we brought out the anchors of the captured ships which had been run aground by the Spaniards and made them in order.

On the second day we started to unload the silver as fast as possible and to divide it among all our ships. After the unloading we figured that there were about 46 lasts* of silver, consisting of minted reals of eight as well as bars or plates of silver and silverware, boxes of cochineal, indigo and other things as shown on the enclosed invoice, about 2,851 pieces.

In the aforesaid Spanish admiral's ship were left about 300 boxes of cochineal, indigo and other things. The hides in our ships together with those in the Spanish ships amount to about 37,375 pieces. We have four galleons with us and hope to bring them, with God's help, to the fatherland; two of these are still mostly filled with pelts.

The Spanish admiral's ship has 24 metal [brass] guns, and five more in the hold. The vice admiral's ship has 22 metal guns, the two other ships each 22 iron guns. We have given these ships provisions for three months from our own ships and a good crew, and also provided them

---

* A unit of weight which varied with the commodity weighed. Seamen used the term for a ton. Forty-six tons of silver was not an unheard of amount in a Spanish treasure fleet.

Silver medal of four-dollar weight commemorating Piet Heyn's capture of the treasure fleet in Matanzas Bay, 1628. Struck from silver captured at that time. Photograph by the author

well with ropes and other equipment. Apart from the aforesaid ships we are also taking with us another small ship of about 100 lasts which is mostly laden with hides and campeche wood.

Of our whole fleet the people are, thank God, all together and unharmed. If you Gentlemen think it risky that we return to the fatherland with the largest Spanish ships because of the winter season, then it would be advisable to send us as soon as possible one or two yachts to cruise near the Island of Wight, or one in the Channel, as we have obviously to pass there in the daytime.

I send you now also the decisions and confessions of the Spaniards, the given orders as usual, as well as my daybook kept during this voyage, and also the names of all persons who died in the fleet during this voyage.

Herewith I recommend your honorable, learned, wise, cautious, and very discreet gentlemen in the mercy and protection of the Almighty.

In the ship *Amsterdam* the 26th of September 1628 about 140 miles west of the island of Bermuda.

P. Pietersz. Heyn[4]

The welcome accorded Piet Heyn on his return was magnificent. The whole country celebrated with bonfires, and he was received in state as a visiting prince might have been. All of this was a little embarrassing to him, and he is supposed to have said on one occasion when he was received in triumph at The Hague and had to dine with the Prince of Orange and the King of Bohemia: "See how the people run mad now, because I bring home such treasures for which I have done but little. When I fought for them before and risked my life, they never turned round to look at me."[5] Even if these were not his exact words, they certainly were characteristic of the man and he probably said something very much like them.

The Spanish captain general, Don Juan de Benavides, having run ashore and ignominiously abandoned his ship and three others to the Dutch, had now to report the incident to his king. On October 7 he wrote from Havana a letter rich in excuses in which he reported the loss of the fleet, carefully avoiding those details which showed him and his men to have been incompetent and even cowardly:

> I would like to be able to excuse myself from telling you of the bad luck which watched over the fleet of my command and to have been so lucky that with my death someone else would have written you,* but since God didn't permit things to happen that way, I have to tell you that having left the port of San Juan de Ulúa the 8th of August after an emergency which unmasted the Capitana, and not having seen a note from Spain, or having word from any other parts, I took thirty days to reach the coast of Havana, which I picked up the 8th of September at dawn, finding myself near the port of Matanzas, and at the same time the Dutch fleet of 32 scows came up on me so mighty, as you may be certain from other sources, and (although very unequal to their strength, having two ships of the Armada and two of the merchant service), I continued my course, resolved to die in such a just and inescapable undertaking, until urged by the ship's company to pass up so great a risk to the silver [belonging to] yourself and your merchants. I agreed with this opinion and decided to put in at Matanzas, when I was informed that I could enter with assurance and with very little room for the enemy, the wind dying at night as is customary, to run the fleet aground or burn the ships after as much treasure as possible was removed. I pulled into the bay at night; although it was very bright under the moon, they ran aground (all four ships) on the shallows. . . . I had to order everyone ashore as fast as possible and the ships burned. . . . I jumped into the boat leaving the Capitana fired to burn itself and the rest and having arrived ashore, I found no one . . . the speed and determination with which the enemy boarded our ships left me isolated on shore; meanwhile they shot at the landing barge. They spoiled my return but although I desired it, they missed me seeing all those around me fall dead or wounded. Thus they overpowered our ships and the wealth they were carrying. The luck being as good to them as unhappy to me since I couldn't do anything.[6]

The same day in the same city, the admiral, Don Juan de Leoz, wrote his version of the incident. He described damage to the *Capitana*, which had occurred just after the fleet left San Juan de Ulúa (Vera Cruz). They were forced to return and transfer the captain

---

* During the action Benavides had not seemed inclined to expose himself to any danger.

general's flag to a large merchantman, which was armed as the *Capitana*. Sailing at last on August 8, they left the sight of land quickly. On the sixth of September the fleet was off the coast of Cuba. That evening neither sails nor land was seen but at dawn the next morning a strange ship was sighted, which refused to answer the hails of the Spanish.

> I made topsail and pursued firing . . . to which she replied. . . . We discovered a great number of sails which I took later to be the enemy. I reached my flagship prepared for a fight and all were ready to fight. . . . At the hour of prayers we saw that the Capitana had entered the port of Matanzas, the enemy being already upon us. I was surprised at such resolution finding myself worried by seeing myself without men in my ship who had been in that port,* and obliged to follow the Capitana which grounded later on a shallow which is in the entrance, and I later went behind her and the other two ships of the fleet. And later the enemy rushed the port, and since I was the furtherest, all the ships fired at me. As they were entering I had no power to do more than fire two stern chasers and found myself without people because they all jumped overboard and so I was determined to blow up the ship, but I couldn't do it because they didn't leave me [alone]. The enemy boarded 100 men and I with eight or 10 comrades did as much as we could, which was little; they overcame us, asking for me, they were told . . . that I had gone with the rest ashore, they put us below decks, where I found it easy to change clothes and heave the old ones overboard so they wouldn't know me.[7]

During his stay on board, the admiral had the presence of mind to secure some intelligence on the strength of the Dutch, which he included in his letter. The next morning he and his companions were put ashore. He concludes by placing the decision to enter Matanzas Bay squarely on the captain general:

> It wasn't with my opinion nor of any of the others that came in the other ships, because the General didn't ask anyone. From 7 A.M. my ship was ready and everything in her, even the religious carried guns and were determined to fight and die. . . . the enemy had it all his way, the weather was favorable, such as we never had; he took us by surprise. You will find out from your minister and other people who sailed with us the truth of what happened and I won't forget it until the pain of following instead of leading dies, but it will console me that he [the captain general] may be imprisoned in this port.

* That is, without pilots.

Action between a Spanish galleon and Dutch warships, 1631. From an engraving of the period. Photograph from the Smithsonian Institution

The fact that the admiral at least stayed on his ship and was captured, the fact that he had the presence of mind to give intelligence of the Dutch to the King, the fact that he was not in supreme command, and probably testimony given by witnesses in the investigation saved him from the block, but he was imprisoned for life at Oran on the coast of North Africa. Benavides was imprisoned for two years and then beheaded. The King did not take the loss of his treasure lightly.

Piet Heyn, at fifty, found himself rich and famous, and able to retire from the sea to a comfortable home in Delft. But his retirement was to be short. Perhaps his wild blood simply could not stand the humdrum of such a quiet life. The following April he was offered command of a fleet to attack the Dunkirk pirates who were raising hob with Dutch shipping in the Channel. At first he refused, but when he was offered the titles of admiral in chief and lieutenant general of Holland, he could not resist and accepted the assignment.

He sailed in May 1629 in a single ship to reconnoiter the Channel off Dunkirk. On June 20 he came upon three pirate vessels. Heyn, of course, attacked headlong and in the battle that followed he fell to the deck, cut in two by an enemy shot. In their rage his men captured the pirates and threw all the survivors overboard in revenge, but their great captain was no more. The grief of the Dutch people was equaled only by the joy of the Spanish at having lost one of the greatest scourges of their commerce in the West Indies.

IX

Bermuda,
A Study in Coral and Gold

These Islands of *Bermudos* have euer beene accounted an in-
chaunted pile of rockes, and desert inhabitation for Diuils; but
all the Faries of the rocks were but flocks of birds, and all the
Diuels that haunted the woods, were but heards of swine.
—Captain John Smith, 1610

LIKE A CONTORTED DRAGON, the tiny archipelago of Bermuda
lies on the tip of a gigantic drowned mountain, a sunken
volcanic cone which thrusts itself up from one of the deepest holes in
the Atlantic Ocean. The islands are formed of windblown shells and
coral sands solidified into limestone.

To the west and north of the archipelago, coral reefs fling themselves seaward as if grasping for the ships sailing by in the deep water
offshore. These are the northernmost coral reefs in the world, and the
enormous flats extend as far as fourteen miles out to sea. Since the
beginning of European commerce in America following the voyages of
Columbus, these reefs have been a deathtrap for ships.

Bermuda lies at the northern end of the great shipping route that
extended from the Caribbean basin to Europe and was a sort of sign-
post pointing toward the Old World. Ships leaving the Florida Straits
would reach for Bermuda and were accustomed to take a last fix on the
islands before departing for the long voyage over the trackless Atlantic. There are days in Bermuda when mist and fog obscure the islands,
and pilots often sailed their vessels right onto the reefs and were
wrecked without ever having seen land. In the winter months especially, storms with much thunder and lightning sweep the archipelago,
and the place takes on the quality of another world. This fearsome
aspect and the real dangers of the reefs gave the islands a terrifying
reputation among the superstitious seamen of the day, and the place

became known as the Islands of the Devils—a reputation refuted only after the first English arrived.

While the name of Juan Bermúdez has been given to the islands, their discovery is still obscure. Bermúdez is supposed to have seen them on a voyage from the Caribbean to Spain in 1515. However, a map in Peter Martyr's *Legatio Babylonica*, published in 1511, contains a woodcut map of Spanish America, clearly showing the island labeled "la Bermuda." Perhaps another Bermúdez was the discoverer—Bermúdez is a very common name in Spain. In any case, by the time Cortés's pilot, Antón de Alaminos, sailed from Mexico with some of the treasure of Montezuma in 1519, the islands were known to Spanish navigators and were on the charts.

The earliest description of the islands is found in Gonzalo Fernández de Oviedo's *Sumario de la Historia Natural de las Indias* (1526):

> In the yeere 1515, when I came first to enforme your maiestie of the state of things in India, and was the yeere following in Flanders, in the time of your most fortunate successe in these your kingdoms of Arragon and Castile, whereas at that voyage I sayled aboue the Island Bermuda, otherwise called Garza, being the furthest of all the Ilands that are found at this day in the world, and arriueing there at the depth of eight yards of water, and distance from the land as far as the shot of a piece of ordnance, I determined to send some of the ship to land, as well to make search of such things as were there, as also to leaue in the Iland certaine hogs for increase. But the time not seruing my purpose by reason of contrarie winde, I could bring my ship no neerer the Iland; being twelue leagues in length, and six in breadth, and about thirtie in circuit, lying in the three and thirtieth degree of the north side. While I remayned here, I saw a strife and combat betweene these flying fishes, and the fishes named giltheads, and the fowles called sea mewes, and cormorants, which surely seemed vnto me a thing of as great pleasure and solace as could be deuised. While the giltheads swam on the brim of the water, and sometimes lifted their shoulders above the same, to raise the flying fishes out of the water to drive them to flight, and follow them swimming to the place where they fall, to take and eate them suddenly. Againe on the other side, the sea mewes and cormorants, take many of these flying fishes, so that by this meanes they are neither safe in the Aire, nor in the water. In the selfe same perill and danger doe men liue in this mortal life, wherein is no certaine securitie, neither in high estate, nor in lowe. Which thing surely ought to put vs in remembrance of the blessed and safe resting place which God hath prepared for such as loue him who shall acquiet and finish the trauailes of this troublesome world, wherein are so many dangers, and bring

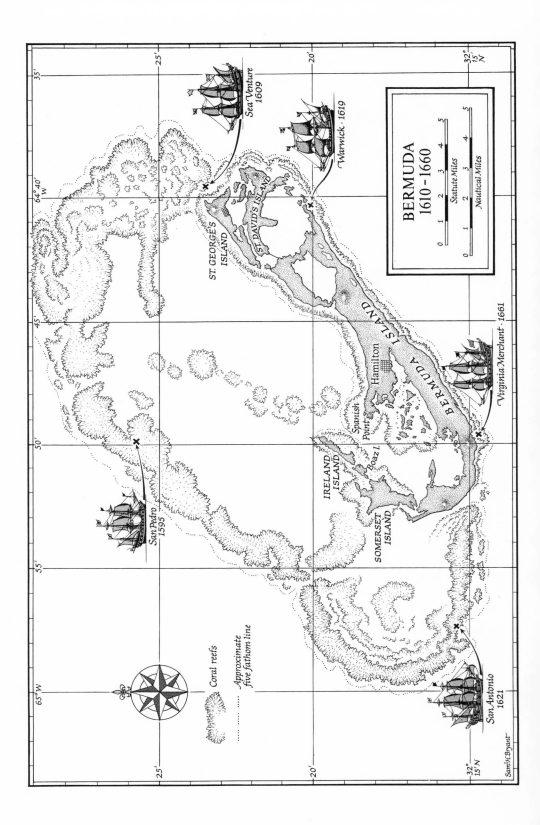

BERMUDA
1610-1660

Statute Miles
0 1 2 3 4 5

Nautical Miles
0 1 2 3 4 5

Sea Venture
1609

Warwick · 1619

ST. GEORGE'S
ISLAND

ST. DAVID'S ISLAND

BERMUDA ISLAND

Hamilton

Spanish
Point

IRELAND
ISLAND

Boaz I.

SOMERSET
ISLAND

Virginia Merchant · 1661

San Pedro
1595

San Antonio
1621

Coral reefs

Approximate
five fathom line

Sam'l Bryant

64° 40' W

65° W

32°
15' N

32°
15'
N

35'

25'

20'

45'

50'

55'

25'

20'

Captain John Smith, who published one of the first accounts of the settlement of Bermuda. From a contemporary engraving

them to that Eternall life where they shall find eternal security and rest.[1]

The statement that hogs were to be landed to increase and presumably to furnish fresh meat to ships going to Spain is interesting. That the islands were overrun by hogs at the time of the settlement by the English is well known. That the islands were a place of great tempests and believed to be inhabited by devils was a current belief in Europe. It is possible that the Spanish did indeed successfully land hogs on the island and that they encouraged the fearsome tales of the place to discourage exploration and possible settlement by the enemies of Spain. The strategic location of the islands in relation to the treasure route from the New World certainly did not escape the Spanish administrators. This thought probably lay behind an offer made in 1527 by a Portuguese named Camelo, a native of the Azores, to transport a colony to the islands and start plantations there after "learning that the king was desirous of peopling the island." Nothing came of this proposal, and the islands remained deserted, although there is no reason to doubt that groups of Spanish sailors visited the islands occasionally in search of provisions and water, or just to have a look. Some of these visits must have been unintentional, since shipwrecks must have occurred on the reefs throughout the sixteenth century. Occasional finds of Spanish coins appear to confirm this. J. Henry Lefroy quotes Sir William Monson as mentioning the wreck of a Frenchman, a Captain Russel, and fixes the date between 1560 and 1570. Captain John Smith states: "Our men [that is, the first English settlers] found divers crosses, pieces of Spanish monies here and there. Two or three wracks also they found by certain inscriptions to be some Spanish, some Dutch, some French."[2]

The first shipwreck of which we have any direct documentation was that of a French vessel commanded by one Captain Barbotière. Henry May, an English sailor who was returning to England in the ship, has left a narrative. In 1591, May had sailed with an English merchant flotilla to the West Indies on a trading venture. After a time, he was transferred by his captain to the French vessel in order that he might return to England with a report on the progress of the trading. He sailed with Captain Barbotière on November 30, 1593, from Laguna, Hispaniola. His dispassionate account of the shipwreck vividly describes these all-too-frequent tragedies and the hardships suffered by survivors:

> The 17 of December next insuing [says he], it was his fortune to haue his ship cast away vpon the Northwest part of the Isle of Bermuda about midnight, the pilots making themselues at noone to be to the southward of the Island twelve leagues, certified the Captain that they were out of all danger. So they demanded of him their wine of height, the which they had. And being, as it should seeme, after they had had their wine, carelesse of their charge which they tooke in hand, being as it were drunken, through their negligence a number of good men were cast away; and I being but a stranger among fifty and odde Frenchmen and others, it pleased God to appoint me to be one of them that were saued. I hope to his seruice and glory. We made account at the first that we were cast away, hard by the shore being hie cliffs, but we found ourseues seuen leagues off, but with our boat and a raft, which we had made and towed at our boats sterne, we were saued some twenty-six of vs; among whom were no more English but myselfe. Now being among so many strangers, and not seeing roome for the one halfe, I durst neither presse into the boat, nor vpon the raft for fear lest they should

haue cast me ourboord, or els haue killed me; so I stayed in the ship, which was almost full of water, vntill the captaine being entred the boat called me vnto him, being at hand, for that it stood vpon life or death: and so I presently entred, leauing the better halfe of our company to the mercy of the sea. After this we rowed all the day vntil an hour or two before night yer we could come on land, towing the raft with the boat. When we came on shore, being all the day without drinke, euery man tooke his way to see if he could find any; but it was long before any was found. At length one of the pilots digging amoung a company of weeds found fresh water, to all our great comforts being only raine water; and this was all the water we found on shore. But there are in this Island many fine bayes wherein if a man did dig, I thinke there might be found store of fresh water. This Island is diuided all into broken Islands; and the greatest part I was vpon, which might be some four or five miles long, and two miles and a halfe ouer, being all woods, as Cedar and other timber, but Cedar is the chiefest. Now it pleased God before our ship did split, that we saued our Carpenters tooles, els I thinke we had bene there to this day; and hauing recouered the aforesaid tooles, we went roundly about the cutting downe of trees, and in the end built a small barke of some eighteen tons, for the most part with tronnels and very few nailes. As for tackling we made a voyage aboord the ship before she split; and cut down her shrouds, and so we tackled our barke, and rigged her. In stead of pitch we made lime, and mixed it with the oyl of tortoises, and as soone as the carpenters had calked, I and another, with ech of vs a small sticke in our hands, did plaister the mortar into the seames, and being in April, when it was warm and faire weather, we could no sooner lay it on, but it was dry, and as hard as a stone. In this moneth of April 1594, the weather being very hot, we were afrayd our water should fayle vs; and therefore made the more haste away; and at our departure we were constrayned to make two great chests, and calked them, and stowed them on ech side of our mainmaste, and so put in our prouision of raine water and thirteen liue tortoises for our food, for our voyage which we intended to Newfoundland.

In the South part of this Island of Bermuda there are hogs, but they are so leane that you cannot eat them, by reason the Island is so barren, but it yieldeth great store of fowle, fish and tortoises. And to the eastward of the Island are very good harbours, so that a shippe of 200 tun may ride there landlocked, without any danger, with water enough.

Also in this island is as good fishing for pearles as is any in the West Indies, but that the place is subject to foule weather, as thundering lightning and raine; but in April and part of May we had very faire and hot weather.

The 11 May it pleased God to set vs cleare of the Island, to the no little joy of vs all, after we had liued in the same almost the space of five moneths, and the 20 of May we fell with the land nere to cape Briton, where we ran into a fresh water riuer, whereof there be many, and tooke in wood, water, and ballast, and here the people of the country came vnto vs, being clothed all in furs with the furred side vnto their skins, and brought with them furres of sundry sorts to sell, besides great store of wild ducks; so some of our company hauing saued some small beads bought some of their ducks. Here we stayed not aboue foure hours, and so departed. This should seeme to be a very good country. And we saw very fine champion ground and woods. From this place we ranne for the banke of Newfoundland, whereas we met with diuers, but none would take in a man of vs, vntill it pleased God that wee met with a Barke of Falmouth, which receiued vs all for a little time; and with her we tooke a French ship. Wherein I left Capitan de la Barbotier, my deere friend, and all his Company, and stayed myself aboord the English barke, and hauing passage in the same, in the moneth of August I arriued at Falmouth, 1594.[3]

A year or two after May's voyage, a Spanish vessel left the Caribbean to return to Spain and was wrecked off Bermuda. She was a small vessel armed with cast-iron falcons that fired balls of about three pounds weight, and with *versos*, long, wrought-iron breech-loading swivels, mounted on her gunwales to defend against boarders. Her sailors were armed with cutlasses and small axes, while the soldiers aboard were equipped with the arquebuses and the heavier muskets. The captain and commander of the soldiers wore steel breastplates and helmets. In the hold were the natural products of the New World— leather, cassia pods, probably some tobacco and cotton, as well as cochineal and indigo. In the cabin, under the protection of the officers, was a treasure of silver pieces of eight and pieces of four, gold bars, gold ingots (called quoits by the English), and jewelry. There may have been a high-ranking churchman aboard the vessel, for when the wreck was discovered and explored 375 years later, the site produced a magnificent emerald-studded cross and a suite of pearl-studded gold buttons suitable for the robes of a bishop. Also on board was an intellectual interested in native cultures, or at least a collector of curiosities, for the site yielded a Carib chieftain's black palmwood staff of office and black palmwood bows and arrows.

It is doubtful if anyone survived the disaster. The ship came over the northwest reef flats in a terrific storm, which probably mortally wounded the hull. It finally struck a large coral head, which tore out the bottom and part of one of her sides, dumping her ballast, artillery, cargo, crew, and treasure into a hole thirty-five to forty feet deep. The great section torn from the bottom plummeted to the sandy bottom of the hole under the weight of the tons of flint ballast and iron guns. The deck and rigging of the vessel were swept on by the rushing wind and water, to sink far away in some yet-undiscovered spot. The end probably came quickly for the unfortunate people aboard, death by drowning or battering on the coral heads ending their terror and suffering. In 1950 the site was discovered by two Bermudian divers, Teddy Tucker and Robert Canton. At first, iron guns and a great copper pot containing the lead ball for the arquebuses and muskets were recovered and sent to the museum of the Bermudian government. Five years later, Tucker and Canton returned to the sand-lined hole, and within a week recovered an archaeological treasure of late-sixteenth-century material without parallel.

The site has taught us much of the weapons with which the ships of the period were armed. For example, we know the small arms fired lead balls joined by copper wire in erratic but deadly flight—the earliest examples yet found. We know the ship was armed with spike or pike shot—a normal round iron cannonball with two spikes projecting from it—which was wrapped with tar-soaked marline and when fired sailed flaming through the air to stick in the sides or masts of an enemy ship, perhaps setting it afire. The guns were able also to fire bar shot, which slid open as it whirled through the air at the target, expanding from sixteen inches to a deadly whirligig over two feet long, ripping sails and rigging and killing personnel on the exposed decks. If an enemy drew close and sought to board, the defenders had fine brass hand grenades with threaded brass fuses, the earliest examples of this important weapon yet found. The swivel guns fired not only lead and iron balls, but also could spray the enemy decks with round flint pebbles, an effective and cheap projectile.

To this date, even though other important sites of the sixteenth century have been uncovered in the New World, the Tucker-Canton find remains the richest historically of any discovery in the Western Hemisphere. The emerald cross is without equal for beauty and historical and intrinsic value, being the most valuable single object known to have come from the sea in modern times. The identity of this ship has not been discovered. Perhaps the secret died with the people in her when she sank, or perhaps it rests, yet undiscovered, in some bundle of documents in the Archives of the Indies in Seville.

We may safely assume that by the time of the settlement of Bermuda, the islands had a long history of shipwreck. Her waters were even then littered with wreckage of the unfortunate victims of the reefs. When settlement came, it also was the result of shipwreck. Two years after the first settlement of Virginia, the colony was a malarial-

Brass case for a small sand glass

Brass navigator's dividers

Gold bar of over forty ounces. Stamps indicate 21 3/10 carats fine gold and that the tax had been paid

Iron falconet firing a three-pound ball. The carriage is a reproduction based on fragments recovered from the site. The carriage is unique in that it slid on skids rather than rolled on trucks.

Top: sections of gold bars and gold filigree buttons studded with conch pearls. Middle: two gold "quoits" and the emerald-studded pectoral cross. Bottom: A gold bar of about forty ounces, marked with carat marks (21 3/10 carats), tax stamps and the name "Pinto," indicating that the gold came from the Pinto River in New Granada

Gold ingot weighing approximately two pounds

Gold bar of about six ounces

infested sinkhole in a swamp. The colonists were sunk in despair, hungry, terrified of the natives, and ready to abandon the place and return to England. The Virginia Company members, in the comparative comfort of England, were not yet ready to quit. Their money was at stake and they were still encouraged to think the project a good one, and relief expeditions with supplies and additional colonists were being sent out.

In the spring of 1609, a small flotilla of nine vessels sailed from England for Virginia. In the group was the newly built *Sea Venture,* the first really decent ship sent to the colony. Some six hundred miles to the northeast of Bermuda, a terrible storm engulfed the ships. The flotilla was scattered. The *Sea Venture* was not seen by the others again. In the early hours of the storm, she sprang a bad leak and the hold was flooded. The words of Sir George Somers, one of the leaders, describe the storm in a matter-of-fact way:

> May yt please yor good honor to bee advertised that sithence our depture out of England in goinge to Virginia about some 200 leagues from the Bermoodas wee weare taken with a verie greate storme or hurricane which sundred all the fleete & on St Jame's daye beinge the 23 of Julie wee had such a leake in our ship insomuch that there was in her 9 ffote of water before wee knewe of any such thinge wee pumped with ij pumpes and bailed in iij or iiij places with certaine Barrackoos & and then wee kept 100 men alwaies workinge night and daie from the 23rd vntill the 28th of the same Julie being ffridaie (at wch time) wee sawe the Iland of Bermuda, wheare our ship liethe vpon the rocke, a quarter of a mile distant from the shoare wheare wee saved all our liues & afterwards saued much of our goodes, but all our bread was wet & lost.[4]

Sir George Somers, one of the real heroes of the first English settlement of North America, was too modest to have recounted his own efforts at saving the *Sea Venture.* His physical courage, doggedness and, above all, optimism in the face of what was apparently a hopeless situation inspired the crew and passengers of the ship to the almost superhuman effort required to save them. A contemporary narrative by Silvanus Jordan, a passenger, published in London in 1610, describes the event:

> I being in ship called the Sea-venture, with *Sir Thomas Gates* our Gouernour, *Sir George Sommers* and captain *Newport,* three most worthy honoured Gentlemen (whose valour and fortitude the world

must needes take notice of, and that in most Honourable designes) bound for Virginia in the height of thirty degrees of northerly latitude, or thereabouts; we were taken with a most sharpe and cruell storme vpon the five-and-twentieth day of July, Anno 1609, which did not onely separate vs from the residue of our fleet (which were eight in number), but with the violent working of the seas our ship became so shaken, torne, and leaked, that shee receiued so much water as couered two tire of hogsheads aboue the ballast: that our men stood vp to the middles, with buckets, baracos and kettles to baile out the water, and continually pumped for three dayes and three nights together, without any intermission; and yet the water seemed rather to increase, then to diminish: insomuch that all our men vtterly spent, tyred and disabled for longer labour, were euen resolued, without any hope of their liues, to shut vp the hatches, and to haue committed themselues to the mercie of the sea (which is said to be merciless) or rather to the mercie of their mightie God and Redeemer (whose mercies exceed al his works). Seeing no helpe, nor hope, in the apprehension of man's reason, that any mother's childe could escape that ineuitable dager, which euery man had proposed and digested to himselfe of present sinking. So that some them hauing some good and comfortable waters in the ship fetcht them, and drunke one to the other, taking their last leaue one of the other, vntill their more joyfull and happy meeting in a more blessed world; when it pleased God out of his most gracious and mercifull prouidence, so to direct and guide our ship (being left to the mercy of the Sea) for her most advantage; That Sir George Sommers sitting vpon the Poope of the ship (where he sate three dayes and three nights together, without meales, meate, and little or no sleepe) couning the ship to keep her as vpright as he could (for otherwise shee must needs haue instantly haue foundered), most wishedly and happily descried land: wherevpon he most comfortably encouraged the company to follow their pumping, and by no meanes to sease bayling out of the water, with their buckets, baracos and kettles; whereby they were so ouerwearied, and their spirits so spent with long fasting, and continuance of their labour, that for the most part they were fallen asleepe in corners, and wheresoeuer they chanced first to sit or lie; but hearing newes of land, where-with they grew to be somewhat reviued, being caried with will and desire beyond their strength, euery man bustled vp, and gathered his strength and feeble spirits together, to performe as much as their weake force would permitte them; through which weake meanes it pleased God to work so strangely as the water was staied for that little time (which, as wee all much feared, was the last of our breathing) and the ship kept from present sinking, when it pleased God to send her within halfe an English mile of that land that *Sir George Sommers* had not long before descried; which were the Ilands of the Barmudas, and there neither did our ship sincke, but more fortunately in so great a misfortune fell in betweene two rockes, where shee was fast lodged and locked, for further budging: whereby wee gained not only sufficient time, with the present help of our Boate and Skiffe safelye to set and convey our men ashore (which were one hundred and fiftie in number), but afterwards had time and leasure to saue some good part of our goods and prouision, which the water had not spoyled.[5]

The escape of the crew and passengers of the *Sea Venture* was no less than a miracle. Lost in a storm which reduced visibility to a few yards, with the ship flooded almost to the point of sinking, with the crew and passengers working through four days and four nights to the point of complete exhaustion, the ship made its way without navigation almost completely in the control of the wind and water over hundreds of miles of ocean and struck the one spot in that vast area which offered any hope of salvation. Even if the *Sea Venture* had made the beach, most of those aboard would undoubtedly have perished in the surf; but the vessel stuck between two coral heads which held it securely until the storm passed. And all of this great good fortune would have been of no use if Sir George Somers had not inspired the crew and passengers by his own heroic efforts.

Soon after landing safely, it was evident to the stranded party that they were still blessed with good fortune. The island was green with foliage, thick with cedars, and literally teeming with birds and wild hogs. The birds, hardly ever having seen man, were so tame they could be taken by hand, and their eggs lay in exposed nests by the thousands. The fearful stories about the place had been largely false, and within days the survivors realized they were indeed in a comparative paradise:

Wherefore my opinion sincerely of this Iland is, that whereas it hath beene and is still accounted, the most dangerous, infortunate, and most forlorne place in the world, it is in truth the richest, healthfullest, and pleasing land (the quantitie and bignesse thereof considered), and meerely natural as euer man sat foote vpon: the particular profits and benifits whereof shall be more Especially inserted, and hereunto annexed, which euerie man to his owne priuate knowledge, that was there can avouch and iustifie for a truth. Vpon the eight and twentieth day of July 1609 (after the extremity of the storme and something qualified) we fell vpon the shore of the Barmudas; where after our Generall *Sir Thomas Gates*, Sir George Sommers, and Captaine Newport, had by their prouident carefulnesse Landed all their men and so much of the goods and prouisions out of the ship as was not vtterly spoyled, euerie man disposed and applyed himselfe to search for and to seeke out such

releefe and sustentation as the countrie afforded: and Sir George Sum-
mers, a man inured to extremities (and knowing what thereunto belonged) was in this seruice neither idle nor backwarde, but presently by
his carefull industry went, and found out, sufficient of many kind of
fishes, and so plentifull thereof, that in half an houre he tooke so many
fishes with hookes, as did suffice the whole company one day. And fish
is there so abundant, that if a man steppe into the water, they will come
round about him: so that men were faine to get out for feare of byting.
These fishes are very fat and sweete, and of that proportion and bignesse that three of them will conveniently lade two men: those we
called Rockfish. Besides there are such store of mullets that with a seane
might be taken at one draught one thousand at the least, and infinite
store of Pilchards, with diuers kinds of great fishes, the names of them
vnknown to me: of tray fishes very great ones, and so great store, as
that there hath been taken in one night with making lights, euen sufficient to feed the whole company a day. The countrie affordeth great
abundance of Hogges, as that there hath been taken by *Sir George
Sommers*, who was the first that hunted for them, to the number of two
and thirtie at one time, which he brought to the company in a boate,
built by his owne hands. There is fowle in great number upon the
Ilands, where they breed, that there hath beene taken in two or three
houres, a thousand at the least: the bird being of the bignes of a good
Pidgeon, and layeth egges as big as Hen egges vpon the sand, where
they come and lay them dayly, although men sit downe amongst them:
that there hath beene taken vp in one morning by *Sir Thomas Gates*
men one thousand Egges: and Sir George Sommers men, coming a little
distance of time after them, haue stayed there whilst they came and
layed their eggs amongst them, that they brought away as many more
with them; with many young birds very fat and sweet . . . with other
birds so tame and gentle, that a man walking in the woods with a sticke,
and whistling to them, they wil come and gaze on you so neare that you
may strike and kill many of them with your sticke, and with singing
and hollowing you may doe the like. There are also great store of
Tortoises (which some call turtles), and those so great, that I have
seene a bushell of egges in one of their bellies, which are sweeter than
any Henne egge: and the Tortose itselfe is all very good meate, and
yieldeth great store of oyle, which is as sweete as any butter: and one
of them will suffice fifty men a meale at least: and of these hath beene
taken great store, with two boates at the least forty in one day.

The party of 140 men and women remained in Bermuda in comparative comfort and plenty until May 10, 1610. Sir George Somers, the
governor, and other officers surveyed the island and organized the
gathering of food fish, hogs, and bird eggs, as well as less palatable
cedar and palmetto berries and prickly pears. Soon after landing, the

longboat was fitted out as a pinnace, decked over with the hatches from the wreck. Under the command of Henry Ravens, master's mate, and a crew of six sailors, the boat got clear of the islands on the southeast on September 1, 1609. With them went Thomas Whittingham, the cape merchant, with letters from the stranded governor to the officers and gentlemen in Virginia. Until the following May when the party escaped the islands, the small community lived in palmetto-thatched huts, with the men devoting most of their time to hunting, fishing, and building two small vessels which were to free them from the islands. Life gained almost a semblance of normalcy, and during the period one murder occurred—the murderer being sentenced to death by hanging, a sentence commuted by the governor after the escape of the prisoner and the intercession of many of his sailor friends. Two babies were born, a boy and a girl, the boy Bermudas and the girl Bermuda. Three mutinies occurred, with the last ending in the execution of the alleged leader, a gentleman named Henry Paine. One marriage ceremony was performed. By the beginning of May 1610, the two small vessels were completed. The work was speeded by the realization that the longboat, not being heard from, must have been lost at sea.

> Wee had brought our Pinnasse so forward by this time, as the eight and twentieth of August we hauing laid her Keele, the sixe and twentieth of February, we now began to calke: old Cables we had preserued vnto vs, which affoorded Ocam enough: and one barrell of Pitch, and another of Tarre, we likewise saued, which serued our vse some little way vpon the Bilg, wee breamed her otherwise with Lime made of Wilkeshels, and an hard white stone which we burned in a Kiln, slaked with fresh water, and tempered with Tortoyses Oyle. . . . Shee was fortie foot by the Keele, and nineteene foot broad at the Beame, sixe foote floore, her Rake forward was fourteene foot, her Rake aft from the top of her Post (which was twelue foot long) was three foot, shee was eight foot deepe vnder her Beame, betweene her Deckes she was foure foot and an halfe. . . . The most part of her timber was Cedar, which we found to be bad for shipping, for that it is wonderous false inward, and besides it is so spault or brickle, that it will make no good plankes, her Beames were all Oke of our ruined ship, and some plankes in her Bow of Oke, and all the rest as is aforesaid. When shee began to swimme (vpon her launching) our Gouernour called her *The Deliuerance*, and shee might be some eighty tunnes of burthen. . . .
>
> About the last of Aprill, *Sir George Summers* launched his Pinnasse, and brought her from his building Bay, in the Mayne Iland, into the Channell where ours did ride, and shee was by the Keele nine and

twentie foot: at the Beame fifteene foot and an halfe: at the Loofe fourteene, at the Transam nine, and she was eight foot deepe, and drew sixe foote water, and hee called her the *Patience*.[6]

On the tenth of May, the vessels were loaded and the party left for Virginia. Three men remained behind. Ten days later, Virginia was sighted after a voyage as peaceful as that to Bermuda had been stormy. Thus rescued, the voyagers joined the Jamestown colony, most of them dying in the starving times which were to come.

Within three years of the wreck of the *Sea Venture*, Bermuda had a permanent colony. The richness of the islands in food and the mild climate had aroused interest in the place, and the Bermuda Company had been organized as an offshoot of the Virginia Company. The struggling colony suffered the poverty which was the lot of most new colonies, but the people never wanted for food as did the starving Virginians.

The colony became a way station on the route from England to Virginia, and ships normally stopped there to take on water and food before continuing the voyage to the American mainland. One such vessel, the *Warwick*, arrived October 20, 1619, with the new governor, Nathaniel Butler. The day after the arrival, the acting governor, Captain Miles Kendall, and his council went aboard the *Warwick* to welcome Butler. After compliments were exchanged, Butler entertained them as best as he could with a dinner on board. The *Warwick* was anchored near the Kings Castle, which guarded the entrance to the harbor and was fortified with gun platforms and heavy ordnance. The governor and council were treated to the dubious pleasure of seeing the gun platform burn accidentally. More disasters were to come as portents of a troubled term for Butler. The last days of November, a terrible storm suddenly arose and drove the *Warwick* against the cliffs of rock below which she was anchored. The ship drove abeam against the shore and then capsized toward the harbor, settling in the thick, light silt on her beams ends. Later some guns were recovered, but other attempts to recover the rest of the ship's battery were frustrated by the lashings which had tightened as they were soaked with water, binding the guns firmly to the slanted deck and preventing their removal by the primitively equipped divers who were working on the wreck. While the loss of the *Warwick* was a financial blow to the owners, in human terms it was not a disaster since the crew escaped. Bermuda was to wait almost forty years before a disaster of major proportions befell a Virginia-bound ship on her shores. But the wreck of the *Warwick* was a portent of trouble for Governor Butler, whose last year in office was clouded with a scandal involving another shipwreck that occurred less than two years after the *Warwick* sank.*

When it became evident to the Spanish that the English heretics were settling Bermuda, there was great concern at the Spanish court. Bermuda, lying as it did across the great treasure route from the New World to Spain and marking a pivotal point on that route, was of strategic interest to the Spanish ministers. In the hands of a well-organized and determined enemy, the islands could become a serious threat to the flow of treasure from America to Spain. What the Spanish did not know at the time was that the Bermudians were poorly organized and less determined. Since they lived on a subsistence level with plenty for themselves but little surplus to send to England for the goods they could not produce, and since they were divided into squabbling factions and not inclined to overwork themselves in fortifying the islands, much less build and maintain a squadron of vessels capable of preying on the passing Spanish fleets, the islands were really no threat at all in themselves. As a base from which armed English vessels might operate against the dons, however, they were a potential threat, and the Spanish kept a close watch on them. On several occasions during the early years of the Colonies, Spanish ships came in to view the harbor and sometimes actually sailed into it, one even blowing up near Kings Castle. The only effect this had on the Bermudians was to temporarily inspire the more desultory to help with the work on the forts, which were being built to protect the entrances to the harbors serving the struggling town of St. George. The real threat of Bermuda to the Spanish fleets remained the natural hazards of the far-reaching coral reefs, waiting to entrap the ships that became lost in the local fogs and storms. Such a ship was the *San Antonio.*

The *San Antonio*, of 300 tons, in the company of other vessels set sail from Cartagena in the summer of 1621. Her cargo was of the usual nature of most American cargos bound to Spain from the Caribbean basin in that period—a treasure of gold, silver, and precious gems, and the more mundane, but no less economically important, products of forest and farm—hides, tanned leather, tobacco, indigo, cochineal, mahogany, and lignum vitae. In addition, the ship carried some goods from the Manila trade, which served Spain with the products of the

* In the summer of 1967, an expedition led by the author and sponsored by the Explorers Research Corporation, an adjunct of the Explorers Club of New York, in company with Teddy Tucker of Bermuda, explored the area in which the *Warwick* was believed sunk. The remains of the ship were located, and a preliminary exploration was carried out. A full-scale exploration and recovery of the remains of the vessel have yet to be done.

Far East by way of the Manila Galleon, Acapulco, and Vera Cruz. These goods must have been put aboard when the ship stopped at Havana to resupply for the voyage across the Atlantic. There were Chinese porcelain and stone beads, but a large shipment of cowrie shells from the Indian Ocean basin was a more unusual item of commerce. These little shells were highly valued on the west coast of Africa by the native chiefs who supplied the Spanish with slaves. There was also a shipment of small copper ingots from the mines of Mexico, also for use in the slave trade.

Sailing from Havana in late August, the *San Antonio* approached the western reefs of Bermuda on the eleventh of September in a storm. The next day the ship drew closer to her doom in weather that obscured the islands and reduced the visibility of the reefs flats. Just before sunset, the ship struck a coral head and stove in her bow planks, sinking quickly by the bow. Seeing their ship lost, twenty sailors seized the only boat and left the officers and passengers to their fate. As the boat was leaving, a boy of fourteen jumped from the ship to get into it but could not reach it. At that moment, a chest from the ship drifted by and the boy climbed on. The chest drifted out of sight in the gloom, and the survivors on the stern, which had remained out of the water, gave up the lad for lost. All through a terror-filled night, the men labored to build a large raft from the timbers of the ship and the next day successfully made the shore near Mangrove Bay in Sandys Parish about seven in the morning. The ship's carpenter landed nearby from a plank on which he had floated to shore. Captain John Smith, in his *General Historie of Virginia*, recounts one poignant episode which ended happily: "There was a Gentlewoman that had stood wet up to the middle upon the raft from the ship to the shore, being big with childe; and although this was upon the thirteenth of September, she tooke no hurt, and was safely delivered of a Boy within three daies after."[7] Smith also reports a happy ending for the young lad who rode the chest off into the night: "It pleased God he got upon a chest adrift by him, whereon they report he continued two daies, and was driuen neere to the cleane contrary part of the Ile, where he was taken up neere dead, yet well recovered."

When the Spanish landed at Mangrove Bay, a great alarm swept the islands. The *San Antonio* and her consorts had been sighted off the western end of the islands before the wreck, and the startled Bermudians at first thought that an invasion was taking place. The governor armed the forts to the east* and marched westward with a party of

---

* The western reaches of the islands were not fortified at this time.

twenty armed men, determined to defend his territory. Here they discovered the distressed Spaniards and set about to relieve their suffering. The twenty sailors who had taken the boat the evening before had also taken some of the treasure from the ship. Captain John Smith in his *General Historie of Virginia* says that the governor of Bermuda recovered the money from the mutineers and restored it to the Spanish captain as a purse to care for the survivors. He also says that the Spanish gentlefolk were lodged and boarded at the governor's expense during their stay and that the common persons were lodged and boarded among the Bermudians at a cost of four shillings a week. Smith also says that when the Spanish were finally able to leave the islands, "to express their thankfulnesse at their departure, [they] made a deed of gift to the Governor of Whatsoever he could recover of the wracked ship."

The *San Antonio* had hardly settled underwater when Governor Butler began organizing the salvage operations which were to bring in a considerable amount of treasure and goods. He saw in the wreck a chance to get some quick wealth, a perfectly normal reaction and one which was usual in these cases at that time. The survival of all the crew and passengers of the ship cramped the governor's style, but he immediately went to the ship and recovered two iron sakers (cannon firing a ball of about six pounds and weighing about three thousand pounds), a cable, and an anchor. It was reported in England "that when the governor came there the ship was split all to pieces and the goods lost."[8] To his credit, Governor Butler also set about to see that the Spanish were cared for as well as Bermuda could provide for them. In a letter to his sergeant major, William Seymour, who handled affairs in the western parishes, Butler said, "I am determined to distribute and disperse them [the Spaniards] throughout the Tribes [parishes], unlesse only such of the principall as goe wth. me to the Towne." He also directed that any money found among the survivors "be ratibly divided for their Generall expense, and that every Baylie [the Bailiff of each Tribe] have a quantity thereof put into his hands for the same purpose, according to the nomber of the Guests his tribe is to find and to quarter, and for the laying out of this money, he be answerable and accountable at their departure from him."[9] This confirms Smith's account of the handling of the Spanish after they landed on the islands.

Before the winds of winter drove the Bermudians from the wreck, several voyages were made to it. The existing records of the colony relating to this are confusing. Butler issued a number of directives in writing to Seymour, and several accounts of the divers with claims for compensation exist, but since some of them are not dated, we cannot tell whether they were issued before the winter weather set in or after diving operations were resumed again in May 1622. We can assume, however, that the salvors used every day of good weather to visit the wreck and recover what they could before the heavier goods sank into the sand or were covered up by the winter storms. In the depositions given in England shortly after the arrival of the Spanish there, silver vessels, silver coins, gold wedges, chains, and coins were mentioned, along with hides, tobacco, and indigo. Some of the tobacco and hides drifted ashore and were picked up, but they proved to be spoiled.

The Spanish were able to obtain passage to England, sailing the last of November. Five were left behind, two because they were diseased and were refused passage. The last days of January, the Spanish landed at Dartmouth, some setting out for London. If we are to believe the depositions given at the interrogation of witnesses on February 22, many of the survivors had gold and silver with which to pay their way. Henry Mansell, cape merchant of the *Joseph*, in which some of the Spanish reached England, stated that "the Spanish boatswain of the ship [*San Antonio*] pawned to him an ingot of gold worth 20 pounds for 8 pounds 8 shillings to pay for their passage.[10] Mansell also testified that he heard Don Fernando de Vera [the ranking Spaniard on the *San Antonio*] and the captain and pilot of the *San Antonio* . . . "acknowledge that they were well used by the Govr. and Inhabitants." A Cheapside goldsmith testified that Spaniards came to him and sold or offered to sell gold ingots and chains. Robert Elliott of Fresh Wharf, Thames Street, London, testified that some of the Spanish had bags of silver coin worth perhaps two hundred English pounds. All of this seems to indicate that the Spanish were not robbed by the Bermudians, but injustices were done to them, or at least they thought so, for the surviviors lost no time in seeing the Count of Gondomar, the Spanish ambassador to the Court of St. James's. In a letter to "Ye Honorable Companie of Marchants of Bermuda" dated February 6, 1621/22,* Gondomar said that

> some of ye passengers having saved themselves by means of ye cockboat,† and ye rest by what other way they could, the said cockboat was taken from them by the English men there without permitting ye Spaniards in no case to return back to save and to benefit themselves of ye goods with which ye said ship was freighted which was great store

* Until the Act of 1750 (which went into effect in 1752) the legal year began March 25. Under the old system dates in the months of January, February and the first twenty-five days of March were expressed with a double year notation. The Act of 1750 changed the date of the beginning of the legal year to January 1.
† The cockboat which, according to Smith, the crew stole and sailed ashore in.

of gold, silver and merchandise to ye value of more than 60,000 crowns*
all which ye English tooke and seized upon even ye artillery and the
rest without giving or restoring anything to ye said Spaniards, not so
much as their apparel.[11]

The ambassador went on to say that the Bermudians had added insult
to injury by offering to sell the Spanish back their clothes "because
they were not made of ye English fashion," even though the Bermudians knew the Spanish had no money left since they had been
robbed of all of it. The ambassador concluded his letter by requesting
that the Bermuda Company "give order that satisfaction may be made
presently for these losses." He further asked that assurance be given
him that the five Spaniards remaining behind as captives would be
released.

Three days later the officers of the Bermuda Company replied to
Gondomar expressing amazement at the ambassador's accusations "instead of those thanks we thought we had deserved for the great respect
and favors which our officers and people there in the Somer Islands
expressed to the company of unfortunate and miserable men so
wrecked."[12] They then went on to deny the recovery of any treasure
from the wrecked ship or pillaging of the Spanish:

> First for the great store of treasure aledged to be taken by or men
> from ye wrack we assure yor excellency we knowe of none at all. for
> gournor affirms to vs that the ship was so suddeinly & violently beaten
> all to shiuers beinge 10 miles of ye land yt he had not recovred any
> thinge of valew out of her saue only two Sakers, the rest of ye goods all
> flotinge away & perishinge in the sea except some little tobacco &
> aneale driuen a shore & taken vp by the people but vtterly spoiled &
> nought worth.
>
> And for yt pillinginge and Riflinge of yor men or Informacōn stands
> thus, yt or gournor vpon complaint by ye captaine and mr of ye ship
> vnderstandinge yt the baser sort of their marinors vpon ye first apre-
> hention of their danger had stolne away from them in ye boate & not
> only left them to ye mercy of ye seas but also caried away wth them all
> such money as could hastily be gotten soe yt the better sort who had
> most right vnto it were thereby vtterly destitute, vpon Justice by them
> herein discreetly demaunded he caused a genrall search to be made &
> recoured from amongst them all to ye quantity of £140 or thereabouts
> the wch before witnes he deliured into ye Captaines hand to be im-
> ployed in a genrall purse towards ye keepinge of them duringe their
> stay there, and soe billited them abrode amongst ye people of yt part

---

* Equivalent to 150,000 pieces of eight.

wherein they were first cast at ye rate of 4s. per week for ye head, only the captaine Pilat & some others of ye chiefest of ye men & women he caused to be conveyed to the towne, wher theie lined ye most part of them at his owne table 9 or 10 weeks and further we knowe not conserninge this nor doe we beleue yt any such misdemeanor.

In conclusion they reminded the ambassador of his faux pas in addressing them as merchants: "And now only conclude for ye better information of yor excellency although you know as well as any what is due to psons of honor & their titles, that we hope it is vpon mistake not purpose yt yor excellency is pleased to stile vs the honorable company of ye Marchants of the Bermudos, we desire yor excellency to know yt sundry of the great peers of this kingdome & knights and gentlemen of quality be aduenturers therein as in a noble action not as marchants wherein we conceyve yor excellency was misinformed."

Two days after the above letter was written, Gondomar replied, addressing the English as "ye right honorable Lords and noble Companie of the Ilands of the Bermudos." The answer given him, he wrote, was not satisfactory, and he would be forced to secure redress by any other means which would offer a way of discharging his obligation to his king and securing satisfaction for the subjects of Spain for their losses and injuries.

The dispute was heating up and the merchants may have received some pressure from the English Crown. At this time James I was pursuing a policy of nonaggression against Spanish possessions in America, quite the opposite to what had happened in the reign of Elizabeth, his predecessor, when the great raids of Drake and Hawkins were carried out even during peacetime. James's policy would have frowned upon the mistreatment of Spanish castaways as alleged by the ambassador. Just eleven days after Gondomar sent his second letter to the Bermuda Company, depositions were being taken of the English crews who had arrived on the ships *Joseph* and *James,* on which most of the survivors had gone to England. Other witnesses having knowledge of the condition of the survivors when they arrived in England were also interrogated on what had actually happened in Bermuda, on the ships bound for England, and after arrival at Dartmouth and London. These depositions were probably taken at the instigation of the Bermuda Company under pressure from the Crown. The records fall silent for several months, and the Spanish busied themselves with getting passage home.

When good weather arrived in Bermuda in May 1622, Butler, without the Spanish on his neck, set his men to work on the *San Antonio* with a will. That winter, probably after the departure of the Spanish, Butler had issued a proclamation directing that any goods from the wrecked vessel, whether fished from the sea or found on the beach, were the property of the company and were to be turned in to the bailiffs. In sending Seymour to the wreck, Butler admonished him to always take with his own men "some other honest men" to allay the suspicions of the Bermudians. To William Elie,* a prominent citizen of Sandys Parish in the western end, he wrote that the Spanish had deeded all the remaining goods of the *San Antonio* to reimburse him for the £100 he said he had spent in keeping the survivors. To Elie and his fellows he gave permission to recover and keep any goods other than silver or gold; all treasure was to be turned over to the governor. The winter must have been a long one for the hungry governor. Writing to Seymour from St. George on February 6, 1621/22, Butler complimented him on setting buoys on the wreck but stated that Seymour would have "done best of all if you could have sent me some newes of the silver bars and chest of Rialls wch certainly must needs lye thereabouts, unlesse some great Rock fish have conveyed them away. . . . In May wee may hope for some further discoveryes."[13] Butler left no doubt who he thought such "Rock fish" might be.

When the summer weather arrived, operations were resumed under the direction of Seymour. Jacob Jacobson, a shipwright of Somerset, apparently built some sort of a diving bell or lifting device, since the records refer to an engine, a term used in that period to describe almost any machine. The party that worked on the wreck included at least four divers and numbers of people from Somerset. Seymour and his party made over twenty-three trips to the wreck and at times remained on the site for as long as ten or twelve days. A William Coxson was chief diver, and during the operations slung underwater ten pieces of heavy ordnance, four small swivel guns, two large anchors and a small one. In all, the list of recovered goods and treasure included ten cannon; six wrought-iron swivel guns; one whole new anchor cable, 4½ inches in diameter; a silver platter; a silver double salt; a silver ewer; a silver dish with handles; a silver basin; a bag containing 150 pieces of eight; an ingot of gold; and a chain of gold. The list is only what was put on paper. There probably was much more. The work continued until the departure of Butler from the islands, which he left without the permission of the company and before the arrival of the new governor, John Bernard. With him, Butler took four anchors and five swivel guns and, no doubt, some

---

* Elie had written the governor requesting permission to go to the wreck.

treasure. When the new governor arrived, Seymour drew up a bill of particulars, listing his work on the wreck and that of the people in his charge, with a list of some of the materials recovered from the wreck and claims for the work done—the best record we have of the actual salvage. It was the custom for a court of inquiry to sit on the administration of a governor at the conclusion of his term of office. The court that sat on Butler heard many complaints of illegal acts and high-handed proceedings. The same commission inquired into the matter of the wreck. Butler must have appeared in very bad light, and his leaving the island before the arrival of the new governor cast great suspicion on him. Nevertheless, he was appointed governor of Providence Island in 1638. Either his crimes were not as great as reputed, or he had strong friends at court.

After the wreck of the *San Antonio*, the islands continued to take their toll of many ships, but the Spanish evidently avoided disaster there until October 22, 1639, when two ships of a passing fleet ran aground on the southwest reefs as the *San Antonio* had done. These were *La Viga*, a stores ship, and her tender, *El Galgo*. An account, written by Juan de Rivera y Saabedra, chief scrivener to the fleet, describes the terror felt by those aboard:

> Our greatest danger lay before our eyes. The fury of the sea foretold our end. A strong wind dashed the waves against the fragile timbers of the *Viga* and, hastened by her pounding on the rocks, began to shatter them. The night was dark, the place unknown, two factors which were a great hinderance, and we expected our plight to become worse and more bitter, and altogether so fearful and horrible that our minds reeled with such dismay and confusion that we felt our senses would leave us as we passed further into the shadow of death, yet we had just enough strength to do what had to be done.[15]

The crew had fired a gun when they found themselves on the rocks, and the rest of the fleet was seen just at sunset to veer off. *El Galgo* was not so fortunate, and when daylight came after a night of terror, she was seen aground about a mile and a half from the *Viga*. The Spanish recognized the islands as the Bermudas. The crew of the *Viga* watched as the people on the *Galgo* built rafts, abandoned ship, and set out for shore. And while this was going on the Bermudians arrived: "While the work was in hand a great many small sailing boats with lateen sails were seen coming in our direction from the Island, like herons in flight twisting and turning as they cut through the restless waves toward us, for even though they were tiny craft they had to use great care to avoid the many shallows. When they reached the tender their crews clambered aboard and must have found the loot they were seeking, for they remained there and would not come to our ship."

A small Bermudian vessel came alongside the *Viga*, and the master informed the Spanish that the governor sent a message of friendship and he would assist them ashore. As they passed their tender, "numerous small boats were gathered round her, and their crews were busy ripping her to pieces to steal whatever they could—like a flock of voracious vultures circling the sky in search of a cadaver and, finding one, pouncing upon it and tearing it apart. So these English troglodytes, coming upon that wooden hull, clambered up and down it in haste, their insatiable appetite not ever sparing her stout timbers."

The Spanish landed and were received in a friendly way by the Bermudians. As in the case of those aboard the *San Antonio*, they were boarded out in private homes at a charge the Spanish considered exorbitant. The Spanish finally escaped the voracious Bermudians by purchasing a locally built ship just being completed, at a price far above its true value. In its essentials the story reads like that of the *San Antonio* of eighteen years before. The plot was the same—the Spanish were kept on the islands while the Bermudians fleeced them. But the Spanish were really quite fortunate: they managed to escape with their lives and some of their money. In that age, just getting back to Europe in one piece after such disasters at sea was no mean accomplishment.

As the Spanish continued to be trapped by the reefs of Bermuda as they sailed toward Europe, ships heading for the English colonies in North America suffered similar catastrophes. While the wrecks of the *Sea Venture* and the *Warwick* were not disasters in human terms, since the crews and the passengers escaped, the first year after the restoration of Charles II to the throne of England witnessed a tragedy of major proportions. In March 1660/61, the *Virginia Merchant* left the harbor near Castle Island and was cast away in a storm on the rocky cliff of the south coast. As she was ripped to shreds on the coral heads, wreckage and victims alike were dashed on the razorlike cliffs of weathered coral rock. The suffering of the victims was quickly ended. Only twelve or so out of more than 180 aboard escaped by being washed by the thundering surf to a small sandy beach. The bow of the ship was washed ashore, the bowsprit almost entering a door of a house on the beach.*

Until the end of the sailing-ship era, the reefs continued to take their

---

* The exact spot lies just west of the Carleton Beach Hotel. The small beach on which the survivors were saved is that now used by guests at the Carleton.

Ivory comb. Luxury goods such as this formed part of the cargo of most ships sailing to the Virginia colony after the first decade of settlement

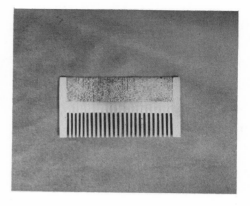

A brass button showing a caricature of a king. At the time, these buttons were worn by antimonarchists. Drawing by Peter Copeland, Smithsonian Institution

Chain plate which held a dead eye

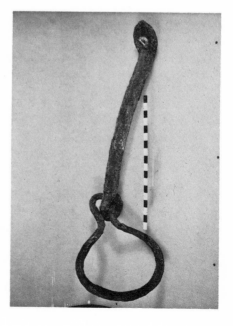

toll. No one knows how many ships are entombed in the sand and coral of the islands, and no one can estimate the wealth entrapped there—precious remnants of that great flood of gold and silver that flowed by the islands en route to the creditors of Spain.

X

The Butchers

"Jesus bless us! Are these devils, or what are they?"
—Words spoken by Spanish sailors on their capture
by Pierre le Grand of Dieppe

 LYING JUST OFF the northwest coast of Hispaniola is a small green-mantled island, oval in shape and rising to a rounded ridge at the center. The shape and color resemble a gigantic turtle floating on the surface of the sea. Because of this resemblance, the Spanish, in early times, named the island Tortuga—turtle. The coast of Hispaniola across the narrow strait is mountainous and lushly green, with the small floodplain of a river visible here and there. To the eastward, the northern part of the island becomes savannah and woodland, and here it was that Columbus built his first settlement, Isabela—a situation which soon proved to be a very bad choice. The capital of Hispaniola was moved to the south coast to a better harbor, nearer the action in the Caribbean, and was named Santo Domingo. These islands—Tortuga and the northern reaches of Hispaniola—were to be the spawning ground of the most ferocious enemy the Spanish Americans faced in their three centuries of history: the buccaneers, who sprang into the arena of war and politics in the Caribbean basin.

As Spain continued into the seventeenth century to pursue her oppressive and thoroughly unwise economic policy of excluding all foreigners from trading in the West Indies, some of the island settlements were brought to the verge of ruin. Of these, Hispaniola suffered as much as any, and by the second decade of the 1600's, much of the land was unpopulated. The savannahs and woodlands of the island, particularly to the north, were largely deserted and soon became overrun by wild cattle, descendants of those abandoned by the planters when they

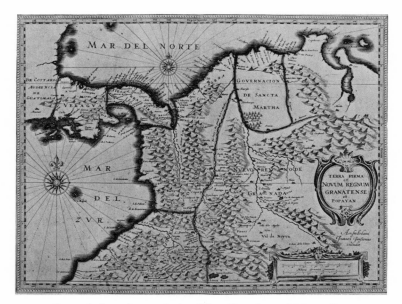

Central America and the Vice Royalty of New Granada, scene of many of the depredations of the buccaneers. Photograph of an eighteenth-century chart
from the Smithsonian Institution

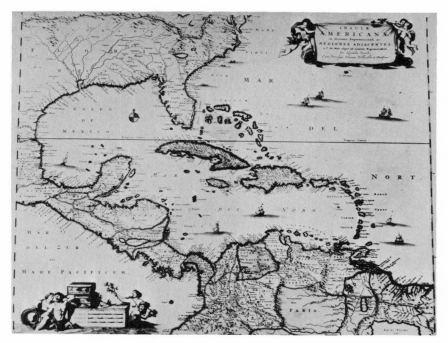

left the land. Soon, shipwrecked sailors appeared on the northern coast and took up cattle hunting, to win a precarious living from the wilderness. Here they learned from the few natives who remained, the process of smoking and drying meat on a boucan, or rack, and before long developed an illicit business in provisions. The sailors were joined from time to time by outcasts from the settlements of the West Indies, by escaped slaves and indentured servants, and by drifters and adventurers unable to adjust to settled society. From St. Christopher and Nevis they came, and from Old Providence, having been harassed and driven out of those islands by the Spanish, who were fearful for the security of their treasure routes and the rise of illicit commerce. By the time these men reached Hispaniola and Tortuga, and joined the buccaneering settlements, they had developed a deep-seated hatred of the Spanish.

The buccaneers, as they were called from their use of the boucan, organized themselves into a loosely knit society with a code of conduct most of them respected. They usually hunted in pairs, and each hunter and his mate shared their possessions and the good and bad fortune that might be theirs. They were a thoroughly wild lot, armed with long muskets and sets of sharp knives, and some used dogs they had tamed from those roaming wild on the savannah. Their life was a rough but apparently healthful one. Food was basic and coarse, and they had few amenities beyond some tobacco and perhaps such foodstuffs as flour, which they might get in trade. One luxury they did insist on, when their fortunes brought them the money to buy it: the pipe of wine they consumed at the annual or semiannual debaucheries they indulged in when they sold their meat. This habit was to become a permanent one, and later, when they took to sea, the drunken orgy ashore was the normal way of celebrating a rich capture. Their way of living and their dress must have appeared bizarre to the ship captains and planters who traded with them. They wore a jacket and breeches of the coarsest cloth, the breeches reaching halfway between knee and ankle. After a short time, the garments became so caked with dried blood it was impossible to tell the material from which they were fashioned. Their shoes were formed from the wet raw leg skins of freshly flayed animals. Maurice Besson describes the process: "Shoes of this kind are made of ox or pig skin, and indeed in this way: as soon as an ox or pig is skinned, the man sets his foot within the piece of skin which covered the leg. His great toe he sets in the place where the knee was, binds it there with sinew and cuts off what he does not need. The remainder is taken three or four inches above the heel and there tied with a sinew till it is dry, and thereafter it stays in position."[1]

A confederacy of French and English drifters had settled the islands of St. Christopher (St. Kitts) and Nevis as early as 1623. Fearing this threat to their shipping, the Spanish attacked them with a powerful fleet and expelled them in 1629. Most of the French removed to Tortuga and the boucan country of Hispaniola, but only a few English came north to join the community at this time. Five years after the expulsion of the French from the Lesser Antilles, a French governor arrived at Tortuga and made this island his capital. The Spanish almost immediately attacked and drove the French out, but they returned even stronger than before and established a secure settlement with a fort. Two years later, in 1641, the French were strong enough to drive out the few English who had settled on the island, and from this time until the capture of Jamaica by Admiral Penn and General Venables in 1655, the English rovers led a precarious life at sea and on certain islands and coasts.

With the firm establishment of the French on Tortuga and in the cattle country of Hispaniola, the business of slaughtering and drying meat, both beef and pork, grew apace and a large trade was established. Other Frenchmen established plantations on the western end of Hispaniola. The constant threat of Spanish attack hung over the buccaneers and rendered just as constant their hatred of the dons. Their settlements lay along the Old Bahama Channel, which was still used by treasure fleets leaving the Indies, even though the Straits of Florida had been opened up a century before and were becoming the principal route of debouchment. Ships leaving Havana and going up the Florida Straits were seen continually by the small French vessels serving the buccaneer settlements as well. These ships were a constant reminder to the French of the wealth that was sailing by their very door, and they could not help comparing these riches to their own rude possessions, won by sweat from the wilderness.

The prime, indeed the only comprehensive, source of information on the buccaneers is the classic *Buccaneers of America* written by Alexander Olivier Esquemelin (or John Esquemeling, as the English called him), one of the participants in the later events he describes. The earlier part of his history is based on word-of-mouth accounts he received from the older buccaneers or on sources which no longer exist. His history has proved to be accurate when checked against the other extant sources, and for many of the events we will quote extensively from his accounts.

Esquemelin was born at Honfleur and came to America in the service of the French West Indies Company as a boy apprentice. His ship, the *St. John*, sailed from Havre-de-Grâce on May 2, 1666, bound for

Tortuga. Soon after his arrival on the island, the company found they could not do profitable business with the inhabitants and withdrew. At this time, Esquemelin and the other servants were sold to new masters for twenty to thirty pieces of eight. Esquemelin describes the terrible result of this act and how he himself became a buccaneer:

> In this occasion I was also sold, as being a servant under the said Company, in whose service I came out of France. But my fortune was very bad, for I fell into the hands of the most cruel tyrant and perfidious man that ever was born of woman, who was then Governor, or rather Lieutenant General, of that island. This man treated me with all the hard usages imaginable, even with that of hunger, with which I thought I should have perished inevitably. Withal he was willing to let me buy my freedom and liberty, but not under the rate of three hundred pieces of eight, I not being master of one, at that time, in the whole world. At last through the manifold miseries I endured, as also affliction of mind, I was thrown into a dangerous fit of sickness. This misfortune, being added to the rest of my calamities, was the cause of my happiness. For my wicked master, seeing my condition, began to fear lest he should lose his monies with my life. Hereupon he sold me the second time to a surgeon for the price of seventy pieces of eight. Being in the hands of this second master, I began soon after to recover my health through the good usage I received from him, as being much more humane and civil than that of my first patron. He gave me both clothes and very good food, and after I had served him but one year he offered me my liberty, with only this condition, that I should pay him one hundred pieces of eight when I was in a capacity of wealth to do so. Which kind proposal of his I could not chose but accept with infinite joy and gratitude of mind.
>
> Being now at liberty, though like unto Adam when he was first created by the hands of his Maker—that is, naked and destitute of all human necessaries, nor knowing how to get my living—I determined to enter into the wicked order of the Pirates, or Robbers at Sea.* Into this Society I was received with common consent both of the superior and vulgar sort.[2]

Until 1672, Esquemelin served the buccaneers as a surgeon's apprentice and then as surgeon. In that year, he returned to France and soon

---

* For the purpose of historical clarity, we will distinguish between the term "buccaneer" and "pirate," using the former to describe only those marauders by land and sea who originated as a group in the Lesser Antilles, Hispaniola, Tortuga, and Old Providence, and were active through 1690. The term "pirate" we will use in a later chapter to describe those sea robbers who were active after the end of the War of Spanish Succession in 1714. Esquemelin does not distinguish between the two but calls the buccaneers pirates in his account.

after wrote his book, which was based on the journals he had kept and on the stories he had heard in the West Indies.

The Spanish treasure ships that sailed by the buccaneer settlements were too much for one Frenchman, Pierre Le Grand of Tortuga, and in 1640 he became the first buccaneer to achieve a major capture at sea. A large, powerful man of Norman descent, who had been born in Dieppe, he made an appearance on the stage of history that was both brief and dramatic. Tiring of his labors ashore, he determined to attempt the capture of a Spanish ship or ships to better his fortune. He assembled a crew of twenty-eight desperadoes, and with an open boat went to the Old Bahama Channel, which ran between the southernmost Bahamas and the northern coast of Hispaniola, to lie in wait for a passing vessel.

A treasure fleet appeared just in time, for the buccaneers were on the verge of starvation. Esquemelin quotes from an account that apparently no longer exists:

The Boat . . . wherein Pierre le Grand was with his companions, had now been at sea a long time, without finding anything, according to his intent of piracy, suitable to make a prey. And now their provisions beginning to fail, they could keep themselves no longer upon the ocean, or they must of necessity starve. Being almost reduced to despair, they espied a great ship belonging to the Spanish flota, which had separated from the rest. This bulky vessel they resolved to set upon and take, or die in the attempt. Hereupon they made sail towards her, with design to view her strength. And although they judged the vessel to be far above their forces, yet the covetousness of such a prey, and the extremity of fortune they were reduced to, made them adventure on such an enterprize. Being now come so near that they could not escape without danger of being all killed, the Pirates jointly made an oath to their captain, Pierre le Grand, to behave themselves courageously in this attempt, without the least fear or fainting. True it is, that these rovers had conceived an opinion that they should find the ship unprovided to fight, and that through this occasion they should master her by degrees. It was in the dusk of the evening, or soon after, when this great action was performed. But before it was begun, they gave orders to the surgeon of the boat to bore a hole in the sides thereof, to the intent that, their own vessel sinking under them, they might be compelled to attack more vigorously, and endeavour more hastily to run aboard the great ship. This was performed accordingly; and without any other arms than a pistol in one of their hands and a sword in the other, they immediately climbed up the sides of the ship, and ran altogether into the great cabin, where they found the Captain, with several of his companions, playing at cards. Here they set a pistol to his breast, commanding him to deliver up the ship to their obedience. The Spaniards seeing the Pirates aboard their ship, without scarce having seen them at sea, cried out, "Jesus bless us! Are these devils, or what are they?" In the meanwhile some of them took possession of the gunroom, and seized the arms and military affairs they found there, killing as many of the ship as made any opposition. By which means the Spaniards presently were compelled to surrender.

Pierre was not only audacious, brave, and decisive, but also possessed of great wisdom, as his subsequent actions demonstrate: "As soon as Pierre le Grand had taken this magnificent prize, he detained in his service as many of the common seamen as he had need of, and the rest he set on shore. This being done, he immediately set sail for France, carrying with him all the riches he found in that huge vessel: here he continued without ever returning to the parts of America."

News of his incredible exploit swept Tortuga, northern Hispaniola, and indeed all the West Indies. The Spanish were flabbergasted by such audacity. Within months other buccaneers took to the sea, and the violent phase of their history began. They were no longer hunters of cattle and illicit traders, but had become predators against Spanish settlements and shipping with a ferocity and cruelty never before seen in the Americas. It might be said that Pierre opened the door to a new and bloody era, which was to bring untold suffering and grief to the Spanish Americans.

The buccaneers were unable to buy or build the boats they needed so they swarmed to sea in their canoes and attacked the Spanish coastal traders who plied their trade in boats between the island settlements and Havana. This commerce involved tobacco, hides, and other natural products, which were taken to Havana for lading on the fleets returning to Spain. Esquemelin describes the results of these attacks:

Hereabouts it was that those pirates at the beginning took a great number of boats, laden with the aforesaid commodities. These boats they used to carry to the Isle of Tortuga, and there sell the whole purchase to the ships that waited in the port for their return, or accidentally happened to be there. With the gain of these prizes they provided themselves with necessaries, wherewithal to undertake other voyages. Some of these voyages were made towards the coast of Campeche and others towards that of New Spain; in both which places the Spaniards at that time frequently exercised much commerce and trade. Upon those coasts they commonly found a great number of trading vessels and many times ships of great burden. Two of the biggest of these vessels, and two great ships which the Spaniards had laden with plate in the port of Campeche to go to Caracas, they took in less than a month's time, by cruizing to and fro. Being arrived at Tortuga with these prizes, and the whole people of the island admiring their progresses, especially that within the space of two years the riches of the country were increased, the number also of pirates augmented so fast, that from those beginnings, within a little space of time, there were to be numbered in that small island and port above twenty ships of this sort of people.

To counter this threat, the Spanish sent to sea two large vessels of war to cruise on their coasts and to attack the buccaneers, but this remedy was applied too late with too little. The buccaneers proliferated and met with success more often than failure in the ensuing years.

As the business of buccaneering grew apace and the buccaneers acquired experience in their new profession, their procedures became organized and more or less uniform. Expeditions were organized in a regular way, articles of agreement were written and signed, and a body of regulation and custom soon arose which was followed throughout the whole period of their activity, to the end of the seventeenth century. Esquemelin describes the preparations for a typical voyage:

> Before the Pirates go out to sea, they give notice to every one that goes upon the voyage, of the day on which they ought precisely to embark, intimating also to them their obligation of bringing each man in particular so many pounds of powder and bullets as they think necessary for that expedition. Being all come on board, they join together in council, concerning what place they ought first to go to wherein to get provisions—especially of flesh, seeing they scarce eat anything else. And of this the most common sort among them is pork. The next food is tortoises, which they are accustomed to salt a little. Sometimes they resolve to rob such or such hog-yards, wherein the Spaniards often have a thousand heads of swine together. They come to these places in the dark of the night, and having beset the keeper's lodge, they force him to rise, and give them as many heads as they desire, threatening withal to kill him in case he disobeys their commands or makes any noise. Yea, these menaces are oftentimes put in execution, without giving any quarter to the miserable swine-keepers, or any other person that endeavours to hinder their robberies.
>
> Having got provisions of flesh sufficient for their voyage, they return to their ship. Here their allowance, twice a day to every one, is as much as he can eat, without either weight or measure. Neither does the steward of the vessel give any greater proportion of flesh, or anything else to the captain than to the meanest mariner.

Their stomachs cared for and supplies of other stores, including ammunition for the heavy guns, laid in, the buccaneers held a meeting under their leaders to determine the target to be attacked. Likely as not this had already been decided on by a well-informed leader, and it was a matter of talking it out with the men. Their organization was democratic in that they all shared alike the provisions and the hardships, but a system of awards based on the importance of the individual to the expedition was adhered to. The agreement, or charter contract, became stereotyped, and terms of a typical one are quoted by Esquemelin:

In this council, likewise, they agree upon certain Articles, which are put in writing, by way of bond or obligation, which every one is bound to observe, and all of them, or the chief, set their hands to it. Herein they specify, and set down very distinctly, what sums of money each particular person ought to have for that voyage, the fund of all the payments being the common stock of what is gotten by the whole expedition; for otherwise it is the same law, among these people, as with other Pirates, *No prey, no pay.* In the first place, therefore, they mention how much the Captain ought to have for his ship. Next the salary of the carpenter, or shipwright, who careened, mended and rigged the vessel. This commonly amounts to one hundred or an hundred and fifty pieces of eight, being, according to the agreement, more or less. Afterwards for provisions and victualling they draw out of the same common stock about two hundred pieces of eight. Also a competent salary for the surgeon and his chest of medicaments, which usually is rated at two hundred or two hundred and fifty pieces of eight. Lastly they stipulate in writing what recompense or reward each one ought to have, that is either wounded or maimed in his body, suffering the loss of any limb, by that voyage. Thus they order for the loss of a right arm six hundred pieces of eight, or six slaves; for the loss of a left arm five hundred pieces of eight, or five slaves; for a right leg five hundred pieces of eight, or five slaves; for the left leg four hundred pieces of eight, or four slaves; for an eye one hundred pieces of eight, or one slave; for a finger of the hand the same reward as for the eye. All which sums of money, as I have said before, are taken out of the capital sum or common stock of what is got by their piracy. For a very exact and equal dividend is made of the remainder among them all. Yet herein they have also regard to qualities and places. Thus the Captain, or chief Commander, is allotted five or six portions to what the ordinary seamen have; the Master's Mate only two; and other Officers proportionate to their employment. After whom they draw equal parts from the highest even to the lowest mariner, the boys not being omitted. For even these draw half a share, by reason that, when they happen to take a better vessel than their own, it is the duty of the boys to set fire to the ship or boat wherein they are, and then retire to the prize which they have taken.

When the buccaneers sailed, they did so under self-imposed discipline, knowing that only through this could they hope to succeed against an enemy that usually outnumbered them. They strictly observed the rules of property: "In the prizes they take, it is severely prohibited to every one to usurp anything in particular to themselves. Hence all they take is equally divided, according to what has been said before. Yea, they make a solemn oath to each other not to abscond, or conceal the least thing they find amongst the prey. If afterwards any one is found unfaithful, who has contravened the said oath, immediately he is separated and turned out of the society."

In the earliest stages, the buccaneers contented themselves with captures at sea, but as they became stronger and better organized, the towns which lined the shores of the Caribbean and the Gulf of Mexico became targets for their rapacity, and Jamaica a principal base of operations. The capture and settlement of Jamaica was the culmination of a generation of effort by the English.

Early in the seventeenth century, English settlers appeared in the Leeward Islands and on Barbados. St. Kitts was settled in 1623, Barbados in 1624–1625, Nevis in 1628, and Antigua and Montserrat in 1632. And in 1635, the French settled Guadeloupe.

On December 4, 1630, Charles I of England issued a patent to the earl of Warwick and certain other noblemen, incorporating the Providence Company. The purpose of the company was the establishment of a settlement on islands lying off the Mosquito Coast (of present Nicaragua and Honduras) adjacent to the Spanish route from Panama to Havana. Here it was hoped to establish an emporium for trading with the hungry Spanish markets on the mainland and, if opportunity afforded, to mount attacks on the Spanish possessions.

Though alarmed at this threat to their treasure route the Spanish could do nothing to expel the superior English force because it exceeded anything they could put together. Providence Island became a base from which attacks were made on the Spanish mainland, especially under the governorship of Nathaniel Butler, the former governor of Bermuda of whom we have already heard. In 1638, Spain suffered two major naval defeats which destroyed her as a major sea power. In the Battle of the Downs, the Dutch admiral Maarten Tromp destroyed a Spanish fleet off the coast of England, killing thousands of

Spanish soldiers and sailors. In another action, a Spanish fleet sent to expel the Dutch from Brazil (Spain ruled Portugal until 1640) was dispersed and largely destroyed by another Dutch fleet. These battles ended Spain's ability to give adequate naval protection to her Caribbean possessions and opened up the entire West Indies to colonizing efforts by the Dutch, English, and French. The same weakness of naval power made possible the rise of the buccaneers. In the entire period, only one major Spanish victory stands out. In May 1641, the Spanish, led by an able and energetic captain general of the galleons, Don Francisco Díaz de Pimienta, invaded and captured Providence, carting off some four hundred English men, women, and children to slavery on the mainland. The English were not to return to Providence until after the capture of Jamaica, the Civil War in England occupying the full energies of the Crown there.

When Cromwell came to power in England with the death of Charles I, a new element was introduced into English foreign policy. Cromwell, the staunch Puritan and Catholic-hater, felt no qualms in planning a large-scale war against the Spanish in the West Indies. At the time he became Protector, he had the strongest fleet in the history of England. Prince Rupert with his Royalist fleet had been driven from English waters and was no longer a threat. The Protector had been a close friend of the founders of Providence, and at one time had even thought of emigrating to the colony. This early experience undoubtedly influenced him in his "Western Design," which the English now developed. With an eye to establishing a base of trade in the Caribbean and a base from which to mount military operations as necessary, Cromwell now turned his attentions to America. He needed an enterprise to distract the English population from conditions at home, and he had as his ready excuse the attacks which the Spanish had made on the early English settlers in the West Indies.* A further motive is found in the jealousy the English felt for the commercial successes of the Dutch there.

During 1654 the English prepared an expedition against Spanish settlements in the Caribbean, primarily against Santo Domingo, still the administrative center of the Spanish West Indies. The fleet sailed in December under the joint command of Admiral William Penn (father of the founder of Pennsylvania) and General Robert Venables. Unfortunately for the English, the commanders were incompetent and in-

---

* Writings such as Thomas Gage's *The English-American: A New Survey of the West Indies,* published in England in 1648 (and extensively quoted in this volume) informed the English of the great wealth and weakness of the Spanish-American colonies and may have influenced Cromwell.

compatible, and the rank and file "a sad miscellany of distempered unruly persons." The attack on Santo Domingo, in April 1655, was mismanaged throughout and a miserable failure.

In fear of the wrath of Cromwell and seeking some way to snatch success from failure, Penn and Venables turned south to Jamaica and here in May they landed their forces and captured the island. The success was as much due to the disorganization, laziness, and poor fighting qualities of the defenders as it was to English skill, and the victory was no credit to the English commanders. Many of the Negroes of the island escaped to the interior hills and formed communities that were later to plague the English colonists there. These were the Maroons, who later waged intermittent warfare against the English intruders and caused endless trouble for decades. When the expedition returned to England, Cromwell was furious at the poor showing of his commanders and put them in the Tower. Later released, Penn retired to his estate in Ireland.

The early history of English Jamaica need not concern us here except as it relates to the buccaneers. It was a sorry story, for the English troops made very poor planters. The Spanish attempted on two occasions to recapture the island, but they were unsuccessful, and it was finally ceded to England by the Treaty of Madrid signed in 1670. The buccaneers had aided the English in the capture of Jamaica —they were supposed to have distinguished themselves—and were received with friendship by the new government. They established themselves at Port Royal, which was being fortified by the English, and from this base they went forth on their greatest expeditions against the Spanish colonies on the mainland. Port Royal grew to be a center of trade, receiving the wealth the buccaneers captured and serving them with the necessities of their violent lives—food, ship supplies, arms, ammunition, and, not least, women and liquor. Port Royal became the richest English city in America and was known as "the wickedest." The waterfront there became the stage for high drama when the marauders returned from their expeditions loaded with gold, silver, jewels, and other rich merchandise, as well as slaves and captive Spanish held for ransom. So lucrative was the trade that property on the waterside street was as valuable as that in central London, and a location there assured a merchant of a fortune if he had any business ability at all.

It was the custom to call some of the buccaneers by the name of the country in which they were born or in which they had lived. Many hesitated to use their real names, and such designations were perfectly satisfactory to identify them to their fellows and to those with whom

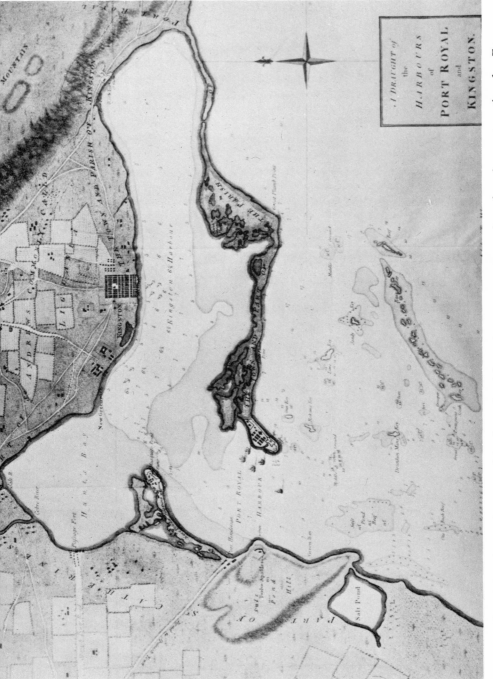

Port Royal, Jamaica, as it appeared in the early eighteenth century, a generation after the great earthquake. Engraved chart published in London

they did business. Such were two buccaneers who resorted to Port Royal immediately after the English captured Jamaica: Bartholomew Portugués and Roche Brasiliano. Bartholomew, as his name indicated, had been born in Portugal and had sailed from Jamaica in a boat with only thirty men and four swivel guns. While cruising off the southern coast of Cuba, he fell in with a great ship of twenty guns out of Cartagena bound for Havana. Without hesitation, Bartholomew and his men attacked the giant. Esquemelin tells us the results of the attack:

> This ship he presently assaulted, but found as strongly defended by them that were on board. The Pirate escaped the first encounter, resolving to attack her more vigorously than before, seeing he had sustained no great damage hitherto. This resolution he boldly performed, renewing his assaults so often that after a long and dangerous fight he became master of the great vessel. The Portuguese lost only ten men and had four wounded, so that he had still remaining twenty fighting men, whereas the Spaniards had double that number. Having possessed themselves of such a ship, and the wind being contrary to return to Jamaica, they resolved to steer their course towards the Cape of Saint Antony (which lies on the Western side of the Isle of Cuba), there to repair themselves and take in fresh water, of which they had great necessity at that time.

Their adventures were only beginning. At Cape San Antonio their ship fell in with three armed Spanish vessels bound from Vera Cruz for Havana. The wind failed, and Bartholomew and his companions soon found themselves dispossessed of their rich prize, put in irons, and cast into the hold of one of the Spanish ships. We can imagine their state of mind at such a turn of fortune, for their prize had been rich indeed, with a cargo that "consisted of one hundred and twenty thousand weight of cacao-nuts, the chief ingredient of that rich liquor called chocolate, and threescore and ten thousand pieces of eight."* Soon after the capture, a severe storm arose and the ships were separated. The one in which the buccaneers were held was blown back to Campeche. Here Bartholomew was recognized as the leader of marauders who had ravaged the coast, robbing and murdering the inhabitants and burning their homes. Several officers of the city came to demand the prisoners so they could be brought to justice ashore, which assuredly meant hanging. Fearing that Bartholomew would escape from jail as he had done on another occasion when a captive there, the city fathers requested that he be held on board the ship until the next day. The

---

* Chocolate was little known in Europe at this time.

BARTOLOMEW PORTUGUES

ROCK. BRASILIANO

View of San Francisco de Campeche, a seventeenth-century engraving

Spanish had resolved to do away with this menace without further ceremony. Word of this got back to Bartholomew and he knew he had to escape that night. After dark he dispatched the sentry with a stolen knife, striking so swiftly that the Spaniard could not cry out. Then, taking two of the earthenware jars in which the Spanish carried wine, Bartholomew leaped overboard and floated ashore. For three days he hid in the bushes and ate only wild herbs.

The next morning, when the sentry was found dead with the knife in his ribs and the prisoner was found gone, panic erupted, and search parties fanned out through the woods near the town where the Spanish were certain their enemy was hiding. The woods were thoroughly searched, but Bartholomew was not found. He had observed the proceedings from the safety of a hollow tree. When the search was given up, a very stiff and sore Bartholomew emerged and started for the Golfo Triste* some 120 miles away, where buccaneers were known to

* Just west of Cape Catoche, the easternmost tip of the Yucatan Peninsula.

resort when they needed to careen their ships and give the crews some recreation. For twenty days, Bartholomew struggled through the wilderness. He almost died of hunger, for all he had with him was a small calabash full of water. He survived on a few shellfish he found on rocks near the shore. Starvation was not his only trouble. There were several rivers to cross, and Bartholomew could not swim. Having left his knife sticking in the sentry, he fashioned one from an iron nail which he found in some wreckage that had washed ashore. With this crude blade he cut small branches and reeds, and made a raft on which he was able to cross the river.

At the cape of the Golfo Triste (probably the modern Punta Holohit), he was overjoyed to find a ship and a party of buccaneers who were old friends of his from Jamaica. He told his story and asked for a boat and twenty men to go back and capture the vessel in which he had been imprisoned at Campeche. His former shipmates obliged, and soon Bartholomew was off to attack the very ship in which he had almost spent his last days on earth. Eight days after leaving his friends, Bartholomew was in charge of the ship again:

> With this great booty he designed in his mind greater things; which he might well hope to obtain, seeing he had found in the vessel great quantity of rich merchandise still remaining on board, although the plate had been transported into the city. Thus he continued his voyage towards Jamaica for some days. But coming near the Isle of Pinos, on the South side of the Island of Cuba, Fortune suddenly turned her back upon him once more, never to show him her countenance again. For a horrible storm arising at sea occasioned the ship to split against the rocks or banks called Jardines. Insomuch that the vessel was totally lost, and Portugues, with his companions, escaped in a canoe. After this manner he arrived at Jamaica, where he remained no long time, being only there till he could prepare himself to seek his fortune anew.

It was not to be, for Bartholomew finished out his wretched life without ever again making a capture.

Roche Brasiliano fared much better than Bartholomew, even though the hardships he suffered were just as severe. Roche had been born in Groningen in the Netherlands, but his surname was never revealed. He had shipped in the service of the Dutch West India Company to their colonies in Brazil. When the Portuguese were finally able to expel the Dutch from their colonies in 1654, Roche had to leave, but the next year found him in Jamaica, where the English had taken over. Here, seeking some means to make his way, he joined a band of buccaneers. For some time he served in the ranks as a common sailor, but his abilities were eventually recognized and he became captain of a dissident group that had split with another commander. With his followers, he fitted out a boat at Port Royal and took his crew to sea. Within a few days, they captured a large Spanish ship which had aboard a large amount of silver. While this gained Roche a great reputation, the success apparently unbalanced his social sense, for Esquemelin tells us that "in his domestic and private affairs he had no good behaviour nor government over himself; for in these he would oftentimes shew himself either brutish or foolish. Many times being in drink, he would run up and down the streets, beating or wounding whom he met, no person daring to oppose him or make any resistance." His peculiar character was also evident in the inordinate cruelty he displayed towards his victims: "To the Spaniards he always showed himself very barbarous and cruel, only out of an inveterate hatred he had against that nation. Of these he commanded several to be roasted alive upon wooden spits, for no other crime than that they would not shew him the places or hog-yards, where he might steal swine."

Soon after the capture of the Spanish ship, which occurred off the coast of Campeche, Roche was wrecked by a violent storm about halfway between the town of Campeche and the Golfo Triste, on the very beach Bartholomew Portugués had walked along in his escape from his captors. Roche and his men saved their lives, their muskets, and some ammunition, but this time the outcome would be different. The Spanish, learning of the wreck and that the buccaneers were making their way down the coast, sent out a party of one hundred horsemen. Roche and his men, hungry and thirsty, turned to face the approaching enemy. Here Esquemelin quotes a speech with which Roche is said to have harangued his men: "We had better, fellow soldiers, choose to die under our arms fighting, as becomes men of courage, than surrender to the Spaniards, who, in case they overcome us, will take away our lives with cruel torments."

Roche had plenty of reasons to fear such torments, for with his wretched reputation he would certainly have been tortured with every device the Spanish could have invented. But the day belonged to the buccaneers. As the horsemen charged the thirty men, their muskets found the mark before the mounted Spanish got within range of pistol shot, and many Spanish were killed at the first volley. This broke the charge and the buccaneers got off volley after volley in a battle that lasted an hour. When it was over, many of the Spanish lay dead or wounded and the others were retreating up the coast. The buccaneers quickly dispatched the Spanish wounded by beating out their brains with the butts of their muskets. Only two buccaneers were killed and two wounded.

After stripping the Spanish of all the weapons and provisions they needed, Roche and his men continued on toward the Golfo Triste. On their way they saw a small vessel lying offshore at anchor, a guardship for wood-gathering parties that had come ashore in canoes. The marauders took the canoes quickly, paddled out to the ship, and captured her. They had no provisions, but this shortage was remedied when they took some of the woodcutters' horses, which they butchered and salted with captured salt. Thus supplied, and armed only with small arms, the buccaneers set out to sea. Soon they fell in with and captured a ship going from New Spain to Maracaibo with a lading of general merchandise and some silver intended for the purchase of coconuts. With these prizes, Roche and his men returned to Port Royal, where they proceeded to celebrate their good fortune with a drunken orgy and a merry time with the prostitutes who abounded there.

The lengths to which the buccaneers went in these celebrations is shown by a story Esquemelin tells of a former master: "My own master would buy, on like occasions, a whole pipe of wine, and, placing it in the street, would force every one that passed by to drink with him; threatening also to pistol them, in case they would not do it. At other times he would do the same with barrels of ale or beer. And, very often, with both his hands, he would throw these liquors about the streets, and wet the clothes of such as walked by, without regarding whether he spoiled their apparel or not, were they men or women." After such an orgy, which sometimes went on for days, the buccaneers would find themselves with big heads and small purses, for it was their habit to spend everything they had in this manner.

After Roche and his men had exhausted their entire fortunes in a few days, they prepared to go to sea again and renew their purses. They sailed to the usual rendezvous point on the coast of Campeche—the Golfo Triste—and from here Roche took a small boat, in which he made off to spy on the harbor of the town of Campeche to see if any potential prizes were there. But instead of getting any information, Roche merely got himself captured. At his wits' end, Roche contrived a trick to secure his release. He wrote a letter purporting to be from other buccaneers and in it warned the governor at Campeche: "he should have a care how he used those persons he had in his custody. For in case he caused them any harm, they did swear unto him they would never give quarter to any person of the Spanish nation that should fall into their hands." The long-suffering governor, having seen his town sacked and burned on many, many occasions and having been unable to prevent the attacks with the soldiers he could muster, apparently felt that the release of these prisoners might win a respite from the buccaneers. He let them go and gave them passage back to Jamaica. The buccaneers showed their gratitude to him by going back to sea and "committing greater robberies and cruelties than ever they had done before; but more especially abusing the poor Spaniards that happened to fall into their hands, with all sorts of cruelty imaginable." Roche was still living in Jamaica when Esquemelin wrote his account.

Despairing of protecting their ships at sea from the buccaneers, the Spanish began to send all the trade they could overland. With opportunities for captures at sea diminishing as the shipping declined, the buccaneers now took to attacking the towns along the coast of Central America and on the islands. The first to do this, according to Esquemelin, was John Scot (again, the buccaneer's name was probably derived from his homeland). He assaulted the town of Campeche, where "he almost ruined the town, robbing and destroying all he could; and, after he had put it to the ransom of an excessive sum of money, he left it."

Scot was followed by Edward Mansvelt, a Dutchman born in Curaçao. This elderly and cunning leader, up to that time, had been regarded as the greatest of the buccaneers. He was the first of his species to cross the Isthmus to the Pacific. In 1664, England and the Netherlands being at war, Governor Modyford of Jamaica asked Mansvelt to lead a force of buccaneers consisting of fifteen ships and five hundred men to attack Curaçao, Mansvelt's own birthplace. Henry Morgan sailed as second-in-command. But instead of Curaçao, Mansvelt's forces attacked the southern coast of Cuba and sacked the town of Sancti-Spíritus lying forty miles inland. The place yielded rich booty, since it had not been looted before. From here, Mansvelt and Morgan sailed to Old Providence, from which the English had been expelled many years before, and captured the island. Unlike his colleagues, Mansvelt was possessed of some humanity and he took his Spanish prisoners to the mainland and released them. From Old Providence, Mansvelt's force ascended the San Juan River and captured Granada, the capital of Nicaragua. This town yielded some treasure, but the buccaneers had not yet finished. They now sailed down the coast of Costa Rica, burning plantations, looting churches, destroying livestock, and cutting down the orchards. Apparently they never did get to Curaçao. Perhaps Mansvelt could not bring himself to attack his birthplace. In any event, when they returned to Port Royal, Governor Modyford only repri-

S.ʳ HEN: MORGAN

manded the leaders. No doubt he shared in the loot and was of the opinion that Old Providence in English hands would be a good base from which to attack the Spanish in the future. But the island was soon back in Spanish hands and these plans came to nothing. Mansvelt died soon after this expedition, and his second-in-command and understudy succeeded him.

Henry Morgan was to become the greatest and most renowned of all the buccaneers, and even today his name is synonymous with "buccaneer" or "pirate." Esquemelin devotes almost half of his book to Morgan, and in the process marks him as the most intrepid, able, ingenious, and ruthless of all his fellows. Morgan was born in Wales in 1635, the son of a prosperous farmer. Before he was twenty, he was taken to Barbados and afterwards went to Jamaica, where he remained for the balance of his life. He had taken part in attacks on the mainland before he joined Mansvelt. On Mansvelt's death, Morgan was chosen by the buccaneers to be their leader.

The earliest governors of Jamaica had encouraged the buccaneers and probably shared in their loot. They saw these marauders as an important armed force that cost the government nothing and kept the Spanish off balance, thus preventing any attempt to recapture the new English colony. This was a perfectly logical extension of Cromwell's policy of using the buccaneers as auxiliary forces. On the restoration of Charles II, the attitude of the government changed. Charles was anxious to develop peaceful trade with the Spanish, and it was necessary to suppress the attacks of the buccaneers if his efforts were to succeed. Thomas Modyford, a Barbadian who was opposed to the buccaneers, was appointed governor of Jamaica and was expected to end the activities of the buccaneers there. He was a statesman of sorts and hoped to develop Jamaica as an international market for the whole of the Caribbean area, with the goods of Europe flowing through the island to the Spanish possessions on the mainland. Modyford's first task, after his arrival in Jamaica in June 1664, was to convince the Spanish of his good intentions, and he set about writing letters to the surrounding colonies telling them of the new policy. His efforts failed. The Spanish simply did not believe Modyford could control the buccaneers, and they were right. Modyford's enlightened policy was being defeated at home, where anti-Spanish and pro-buccaneer elements in the government were on the ascendant. In 1663, Charles had dropped his intentions to establish a peaceful trade with Spain, and Modyford soon loosened his restrictions on the buccaneers and began to grant commissions of reprisal to them. Thus, the policy of using the buccaneers as an arm of the colonies' military forces was reestablished. The response from the buccaneers was enthusiastic, and Port Royal again bustled with activity as the marauders prepared their ships and crews to sail against the Spanish. The undisciplined buccaneers, however, contributed very little toward furthering royal policy but went their own way, waging private war against the Spanish. They, not the King, determined what their policies would be. Throughout 1665 and 1666 negotiations had been going on in Madrid between the English and Spanish on a commercial treaty. Finally in May 1667, Lord Sandwich signed such an agreement, but this had no effect on events in the West Indies, for Modyford was given no definite instructions concerning it. The buccaneers were permitted to arm a fleet in preparation for further depredations. By 1668, Modyford had information that the Spanish were planning an attack on Jamaica. Apparently the old rule of "no peace beyond the line" was to apply despite the new agreement with Spain.

Modyford commissioned Morgan to go to Cuba and seek intelligence of the Spanish intentions. Morgan, joined by other buccaneers

The Towne of Puerto del Principe taken & fackt

Morgan's atack on Puerto Príncipe, Cuba. Engraving from Exquemelin's *Bucaniers of America* (London, 1684)

who lurked about the keys off the south coast of Cuba, landed and marched inland fifty miles to Puerto Príncipe. Why he had to go there for information on the expected attack by the Spanish is clear enough. He was simply after plunder, and the intelligence mission was just a cover-up, although he probably did gather some information for Modyford. Esquemelin's account makes no mention of the intelligence mission, although he might not have been aware of it.

After two months on the coast Morgan had raised a force of twenty boats and 750 men. With his lieutenants he discussed the possibility of attacking Havana under cover of night, but some of the men, who had been captives there, asserted that the city could not be taken with less than fifteen hundred men. It was then proposed that they recruit the necessary men from the Isle of Pines and other islands the buccaneers frequented, but this idea was discarded as impractical and the plan was abandoned. Then someone proposed that they attack Puerto Príncipe (Camagüey) since it had never been sacked, being too far inland. This proposal was adopted, and the buccaneers landed at El Puerto de

Santa María on the south coast, preparing to march into the interior. The operation did not go as planned. A Spaniard held on one of the ships had heard the plans discussed—the buccaneers did not know he understood English. When the forces approached the port, this Spaniard slipped overboard undetected, swam ashore, and made his way to Puerto Príncipe, where he warned the town. "The Spaniards, as soon as they received this fortunate advice, began instantly to hide their riches, and carry away what movables they could. The Governor also immediately raised all the people of the town, both freemen and slaves." Trees were felled along the road into town and ambuscades placed there. Cannon were mounted to sweep the intended route of the buccaneers and the remaining Spanish were drawn up in military formation before the town.

When Morgan arrived with his forces and found the way blocked by the fallen trees, he gave orders to approach the town through the woods. In thus avoiding the barriers, the buccaneers also avoided the ambuscades. Arriving on the savannah before the town, the buccaneers beheld the governor there with his foot soldiers and mounted troops drawn up ready to give battle. The action opened with a charge of Spanish horse, but this was repulsed, as Esquemelin tells us:

> For the Pirates marched in very good rank and file, at the sound of their drums and with flying colours. When they came near the horse, they drew into the form of a semicircle, and thus advanced towards the Spaniards, who charged them like valiant and courageous soldiers for some while. But seeing that the Pirates were very dextrous at their arms, and their Governor, with many of their companions, killed, they began to retreat towards the wood. Here they designed to save themselves with more advantage; but, before they could reach it, the greatest part of them were unfortunately killed by the hands of the Pirates. Thus they left the victory to these new-come enemies, who had no considerable loss of men in this battle, and but very few wounded, howbeit the skirmish continued for the space of four hours.

Having killed many of the Spanish and dispersed the remainder, the buccaneers entered the town, but the skirmishing was not over. The inhabitants shut themselves up in their houses and, being joined by soldiers from the battlefield, fired on the marauders. With this, the buccaneers threatened to burn the town and kill everyone in it, including the women and children. At this threat, the Spanish submitted, with horrifying results:

As soon as the Pirates had possessed themselves of the town, they enclosed all the Spaniards, both men, women, children and slaves, in several churches; and gathered all the goods they could find by way of pillage. Afterwards they searched the whole country round about the town, bringing in day by day many goods and prisoners, with much provision. With this they fell to banqueting among themselves and making great cheer after their customary way, without remembering the poor prisoners, whom they permitted to starve in the churches. In the meanwhile they ceased not to torment them daily after an inhuman manner, thereby to make them confess where they had hid their goods, moneys and other things, though little or nothing was left them. To this effect they punished also the women and little children, giving them nothing to eat; whereby the greatest part perished.

After pillaging the houses and churches of all visible loot, Morgan now turned his attentions to the remaining prisoners and the wealth they had hidden, intending to extract it from them as ransom for their lives. At first, he merely threatened them with transportation to Jamaica as slaves. He freed four of their number to go into the country and try to raise the ransom he demanded. They returned to tell him that they could find nothing and pleaded for more time.

The Spanish were stalling, a fact Morgan suspected but did not know for certain until he intercepted a letter. This fell into his hands when a small party of buccaneers returned to town from the countryside with loot they had found buried and some prisoners they had taken. On one of them, a Negro, was found a letter from the governor at Santiago which told the townspeople that "they should not make too much haste to pay any ransom for their town or persons, or any other pretext. But, on the contrary, they should put off the Pirates as well as they could with excuses and delays; expecting to be relieved by him within a short while, when he would certainly come to their aid." With this, Morgan gave orders for all the loot to be taken toward the ships lying at Santa María and told the prisoners they must raise the ransom by the next day or he would burn their town. Not wishing to face another Spanish force, Morgan finally settled for five hundred cattle and the salt necessary to preserve the meat. When the cows were delivered to the ships, he forced the Spanish to butcher and salt them before he released the hostages he had held, to ensure the terms of the contract. In the latter days of the occupation of the town, the question of ransom had become largely a moot one, since many of the prisoners had already died of hunger and more were to follow as a result of their imprisonment without food or water.

Seventeenth-century fortifications of Porto Bello, Panama. Photograph
from the Smithsonian Institution

When Morgan returned to Jamaica, he was received by Governor
Modyford and very probably congratulated on his "intelligence-
gathering" mission. Indeed, Morgan claimed he had turned up evidence
that the Spanish were planning to attack Jamaica. On this evidence, he
persuaded Modyford to abstain from interfering with his next design.
Soon he was making plans for a greater and more lucrative operation.

As Drake had done almost a century before, Morgan now planned to
strike at the heart of the Spanish treasure system and attack Porto
Bello. He gathered together a squadron of nine ships and a force of 460
buccaneers. He would not reveal their destination but told his followers only that "he should make a good fortune . . . if strange oc-
curances altered not the course of his designs." The French buccaneers
did not take part in this expedition.

Early in the summer of 1668, Morgan sailed with his fleet to the
coast of Costa Rica, where he gathered together his commanders and
told them of his plans: they would attack at night and plunder the
whole place. He added that the surprise would be complete since he
had not revealed his plans to anyone and no word of them could have
reached the Spanish. At this, some of the commanders declared they

had not sufficient numbers to attack such a place with a regular army garrison. But, according to Esquemelin, Morgan replied, "If our number is small, our hearts are great. And the fewer persons we are, the more union and better shares we shall have in the spoil." Morgan, like Drake before him, understood perfectly well the minds of the men who followed him and was always able to find the right words to spur them on in moments of discouragement and fear. The commanders agreed to follow, and later the men were briefed.

Early in July the attack was mounted. Morgan knew that the landward side of the town was undefended. Only the seaward side of the fortifications boasted any heavy guns or ramparts that could be held. They had been designed to repel an attack only by sea. On these facts, Morgan decided to launch the assault from the woods opposite the undefended side of the town and to strike at night, when all but the sentries would be off their guard. The fleet arrived at Puerto de Naos west of their target and sailed up the river there to a harbor called Puerto Pontín. Here the men left the ships in boats and canoes. Only a small crew remained aboard the ships to bring them to Porto Bello the next day. At midnight, the company reached a spot named Estra longa Lemos and disembarked, leaving sentries at their boats.

Led by an Englishman who had been a prisoner in the town, the buccaneers marched silently through the woods. A few men, including the guide, went ahead as an advance guard and captured a Spanish sentry before he could cry out or fire his musket. The sentry was brought to Morgan and under threat of death revealed all he knew of the garrison and the situation in the town. As early morning approached, the buccaneers surrounded a castle on the outskirts of the city. Here, the sentry was made to hail his companions within, "charging them to surrender, and deliver themselves up to his discretion; otherwise they should be all cut to pieces, without giving quarter to any one."

The garrison answered with musket fire. The buccaneers attacked, scaling the walls and overwhelming the garrison after much bitter fighting. When many Spaniards were dead and the survivors had thrown down their arms, the buccaneers kept their promise. They herded well and wounded alike into one room of the fortress, laid a powder train to the magazine, and blew the entire structure and prisoners to bits. With this they entered the city, "which as yet was not in order to receive them. Many of the inhabitants cast their precious jewels and moneys into wells and cisterns or hid them in other places underground, to excuse, as much as were possible, their being totally robbed."

A party of buccaneers attacked the local monasteries and convents, and captured as many priests and nuns as they found. In the confusion the governor had retired to one of the castles with his remaining soldiers and from here fired on the town with the heavy guns. The buccaneers returned the fire, killing many Spaniards who exposed themselves on the walls of the fort to reload the cannon. The furious assault lasted from daybreak to noon, and the buccaneers were at a stand. At each attempt to enter the castle or to scale the walls, the defenders showered the marauders with pots full of gunpowder, stones, and burning tar. The attackers answered with firepots, which they threw over the walls and against the doors of the fortress. The valiant defense of the Spanish depressed Morgan and his lieutenants, and at this moment when the battle was in the balance, an English standard fluttered from the top of one of the bastions. With this, the corner was turned, and Morgan and his fellow commanders resolved to renew the attack with a new weapon. Ladders wide enough to accommodate three or four men abreast were quickly fashioned from poles and lumber found in the town, and the weeping and terrified nuns and monks from the cloisters were assembled. Morgan again hailed the governor of the town in the fortress and asked him to surrender. The Spaniard answered that "he would never surrender himself alive." With this, the religious were sent forward carrying the ladders to place them against the walls. Morgan had thought the Spanish would never have fired on the nuns and monks, but the governor was made of strong stuff and musket fire opened on the clergy:

> The Governor, who acted like a brave and courageous soldier, refused not, in performance of his duty, to use his utmost endeavours to destroy whoever came near the walls. The religious men and women ceased not to cry to him and beg of him by all the Saints of Heaven he would deliver the castle, and hereby spare both his and their own lives. But nothing could prevail with the obstinacy and fierceness that had possessed the Governor's mind. Thus many of the religious men and nuns were killed before they could fix the ladders. Which at last being done, though with great loss of the said religious people, the Pirates mounted them in great numbers, and with no less valour; having fireballs in their hands, and earthen pots full of powder. All which things, being now at the top of the walls, they kindled and cast in among the Spaniards.

The rank and file of the Spanish and the remaining officers threw down their arms and asked for quarter, but the valiant governor refused. He stood firm and killed several of his own men who tried to surrender. When called on to give up, the governor is quoted by Esquemelin as saying, "By no means: I had rather die as a valiant soldier than be hanged as a coward." He fought on until he had to be killed by the now-admiring buccaneers, in spite of the entreaties of his wife and daughter who were present and witnessed his death.

With the main castle in their hands, the buccaneers placed all the prisoners in it after robbing them of any valuables they had. Then the celebration started: "They fell to eating and drinking after their usual manner; that is to say, committing in both these things all manner of debauchery and excess. After such manner they delivered themselves up to all sort of debauchery, that if there had been found only fifty courageous men, they might easily have retaken the city, and killed all the Pirates." The next day began the interrogation of the prisoners, as the captors sought the treasure which the townspeople were supposed to have hidden. Many of the prisoners were put on the rack and tortured with the utmost brutality to reveal where they had hidden money and jewels. Many so tortured had hidden nothing and died on the rack while trying to convince the buccaneers of this. The debaucheries and the torture of prisoners continued for two days. Then word arrived that the president (governor) of Panama was coming with troops to rescue the town, but the invaders paid scant attention to this, having their ships close at hand. Morgan now demanded of his prisoners a ransom of 100,000 pieces of eight on threat of burning the town. While the negotiations were going on, the president of Panama appeared on the road from that city some miles from Porto Bello. A welcoming committee of one hundred buccaneers was sent out and laid an ambush at a narrow part of the trail where it passed through woods. Here they received the president and his troops with a withering fire, and the Spanish turned and fled, leaving the citizens of Porto Bello to work out their own arrangements with Morgan. Somehow the ransom was raised, and the 100,000 pieces of eight were brought to Morgan and his officers. With nothing remaining to be done, Morgan and his men embarked and left the town and its sorrowing people. The fleet sailed to the deserted south coast of Cuba, there to divide the loot. In coin alone the buccaneers had captured 250,000 pieces of eight, besides much rich merchandise, such as silks, linen, and other goods. The share per man amounted to about 400 pieces of eight, a very substantial sum at that time. With this treasure, Morgan and his men returned to Port Royal to enjoy the adulation of local merchants, tavernkeepers, and prostitutes, who soon relieved most of them of their hard-won wealth.

With their purses empty again, the buccaneers were ready for another enterprise. Morgan spread the word for the buccaneer captains and their men to assemble at Vaca Island, a favorite rendezvous. This small island lying off the western end of Hispaniola and due east of Jamaica became, during the winter of 1668–1669, a scene of great activity as the ships gathered and the captains conferred with Morgan while they made plans for the next assault on the Spanish mainland. Morgan, "now rendered famous in all the neighboring countries, for the great enterprizes he had performed," had no trouble recruiting men in great numbers. He was joined on Vaca by a fine ship from New England, mounting thirty-six guns, which had come to strengthen his forces on orders from Governor Modyford. Also in the harbor was a French buccaneer vessel of twenty-four guns, which Morgan tried to recruit, but the French captain refused, "not daring to repose any trust in the English, of whose actions [the French] were not a little jealous." Then with great dissimulation, Morgan invited the French captain and his officers to dine with him on his new flagship. When they came aboard, he made them prisoners and then called a council of his commanders in the great cabin of his ship. Esquemelin describes what follows, seeing in it the hand of God:

> This unjust action of Captain Morgan was soon followed by divine punishment, as we may very rationally conceive. The manner I shall instantly relate. Captain Morgan, presently after he had taken the French prisoners abovesaid, called a council to deliberate what place they should first pitch upon, in the course of this new expedition. At this council it was determined to go to the Isle of Savona,* there to wait for the *flota* which was then expected from Spain, and take any of the Spanish vessels that might chance to straggle from the rest. This resolution being taken, they began on board the great ship to feast one another for joy of their new voyage and happy council, as they hoped it would prove. In testimony hereof, they drank many healths, and discharged many guns, as the common sign of mirth among seamen used to be. Most of the men being drunk, by what accident is not known the ship suddenly was blown up into the air, with three hundred and fifty Englishmen, besides the French prisoners above-mentioned that were in the hold. Of all which number, there escaped only thirty men, who were in the great cabin at some distance from the main force of the powder. Many more 'tis thought might have escaped, had they not been so much overtaken with wine.

Morgan himself and his lieutenants had escaped because the forward magazine had exploded. They were blown through the stern windows of the great cabin and in an instant found themselves in the water. The

---

* Saona, lying off the southeastern tip of Hispaniola.

practical effect of the disaster was to deprive Morgan of his most powerful ship and almost a third of his men.

Looking about for those to blame, the English decided the French must have fired the magazine in revenge for their imprisonment, manifestly an excuse which enabled Morgan to seize the French ship whose officers and captain had been killed in the explosion. Another technicality was invoked to bless the seizure with legality. It was found that the French had previously taken some supplies from an English ship, for which they had given bills of credit against money in Tortuga. This now was interpreted as technical piracy by Morgan, and he seized the ship and sent it to Jamaica as a prize. It is a little unclear why Morgan did not make the French vessel his flagship, since he had lost his own. The French ship was much larger and more powerful than the one Morgan now had—a small vessel carrying fourteen guns of small caliber. Morgan at this time had fourteen ships and about nine hundred men. The first problem was to top off provisions of the fleet, and this was done on the coast of Hispaniola with the capture of a number of cows and horses. The defending Spanish attempted to lay an ambuscade with troops from Santo Domingo, but they were driven off with severe losses. When some of Morgan's ships did not join him as expected, he decided to go to the coast of Venezuela, and Lake Maracaibo became the next destination. He now had only five hundred men and eight ships, four hundred being on the six ships which deserted. In this decision, he was influenced by one of the captains with him, a Frenchman who had served with Captain Jean-David Nau, called L'Ollonois, about whom we shall hear later. The Frenchman had plundered the area of Lake Maracaibo two years before and had taken rich loot. He knew the waters of the lake and the surrounding country well, and this was an important factor in Morgan's decision. The fleet set out, stopping near Curaçao to obtain water, meat, and wood, and continued on to the coast of Venezuela. Lake Maracaibo, one of the natural wonders of the northern coast of South America, spreads out from a narrow strait and extends fifty miles inland as a great oval. The town of Maracaibo lay down the narrow entrance some twenty miles below the bar at the entrance of the strait. At the mouth of the strait, there was a fortified tower on one side near the bar to protect the entrance of the lake. Unknown to the Frenchman, who had not been there for two years, there was also now a fortress built as a result of the raid of L'Ollonois.

As Morgan's little squadron approached the strait, it was decided to enter after dark in the boats and on the side opposite the fortified tower. In the darkness, the boats crept along the shore, but when

The destruction of the Spanish squadron at Maracaibo by Henry Morgan.
Engraving from Exquemelin's *Bucaniers of America* (London, 1684)

daylight came, they were astonished to find themselves directly under
the new fort as they prepared to land to attack the tower. Esquemelin
describes the hot action which ensued and an unsuccessful trap placed
by the Spanish:

> The dispute continued very hot on both sides, being managed with
> huge courage and valour from morning till dark night. This being
> come, Captain Morgan, in the obscurity thereof, drew nigh the fort;
> which having examined, he found nobody in it, the Spaniards having
> deserted it not long before. They left behind them a match kindled near
> a train of powder, wherewith they designed to blow up the Pirates and
> the whole fortress, as soon as they were in it. This design had taken
> effect, had the Pirates failed to discover it the space of one quarter of
> an hour. But Captain Morgan prevented the mischief by snatching
> away the match with all speed, whereby he saved both his own and his
> companions' lives. They found here great quantity of powder, whereof
> he provided his fleet; and afterwards demolished part of the walls,
> nailing sixteen pieces of ordnance, which carried from twelve to four
> and twenty pound of bullet. Here they found also great number of
> muskets and other military provisions.

The ships were brought in, and Morgan and his men set out for the town of Maracaibo, but after going into the strait some distance, they found the water too low to admit their vessels. Morgan transferred his forces to boats and had the men continue with their side arms and only some small boat guns as their artillery. Two days after passing the straits, the buccaneers landed at the town and attacked the fort called De la Barra. It was an easy capture: the garrison and most of the townsfolk had fled to the woods with everything of value they could transport. Only a few pitiful old and sick people remained behind. When the buccaneers entered the town, they searched every house and hiding place but found no loot. They then quartered themselves in the houses, assembled provisions, and set up the office of the watch in a church, "where they lived in their military manner, committing many insolent actions."

Their next move was to send a party of one hundred men into the surrounding country to search for the inhabitants and their wealth.

These returned the next day following, bringing with them to the number of thirty persons, between men, women and children, and fifty mules laden with several good merchandize. All these miserable prisoners were put to the rack, to make them confess where the rest of the inhabitants were and their goods. Amongst other tortures then used, one was to stretch their limbs with cords, and at the same time beat them with sticks and other instruments. Others had burning matches placed betwixt their fingers, which were thus burnt alive. Others had slender cords or matches twisted about their heads, till their eyes burst out of the skull. Thus all sort of inhuman cruelties were executed upon those innocent people. Those who would not confess, or who had nothing to declare, died under the hands of those tyrannical men.

These horrors continued for three weeks, every day more victims being brought in and tortured and every day more victims dying an agonizing death. Morgan was able to capture members of about one hundred of the leading families in the town and their goods. Presently he decided to leave Maracaibo to its agonies and give his attention to Gibraltar, a town lying some distance down the lake shore. To prepare the people of Gibraltar for their arrival, Morgan had sent a few victims from Maracaibo to the town to warn the citizens that "they should surrender: otherwise Captain Morgan would certainly put them all to the sword, without giving quarter to any person he should find alive."

Within a day or two of sending his warning, Morgan and his men approached the town in their boats, to be received by a shower of cannonballs. With the attack of L'Ollonois only two years past, the townspeople were not in a mood to negotiate. At this, Morgan led his men to another place on the coast and landed in the early hours of the next morning. The Frenchman who had been at Gibraltar with L'Ollonois two years before led the buccaneers through the woods to the town, avoiding the road. Morgan expected stiff resistance and marched warily, but not a shot was fired. The wondering buccaneers entered a deserted town. The inhabitants had fled to the woods with all the goods they could carry, after having spiked the cannon defending the place. Only one man was found, a poor old demented citizen dressed in rags. The buccaneers put him to the rack, assuming his rags were a disguise. After intense suffering, he agreed to lead them to his "treasure." This proved to be two pieces of eight and some earthernware pots, which was all he owned. The buccaneers then strung him up to the rack, "lifting him up on high with cords, and tying huge weights to his feet and neck; besides which cruel and stretching torment, they burnt him alive, applying palm-leaves burning to his face, under which miseries he died in half-an-hour. After his death they cut the cords wherewith they had stretched him, and dragged him forth into the adjoining woods, where they left him without burial."

Having settled down in the town, the buccaneers now sent out their search parties to ferret out the refugees hiding in the countryside. One party brought back a farmer and his two daughters, and on being threatened with the rack, he consented to lead the marauders to the refugees. But the refugees had moved farther out into the country, and none could be found. Thinking the farmer had deceived them, the buccaneers promptly hanged him on a tree. What happened to the daughters we must imagine, for Esquemelin does not tell us. Morgan and his men knew that the Spanish refugees could not live long in the woods with the supplies they had carried with them, so parties were sent to the surrounding plantations. In one, a Negro slave was found who promised to lead them to the Spanish if they would take him to Jamaica and give him his liberty. This man led the buccaneers to a party of refugees, which was surrounded and captured. To assure their hold on the Negro for the rest of his life, the buccaneers commanded him to kill some of the Spanish in view of the rest "that by this perpetrated crime he might never be able to leave their wicked company. The negro, according to their orders, committed many murders and insolent actions upon the Spaniards, and followed the unfortunate traces of the Pirates." About 250 persons were captured, and for eight days, the buccaneers "examined" them, repeating the same tortures to the obstinate that they had applied to the man they had found in the town.

When they returned to Gibraltar, they brought mules loaded with pieces of eight, plate, and jewelry. In questioning another Negro slave, they heard of a richly laden vessel and four boats lying up a stream which flowed into the lake. This slave also revealed that he knew where the governor of Maracaibo was hiding.

Morgan sent two large boats with a hundred men in each after the ship. He himself led 250 others to find the governor, who had fortified himself on a small island in the middle of the same river in which the ship was anchored. On hearing Morgan was coming, the governor took himself and his small force to the top of a steep hill which he prepared to defend. It was days before Morgan arrived at the island, and in this time, the governor prepared his defenses carefully. Meanwhile, a great rain had fallen, flooding the river and drowning several of the buccaneers and captured refugees as they tried to cross with a muletrain loaded with loot. The force with Morgan was thoroughly discouraged by the rain and the fact that the governor was well fortified and armed with good weapons and plenty of ammunition. The buccaneers' ammunition and muskets were soaked and in no condition for a battle. Morgan gave up his plans to attack and returned to Maracaibo twelve days after they set out. While they had failed to take the governor, they captured many more prisoners and considerable booty.

Two days after Morgan returned, the boats sent to capture the ship entered with some parcels of goods the Spanish were unable to take away from the ship before the buccaneers arrived: "Thus, after they had been in possession of the place five entire weeks, and committed there infinite of murders, robberies, and suchlike insolences, they concluded upon their departure. But before this could be performed, for the last proof of their tyranny, they gave orders to some prisoners to go forth into the woods and fields, and collect a ransom for the town; otherwise they would certainly burn every house down to the ground." Those who could walk returned to the surrounding woods to search everywhere for any loot that might appease the wolves. They found no treasure but collected among themselves an additional five thousand pieces of eight. They offered to try to raise more, leaving hostages with Morgan even though the governor had prohibited their giving any more ransom.

Morgan was now anxious to get out, fearing that the Spanish at Maracaibo might have prepared a trap to keep him in the lake. He freed all the prisoners, setting a ransom on each, kept four hostages to assure the ransom's being paid, and retained the slaves he had captured. The loot from Maracaibo and Gibraltar had been meager. L'Ollonois had done an efficient job of cleaning out the place two years before. Morgan was disappointed in the results, but his anxiety about what might be happening at the entrance to the lake persuaded him to leave.

Four days later, the buccaneers arrived at Maracaibo. Here Morgan learned that his hunch about the Spanish was right. Several old and sick Spaniards who remained in the town told him that three large Spanish men-of-war were waiting for him at the entrance of the lake and that the castle there had been put in order for defense, with larger cannon emplaced and much ammunition on hand. The future of the buccaneers looked very bleak. What followed demonstrated the devilish ingenuity and intrepidity of Morgan and his men. Morgan knew he had no chance in a battle with the Spanish ships, which mounted forty, thirty, and twenty-four guns respectively. To face them, he had five or six small vessels mounting only guns of low caliber and a fleet of boats loaded with loot. He had lost several men killed and wounded and others drowned in the disastrous flood.

His first move was psychological, as Esquemelin tells us:

> Hereupon, being necessitated to act as well as he could, Captain Morgan resumed new courage, and resolved to show himself as yet undaunted with these terrors. To this intent he boldly sent a Spaniard to the Admiral of those three ships, demanding of him a considerable tribute or ransom for not putting the city of Maracaibo to the flame. This man (who doubtless was received by the Spaniards with great admiration of the confidence and boldness of those Pirates) returned two days after, bringing to Captain Morgan a letter from the said Admiral.

The admiral informed Morgan that he had been ordered to Maracaibo to destroy him but offered to let the buccaneers pass out of the lake if they would restore all the prisoners and loot they had taken. If Morgan would not agree to these terms, he wrote,

> I will command boats to come from Caracas, wherein I will put my troops, and coming to Maracaibo, will cause you utterly to perish, by putting you every man to the sword. This is my last and absolute resolution. Be prudent, therefore, and do not abuse my bounty with ingratitude. I have with me very good soldiers, who desire nothing more ardently than to revenge on you and your people all the cruelties and base infamous actions you have committed upon the Spanish nation in America. Dated on board the Royal Ship named the *Magdalen*, lying

at anchor at the entry of the Lake of Maracaibo, this 24th day of April, 1669.

DON ALONSO DEL CAMPO Y ESPINOSA.

Don Alonso had every reason to be haughty, seeing that his forces were vastly superior to those of Morgan. Confident of victory, he could not have foreseen what fortune had in store for him.

When Morgan received the letter, he called his men into the market-place in Maracaibo, read them the letter, explained the military situation, and asked them whether they would surrender or fight for their loot and their freedom. To a man they chose to fight. Then, one of Morgan's men stepped up to his leader with a suggestion—he proposed to build a fireship from one of their vessels and float it down on the Spanish squadron. The buccaneers approved this plan, but Morgan continued to negotiate with the Spanish admiral, preferring an accommodation to a battle. Morgan offered to quit the lake if he were allowed to keep the loot. To this, the admiral replied: "That in case they surrendered not themselves voluntarily into his hands within the space of two days, under the conditions which he had offered them by his letter, he would immediately come and force them to do it." Morgan now knew he must fight and began preparations. The prisoners and slaves were tied up and given extra guards. Flammables, such as sulphur, pitch, and tar, were gathered from the town to prepare the fireship.

> Likewise they made several inventions of powder and brimstone, with great quantities of palm-leaves, very well anointed with tar. They covered very well their counterfeit cannon, laying under every piece thereof many pounds of powder. Besides which, they cut down many outworks belonging to the ship, to the end the powder might exert its strength the better. Thus they broke open also new port-holes; where, instead of guns they placed little drums, of which the negroes make use. Finally, the decks were handsomely beset with many pieces of wood dressed up in the shape of men with hats, or monteras, and likewise armed with swords, muskets and bandoliers.

The male prisoners were loaded in one of the large boats, while the women, jewels, and silver were loaded into another. Other boats carried the bales of rich merchandise. Each of the boats was guarded by twelve well-armed men. The fireship was sent ahead with a small crew to bring her alongside the largest Spanish vessel. Morgan's flotilla got under way on April 30, 1669, and arrived in the vicinity of the Spanish ships as darkness fell. Posting extra watches, the buccaneers rode at anchor through the night not far from the enemy. At dawn, the action started. "The fire-ship, sailing before the rest, fell presently upon the great ship, and grappled to her sides in a short while. Which by the Spaniards being perceived to be a fire-ship, they attempted to escape the danger by putting her off; but in vain, and too late. For the flame suddenly seized her timber and tackling, and in a short space consumed all the stern, the forepart sinking into the sea, whereby she perished."

With their admiral's ship destroyed before their eyes, the Spanish on the thirty-gun vessel panicked and drove their ship aground, sinking her near the castle. The smallest of the Spanish flotilla, left alone to face the swarming buccaneers, was soon taken and joined to Morgan's squadron. As the crew of the thirty-gun ship left their vessel, they fired her to prevent her salvage by the marauders. A number escaped, as well, from the admiral's vessel as she burned, making their way to the castle and joining the defenders. The admiral was among them.

The victory over the Spanish flotilla gave the buccaneers new spirit and courage, and they determined to assault the castle immediately with only small arms, firepots and a few small swivel guns in their boats. Until nightfall they showered the fortress with fire but this was returned by the defenders, who retaliated with showers of scrap iron and solid shot from their heavy guns. In the face of this the attackers retired to their ships.

The Spanish in the castle believed that Morgan intended to attack again the next day and spent the entire night clearing small hillocks in front of their guns and preparing the fortifications for the worst. Morgan, with many of his men dead or wounded, a considerable amount of wealth in his hands, and the problem of passing the great guns of the castle yet to be solved, had no intention of renewing the attack but busied his men with picking up more Spanish prisoners from the water where they had floated all night on wreckage from the ships. Among these was the pilot of the thirty-gun ship, which had been run aground and sunk near the fort. Morgan questioned this man at length, learning that the three ships had been part of a squadron of six gathered on orders of the Supreme Council of State in Spain under the Queen Regent, who was determined to chase the buccaneers from Spanish waters. He learned of the strength of the other vessels, which included the *Nuestra Señora de la Soledad* of forty-eight guns, the ship of Admiral Don Agustín de Bustos, commander of the entire squadron. The vice admiral, whom Morgan had just defeated, had sailed in *La Concepción* of forty-four guns. On arriving at Cartagena, the two largest ships were ordered back to Spain with the fleet, being found too large for chasing marauders in West Indian waters. Don Alonso

The English first rate, built in 1637. With stately ships of this type the English contested control of the seas. Early engraving from a painting by Vandervelde. Photograph from the Smithsonian Institution

French first rate of the late seventeenth century. From a contemporary water-color. Photograph from the Smithsonian Institution

had transferred his flag to the forty-gun ship and had assumed command of the squadron. While cruising off Campeche, he had lost his smallest vessel in a storm and had then proceeded to Lake Maracaibo when reports of Morgan's raid had reached him. The pilot also gave Morgan a most tantalizing piece of information. The vessel in which he sailed, now lying sunk in the strait, had aboard 40,000 pieces of eight. Morgan now had two major problems: how to get out of the lake with a whole hide, and how to salvage the money before he escaped. The expedition had not paid as he had wished, and he saw in the sunken treasure the chance to recoup his fortunes.

Morgan left a ship at the site of the wreck to see to salvaging the treasure and then returned with his flotilla to Maracaibo. Here he transferred to the ship he had captured off the fort, "giving his own bottom to one of his captains." Shortly after, he sent another message to the vice admiral in the fort, threatening to burn Maracaibo unless a ransom was paid. The vice admiral refused and furthermore forbade the townspeople to pay. In spite of the Spanish leader's instructions, the citizens agreed to scrape together a ransom to save their homes. This was set at 20,000 pieces of eight and 500 cattle. The buccaneers set to slaughtering the cows and salting the meat while they waited for the arrival of the money. It was duly delivered, but Morgan refused to release his prisoners, in the hope that they would be a means of his getting past the guns of the fort and out to sea:

> Thus he set sail with all his fleet in quest of that ship which he had left behind, to seek for the plate of the vessel that was burnt. He found her upon the place, with the sum of fifteen thousand pieces of eight, which they had secured out of the wreck, besides many other pieces of plate, as hilts of swords and other things of this kind; also great quantity of pieces of eight that were melted and run together by the force of the fire of the said ship.

With the additional ransom and the treasure secured from the wreck, Morgan now considered the expedition a success, especially since the deaths of numbers of his men made the individual shares larger. The passage of the fort now became the last problem to be reckoned with, and Morgan solved it with characteristic ingenuity. First, hoping to pay his way out with the lives of his prisoners, he sent a deputation of them to the vice admiral in the fort, proposing a free passage for his fleet in return for their lives. The vice admiral, instead of sending the word which they hoped would save them from death, sent them a lecture on loyalty: "If you had been as loyal to your King in hindering the entry of these Pirates as I shall do their going out, you had never caused these troubles, neither to yourselves, nor to our whole nation; which have suffered so much through your pusillanimity. In a word, I shall never grant your request; but shall endeavour to maintain that respect which is due to my King, according to my duty."

Now Morgan prepared his next move. First, he divided the booty equally between the boats and ships according to the crews of each. The entire take amounted to 250,000 pieces of eight in money and jewels, large quantities of merchandise, and slaves. Then the buccaneers

made use of a stratagem, of no ill invention, which was as follows. On the day that preceeded the night wherein they determined to get forth, they embarked many of their men in canoes, and rowed towards the shore, as if they designed to land them. Here they concealed themselves under the branches of trees that hung over the coast for a while till they had laid themselves down along in the boats. Then the canoes returned to the ships, with the appearance only of two or three men rowing them back, all the rest being concealed at the bottom of the canoes.

This operation was repeated during the day and the Spanish, convinced they were to be attacked from the landside, moved their great guns to that side of the fortress, leaving the waterside without a battery.

As night came the buccaneers raised anchors and set sail. The furious Spanish, realizing they had been duped, tried to rush their heavy artillery back to the waterside of the fortress. But great guns cannot be rushed and the Spanish were too late. Morgan's fleet escaped with little damage and only a few casualties. A day after sailing, a great storm struck the little squadron and the vessels were forced to anchor. For a while, it appeared that they would be wrecked on the shore they had just left and be at the mercy of their frustrated enemies. But the anchors and lines held, and once the storm had cleared, they set sail for Port Royal. Here they arrived safely and spent their loot in the usual debaucheries.

Morgan knew that both officers and men would soon be destitute and ready for another adventure to restore their fortunes. Not only were they spending everything they had, but many of them had gone deeply into debt to the merchants and tavernkeepers. He lost no time in planning the biggest operation of his life—the raid on Panama.

As before, he proclaimed the place of rendezvous as Vaca Island and spread the word throughout the islands. The buccaneers of all nationalities flocked from everywhere to join. Morgan sailed from Jamaica on August 12, 1670. The next day, Governor Modyford received a message from King Charles that the buccaneers should refrain from attacking the Spanish on land, since the earl of Arlington was in Madrid negotiating an agreement for "peace and friendship in America." The message had left England two months before. Modyford immediately recalled Morgan to Port Royal and asked him to obey the wishes of the King and "strictly charging him to observe the same and behave with all moderation possible in carrying on the war."[3] Morgan told the governor that he might have to land on Spanish territory for supplies—the understatement of the century as it turned out.

Sailing again on August 14, Morgan went to Vaca Island to organize his forces, and here he was joined by a large party of French as well as another party of English buccaneers, who had returned to Jamaica from a raid on the mainland and had been immediately sent by Modyford as reinforcements. The governor was undoubtedly involved in the plan with Morgan and was only paying lip service to the King's wishes.

With many ships and men at hand, Morgan now sent his vice admiral, Edward Collier, to the mainland for beef and other provisions. Here Collier captured Spanish ships loaded with provisions, sacked the town of Río de la Hacha, and held it for a ransom of corn, beef, salt, and other foodstuffs. Collier returned to Vaca, heavily laden, on October 28. By December, everything was in readiness, and Morgan and his officers, in general council, agreed they should mount an overland attack on Panama by way of Old Providence Island and the Chagres River.* Before sailing, Morgan called his commanders together where they signed the customary articles of agreement. Morgan then gave orders to depart and, on December 16, 1670, the fleet cleared Cape Tiburón. Old Providence was sighted on December 20, and the landing made the next day. The larger of the two islands that formed the Old Providence colony was taken without resistance, the Spanish having retired to the smaller, heavily fortified island. While the buccaneers were waiting out the night before attacking, they were drenched by a violent rainstorm, which soaked them to the skin, wet their ammunition, and caused great discomfort, for they were dressed only in seaman's breeches and thin shirts without shoes or stockings. The rain stopped as day came, and the buccaneers set about drying their arms and powder, but just after they started to march toward the forts, another rain struck them.

* See the map on p. 139.

The Pirates were now reduced to great affliction and danger of their lives through the hardness of the weather, their own nakedness, and the great hunger they sustained. For a small relief hereof, they happened to find in the fields an old horse, which was both lean and full of scabs and blotches, with galled back and sides. This horrid animal they instantly killed and flayed, and divided into small pieces among themselves as far as it would reach, for many could not obtain one morsel, which they roasted and devoured without either salt or bread, more like ravenous wolves than men. The rain as yet ceased not to fall, and Captain Morgan perceived their minds to relent, hearing many of them say they would return on board the ships.

Facing a mutiny, Morgan as always was ready with a solution. He decided to bluff the Spanish commander on the fortified island, and sent a boat and flag of truce with a message: "that if within a few hours he delivered not himself and all his men into his hands, he did by that messenger swear to him, and all those that were in his company, he would most certainly put them all to the sword, without granting quarter to any." The Spanish commander asked for two hours in which to discuss the terms with his staff before replying. This he was given. After this time, two canoes arrived from the fort with Spanish officers carrying flags of truce. After hostages were furnished the Spanish for the security of their emissaries, the Spaniards conferred with Morgan and his officers. To their delight the spanish governor and his officers proposed to deliver up the main fortress, St. Jerome, to the buccaneers on the condition that Morgan would feign a furious attack by land while their ships bombarded the place from the sea—all with blank ammunition. With St. Jerome in his hands, for the governor proposed to surrender after a decent interval, the other forts would easily fall to Morgan.

The proposition was readily accepted by Morgan and his staff, and the charade was enacted the next day with great noise and commotion and no casualties. In this way, Providence was won, the Spanish commander saved his head, and he and his troops were later transported to Panama and released. With the islands in their hands, "the Pirates began to make a new war against the poultry, cattle and all sort of victuals they could find. This was their whole employ for some days, scarce thinking of anything else than to kill those animals, roast and eat, and make good cheer, as much as they could possible attain unto. If wood was wanting, they presently fell upon the houses, and, pulling them down, made fires with the timber, as had been done before in the field." The unfortunate civilian inhabitants were set to work gathering provisions for the invaders. Their stomachs being satisfied, the buccaneers now took inventory of the trophies they had captured. These included forty-seven cannon, numerous muskets, thirty thousand pounds of powder, and all sorts of other ammunition. The invaders spiked all the guns and demolished the fortresses, saving that of St. Jerome, the main castle. Here the buccaneers made their headquarters. The muskets and small-arms ammunition were all taken aboard the ships, a welcome addition to the magazines for use in the coming actions. All things being in order on Providence, Morgan now sent four ships with four hundred men to attack the Castle of San Lorenzo at the mouth of Chagres River in Panama. The admiral and the remainder of the forces stayed at Providence. To appear on the Panamanian coast with such a large force might alert the Spanish to the planned attack on Panama. On Providence, Morgan anxiously awaited word of the assault.

The troops were under the command of Captain Brodely, who had been on the coast with Mansvelt and was familiar with the area. He also had with him the Spanish deserters who were to serve as guides. His target, the Castle of San Lorenzo, stood on high ground, defended on the landward side by a bluff. On the other side, the river formed a defense and the whole was surrounded by strong palisades. Several bastions formed the outer works. Entry into the castle was by a single drawbridge behind the secondary fortifications. It was a very strong place to attack with small arms only. Brodely and his men arrived within sight of it three days after sailing from Providence. They landed about three miles down the coast from the castle, intending to attack from the landward side. On their march, they were inadvertently led into an open place by their Spanish guides and caught some severe gunfire from the fortress. Several men were killed. Because of the difficult way through the swamps and woods, they had not arrived until two o'clock in the afternoon, but they resolved on an immediate assault, even though they had no cover. They rushed on the fort with swords and fireballs in hand and pistols in their belts, but were repulsed with loss by the defenders. When night fell, the buccaneers attacked again, this time trying to set fire to the palisades with fireballs. During the attack, a peculiar accident occurred which ultimately led to the fall of the stronghold:

> One of the Pirates was wounded with an arrow in his back, which pierced his body to the other side. This instantly he pulled out with great valour at the side of his breast; then taking a little cotton that he had about him, he wound it about the said arrow, and putting it into his musket, he shot it back into the castle. But the cotton being kindled by

the powder, occasioned two or three houses that were within the castle, being thatched with palm-leaves, to take fire, which the Spaniards perceived not so soon as was necessary. For this fire meeting with a parcel of powder, blew it up, and thereby caused great ruin, and no less consternation to the Spaniards, who were not able to account for this accident, not having seen the beginning thereof.

Taking advantage of the confusion of the Spaniards, who were busy trying to extinguish the fire, the pirates ignited the palisades in several places, thereby ultimately gaining entrance to the inner defenses. The battle and the fire continued through the night, with the buccaneers killing many Spaniards who were silhouetted against the flames. The defenders brought up big guns to defend the breaches and fought like madmen, having been given orders by the Spanish commander not to retreat under pain of death. Finally at noon the day after the battle had begun, the buccaneers assaulted a breach defended by the Spanish commander himself with twenty-five soldiers:

Here was performed a very courageous and warlike resistance by the Spaniards, both with muskets, pikes, stones and swords. Yet notwithstanding, through all these arms the Pirates forced and fought their way, till at last they gained the castle. The Spaniards who remained alive cast themselves down from the castle into the sea, choosing rather to die precipitated by their own selves (few or none surviving the fall) than ask any quarter for their lives. The Governor himself retreated to the *corps du garde*, before which were placed two pieces of cannon. Here he intended still to defend himself, neither would he demand any quarter. But at last he was killed with a musket shot, which pierced his skull into the brain.

With the death of the governor, the battle ended. The buccaneers found only thirty survivors among the garrison, and of these, more than twenty were wounded. Only these men of a garrison of 314 remained alive. No officers survived. From the prisoners, the buccaneers learned that several of the garrison had escaped and were on their way to Panama to tell the president there of the attack. Captain Brodely also learned that the Spanish at Cartagena knew of the buccaneers' intention to assault Panama overland and had warned the president of Panama, who sent reinforcements to San Lorenzo shortly before the buccaneers attacked. The captives also told Brodely that the president had placed ambuscades along the Chagres River and had a large force at Panama waiting for the arrival of Morgan and his men. The buccaneers were not to have surprise as their ally. Word was sent

back to Morgan at Providence of the capture but also the bad news—
that the victory had cost the buccaneers many killed and wounded,
and that the president of Panama was waiting with an aroused army of
thirty-six hundred men, intending to defend his city.

After receiving the news of the fall of San Lorenzo, Morgan prepared to leave Providence. All the provisions to be found on the island
were loaded on the ships, the guns of the fortification were thrown
into the sea, and all but one of the castles and houses remaining were
leveled. Because Morgan intended to return to the island and fortify it
as a base, he preserved the one castle to use as his headquarters. All of
the prisoners were secured and taken aboard the ships which were soon
under way for Panama.

When Morgan's squadron approached San Lorenzo, the buccaneers
gave a tumultuous cheer as they saw the English flag flying over the
fortress. The fleet entered the river and here disaster struck. Four ships
ran aground, including Morgan's. All the men and supplies were saved,
but a sudden storm prevented refloating the vessels, and they were cast
on a submerged rock in the river and sunk. This misfortune hardly
dampened the spirits of the buccaneers, and when Morgan entered the
castle, he was greeted "with great acclamations of triumph and joy."
In the river nearby, his men found some of the boats the Spanish used
in carrying their goods up and down the stream from Los Ventos.
These were armed with two small carriage guns and four small brass
swivels. All that were seaworthy were taken and prepared for the trip
up the river and the assault on Panama. Morgan left a garrison of five
hundred men in the castle to protect his rear and one hundred fifty
men to guard the ships. Taking twelve hundred men in five Spanish
boats and thirty-two large canoes with scant provisions, he set out up
the river on August 18, 1670. He intended to live off the country.
Here he miscalculated the determination and efficiency of the
Spaniards.

The first day, the invaders covered eighteen miles and then went
ashore to sleep. Parties went out to find food but returned with almost
nothing. The Spanish living in the surrounding country had gone,
taking all their provisions with them. Esquemelin tells us that the
"greater part were forced to pass with only a pipe of tobacco, without
any other refreshment." Early the next morning, the hungry buccaneers continued their journey up the river and, in the evening, came to
a place called Cruz de Juan Gallego. Here they came to a stretch
almost devoid of water and clogged with fallen trees and had to abandon their boats. They left a guard of one hundred sixty men in the
boats, and the next morning continued on land. The guides had said

that open country lay ahead about six miles, but Morgan found the way "so dirty and irksome" that he had some of the men proceed in canoes which, with great labor, were dragged over the obstructed reaches of the river and paddled to the area of savannahs. As night fell, the canoes then returned and brought the remainder of the force to rejoin those who had gone ahead. The march without food had worn out the men, and they "were extremely desirous to meet any Spaniards, or Indians, hoping to fill their bellies with what provisions they should take from them. For now they were reduced almost to the very extremity of hunger."

The next day (the fourth day of the march), most of the men went on by land while the remainder went by the canoes up the river. Mounted Spanish spies watched the buccaneers constantly, and Esquemelin tells us that these spies could give six hours' warning to the Spanish upstream. At noon on the fourth day, the party arrived at a small settlement where the guide warned of an ambuscade. To this, the men reacted with joy, hoping to disperse any Spaniards there and capture their food, but the place was deserted, and no food was to be found. Had the buccaneers come upon any Spanish there they most certainly would have killed, cooked, and eaten them.

> Being angry at this misfortune, they pulled down a few little huts which the Spaniards had made, and afterwards fell to eating the leathern bags, as being desirous to afford something to the ferment of their stomachs, which now was grown so sharp that it did gnaw their very bowels, having nothing else to prey upon. Thus they made a huge banquet upon those bags of leather, which doubtless had been more grateful unto them, if divers quarrels had not risen concerning who should have the greatest share.

After their feast of leather bags, the company pushed on up the river. Soon they came to another place where the Spanish had laid an ambuscade which they had abandoned. There was not a crumb to be seen. The more far-sighted men had reserved some pieces of the leather from the bags on which they dined and ate them here. Esquemelin explains to his reader the manner of preparing this delicacy: The men "first took the leather, and sliced it in pieces. Then did they beat it between two stones, and rub it, often dipping it in the water of the river, to render it by these means supple and tender. Lastly, they scraped off the hair, and roasted or broiled it upon the fire. And being thus cooked they cut it into small morsels, and eat it, helping it down with frequent gulps of water, which by good fortune they had near at hand."

In council

Blood letting

On the march

Those who had consumed all of their leather for lunch had none for dinner and went to bed with their ever-growing hunger. On the fifth day, the buccaneers came to another small settlement and here in a cave found two bags of meal, some wheat and other grain, two jars of wine, and some bananas. Morgan realizing that some of his men were actually in danger of their lives from hunger, distributed the food to those in the worst physical condition. With their strength somewhat renewed, the men marched on until dark and then lay down to a restless night again without food.

The next (sixth) day, the company arose to continue their advance, but now had to rest more frequently because of the roughness of the country and their extreme weakness from lack of food. They were reduced to eating grass and young leaves to relieve their stomachs. At noon, their fortune changed: they came upon a barn full of corn. "Immediately they beat down the doors, and fell to eating of it dry, as much as they could devour. Afterwards they distributed great quantity, giving to every man a good allowance thereof." Soon after, they ran into an ambuscade of Indians. In the skirmish some of the buccaneers were killed and the Indians fled before they could be captured. That night in camp, "great murmurings were heard . . ., many complaining of Captain Morgan and his conduct in that enterprize, and being desirous to return home." But some of the more resolute condemned this talk and nothing came of it.

The next morning, Morgan ordered each man to test and clean his pistol and musket. Each weapon was fired without ball to test the lock and was then cleaned and reloaded. They then crossed the river to continue their journey, for the side on which they lay was not passable. The next day, the buccaneers were overjoyed to see smoke rising in the distance. They were certain that all the inhabitants of the village to which they were marching had hearth fires going and were cooking the noon meal. Rushing forward with the strength of their vision, they arrived at the place only to find that the settlers had abandoned it after setting fire to their own homes. A few dogs and cats were found, which they instantly killed and ate, and then, in the King's warehouse, they found some bread and jars of wine. They fell to with the results Esquemelin describes:

But no sooner had they began to drink of the said wine when they fell sick, almost every man. This sudden disaster made them think that the wine was poisoned, which caused a new consternation in the whole camp, as judging themselves now to be irrecoverably lost. But the true reason was, their huge want of sustenance in that whole voyage, and the manifold sorts of trash which they had eaten upon that occasion. Their sickness was so great that day as caused them to remain there till the next morning, without being able to prosecute their journey as they used to do, in the afternoon.

The village was the final point that could be reached on the Chagres River, and Panama lay only twenty-four miles away, but to the worn-out and starving men, this seemed an impossible distance. Here all of them, even the weakest, had to come ashore and prepare to continue the journey on land. Morgan sent the canoes back to the point where the boats waited, saving one canoe, which he hid for use as a dispatch boat later. The next morning (the eighth day of the march), he sent an advance party of two hundred of the stronger men ahead to scout the way to Panama. They found the road narrow and rough and at one point were attacked by Indians, who showered them with arrows and wounded several of the men. The chief of the Indian party was killed, but the remainder escaped, easily outrunning the hungry and tired buccaneers. As the main party came up, the woods about were swept by groups of men to root out any possible ambuscade, but only parties of Indians were found. Later, they entered mountainous country, where they saw a small number of mounted Spanish soldiers who were scouting them. That night, a great rain fell, and the arms of the men were stored in a few shepherds' huts they had found, while the majority spent a miserable night in the rain.

The next day, early in the morning, the buccaneers began their march before the heat of the day. They ascended a mountain trail, and when they reached the top they were able to see the Pacific. "This happy sight, as if it were the end of their labours, caused infinite joy among all the Pirates. Hence they could descry also one ship, and six boats, which were set forth from Panama, and sailed towards the islands of Tovago and Tovagilla." It was downhill now and the worst was over. The men stumbled along the trail, tired, hungry, and on the verge of collapse, but the psychological boost given them by seeing their objective furnished the necessary strength to carry on. In a small valley they soon entered, they found a herd of cattle, which they fell to slaughtering, and soon joints of beef were roasting over their fires: "Thus cutting the flesh of these animals into convenient pieces, or gobbets, they threw them into the fire, and, half carbonadoed or roasted, they devoured them with incredible haste and appetite. For such was their hunger that they more resembled cannibals than Europeans at this banquet, the blood many times running down from their beards to the middle of their bodies."

Strengthened with the food, the buccaneers now marched with new courage and vigor. Morgan sent an advance party of fifty men to scout the way. In the evening, the advance party spotted a company of mounted men who shouted to them in Spanish. Before night fell, they sighted a church steeple in the city of Panama. It had been nine days since they had left the Atlantic coast of the Isthmus. The men were overcome with joy, the trumpets were blown and the drums beaten. The sound was of course heard in the city, and that evening there appeared a company of fifty horsemen, who shouted to the invaders, "Ye Dogs! We shall meet ye." The company left without attacking, but several remained behind to observe the buccaneers during the night. After the horsemen returned to the city, the heavy guns there began to fire at the encampment, but the camp was well beyond the range of any of the cannon and no harm was done, although the biggest guns continued to fire throughout the night. As evening fell, the company of cavalry that had been seen by the advance guard during the afternoon surrounded the camp as if to lay siege. The buccaneers posted their sentries and proceeded to dine on the remains of the beef they had eaten for lunch. With full bellies, the bone-tired buccaneers then settled down for the first good night's sleep since they had started their march. Even the gunfire from the defenses of Panama failed to disturb most of them.

In the morning, the tenth day of the journey, they assembled in military order and marched with trumpets sounding and drums rolling. On the advice of one of the Spanish guides, Morgan led his men through the countryside and not along the road where ambuscades would be found, thereby outflanking the traps laid for them. With this, the Spanish were compelled to come out of the city and engage the buccaneers. The president of Panama drew his forces up in a large field lying outside the city across the route of the buccaneers. He had two squadrons of cavalry, four regiments of foot, and his auxiliaries, which consisted of a large number of wild bulls. When the invaders saw the battle array before them "they were suddenly surprised with great fear." But with the courage of desperation, they prepared to attack. Morgan divided his troops into three bodies and sent as an advance guard two hundred men who were expert musketmen. The Spanish cried out, "God save the King!" and sent a company of mounted troops toward them. The land being soft and rough, the cavalry could not maneuver as they wished and were caught in the fire of the advance guard, which fired from a kneeling position. The Spanish fought with great courage and many were killed. Finally, they drove the wild cattle against the invaders but many of the bulls ran off, frightened by the gunfire, while a few were killed and furnished food for the buccaneers after the battle.

After two hours of heated action, the Spanish horsemen had almost all been killed, and the foot were in full retreat, having thrown away their muskets. The buccaneers, weary with the march and still suffering from the effects of the recent starvation, could not summon the strength to follow their defeated enemies. Some of the Spanish tried to hide in the bushes near the battleground, but most were found by the more energetic buccaneers and killed without mercy. Some captured clergymen were brought before Morgan crying for mercy, but they were shot without exception. A Spanish captain of troops was also found who, when questioned by Morgan, revealed the strength of the defeated forces and gave the commander details of the defenses of Panama. He told Morgan "that in the city they had made trenches, and raised batteries in several places, in all which they had placed many guns, and that at the entry of the highway which led to the city they had built a fort, which was mounted with eight great guns of brass, and defended by fifty men." On hearing this, Morgan resolved to march against the city by another route. In the battle, the buccaneers lost many killed and wounded, but six hundred Spanish bodies lay on the field, and the strength of the invaders in proportion to that of their enemies had actually increased. After some rest, Morgan ordered his men forward.

As they approached the city, they were greeted by scrap iron and musket balls fired from cannon placed at strategic spots about the edge of the place. Under this deadly and continuous fire, the buccaneers continued their advance, and in three hours, during which many of the invaders were killed, the city was taken. The streets of the city were littered with Spanish dead. The fighting over, Morgan assembled his men and warned them not to drink any wine—he had intelligence that it had been poisoned. In this manner, he prevented the drunkenness that usually followed a capture and that here would have exposed them to excessive danger from the Spanish forces still in the country surrounding the city. After this the looting began. The fleeing citizens had taken most of their small valuables with them, but a rich prize was found—"several warehouses, very well stocked with all sorts of merchandize, as well silks and cloths as linen, and other things of considerable value."

Soon after capturing the city, disaster struck. Morgan had given orders for certain buildings to be burned. But the fires got out of hand and most of Panama went up in flames. The Spaniards joined their captors in attempting to stop the fire. Houses were blown up to make fire lanes, but nothing could stop the holocaust. When the fire had burned itself out, most of the city lay in ruins, including many rich residences of the wealthy merchants. For three weeks, Morgan and his men remained there, camping in the fields with sentries posted until the heat of the fire died down and then quartering themselves as best they could in the few houses that were not burned. During this time, the invaders found many pieces of gold and silver plate and pieces of eight hidden in the wells of the burned houses, and this loot swelled that taken from the warehouses before the fire. The usual procedures were followed in sending searching-out parties through the country to capture prisoners and loot. The prisoners were interrogated in the most brutal manner to make them reveal the hiding places of their wealth, and much booty was obtained. More money was obtained by ransoming the prisoners. Some of them told Morgan of a large galleon that had sailed, loaded with wealthy residents of the city and their jewels and plate. The ship had only topsails rigged and was lightly defended. The buccaneers found a large boat aground in the harbor. This was quickly fitted out and sent cruising to find the galleon among the islands lying offshore. The rich ship was never found, but other prizes with money and valuable goods were recovered and brought in. Morgan had sent a column of one hundred fifty men to the Chagres to tell the garrison there of the victory and to deliver some of the loot. They returned with the good news that the buccaneers at San Lorenzo had gone cruising on the coast and had captured Spanish ships loaded with provisions, of which there was a great shortage at the fort. This good news had influenced Morgan to stay longer in Panama.

During the occupation, there occurred an incident that has found its way into the romantic literature of our time. This was the story of how Morgan tried to win the favors of a beautiful Spanish lady of Panama. When the buccaneers brought back their prisoners from islands lying off the Pacific coast, there was found among them "a gentlewoman of good quality, as also no less virtue and chastity, who was wife to one of the richest merchants of all those countries. Her years were but few, and her beauty so great as peradventure I may doubt whether in all Europe any could be found to surpass her perfections either of comeliness or honesty. Her husband, at that present, was absent from home, being gone as far as the kingdom of Peru." The lady had taken refuge in the country but was brought in a prisoner. When Morgan saw her he was struck by her beauty and was immediately infatuated. He had his fair prisoner lodged in an apartment near his and fed her from his own table. She begged to be returned to the other prisoners but Morgan continued to court her with all the charm he could muster, which was considerable. He attempted to give her rich presents, but when she refused them the furious Morgan, his vanity badly bruised, cast her into a "darksome and stinking cellar."

Morgan was now convinced of her invulnerability and became concerned with a wave of sympathy for her which was sweeping his followers. To counter this and explain his conduct, he spread a report that the lady was a spy and in correspondence with the Spanish outside the city. Esquemelin insists these were "false accusations" and describes the lady as having unbelievable "constancy of mind and virtuous chastity."

With the departure of the buccaneers imminent, a faction of them plotted to steal away on a ship found in the harbor and cruise in the Pacific. For this purpose, they began secretly to lay in provisions, weapons, and ammunition, thinking to seize the vessel without warning and get away before Morgan got wind of the plan. Word of the conspiracy came back to the commander, and he frustrated their designs by simply cutting down the main mast of the vessel they planned to use. With this, the plot fell apart. In the last days of the occupation, the buccaneers were busy trying to raise ransom for the prisoners they held, and messengers were permitted to go into the country for this purpose. By this means, thousands of additional pieces of eight were gathered and added to the treasure looted from the city. Among those attempting to raise a ransom by messenger was the beautiful lady who had rejected Morgan's advances, but she was deceived. Her messengers were clergymen in whom she trusted, but after receiving the money to win her release, they returned to the city and ransomed friends instead. When Morgan began his march back to the Atlantic, the lady was taken along and "her lamentations did pierce the skies, seeing herself carried away into foreign captivity." Finally Morgan, realizing she had been betrayed by her friends who had brought her ransom, freed her and she returned to Panama. Thus, she left the pages of history and entered those of fiction, where her story in more romantic guise is still told.

Morgan and his cutthroats left Panama on February 24, 1671. They left a place so ruined it never recovered—the new city of Panama was established in another location. To appreciate the enormity of the crime, we must consider the description of the city as Esquemelin saw it before it was burned:

There belonged to this city (which is also the head of a bishopric) eight monasteries, whereof seven were for men and one for women, two stately churches and one hospital. The churches and monasteries

were all richly adorned with altar-pieces and paintings, huge quantity
of gold and silver, with other precious things; all which the ecclesiastics
had hidden and concealed. Besides which ornaments, here were to be
seen two thousand houses of magnificent and prodigious building, being
all or the greatest part inhabited by merchants of that country, who are
vastly rich.

In addition, two hundred warehouses were destroyed, along with
many slaves who had hidden in them.

Behind him Morgan left complete devastation and ruined fortunes.
With him he carried the greatest quantity of loot ever taken from a
Spanish city, exceeding even the wealth extracted by Drake almost a
century before. Esquemelin lists the plunder: "He carried with him
one hundred and seventy-five beasts of carriage, laden with silver, gold
and other precious things, besides six hundred prisoners, more or less,
between men, women, children and slaves." The strange assemblage
made its way slowly over the trails toward the Atlantic coast. The
clanging of the loaded mules and the tramp of the marching men was
drowned out by the weeping and cries of the women and children
among the prisoners, who suffered terribly during the journey. All of
the Spanish were convinced they were being taken to English territory
to be made slaves.

At the village of Venta Cruz, Morgan stopped to rest his men and to
gather provisions for his fleet, and here some of the prisoners were
ransomed by friends who arrived with money. Those less fortunate
were taken along to the coast when Morgan left the village on March 5.
With him went some new prisoners, who had returned to Venta Cruz
after the buccaneers had passed through on their way to Panama and
had just been taken. Halfway between Venta Cruz and San Lorenzo,
Morgan stopped the march and made a search among the buccaneers
for spoils, according to the custom. This event, which Esquemelin
describes, casts an interesting light on the habits of the buccaneers and
how, on this occasion, Morgan added a precaution not before taken:

Captain Morgan commanded them to be placed in due order, according
to their custom, and caused every one to be sworn, that they had
reserved nor concealed nothing privately to themselves, even not so
much as the value of sixpence. This being done, Captain Morgan having
had some experience that those lewd fellows would not much stickle to
swear falsely in points of interest, he commanded every one to be
searched very strictly, both in their clothes and satchels and everywhere it might be presumed they had reserved anything. Yea, to the
intent this order might not be ill taken by his companions, he permitted

himself to be searched, even to the very soles of his shoes. To this effect, by common consent, there was assigned one out of every company, to be the searchers of all the rest. The French Pirates that went on this expedition with Captain Morgan, were not well satisfied with this new custom of searching.

With this, the march continued to San Lorenzo. Here they found that most of the wounded men they had left behind for care had died of the infections that usually followed. The remaining buccaneers held the fort with provisions and ammunition in plenty.

Before preparing to leave the Isthmus, Morgan now made one last effort at raising more ransom. He sent a large boat to Porto Bello with all the prisoners he had taken at Providence, with a demand that the governor send a substantial amount as ransom for the Castle of San Lorenzo, or otherwise he would raze it to the ground. The governor replied he would give nothing as ransom and Morgan could do what he wanted to the castle. With this, Morgan divided the loot, and here he deceived his own men, who had suffered so greatly and had fought so hard for what they had stolen. Blackguards that they were, one can almost sympathize with them, for now they were grossly cheated by the leader in whom they had trusted. Esquemelin describes the division and the anger of the men when they realized they had been duped. Morgan had wind of the political situation in Europe and probably realized that this was his last expedition. He accordingly made the most of his opportunity to run off with the major share of the loot: "The dividend was made of all the spoil they had purchased in that voyage. Thus every company, and every particular person therein included, received their portion of what was got: or rather, what part thereof Captain Morgan was pleased to give them," amounting to only two hundred pieces of eight per person. The men feared to complain to Morgan and had to content themselves with grumbling. As the grumbling increased, Morgan began to fear a mutiny and secretly prepared to leave. The fortress was demolished and the cannon from it loaded on the flagship. Then "he went secretly on board his own ship, without giving any notice of his departure to his companions, nor calling any council, as he used to do. Thus he set sail, and put out to sea, not bidding anybody adieu, being only followed by three or four vessels of the whole fleet. These were such (as the French Pirates believed) as went shares with Captain Morgan, towards the best and greatest part of the spoil which had been concealed from them in the dividend."

And so with one last act of infamy, this time to his own followers, Morgan the pragmatist sailed into retirement from buccaneering. He had caused untold human misery and suffering. Every piece of eight he had stolen had a price in human anguish, and even by the standards of his day, he was judged a brutal person. Yet, later in England, he was to be lionized. America was far away from London, and the violence Morgan did in the towns of Spanish America did not seem real to his English admirers.

When Morgan reached Port Royal, he found the climate slightly different from that when he had sailed in August. At the very time he and his men were spending the loot of Maracaibo and planning the Panama operation, Sir William Godolphin, as envoy extraordinary to the court of Madrid, was beginning negotiations for a treaty of peace and friendship. Spain wanted it because of her fears of the expansionist policies of Louis XIV. England desired it because she wanted to retain her commercial foothold in the West Indies and because Spain was threatening to declare a formal war beyond the line if England did not curb her buccaneers. Godolphin had instructions not to agree to any compensation for the collusion of Governor Modyford with Morgan after the general peace treaty of 1667, as the English maintained that treaty did not extend beyond the line. There was opposition in Spain to the treaty, since certain factions recognized it as the abandonment of Spain's long policy of exclusion of other powers from the New World and recognition of the right of the English and, by inference, other powers to colonies in the West Indies. But the power of Spain had been broken. With her effective naval power destroyed and her government almost bankrupt, the Queen Regent and her ministers had nothing left but diplomacy to stop the depredations that were bleeding the Spanish colonies white and bringing such suffering to their people.

The Spanish finally accepted the English conditions, and in July 1670 the Treaty of Madrid was signed. It was supposed to have ended hostilities beyond the line, and it gave England title to her West Indies colonies for the first time. Modyford and Morgan ignored the treaty, and the Panama operation went forward after word of the peace had arrived in Jamaica. For this, Morgan and Modyford were recalled to London and placed in the Tower for a period, but the punishment was only window dressing to placate the disappointed and furious Spanish. After his release, Morgan became the hero of the day in London, was knighted, and later returned as lieutenant governor of Jamaica. While in this office, which he disgraced with his conduct, he found himself on the other side of the fence, being instructed to suppress the buccaneers in Port Royal, among whom were many of his former shipmates. This he did with indifferent efficiency, and he was finally relieved of his office. He died rich and still respected by the rougher elements in

FRANCIS LOLONOIS.

Jamaica in 1688. He was buried in Port Royal, and there in the terrible earthquake, his grave sank into the sea with two-thirds of the town. It has been said that "romantic adventure is violence in retrospect" and whoever said it must have been thinking of Henry Morgan.

With the retirement of Morgan, the leadership of the buccaneers passed to the French, now securely established at Tortuga and the western end of Hispaniola as sometime planters, sometime hunters, and sometime marauders. The French continued, and even enlarged upon, the cruelty and violence that had been the code of the buccaneers under Morgan, and the sufferings of the Spanish colonials continued unabated after the Treaty of Madrid.

Of all the French who preyed on the Spanish, none has a reputation for cruelty greater than that of Jean-David Nau, called L'Ollonois from his home, Les Sables-d'Olonne, near La Rochelle. L'Ollonois came to Dominica as an indentured servant when a young man. Here he served out the term of his indenture and then went to Hispaniola and joined the buccaneers. As a sailor, he served well and bravely in action against the Spanish. These deeds brought him to the attention of the French governor of Tortuga, who entrusted a vessel to his command. On his first voyages, L'Ollonois captured numbers of Spanish vessels, and his reputation as a leader grew among his companions. His great talents were marred by a psychopathic predilection for treating his prisoners with extreme cruelty, and he soon had the deserved reputation of being an inhuman monster. This very cruelty became a disadvantage of L'Ollonois, as Esquemelin tells us: "But, withal, his cruelties against the Spaniards were such that the very fame of them made him known through the whole Indies. For which reason the Spaniards, in his time, whensoever they were attacked by sea, would choose rather to die or sink fighting than surrender, knowing they should have no mercy nor quarter at his hands."

After these initial successes, L'Ollonois's fortunes changed. In a violent storm on the coast of Campeche, his ship was wrecked. He and his men escaped to shore, "but coming upon dry land, the Spaniards pursued them, and killed the greatest part of them, wounding also L'Ollonais, their captain. Not knowing how to escape, he thought to save his life by stratagem. Hereupon he took several handfuls of sand and mingled them with the blood of his own wounds, with which he besmeared his face and other parts of his body. Then hiding himself dextrously among the dead, he continued there till the Spaniards had quitted the field."

For a time, L'Ollonois lived in the woods while his wounds healed. Here he lived on the land, eating what he could find in the forest and along the shore. Having gotten some Spanish clothes, he then went into Campeche and there conspired with some slaves to steal a canoe and go to sea. Some of L'Ollonois's companions lay in jail in Campeche, and when repeatedly asked by the Spanish what had become of their leader, answered that he was dead, for indeed they thought he was.

When the Spanish were convinced the monster had really been killed, they gave themselves up to celebrating their deliverance from this scourge and said prayers of thanksgiving in their churches. L'Ollonois was still in the town when these celebrations took place, and "having seen these joys for his death, made haste to escape with the slaves above-mentioned, and came safe to Tortuga, the common place of refuge of all sorts of wickedness, and the seminary, as it were, of all manner of Pirates and thieves."

L'Ollonois's reputation being what it was, he contrived to get himself another ship, which he manned with twenty-one well-armed buccaneers. With this, he set out to attack the southwestern coast of Cuba and the village of De los Cayos, a center for trade in hides, sugar, and tobacco which was carried on in boats, the water being too shallow to accommodate ships. Some fishermen saw the buccaneers and warned the town, which sent a dispatch rider overland to beg the governor of Havana for help. This worthy official immediately sent a fast frigate to the waters off the town. The frigate was armed with ten guns and carried a well-armed crew of ninety men. The governor, hardly believing the leader of the buccaneers to be the supposedly dead L'Ollonois, nevertheless sent a Negro hangman with the ship and orders to hang all the buccaneers on the spot. The exception was L'Ollonois himself. He was to be brought to Havana for some special treatment the Spanish had devised for him. The ship was waiting for L'Ollonois in a river port near the village when the buccaneers arrived. They immediately decided to attack the vessel and forced some captured fishermen to pilot them up the river to within speaking distance. At two o'clock in the morning the watch on the Havana ship hailed the new arrival and asked if they had seen any pirates, to which L'Ollonois replied that they had seen none. With this, the Spanish were deceived into thinking that the buccaneers, having seen the large ship lying in the river, had decided not to attack.

But they experienced very soon the contrary; for about break of day the Pirates began to assault the vessel on both sides with their two canoes. This attack they performed with such vigour that, although the Spaniards behaved themselves as they ought and made as good defence as they could, shooting against them likewise some great guns, yet they were forced to surrender, after being beaten by the Pirates, with swords in hand, down under the hatches. Hence L'Ollonais commanded them to be brought up one by one, and in this order caused their heads to be struck off.

With the Havana ship in his hands, L'Ollonois now had a vessel that could attack almost any target, but he required provisions and additional crew. To supply this need, he went cruising, and finally, off Maracaibo, captured a ship with provisions and a considerable amount of plate aboard. With this booty, he returned to Tortuga, and the resulting fame brought him the crew he needed. While off Maracaibo, he had viewed the rich settlement and resolved to return and sack it. He soon had a fleet of eight ships and 660 men at his command. With him went several prisoners who were familiar with the town and the surrounding country. An old buccaneer who had campaigned with an army in Europe was given command of the land forces.

The fleet left Tortuga at the end of April 1668, and touched at the north coast of Hispaniola, where some French joined. Finally, the fleet got away from Hispaniola on July 31. Soon the buccaneers fell in with a Spanish vessel on the way from Puerto Rico to Vera Cruz, and after an action of three hours it was taken. In the prize were found a valuable cargo of 120,000 pounds of cacao, 40,000 pieces of eight, and jewels worth £10,000. This prize was sent to Tortuga with orders to return, as soon as it was unloaded, to the island of Saona. Thus, a fine sixteen-gun ship was added to the fleet. At Saona, L'Ollonois captured another Spanish vessel loaded with military supplies and provisions. This vessel of eight guns was added to the growing fleet and provided many of the supplies needed for the expedition, including 7,000 pounds of powder and a large number of muskets, as well as 12,000 pieces of eight.

With this prosperous start, the buccaneers finally sailed to Maracaibo, assaulted the fort, and took it. When they entered the town soon after, they found that the inhabitants had fled down the lake to Gibraltar. The operation then proceeded almost exactly as it did two years later, when Henry Morgan took the place, an event we have already described. Afterwards, L'Ollonois took Gibraltar, and when he and his men left, they were loaded with 260,000 pieces of eight and many bales of valuable goods, such as silks and fine linen as well as a considerable quantity of jewels. Reaching Vaca Island, L'Ollonois divided the loot, setting aside extra portions for the wounded and for the families of those killed. When the buccaneers arrived back at Tortuga with the bags of pieces of eight, they found in the port two French merchant ships loaded with wine, brandy and other French luxuries. Prices for the goods on the French ships took a rapid spiral upward, and Esquemelin tells us that a gallon of brandy finally sold for four pieces of eight, a great bargain now, but an enormous price at that time. Tortuga celebrated the success of the raid with the usual carousing.

L'Ollonois was now riding the crest of a wave. His voyage to Maracaibo and Gibraltar had made him the hero of the buccaneer community at Tortuga and the most sought-after commander there. He now planned his next foray, put another fleet together, and set out for the south coast of Cuba to steal provisions from the fishermen there. Here his fleet was becalmed and drifted into the Gulf of Honduras. The ships were short of provisions and the men were soon in a desperate condition. Putting into the first port they reached, that of Xagua, an Indian settlement, they totally destroyed it, robbing the place of hogs, millet, and chickens. Thus provisioned, they decided to remain on the coast and loot all the settlements in that area. At Puerto Caballos, they found a large Spanish ship of twenty-four guns and instantly took her.

In the port, they robbed two great warehouses loaded with goods and then burned them down. The prisoners were treated with unspeakable cruelties according to the custom of the psychopath who led the raiders:

> They took prisoners, and committed upon them the most insolent and inhuman cruelties that ever heathens invented, putting them to the cruellest tortures they could imagine or devise. It was the custom of L'Ollonois that, having tormented any persons and they not confessing, he would instantly cut them in pieces with his hanger, and pull out their tongues; desiring to do the same, if possible, to every Spaniard in the world. Oftentimes it happened that some of these miserable prisoners, being forced thereunto by the rack, would promise to discover the places where the fugitive Spaniards lay hidden; which being not able afterwards to perform, they were put to more enormous and cruel deaths than they who were dead before.

Among the prisoners only two remained alive, and they consented to lead the buccaneers to the town of San Pedro some thirty miles distant. L'Ollonois set out with three hundred men and ran into Spanish ambuscades along the way nine miles from Puerto Caballos. The buccaneers attacked with fury. Many of the Spaniards were either killed or taken prisoner, only a relatively few escaping through the woods. It was here that L'Ollonois, having lost numbers of his men killed and seeking another route, vented his insane rage on one Spaniard:

> There were still remaining some few prisoners who were not wounded. These were asked by L'Ollonois if any more Spaniards did lie farther on in ambuscade? To whom they answered, there were. Then he commanded them to be brought before him, one by one, and asked if there was no other way to be found to the town but that? This he did out of a design to excuse, if possible, those ambuscades. But they all constantly answered him, they knew none. Having asked them all, and finding they could show him no other way, L'Ollonois grew outrageously passionate; insomuch that he drew his cutlass, and with it cut open the breast of one of those poor Spaniards, and pulling out his heart with his sacrilegious hands, began to bite and gnaw it with his teeth, like a ravenous wolf, saying to the rest: "I will serve you all alike, if you show me not another way."

Finally, after fighting through other ambuscades and a valiant defense of the town by the Spanish soldiers and civilians, the place was taken, sacked, and burned. The buccaneers subsequently stayed on the coasts of Honduras and Yucatan, looting and burning. Finally, L'Ollonois determined to go to Nicaragua, but several of his lieutenants decided for Costa Rica and left in the smaller vessels. L'Ollonois, with a ship too deep to get out of the gulf during the dry season when the water was low, soon ran out of provisions, and he and his men were reduced to eating monkeys. While attempting to sail down the coast, the great ship ran aground on a small key and could not be gotten off. L'Ollonois and his crew were forced to abandon ship and built a boat from timber salvaged from the wreck. For five or six months, the buccaneers worked on their boat and cultivated a garden on the key to provision their new craft. Since it was not large enough to hold them all, when it was finished, a party chosen by lot went to Nicaragua to the Río Grande to capture canoes in which to take away some of the stranded buccaneers. On the Nicaragua coast, they were attacked by Indians and Spanish, and many were killed. L'Ollonois escaped with some of his men and set out for the vicinity of Cartagena to capture a vessel so he could return for his stranded companions. Here fate caught up with him. He landed on the coast of Darién on the way and was captured by the Indians. The savages contrived a manner of execution for the hated buccaneer appropriate to his unbelievable cruelty. One of his companions escaped capture and finally returned to Tortuga, bringing with him the story of L'Ollonois's death, and this account is given in Esquemelin: "But the Indians within a few days after his arrival took him prisoner and tore him in pieces alive, throwing his body limb by limb into the fire, and his ashes into the air; to the intent no trace nor memory might remain of such an inhuman creature." So ended the career of the most inhuman of the buccaneers.

By the 1670's, the nature of buccaneering had changed. Finding prizes in the Caribbean scarce, the marauders began to go to the Pacific. This they accomplished by marching over the Isthmus of Panama, stealing or building canoes, and then cruising the coasts until they captured a ship. In this way, a fleet of buccaneers was built up in the islands off the Panama coast, and from here they preyed on Spanish shipping and raided towns. Some of the buccaneers even navigated the Straits of Magellan, as Drake had a century before, and joined their companions. Ships and squadrons were sent against them by the viceroy of Peru, and fortifications were built along the coast to meet this new threat, but the buccaneers wreaked havoc. In the West Indies, the buccaneers of Santo Domingo and Tortuga were commissioned as privateers in times of hostilities between the European powers. So it was in the early 1680's, when the governor of Santo Domingo sent buccaneers cruising against Spanish ships and settlements. And so it was when war broke out between France and England in 1689. The buccaneers, of necessity, took sides, and former companions in arms found themselves facing each other as enemies as they cruised under privateering commissions. In the almost continuous warfare that prevailed in Europe from 1689 to 1715, the buccaneers lost their identity as a community and were dispersed among the numerous privateers that sailed the seas on both sides of the conflicts. When peace came to Europe with the end of the War of Spanish Succession in 1713, most of the old buccaneers were gone. Of those that remained, many identified themselves with the pirates, who now took to the seas in great numbers, bringing on the last great age of piracy.

XI

Two Lost Treasure Fleets

Even though I am greatly distressed it doesn't excuse my obligation to inform you of the unfortunate loss of the whole Fleet of Mexico and the Galleons of Terra Firma, which occurred on July 31.
  —Letter of Admiral Don Francisco Salmón to Philip V of Spain, September 20, 1715

 TWO MAJOR WARS racked Europe between 1688 and 1715, brought on by the expansionist policies of Louis XIV. During the first of these, the War of the Grand Alliance, the buccaneers who entered the service of their respective kings, as privateers or auxiliary troops, lost their identity, and their history may be said to end. The war not only disrupted the continent of Europe but also the American trade, and Spain, depending as she did on her American treasure to finance her way in European politics, suffered badly. With the Dutch, English, and Spanish on one side and Louis XIV on the other, the buccaneers in the West Indies split into English and French factions. In the ensuing struggle, the French buccaneers continued the depredations against the Spanish which they had formerly carried on in alliance with their English counterparts. In 1697, eluding an English fleet under Vice Admiral John Nevell, the sieur de Pointis with a French fleet joined by buccaneers from Tortuga, attacked, captured, and sacked Cartagena. This event may be said to mark the end of the buccaneers and brought the Crown of Spain close to bankruptcy.

The War of the Grand Alliance ended with the Treaty of Ryswick in 1697, but war broke out again over the succession to the Spanish throne in 1701 after Charles II had died childless. On his deathbed, Charles had named Philip, the grandson of Louis XIV, as his heir. The Holy Roman emperor Leopold I, wanting the succession for his son, Archduke Charles, and wishing to prevent a close alliance between Spain and France, went to war. When the lines were drawn, the Emperor, the Dutch, and England found themselves in alliance, opposing France, Spain, Bavaria, Portugal, and Savoy. As the seas became flooded with the regular naval vessels and privateers of the belligerents, Spain's routes to and from America were again threatened, and the flow of American treasure to the mother country was reduced to a trickle. In 1702 a powerful English force sailed into Vigo Bay on the northwest coast of Spain, capturing a large treasure, sinking a number of ships and making off with the rest. The haul was large enough that a special issue of coins was struck by Queen Anne, with the word VIGO below the bust to identify the source of the bullion and, no doubt, to advertise the victory. Another English squadron destroyed a Spanish fleet off Cartagena in 1708. Not only human enemies but capricious nature continued to take a toll of Spanish shipping. In 1711 a storm wrecked a fleet on the coast of Cuba.

The War of the Spanish Succession was ended by a series of treaties known to history as the Peace of Utrecht. The treaty between Great Britain and France confirmed Philip V's succession to the throne of Spain. In it, Philip renounced his rights to the French throne, a commendable precaution on the part of Great Britain, since the combined kingdoms of France and Spain would have been a threat to the balance of power on the Continent. The British were also given Newfoundland, the Hudson Bay territory, and the island of St. Christopher. The series of treaties signed between Spain and Great Britain advertised to the world the low depths to which the formerly powerful Spanish kingdom had sunk since the days of the early Hapsburgs. Gibraltar was ceded to the British, and by the "Asiento Treaty," British merchants were permitted to lade one ship each year for the fair at Porto Bello and were given a monopoly of the slave trade with the Spanish possessions. The British very soon learned to circumvent the terms of the treaty by simply unloading an entire fleet over the deck of the one ship, after it docked at Porto Bello. The Treaty of Madrid had given the British title to her earliest West Indian colonies; now the Asiento Treaty gave them the commercial privileges they had sought since the days of John Hawkins. The war had ended officially, but in reality it continued on a smaller scale: the Spanish coast-guard vessels that cruised against smugglers occasionally took a British ship illegally and the British retaliated. Eventually, this unofficial warfare broke into open hostilities.

When the War of the Spanish Succession ended, the Spanish Crown was in truly desperate straits. The King ordered a fleet to America to bring back to his empty coffers the gold and silver that had been piling up in America during the war. The combined fleet consisting of the

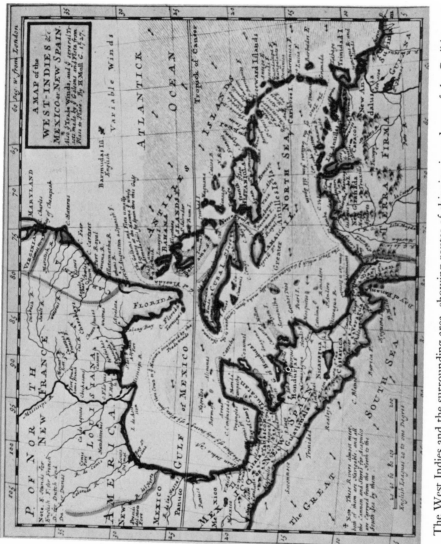

The West Indies and the surrounding area, showing routes of shipping in and out of the Caribbean and the Gulf of Mexico. From Hermann Moll's *Atlas Minor* published in London in 1727. Photograph from the Smithsonian Institution

Squadron of Tierra Firme, serving the South American trade out of Cartagena, and the Flota, serving the New Spain and Manila Galleon trade out of Vera Cruz, assembled at Havana early in the summer of 1715.

The Squadron of Tierra Firme, under the command of Captain General Don Antonio de Echiceis y Zubiza, consisted of six ships. The *Capitana*, the flagship of the captain general (which had been the *Hampton Court*, an English-built ship), was laden with gold in coin, bar, and dust, and with jewelry, silver in coin, cacao, and dyewood. The *Almiranta*, the flagship of the admiral, was laden with gold in coin and bars, silver in coin, dyewood, cacao, vanilla beans, tortoise shell, and many cured hides. The *Nuestra Señora de la Concepción* carried gold in coin and bar, cacao, vanilla beans, cured hides, tobacco. The *El Ciervo* sailed with almost one hundred tons of dyewood. The frigate *San Miguel* and a patache completed the squadron.

The New Spain Flota, under the command of Captain General Don Juan Esteban de Ubilla, was composed of five ships. The *Capitana* was laden with over 3,000,000 pieces of eight, including almost 800,000 pieces for the account of the King and the Council of the Indies, all contained in thirteen hundred chests. There were silver bars and chests of worked silver, gold in coin, bars, disks called quoits, and jewelry. Also included were pearls, Chinese porcelain from the Manila Galleon trade, indigo, cochineal, various drugs, hides, dyewood, copper in large disk-shaped ingots, and some ceramics, probably of native manufacture. Also on board was treasure salvaged from a Spanish ship and loaded in Havana. This included 36,000 pieces of eight, gold quoits, and silver bars. The *Almiranta* carried almost a thousand chests of coined silver, each chest containing about 3,000 pieces of eight. This was the property of the King and private persons, in about the same proportion as the coin carried on the *Capitana*. Also in the hold of the *Almiranta* was a similar cargo of natural products, including sarsaparilla and cacao. The *Refuerzo* carried eighty-one chests of silver coin valued at 252,171 pieces of eight (all the property of private persons), over fifty chests of worked silver, and a cargo of natural products, among them snuff and balsam. A patache was laden with silver coins in chests and bags to the value of 44,000 pieces of eight and natural products including incense, probably from the Manila Galleon trade. One frigate completed the Flota.

Joining the combined fleet in Havana was a French ship, the *Griffon*, commanded by Captain Antoine Dairé who had received permission to sail with the Spanish ships. The total registered lading of the combined fleet in gold and silver was almost 7,000,000 pieces of eight, which at that time represented a real value of about $86 million of our money. In addition, there was probably a fortune in gold and silver being smuggled to Spain.

The fleet had been delayed, as most fleets were in that day, by provisioning, watering, and lading the treasure, which had to be registered by the master of plate. The general cargoes coming in from the country were frequently held up, and this in turn held up the fleet. Added to this was the languor which comes to Europeans living in the tropics. The fleet remained in Havana until after the start of the hurricane season, a delay that was to prove fatal.

The last preparations were being made. The water casks were topped off, the last fresh provisions were brought aboard—chickens, possibly turkeys, and some hogs, all to be carried in pens on deck. Dried onions, strings of garlic, and cassava bread were carried in baskets or hung about the ship. The usual provisions were added— peas, millet, ship's biscuit, and dried corn. Biscuit, salted pork, beef, and fish were carried in barrels and clay jars in the hold. Wine in jars swung in fiber net bags from the overhead beams. On the better- supplied ships, there would be raisins and other dried fruit. The fresh provisions would belong to the more opulent passengers and the officers, who supplied themselves with delicacies the sailors, soldiers, and poorer passengers could not afford. These would include pickles and olives in earthen jars, fruits preserved in brandy and honey, dried and honeyed almond hard cakes, and special wines and liquors. The wealthier passengers and the officers would be served these things at their tables in the cabins. The rank and file would squat on the deck and eat from a bowl which served a "mess" of three or four. The food of the aristocrats would be prepared on braziers in the cabins, while the rest would eat dishes boiled up in large pots on the brick stoves amidships on the lower deck. The weatlthy would sleep in beds with hair matresses, while the rest would swing in net hammocks or stretch out on the deck with a thin pallet or nothing under them. Travel in those days was hard at best, and even the wealthy suffered intense discomfort on the long voyages to and from America. They could at least travel half drunk if they chose, while the poorer sort had to suffer the horrendous odors of the hold, the pitching and rolling of the ship, and the heat or cold without the consolation of liquor.

While all of the last supplies were being loaded and the baggage of the passengers was being brought aboard, the master of plate would have checked on any plate to be shipped from Havana and would have placed it with the other in a guarded area near the aftercabins. Everything in the cargo of the ship, theoretically at least, would be on a manifest prepared in several copies. One would go with the ship, one would go in another vessel, and one would remain with the authorities at the port from which the ship sailed. In actuality, much got into the ship without being listed, for the art of smuggling was highly developed at this time.

Everything loaded and the papers completed, the people now took themselves to the nearest church or to the nearest tavern or bawdy house, according to their inclinations, and here performed their last preparations for the long and arduous voyage. This done, they went aboard ship to await the signal to sail. When the captain general, the admiral, and their pilots and other officers consulted among themselves and reached a decision to put out to sea, the *Capitana* fired a gun, sails were unfurled, and the ships would slowly file out of the harbor on a land breeze or would be warped out to catch a breeze outside the harbor.

The combined fleet of 1715 sailed from Havana early on the morning of July 24 of that year. At the very moment they sailed, a large tropical storm was churning up the waters of the Atlantic to the southeast of Havana. The fleet had been in the Indies almost two years, and the impatience of the captain general to leave for Spain must be imagined. This impatience must have influenced Ubilla in deciding to sail when he did, even though it was late into the hurricane season, but we do not know whether any of his officers advised against going at the time. Apparently there was no evidence at Havana to indicate that a storm was brewing, and without modern weather observation equipment the Spanish had to rely on the trick knee and other homely devices to do any weather predicting at all.

The ships moved slowly out around the Morro Castle and caught the breeze which would carry them to the Florida Current rushing along offshore and up the Straits of Florida. The eleven ships, including the *Griffon*, moved slowly along. Once they entered the current, their speed increased by two or three knots. The voyage continued without incident for five days, the weather remaining good and showing no evidence of the coming storm until July 29. On this day, the atmosphere was misty on the horizon to the southeast, and the sun was reddened as it rose through the vapor that morning. The sea was smooth, but long swells were coming from the southeast, and the ships dipped and rolled gently. The old hands began to worry. They recognized the signs of an approaching hurricane.

The storm now lay to the east of the convoy and was running north, roughly paralleling the fleet, hundreds of miles away. The winds at the center of the storm had reached ninety to one hundred miles per hour.

This was an adult hurricane, and like all of this species was erratic. By evening, the storm had turned west and was heading directly for the Florida Straits. The weather there was still good, with winds lower than normal. The next morning, the winds began to pick up, and by noon they had suddenly increased to 20 knots, and the ships were rolling and pitching as the sea responded to the wind. All the sailors and passengers were apprehensive by now, for they realized that a bad storm was approaching and they were in the worst place to be caught —narrow straits with a lee shore fringed by reefs and sandy shallows. As the afternoon passed, the skies darkened and the wind increased to 30 knots, with the seas running in waves fifteen to twenty feet high. The ships were now being battered by the winds and water, but the worst was yet to come.

The captain general ordered the ships to face toward the direction of the wind but to sail off the wind at an angle calculated to bring them clear of the reefs to their lee. The ships were brought about as best they could be. Only the captain of the *Griffon*, who was not under Ubilla's orders, disobeyed and turned as close to the wind as his ship would sail. At nightfall, the storm was still worsening. The gusts of wind, which were hitting the ships in bursts, were now making a continuous whine in the rigging, and the velocity kept increasing.

Early the next morning (July 31), the hurricane struck the helpless ships in all its force. Nothing could save them now. One after another they were driven onto the reefs or beaches. The blackness of the night was broken only by the stern lanterns that continued to burn until the ships broke up. One by one, the lights went out as the doomed vessels crashed on the fringing reefs beneath the wildly raging seas or were beached in the sand. Some of the ships were smashed like matchsticks. Ubilla's ship was crushed on the reef, breaking up as it passed over it, and the wreckage was strewn for hundreds of yards toward the beach, and later, fragments were carried by the current a quarter of a mile up the coast. Almost all aboard, including the captain general, drowned or were crushed by wreckage. All of the convoy was destroyed in the same manner. Of the twenty-five hundred persons aboard the ships, over one thousand lost their lives.

There were miraculous escapes in that wild night, as some survivors got ashore on large pieces of wreckage or were simply washed onto the beach. Some ships were beached and the people escaped before the vessel broke up. In one instance, a sizable portion of the weather deck of a vessel broke away and carried a large number of people to safety. Of the fifteen hundred or so who reached the land alive, many died soon after from exposure or wounds. Only the *Griffon* escaped. In sailing as close to the wind as his ship would let him, Captain Dairé saved his vessel and the lives of all in her. He was able to pull away from the reefs and ride out the storm.

When morning came, the beaches below Cape Canaveral were littered with wreckage, dead bodies, and exhausted survivors. The ships had been scattered by the storm. According to a deposition of one of the pilots, they had gone aground or had been wrecked between 27°15″ and 27°50″ north, a distance of about thirty-five miles. The survivors of each vessel were in some instances separated from the survivors of other ships and had no way of knowing the full extent of the disaster. Between July 31 and August 6 or 7, Admiral Don Francisco Salmón surveyed the damage to the combined fleet and found all vessels wrecked or beached. Among the latter were three frigates. The people were without food, drink, or medical supplies, and many of the injured were dying each day. On August 6 or 7, he sent a launch with eighteen men and Ubilla's pilot, Nicolas de Inda, toward Havana. With the pilot went letters to the governor of Cuba, the Marqués de Casatorres, from both Salmón and a deputy of the fleet, Don Alonso de Armenta. The launch arrived at two o'clock in the afternoon of August 16. De Inda delivered his letters to the governor and gave a deposition in which he recounted what had happened:

> He said at first, that the 30th day of the last month, July, being at latitude 28 degrees open sea, the said fleet and squadron of Tierra Firme, under the Captain of Sea and War Don Antonio Echiceis y Zubiza was attacked by a storm so strong that having maintained itself through to the next day on which they lost the greater part of the sails and masts and seeing it impossible to maintain themselves in the severe weather obliged the ships to beach themselves, with the loss of General Don Juan Esteban de Ubilla, their Captain and according to the news that came in later 200 men drowned with their Captain, the same thing happened to the flagship and most of the other ships, so of the said fleet as of the squadron, that in total there are eight lost that may be found from 27 degrees 15 minutes to 27 degrees 50 minutes [north].[1]

Admiral Salmón's letter told of the suffering of the survivors and of their need for help: "I find myself on an island, in the greatest possible necessity, without anything to eat, in the same anguish the whole fleet finds itself. . . . I hope in the benignity of your Lordship, you will succor us [by] sending us supplies and ships for the transportation of these people." The admiral went on to say that no salvage had been done: "Nothing has been taken out, only what came in the staterooms, in some boxes."²* To provide the governor with funds for the rescue, Don Alonso wrote two other letters to two wealthy merchants of Havana requesting them to furnish the money to the governor.

Within a few days ships with supplies were on their way to the coast of Florida, and salvage operations began soon after they arrived at the survivors' camp. In a letter dated August 28, Admiral Salmón informed the governor at Havana that one of the salvage sloops had been dragging for the hulk of the flagship, and had found the bottom of the vessel. In it were some of the chests of coined silver, two of which were dragged up and brought back to the admiral. He apparently had three other sloops working on the salvage as well. In another letter to the governor, dated the same day, the admiral tells of the return of his launch with native divers from Havana and of the need for small boats to drag for the sunken hulks. By September 2, substantial amounts of silver had been saved. In a letter from Deputy Don Alonso de Armenta to the governor, dated that day, he tells of the progress in salvaging the treasure. In just a few days there were recovered "147 closed chests and the silver loose as pesos, in boxes that they consider to be about 80 or 90 thousands pesos worth." The same day, the admiral wrote the governor: "With the sloop from Florida which has arrived at this camp I send with the master of silver, in whose charge it is, and it must be all that he will carry to this city, he takes a little silver now, which is all that we could save, because of bad weather, and I ask you to send me in the first sloop 25 soldiers and munition for them, because it is good to guard the king's gold."³

By this time, sloops were shuttling back and forth between Havana and the wreck sites, carrying survivors, salvaged treasure, cargo, and letters. Two weeks after the admiral asked for soldiers to guard the King's treasure, they still had not arrived, and on September 16, he again asked the governor for an armed guard: "Please do me the pleasure of sending those 25 soldiers (with their arms); I ask it because I find myself with no one to guard the king's treasure here, because of all those saved from the second flagship many have died and I have sent most of the rest to Havana, sick. Those very few who escaped from the flagship are now in no condition to stand guard."⁴ At the same time, he mentions the plan to post armed sloops in the area to guard against the incursions of pirates. By this time, 589 chests of silver, each with 3,000 pieces of eight, had been recovered and sent to Havana.

---

* After breaking up, the superstructures of the ships had floated ashore, carrying some of the goods and treasure of the wealthy cabin passengers. The island to which the admiral referred is the long sandy key which lies directly off the mainland and is separated from it by the Indian River.

This salvage was being carried on with the crudest of equipment and with native divers working on lung power alone. They were directed by the sergeant major of Havana, Don Juan del Hoyo Solorzano.

Now that the survivors were being cared for and were being sent to Havana as quickly as transportation could be had and the salvage was proceeding well, Admiral Salmón could perform the task of informing King Philip V that his fleet was wrecked and that the royal and private treasure was now partially recovered. On September 20, he completed a letter to the King, in which he gave the account of the disaster in detail:

> Even though I am greatly distressed it doesn't excuse my obligation to inform you of the unfortunate loss of the whole fleet of Mexico and the galleons of Tierra Firme, which occurred on July 31, having left Havana on the 24th, and having entered the canal we were hit by a great storm the 28th, which grew worse every hour. At first I had to run on the two lowest sails, then even though I lowered them the wind carried them away, broke the mainmast and shattered the rudder and tiller, and the bow was stove in. I dropped anchor in 12 "brasas" of water, then both cables broke, in 2 hours I was in 4 brasas of water, on the rocks, and at the second blow on the reef the ship split into 3 parts, the bottom sunk, and the bow and stern washed up on the beach, from which almost all were saved, although 82 were drowned. The flagship had sunk 2 leagues away 4 hours earlier with the loss of the General and 200 persons.
>
> The leading Galleon and their flagship beached 5 leagues away and all the rest close together on the same island. The number thought lost is 9, and 2 missing but surely sunk, because we have sighted wreckage on the n. coast of San Agustín, Florida. . . .
>
> From the 2 flagships they have saved 1,450 trunks each with 3,000 pesos including your treasure and several bars, and because the bill of lading and the master of silver were lost, I couldn't give you a specific account of the royal treasure, but I think it was 1,400,000 pesos which is now in Havana.
>
> One owes to don Manuel de Mirallas, neighbor of Havana, the help of 9 sloops, and the Governor offered his total wealth to save the sailors and is still helping us on the island.
>
> This silver, which we later saved, was verified by don Alonso de Armenta, Deputy of the Fleet, and 4 men that the merchants named.
>
> I remain on this island in bad health without clothes and I stay and will give my life as I have done many times in your service.[5]

The admiral must have felt the greatest anxiety during the months he waited for the King's reaction to his letter. Almost every high-ranking commander had enemies as well as friends at court, and a charge of neglect might be sustained against him if the wrong courtiers got the King's ear. This was an age when commanders were given high rewards for success but on the other side of the scale were punished with the utmost severity when they had been careless or negligent, or the fates had crossed them. The death penalty was not unheard of in such cases, and long imprisonment for loss of the King's ships or treasure was common enough. The distressed admiral could not allow himself to think of the possible consequences, but applied himself to the salvage, realizing that if this were successful the chances of avoiding punishment were much greater.

Later, he discovered that the governor at Havana had held up his letter, and it was delayed for months while the governor's reports of September 17 and 29 were sent promptly to the King. The Spanish officials were taking every opportunity to come out of the disaster looking good to the King, and this required that some of their rivals look bad. There appears to have been collusion between the governor and the deputy. While Deputy Armenta was at the site, he and the governor corresponded frequently, and the governor sent a letter from Armenta to the King with a covering letter of his own, dated September 30, in which he described Deputy Armenta as "Royal representative directing the diving operations at Palmer de Ais, the site of the wrecks." No mention was made of the admiral, who by law was in charge. Both the governor and the deputy wrote the King again on October 28, and each praised the other in the salvaging. Again, no mention was made of the admiral, who had remained at the site as long as the deputy had.

The admiral and the deputy had returned to Havana late in October, when the water at the sites had become too cold for the divers to work. At this point, the deputy reported that 5,000,000 pieces of eight had been recovered, of which 3,000,000 had been sent to Havana, the remainder staying at the salvage camp guarded by soldiers and two armed sloops. The balance of the money would be sent on to Havana when the weather permitted. All during the salvage, which was substantially completed but continued with diminishing returns into 1718, every official concerned in it wrote the King directly, praising his own services and taking for himself as much credit as he could.

News of the disaster had swept America from the West Indies to the English colonies in the north. It was customary for the French, English, and Dutch to keep close account of the comings and goings of the Spanish fleets. In times of war in the eighteenth century, the information was needed to direct naval operations against the Spanish when the treasure fleets became military targets. In earlier times when the principle of "no peace beyond the line" was followed, the treasure fleets were targets at all times, and watching their movements was a regular habit. This habit carried over into the more-enlightened eighteenth century, when England had established some commercial rights in the West Indies and in Spain, and the movement of a treasure fleet was commercial as well as military intelligence of value. It was customary for colonial governors in the non-Spanish colonies to report to their governments the movements of the annual treasure fleet from arrival in America to departure for Europe. So it was with the fleet of 1715. The activities of the ships had been watched closely by non-Spanish shipmasters in the West Indies, and news of the movements of the Squadron of Tierra Firme and the Flota of New Spain were duly reported. For example, in a letter dated at Jamaica, April 26, 1715, Governor Archibald Hamilton reported to the Lords Commissioners for Trade and Plantations in London: "By late advices from the Havana I am told the Gallions from Vera Cruze were dayly Expected there in order to join Two Spanish Ships of War, one of which was the Hampton Court, who are Said to have great Treasure on Board for Old Spain."⁶ With such intelligence, it is little wonder that the officials of other nations knew almost as much about the movement of Spanish fleets as did the Spanish Crown and the Spanish colonial officials. When news of the disaster reached non-Spanish colonies, the governors and mariners became very much interested in what was going on at the site of the wrecks. Merchant ships passing up the Straits saw the operations in progress, and many merchant captains soon knew of what was happening. Within weeks, ships of outsiders were snooping about the scene, and when diving operations by the Spanish were reduced because of the winter weather, some English adventurers even tried their hands at fishing and attempting to dive on the wrecks.

Governor Hamilton of Jamaica had watched the events with increasing interest. On November 21, three weeks after Admiral Salmón and Deputy Armenta had returned to Havana from the salvage camps, Hamilton had commissioned two armed sloops to "cruize against pirates." These were the twelve-gun *Eagle*, 35 tons, commanded by John Wills, and the eight-gun *Barsheba*, 40 tons, commanded by Henry Jennings. Both were commissioned for a period of six months.

The ships were well armed with small arms of all kinds including grenades. During the following month, eight more sloops were commissioned. At this time, some of the merchants were complaining of depredations by Spanish coast-guard ships, who were seizing English vessels on flimsy pretenses and sending them into Spanish ports as prizes. Governor Hamilton ostensibly commissioned the sloops to cruise against the Spanish "pirate," but what they proceeded to do was to attack the ships bringing treasure from the site of the wrecks to Havana, and even to attack the site and fish for treasure on the wrecks.

Early in January, Jennings and Wells cast anchor off the site of the Spanish salvage camp. Juan Francisco del Valle, who was later sent to protest the action to the governor of Jamaica, described the events that followed:

> They laid still till night, & then landed their people, who the next Morning march'd to the Camp with their Arms. Upon which the Spanish Commanding Officer ask'd them, if it was war, they answer'd no, but that they came to fish for the Wrecks, to which the Officer said, that there was nothing of theirs there, that the Vessels belonged to his Catholick Majesty and that he & his people were looking for the said Treasure; But seeing that his Insinuations were of no use, he profer'd them 25,000 pieces of Eight, which they wou'd not be satisfy'd with, but took all the Silver they had & stript the people taking likewise away four small Cannon, two of them Brass, & nail'd two large ones (all which were to defend a parapet they had thrown up to defend themselves from the Indians) they carried away to the Value of 120,000 pieces of Eight, besides the wrought Silver.[7]

On January 26, the sloops returned to Port Royal with their loot, and there some of the men were heard bragging openly of the robbery. Later, some of the money was traced to the governor's house. The senior naval commander, Captain Balchen, took a dim view of these activities, and when the governor told him the sloops had been armed to cruise against the Spanish who were illegally seizing English merchant ships, the captain reminded the governor that His Majesty's ships were available for that purpose. Later, the governor was to state that "His Majesty's ships and vessels which have been on this station [have] not been sufficient, and indeed of little use for preventing such assaults being restrained by their orders from cleaning abroad, and thereby as well as bigness rendered unfit to goe after clean, light and nimble vessels."[8] Hamilton not only brushed aside the objections of the captain, but also tried to interest another captain in the Royal Naval Squadron in taking his ship to the Spanish camp to fish for silver on the wrecks. He approached Captain Davis, commanding officer of the naval sloop *Jamaica*, attempting to interest him in fishing on the Spanish wrecks for shares. Davis rejected the idea forthwith. The recruiting of sailors to man Hamilton's sloops had started a rush among those on ships of the Royal Navy present at Port Royal. Captain Balchen of the

Diamond reported when he arrived in England: "If I had stay'd a Week longer, I do believe I shou'd not have had men enough to have brought [my ships] home, I lost ten in two Days before I sailed being all mad to go a wrecking as they term it; For the Generality of the Island think they have Right to fish upon the Wreck, although the Spaniards have not quitted them."[9]

While Jennings and Wills were busy with the Spanish treasure, another sloop, the fourteen-gun *Bennett*, 40 tons, sailed from Port Royal under the command of Fernando Hernández. She had been commissioned by Governor Hamilton on December 12 and had put to sea soon after. In a representation of the merchants of Jamaica to the Lords Commissioners for Trade and Plantations, the cruise of this sloop is described:

> One of these Sloops commanded by a Tawny moor called Fernando Hernández, carrying in guns 6 mounted & 8 in the hold by Reason of the bad Weather on the 11th Day of January of this present Year, Off the Hills del Rosarrio he gave Chace to a Spanish Sloop commanded by Don Manuel de Aranburu wch went as a Register Ship from the Vera Cruz to the Havana & about eight at Night he took her, and Don Manuel and his men complaining of this Tyranny, the Capt. told them he had Orders from the Govr. of Jamaica to do so by all the Ships he should meet with either Spanish or French & removed from on Board the said Aranburu's Sloop to his own, all that he found in her of Value.[10]*

The haul was a rich one of coin, jewelry, and fine goods valued at 250,000 pieces of eight. As his excuse for taking the ship, Hernández alleged that she had been a vessel of Jamaica which had been taken by the Spaniards. He sent his prize into port with the bulky goods but kept the money and jewelry with him until he was sure of the condemnation of the prize. This was duly performed, probably being a conspiracy between the governor, the attorney general, and Hernández.

Word of these outrages began to get back to the Lords Commissioners for Trade and Plantations in letters and in representations of the merchants of Jamaica such as that just quoted. Meanwhile, the Spanish governor at Havana, to protest Jennings's raid on the Spanish treasure camp and other attacks on Spanish commerce, sent an envoy to Jamaica to Governor Hamilton. We have already quoted his description of Jennings's raid on the silver camp. Peace with England and

* "The hills of Rosarrio" refer to Rosario Key off the south coast of Cuba; the prize was off course.

the wreck of the treasure fleet had brought a wave of attacks against Spanish commerce which had reached the proportions of an epidemic. The disaster of the combined fleet had advertised to the world the enormous wealth that still flowed from the weak Spanish colonies, which were now unable to defend their commerce as they had in the great days of the Hapsburg kings. This was too much for the idle captains and men who had been put out of work by the end of the war.

When the governor at Havana heard of the raid by Jennings and Wills, he called his council together to determine what was to be done. As a result, five vessels were armed and sent to the scene of the salvage while the governor's envoy was on his way to Jamaica. He was Juan Francisco del Valle, a deputy of the Council of Commerce with Ubilla's fleet. After a short stay, he filed a protest with Governor Hamilton, pointing out that while he was there in Port Royal, Jennings and Wills had returned with 120,000 pieces of eight and worked silver which the captains and their crews openly admitted had come from the wrecked fleet. The envoy addressed Hamilton in the elaborate language of eighteenth-century diplomacy:

> The Govr. & the said Council of Trade at the Havana entertaining the highest Opinion of the Clemency, Piety & Justice of his said most serene Britannick Majesty, and having repeated Experience of your Excys great Wisdom as well as Justice; having sent the underwritten Deputy to represent unto your Excellency that notwithstanding the perpetual Peace Amity & friendship between their said Majesties the King of Spain & Great Britain, divers of his said Britannik Majesty's subjects in Warlike Manner committed Hostilities upon the Subjects of his said Catholick Majesty of which I lately had the Honour to acquaint your Excy.
>
> But since the said Deputys Arrival to Jamaica, to his great Surprize is given to understand that divers others of his said Britannick Majesty's Subjects, with two Sloops belonging to this Island have lately in a Hostile & Pyratical Manner landed upon his said Catholick Majesty's Dominion in the Channel of the Bahamas on the Coast of Florida, under pretence of looking for Pyrates but in Reality have committed the highest Act of Piracy, upon his said Catholick Majestys subjects; by forceably taking from them in value above 120,000 Pieces of Eight which being not only against the Treaty of Peace & Commerce between their said Majesties whereby all Plunderings, depredations, injuries & annoyances whatsoever are to cease as well by Land as by Sea. . . .
>
> Therefore the said Deputy should think himself wanting to the Respect he owes to the said Govr. & Council of Commerce; who have

charged him as well with Letters to your Excy., as humbly to represent unto you the Mischiefs that may ensue such Proceedings as likewise to pay your Excellency to inhibit & Discountenance the like Practices for the future.[11]

Del Valle asked the governor, first, to issue a proclamation prohibiting the sailing of private men-of-war from Jamaica and prohibiting any of his subjects from diving on any wrecks on the coast of Florida; second, to impound the treasure brought into Jamaica; and third, to arrest those involved in the incidents, charge them with piracy, and bring them to trial. While del Valle waited for the governor's reply, the sloop taken by the *Bennett* came into port adding further outrage to the envoy's feelings. Del Valle must have had grave doubts that Hamilton would do anything to suppress the privateers, since it was increasingly evident that he was in collusion with them. In his reply, Hamilton pointed out the alleged attacks committed by the Spanish on English shipping, and his final answer was that the loot brought back by the privateers "should be put into the Royal Treasury, until the Spaniards had made Satisfaction to the Inhabitants of Jamaica, for what they had taken from them."[12] Receiving no satisfaction and expecting none after he became aware that some of the captured money had found its way to the governor's house, del Valle returned to Cuba.

A copy of del Valle's letter reached the clerk of the Lords Commissioners for Trade and Plantations on May 19 and was read immediately. At the same time, a memorial from some of the merchants of Jamaica was received, in which they protested that the activities of the privateers were ruining legitimate trade with the Spanish and subjecting their ships to retaliation. Captain Balchen's letter written from the Nore on May 13 arrived about the same time, and the bureaucratic pot began to boil. Later accounts of the situation in Jamaica, written by Walter Arlington, a prominent merchant, and Samuel Page, secretary and commissary at Jamaica, reached the Lords. An inquiry was ordered, and Hamilton was removed from office. The pirates were ordered seized and sent to England with their loot as evidence. They escaped, Jennings finally settling in the Bahamas at New Providence, where he became a founder of what was to be known as the "pirate republic."

In a long letter dated at Jamaica, June 12, 1716, Hamilton defended or at least attempted to explain the charges against him:

Since the Cessation of arms and the Conclusion of the Peace with Spain His Majestys Subjects in these parts have contrary thereto been often robb'd and plunder'd both by sea and land by Spaniards, and Severall British vessels, have been taken on the seas passing on their Lawfull occasions by Spanish Vessels under Colour of Comissions for Guarding their Coasts, and frequently by Vessels having no Comissions for which no other pretence has in some casses been found, then that some few Spanish pistolls or inconsiderable sums of coin'd silver of that Nation (which is our Court Money) has been found on board which they have pretended was counterband goods, Some vessels indeed have been seized on their coast on Suspitions of Trade, and Have been detained and keept without any proof of their having traded and without any Legall Condemiration.

Of all which I have made repeated instances and demands for restitution to the respective Spanish Governments without being able in any one Instance to obtain the least Satisfaction to the partys aggriev'd, tho I had given an Example of that kind Immediatly after the Cessation by causeing exact restitution to be made for goods of a considerable Vallue taken off Hispaniola the cessation being then even unknown to the Captors.

These frequent losses and injurys sustain by our Merchts. and trading people, and our navigation being rendered extreamly dangerous, even beyond what it was in time of open War; His Majstys Ships and Vessels which have been on this Station haveing not been Sufficient, and indeed of Little use for preventing such insults being restraind by their orders from cleaning abroad, and thereby as well as by their bigness rendered unfitt to goe after clean light and nimble Vessels.

And having been frequently Importuned by the Clamours of our Trading people I was prevail'd upon at last to grant Comissions to some to arm and cruise upon Pirates and all necessary precaution were taken to prevent any Inconveniencys by such Comissions but the Spanish Flota hapening to be Shipwreck't about the same time two or three of these Comission'd vessels and severall others have gon thereon.[13]

Hamilton states in his letter that "finding reason to believe some ill uses had been made of these commissions I thought proper to recall them by preoclaimation as likewise to prohibit fishing or diving on those wrecks." The Spanish envoy was unaware of any such action and was given no satisfaction by Hamilton at all in late January when he met the governor and complained of Jennings and Wills. When the storm in England arose from the complaints of Page and Arlington, Hamilton, in collusion with his council, may have attempted to doctor the record and make it appear that he had actually exerted a little effort to curb his privateers.

The Spanish continued to work the wrecks until 1718, when the Spanish party withdrew to Havana. Much of the treasure remained on the ocean bottom, and the rotting hulks were visible underwater for some years after the disaster. It became customary for merchant ships passing the site to fish for treasure and some was recovered in this way. The treasure then remained undisturbed for two and a half centuries, the site being largely forgotten, although the general area is indicated on a map of Florida by Bernard Romans dated 1774. In 1964, a party of salvors led by a treasure hunter, Kip Wagner, found a deposit of silver and gold coins, ingots, and jewelry in the turbulent, milky shallows off the beach indicated on the map. The treasure was the largest of Spanish origin taken from the sea in modern times. Some of the illustrations in this volume are of objects from this find.

The old adage "war makes pirates and peace hangs them" best describes what happened after the end of the War of the Spanish Succession. Seamen, having lived the comparatively free and democratic life of the privateer, found it difficult to readjust to the discipline of the navy or merchant service and to the tyranny of the officers and mates. Many of these sailors were on the beach with no means of support, even if they had wanted to work honestly. To these disaffected and desperate men, the life of the pirate seemed to be the answer, and many took to sea with pirate leaders at the first opportunity. The feats of Jennings and his companions became famous throughout the West Indies and in the English colonies to the north, and undoubtedly helped to spark the new age of piracy that began when the war ended in 1713.

Since most islands in the West Indies were being closed to the pirates, a new base of operations had to be found, and the man who led the way was Henry Jennings. Escaping in his ship before he could be seized on the charges stemming from the raid on the Spanish salvage camp, Jennings now sailed to New Providence Island and settled there. At this time, the Bahamas were under the jurisdiction of a private company and were in a deplorable state. No authority was being exercised, and the arrival of Jennings soon attracted other pirates, until the community became known as the pirate republic.

The raid on the Spanish plate fleet and the gathering of the pirates in the Bahamas may be said to mark the beginning of what has been celebrated in literature as the golden age of piracy. In the next chapter, we shall see how these wolves of the sea harassed shipping in the West Indies, the Florida Straits, and the waters of the English colonies in North America. But we must now turn to another disaster that virtually spelled the end of the Spanish treasure fleets and marked the passing of another era in the steadily declining fortunes of Spain.

On *Friday, July 13,* 1733, the Flota of New Spain, under the command of Don Rodrigo de Torres, knight of St. John, left Havana for Cádiz. The first day the voyage proceeded smoothly, but the wind increased and the air was misty. On Sunday, July 15, the fleet was caught by a full-fledged hurricane off the central Florida Keys. When the fringes of the storm hit Cuba the same day, the officials at Havana were apprehensive for the safety of the fleet and sent a ship, under a local pilot, to the mouth of the Florida Straits to discover what had happened. Before the pilot could return, another sloop arrived in Havana "with news of having seen on the Keys near the place called Head of the Martys, 12 big ships grounded and we guessed it was our fleet. Immediately we got ready all available ships that were in the port together with this sloop, 9 ships in all, and with a good many people we loaded them with all kind of supplies and food, and left within 24 hours for the channel and islands around its entrance to rescue the fleet."[14] Just as the relief ships were about to sail, a letter arrived from the wreck site of the *Almiranta*, written by Deputy Don Pedro de Córdoba, giving Havana and Madrid a brief account of the event: "Having left there on the 13th of July, our fleet of 19 sails was overtaken on the 15 by so strong a hurricane that it is impossible to explain by the knowledge of the experienced pilots. We awoke to the results the following day; all the ships were grounded except the *San Ignacio* which sunk (from which only 12 survived, but about which we know no more), within the reefs on the coast of Florida, 30 leagues from Havana." When the relief fleet arrived, much to the joy of Admiral de Torres and his stranded companions, they found a scene of devastation: "all the ships wrecked except the *San José*. . . . and this aid arrived just in time, if it had been held up a few days more surely most of the men would have perished, because although a few ships could save their supplies the distance between wrecks was so great made communication impossible."*

The relief ships sent from Havana were not the only vessels used in the rescue. One small vessel from South Carolina, commanded by Master John Calcock was pressed into service by the Spanish, and his story, which he gave under oath before the governor of South Carolina when he returned the middle of September, throws an interesting light on the methods used by the Spanish:

So. Carolina

MEMORANDUM. That on the 17th Day of September One Thousand Seven hundred and thirty three Before me Robert Johnson Esq. Captain

* The *San José* had sunk; this was not known at the time.

General and Commander in Chief of His Majesty's Province of So. Carolina &c personally appeared John Calcock of Charles Town aforesaid mariner, who being duely sworn on the Holy Evangelists of Almighty God saith that the account following is to the best of his knowledge (and what he could learn at the Havanna) the particulars of the loss of the Flota who sailed the 2d July last under the Comm. of Dr. Rodriguez de Torro as Admiral in a ship of 60 guns, one ship of war of 60 guns built in the Havanna, and commanded by Captain Daniel Chany two other ships of 60 guns each, commd. unknown, 15 merchant ships, a snow bound to St. Augustine, and a small sloop, in all which were about fifteen millions of money of Register, Chochineal, Indigo &c unknown. That on the 4th day of July* a very violent storm of wind arose about north which kept increasing and going against the course of the sun at. S. E. it proved a hurricane, in which this deponent very hardly escaped, being about 35 leagues to the westward of the Spanish Flota near the Tortugas Bank in a schooner bound to this port, the manner of their working their vessels in the storm is unknown, but that . . . as he was entering the Gulph, the wind being scant, was obliged to stand close in shore, were on the Islands called (in Genl.) the Martiers, he saw three large ships, and presently after it failing calm perceived a launch with about 20 or 30 hands, who very civilly accosted this deponent and informed him they were part of the Spanish Flota cast away, that one of the men of War commanded by Cap't Ohany they believed was saved, all the rest being ashore except the snow, which foundered the beginning of the storm, and the little sloop which was saved amongst the Keys, and in the end desired this Deponent to take in some of the passengers to the Havanna, which accordingly he did, and at his arrival was immediately seized for the service of the King himself and people, with his cargo of skins turned ashore; and he obliged to maintain his people almost five weeks, which time they had kept his vessel, and at the delivering of her up, gave this deponent only 124 8/8 and 5 Rials, the mens wages only—amounting to near that sum, without their victuals, hire of the schooner or detriment of his cargo considered, but on his complaint was told he had but two remedies, patience or beating his head against the wall.[15]†

The salvage of the ships proceeded quickly after the arrival of the laborers, divers, and relief ships from Havana. Some of the grounded vessels stood with their decks awash, and the salvage of the cargoes was much easier than with those that had sunk. Within two weeks, Deputy

---

* The English calendar was ten days behind the Spanish.

† The Spanish paid Calcock 124 pieces of eight and 5 reals (1 real = ⅛ piece of eight).

Don Pedro de Córdoba reported that 1,839 boxes of coined silver and bars and 26 cases of worked silver had been brought up, along with some cochineal and indigo, although some of this had been water-soaked and was not worth salvaging. As quickly as the silver was brought in, it was sent to Havana and stored in the fortress there. By August 18, most of the silver—3,012 boxes—had been salvaged from the *Capitana* and the *Almiranta*. Once much of the salvage had been completed, Admiral Don Rodrigo de Torres left the camp on August 20, but calms and contrary winds delayed his vessel, and eight days were required to cover the distance to Havana. One month later, he wrote a report to Madrid, in which he praised the quick relief sent by the governor at Havana and his officials, which included ships, food, medical supplies, laborers, and more than twenty divers. He reported that there still remained one hundred and twenty men near the wreck of the *Capitana* and forty near the hulk of the *Almiranta*. One of the merchant ships, the *Nuestra Señora del Rosario*, had been refloated, returned to Havana, and refitted. The captain of the vessel had requested permission from de Torres to go on to Spain as a ship of register, but de Torres reported in his letter that he would not give such permission "unless by special necessity or by a Royal order." Later, the ship did sail with letters for Madrid.

When the salvage was completed, a summary of goods recovered was prepared and forwarded to Spain. A total of 11,500,000 pesos (pieces of eight) in treasure and cargo had been recovered, through hard work and good luck. The salvage had been very successful, since most of the ships had run aground and had not broken up badly. The summary presents us a remarkable picture of the lading of a treasure fleet and the value of goods and treasure shipped in it and is given here in its entirety:

Capitana

In minted, worked, and bar silver and some gold, all of private interests	5,258,035 pesos*
In 4,145 arrobas 23 tomines of cochineal,† most wet	105,981 pesos 6 reales
In 995 arrobas 4 tomines of anil [indigo], damp	4,478 pesos 3 reales
His Majesty's silver, minted and in bars	727,733 pesos 7½ reales
584 plates of copper weighing 290 quintals‡ '90 tomines of the King's account	no value given

The Funnel of Gold

Almiranta

In minted and worked silver and gold, all of private interests	4,998,397 pesos 6⅜ reales
In 4,820 arrobas of cochineal, wet and dry	138,455 pesos§
In 1,420 arrobas 14 tomines wet anil	6,392 pesos 4 reales
In coined, worked, and paste‖ silver of the King's account	729,951 pesos 5 reales
439 plates of copper with 232 quintals 85 tomines of the King's account	no value given

Infanta

In minted and worked silver	567,384 pesos 4 reales
In 1,184 arrobas 24 tomines 14 grains of wet cochineal	29,611 pesos 3½ reales
In 103 arrobas 18 tomines of wet anil at 4 pesos 4 reales the arroba	466 pesos 6 reales

Nuestra Señora de Belén

In 5 cases of worked silver	2,792 pesos
In 173 arrobas 14 tomines 7 grains of wet cochineal	4,332 pesos 1¾ reales
In 320 arrobas 8 tomines of wet anil at 4 pesos 8 reales the arroba#	1,441 pesos 3 reales

Nuestra Señora de los Dolores

In 2 cases of worked silver	1,328 pesos
In 424 arrobas 18 tomines 6 grains of wet cochineal	10,609 pesos 1½ reales

* Pieces of eight.

† 4,145 arrobas = about 105,283 pounds (1 arroba = 25.356 pounds). The 23 tomines = a little more than ⅓ ounce troy. Cochineal is a red dyestuff consisting of the bodies of scale insects.

‡ Copper was frequently shipped in rough-cast disks of about fifty pounds each; "plate" refers to this form. The quintal was equivalent to a little more than 100 pounds avoirdupois. The King's copper was used principally in coinage and in the manufacture of bronze cannon.

§ The wet cochineal was valued at 1 peso a pound, while the dry was worth 2.4 pesos a pound.

‖ Paste apparently refers to silver cast in rough cakes.

There is no explanation of the difference in the value of the cochineal on the *Almiranta* and on *Nuestra Señora de Belén*.

In 102 arrobas 12 tomines of wet anil	461 pesos 1 real
In 35 botijas of balm [earthenware jars of balsam] at 20 pesos per botija	700 pesos

San Fernando

In 3 cases of worked silver	4,211 pesos
In 815 arrobas 13½ tomines of wet cochineal	20,381 pesos 6 reales
In 231 arrobas 8 tomines of wet anil	1,040 pesos 7½ reales

San Felipe

In 4 cases of worked silver	3,414 pesos
In 639 arrobas 24 tomines of wet cochineal	15,987 pesos
In 642 arrobas 13 tomines of wet anil	2,891 pesos 1½ reales

San Pedro

In 125 arrobas 19 tomines of wet cochineal	3,144 pesos
In 402 arrobas 18 tomines of wet anil	1,812 pesos 2 reales

San Francisco

In 797 arrobas 9 tomines of wet cochineal	19,934 pesos

Nuestra Señora del Carmín

In 919 arrobas 14 tomines of dry anil*	11,494 pesos 4 reales
In 936 arrobas 24 tomines of purgative of julap† at 12 pesos the quintal	2,891 pesos 7 reales
In 10,000 vanilla pods	1,200 pesos
In 17 cases of gifts‡ at 30 pesos a case	510 pesos
In 5 crates of Chinese paving stone [from the Manila Galleon trade] at 30 pesos the crate	150 pesos
In 28 botijas of balm	560 pesos

* Dry anil was worth about four times as much as wet anil.

† Julap is from the Arabic *julab*, a sweet drink prepared with herbs, in this case a laxative. The herbs must have been in a raw state since the value was so low. Our word *julep* comes from the same Arabic word.

‡ Archaeological evidence recovered from wreck sites indicates that these gifts were largely native ceramics and woodenware.

San José

In minted silver	227,084 pesos
In 150 arrobas 3 tomines of wet cochineal	3,753 pesos
In 28 botijas of balm	560 pesos

Nuestra Señora del Rosario of Santo Domingo

In 9 cases of worked silver	5,486 pesos
In 835 arrobas 21 tomines of dry cochineal at 70 pesos per arroba	50,508 pesos 6½ reales
In 903 arrobas 11½ tomines of dry anil	11,293 pesos 2 reales
In 3,358 arrobas 18 tomines of tobacco at 3 reales per arroba*	1,259 pesos 4 reales
291 arrobas 1½ tomines tobacco at 8 reales per arroba	291 pesos 1½ reales
28 cases of gifts at 30 pesos each	840 pesos
3,353 arrobas 16 tomines white sugar, 2,107 arrobas 14 tomines rough sugar, all at 8 reales the arroba	5,461 pesos 2 reales
2,071 arrobas of tobacco powder at 3 reales the arroba	776 pesos 5 reales
1,410 arrobas 14 tomines purgative of julap	4,231 pesos 5 reales
60,800 vanilla pods at 20 pesos per 1,000	1,216 pesos
176 arrobas 13 tomines of annatto tree†	1,103 pesos 2 reales
9 sacks of cacao	170 pesos

Nuestra Señora del Agustín

Lot of worked silver	4,680 pesos

When the royal deputies' reports of the disaster and salvaging reached Madrid, the King ordered a squadron of four warships to Havana to bring the treasure and cargo to Spain. These were the *San Carlos* (*Capitana*), the *Africa* (*Almiranta*), the *Santa Rosa*, and the *Xavier*. The same day, December 18, letters announcing this were sent to the viceroy of New Spain, the royal officials at Havana, and the deputy of the fleet, Don Pedro de Córdoba. Meanwhile, the ship

* Seemingly a very low price, perhaps a low quality of leaf in the rough.
† Refers to a yellowish-red dyestuff made from the pulp that surrounds the seeds of a tropical tree. The name of the tree comes from the Carib language.

Sand-encrusted cannon and silver coins recovered by Captain Tom Gurr from the wreck site of the *San José*, a ship in the ill-fated fleet of 1733. Photographs by Ed Reimard

Nuestra Señora del Rosario had been sent by Admiral de Torres to Spain with his report of the events. Because of bad weather, she put into Villanueva in the Algarve (south coast of Portugal). Lieutenant of Infantry Don Francisco Cumpledo, the officer carrying the admiral's letters, went ashore and continued on to Madrid by land, arriving there shortly before December 25, 1733. In his letters, de Torres gave a complete account of the disaster, the salvage, and a subsequent dispute he had with the royal deputy, Don Pedro de Córdoba, and some merchants. These people wanted to have access to the salvaged silver in Havana and have it distributed to the owners there, using the reasonable excuse that the chemical effects of the sea water would damage the metal. They also requested permission to send their shares on to Spain in two ships unescorted. De Torres had refused their request and had ordered that the silver be kept in the fortress at Havana and that no ships sail without escort, maintaining that he was still responsible for the fleet and treasure whether sunk or not and that his authority over it did not cease until he had returned it to the officials at Cádiz or he had been relieved by another admiral by order of the King. De Torres undoubtedly suspected the merchants and possibly even the deputy of wanting to get their hands on the treasure, because much of it was being smuggled and did not appear on the manifests being checked against it. In any case, de Torres's decision proved to be a wise one. The King and his ministers completely approved the admiral's actions. In the same letter advising de Torres of the arrival of his envoy, Lieutenant Cumpledo, with the reports, the court officials informed the admiral:

> His Majesty agrees with your stand and he has reprimanded the irregular pretension of the deputy Córdoba and his friends in wanting to deprive you of the trust his Majesty gave you over the lost fleet and goods salvaged from it. They should know that the accident doesn't diminish your authority so you make the provision most suitable for the king and the merchants concerning the salvage, transport and warehousing, leaving you free of the deputies in the use of this jurisdiction and even the disposition of the expenses and people which have discussed them; in consequence of which to the deputies is made known that his Majesty will give you recognition by the enclosed letter and the merchants should obey you.[16]

With the letter to de Torres was enclosed another to the deputies at Havana and the troublesome merchants. In no uncertain terms they were directed to follow the orders of the admiral: "The King is displeased with the opposition given de Torres by a deputy and various merchants . . . intending that you should be the arbiters to determine the matter. The king has asked me to tell you he doesn't like what you are doing and that everyone in the fleet is under the strict command of de Torres and everyone is to obey him in matters pertaining to each."[17] This settled the matter of authority, and de Torres continued preparing the treasure and supplies for transportation to Cádiz whenever the ships should arrive. One of the letters which arrived with the lieutenant in Madrid in late December had mentioned details of preparing for the voyage. De Torres tells of a supply barge coming from Vera Cruz in New Spain with flour, which fought stormy weather for forty-four days en route and arrived "with the mainmast overboard and the deck boards ripped up."[18] He added that they would soon begin making sea biscuit for the fleet. He also reported on a ship under construction which they apparently were thinking of adding to the squadron: "The new ship remained planked all the first deck and starting to do the bottom, the caulking and clamps of the cross members are going ahead. The breasthooks and knees are being set up and elsewhere the sails and gear are coming along well, she should be ready to sail by March." In the middle of December, the *Incendio* arrived from Vera Cruz with additional treasure of 3,500,000 pieces of eight for the King. This ship was held until the relief fleet was ready to go to Spain.

When the relief vessels arrived early in 1734 and preparations were completed, the fleet returned to Cádiz with the salvaged treasure and goods. The disaster, while expensive in human life and ships and in some of the merchants' goods, was not a severe blow to the finances of the Crown, although they were bad enough in any case, for most of the King's treasure was saved. In a larger way, the incident symbolizes the impotence to which the once-great Spanish kingdom was being reduced. In June, before the fleet of de Torres had sailed to its fate in the Florida Straits, an English sea captain had been in Havana harbor and described the fleet as consisting of one Mexican ship, one ship built in Genoa, one Dutch ship built in New England, one built in Havana, eleven built in Great Britain, and two smaller vessels he could not identify. Of this fleet, then, probably only four at most were Spanish-built. How far Spain had sunk from those proud days when Philip II could decree that none but Spanish-built ships could sail in the American trade.

De Torres's handling of the salvage and his administration of the affairs of the wrecked fleet were approved by the Crown, and he returned to sea in the same rank. Three years after he escaped death in the hurricane, his flagship *Invencible* was struck by lightning while lying in the harbor of Havana. The lightning set off the magazine and the ship was blown up, but the apparently indestructible admiral survived.

In the period between the raid of Henry Jennings on the Florida salvage camps of the fleet of 1715 and the disaster of 1733, a new wave of hostilities swept the West Indies, the Florida Straits, and the eastern seaboard of North America. This violence was the result of an informal war being waged against ships of all nations by sea robbers of every nationality to be found in the New World. The first nest of these robbers was New Providence Island in the Bahamas, where Henry Jennings had fled when he left Jamaica to escape prosecution for the outrage he had committed.

XII

Housecleaning in Providence

Then for work they mortally hate it . . . they thus live poorly
and indolently, with a seeming content.
                    —Woodes Rogers, governor of the Bahamas,
                       in a letter to London, May 29, 1719

 EVEN THOUGH the Bahama Islands lie alongside the two major
routes by which shipping left the Caribbean basin, the Spanish
failed to settle and fortify them. It was as if they had left one side of a
double gate open. After first touching here, Columbus sailed to the
south and never returned to explore them further. This was the task of
later Spanish explorers and the slave raiders who largely depopulated
the archipelago in the first years of Spanish mining and farming activity
on Hispaniola. The islands became a geographical backwater and were
deserted. Pirates and privateers moved into the void. The hundreds of
small inlets, ideally suited to the swift shallow-draft vessels of sea
marauders, offered hiding places for ships and men secure from the
deep-draft Spanish vessels of war. As the problem increased, the Spanish
sporadically sent smaller armed ships and galleys into the islands to clean
out the enemy, but these attempts were like trying to remove a wide-
spread infection with a scalpel.

As early as 1627, Charles I included the islands in a grant to Sir
Robert Heath, but nothing came of this. Visitors from Bermuda called
at the islands largely to rake salt, and they formed temporary settlements that were occupied during the winter months. In 1647–1649, the
Company of Eleutherian Adventurers was organized in London for the
development of planting in the islands. Eleuthera was settled and plantations laid out with some success. In spite of this, Charles II in 1670
granted the Bahamas to the Proprietors of Carolina headed by the duke
of Albemarle. In 1671 a governor (who had already been elected by

the settlers) was confirmed in his office by the proprietors. New Providence now became the center of government because of its central location and fine harbor, and a representative form of government was set up. All the schemes of the proprietors came to nothing during the following decades, and the islands were frequently attacked by the Spanish and the French. The Spanish saw the settlers as squatters on Spanish soil as well as a threat to their shipping. In 1684 the settlement on New Providence was almost wiped out by an attack. The early history is a dismal one of little accomplishment. In 1694 a new governor, Nicholas Trott, arrived and instilled some energy and enthusiasm into the colony. Nassau, named for the family of William III, was laid out, and Fort William was built to guard the harbor. Trott also set plans for plantations on New Providence to raise sugar, tobacco, cotton, and indigo, but nothing substantial came of them. By the end of the War of the Grand Alliance in 1697, sailors and privateersmen thrown out of work by the Peace of Ryswick swarmed to the islands, and by 1700 there was a pirate for every honest citizen living there. Using the islands as a base, the pirates attacked ships of all nationalities coming up the Florida Straits, not excluding those of England, even though most of the pirates in the islands were English.

When the War of the Spanish Succession began in 1702, New Providence became a target of the French and Spanish (who were now allies), and in 1703 a combined force invaded the island, burned Nassau, and destroyed the fort. Two years later, they returned and wiped out the town. By this time, only twenty or so families remained, and the colony seemed to be doomed. In 1706 the British Admiralty made plans for refortifying the island and actually produced drawings of the project; but drawings do not defend islands, and during the nine years the Lords of the Admiralty spent mulling over the plans, the pirate community infesting New Providence grew to such strength that the place was referred to as a pirate republic.

In 1716 the Spanish invaded the logwood-cutting settlements on the Gulf of Campeche and expelled the woodcutters. These, like the buccaneer communities on Hispaniola in the previous century, consisted of drifters, privateersmen thrown out of work by the Peace, deserters from the navy and merchant ships, and other social misfits who came to the Mosquito Coast to win a living cutting the dyewood there. This band of ne'er-do-wells now put to sea with nowhere to go, determined to join the first pirate who came in sight. The pirate turned out to be Henry Jennings, who was fleeing Jamaica to avoid prosecution for plundering the Spanish treasure-salvage camp after the disaster of 1715. The men from the Mosquito Coast joined Jennings, and they went together to New Providence and settled at Nassau. The town then became a base of operations against shipping in the West Indies, the Florida Straits, and the coast of the English colonies to the north. To Nassau there resorted pirate captains known and feared throughout the Caribbean and the Atlantic, among them Charles Vane, John Auger, Edward Teach called Blackbeard, Benjamin Hornigold, and Calico Jack Rackam. For almost three years, the pirates controlled the town of Nassau. What legal authority there was could not resist them.

Though all these captains were known for their bravado and love of a fight, one incident of piracy, perhaps the first to occur in the Bahamas, was carried out with good planning, official collusion, and diabolical ingenuity rather than violence. It was committed in September 1713, five months after the end of the War of the Spanish Succession. Early that month, there sailed from Santo Domingo a ship owned by the Royal French Company of Senegal bound for Havre-de-Grâce in France. She was loaded with sugar, indigo, ambergris, gold dust, and other merchandise. Her master was a Bermudian, Lewis Doyer; her pilot, a Frenchman, Jean de la Croix, who was part owner of the cargo. A few days out of port, off the island of Inagua in the Bahamas, a fire suddenly broke out in a cask of brandy. While the pilot worked to extinguish the fire, the master, taking control of the ship, ran her aground. The vessel piled up on a sandbank, but her hull remained intact and was apparently not severely damaged. The master went immediately ashore, taking with him the gold dust and ambergris. Some of the men were sent to look for small vessels to "save" the cargo, no attempt being made by the master to refloat her. In the vicinity, there "happened" to be several sloops of Bermuda, commanded by friends of the master. They straightway came to the ship and "saved" the cargo for themselves. These sloops, commanded by Captain William Richardson, a Captain Tynes, and Captains William Joel, John Penniston, and Richard Penniston, all Bermudians, came alongside the intact ship, tied up, and over the protests of the pilot and the crew, began loading her cargo into their vessels without delay. Sugar, indigo, tobacco—everything aboard—was hoisted out of the hold and distributed to the sloops. They stole not only her cargo but also broke up the ship itself, taking everything of her running and standing rigging and equipment they could move. When nothing else could be stripped from her, the Bermudians set sail for home. One sloop, Captain Richardson's *Susanna*, with Pilot de la Croix aboard, went home by way of Virginia and put into Williamsburg in November. De la Croix at once appeared before Governor Alexander Spotswood and accused Richardson and his companions of the robbery of the French ship. The governor forthwith seized Richardson, his crew, and his sloop, charging him with bringing goods into Virginia contrary to the acts of Parliament and ordering a hearing on the other charges. At his hearing, Captain Richardson admitted taking from the French vessel "five or six hundred pounds of indigo, several casks of sugar, about 2000 pounds of junk,* one cask of brandy and about 4000 pounds of old iron, which he sent to Bermuda by Daniel Gibbs Master of the Sloop Samuel and Abraham Adderly Master of the Sloop Mary both of the Island of Bermuda."[1] On board the *Susanna* were found 5⅔ hogsheads of sugar and some 150 pounds of indigo, which the governor seized to be sold for the benefit of the owners when they should file claim for it. De la Croix had been stripped clean by Richardson, and to enable him to continue to France, the governor furnished him with £12 10s. of "current money." De la Croix also took with him other testimony of the crew of the French ship to be used in filing claims in Great Britain. Richardson was not charged with piracy, it being the conclusion of Governor Spotswood's council

> that no information was given by the said La Croix till a considerable time after his arrival here, and then only upon a quarrel between him and the said Richardson; that none of the goods alleged to be piratically taken have been found upon the searches made except about 150 pounds of indico [the council did not mention the sugar], which the said Richardson owns to have been taken from the French Wreck and that it is also very improbable that Richardson should bring along with him a person on whom he had committed piracy. It is therefore the unanimous opinion of the Council that the single testimony of the said La Croix [is] so circumstantial, and without any other corroberating evidence is not a sufficient or legal proof so as to bring the said Richardson to a tryal upon the aforesaid accusation.[2]

Richardson was tried on the lesser charge of illegal entry of goods. As for his admission that he had sent substantial goods "saved" from the "wrecked" ship to Bermuda, it was up to the governor and courts of the island to hear the case on the more serious charge. Subsequent testimony in London by persons who were in Bermuda at the time of the arrival of the goods indicated that Governor Bennett of Bermuda and members of the council there received shares of the goods taken from the French ship and these were the men who were to try the Bermudians who had taken them! Later in London, a petition was filed by Sir John Lambert on behalf of the owners of the French ship to

---

* Old worn-out cordage that was pulled apart and used for caulking.

transfer the case to Great Britain, and this was done. Here it was referred to the Lords Commissioners for Trade and Plantations three years after the event, and the case disappears into a limbo of official papers. The evident collusion of the governor of Bermuda in this piracy typifies one of the main features of the piracies committed in the period that began with the Peace of Utrecht. Piracy was a big business with some colonial governors and other officials, and with some merchants—the profits reaped from the traffic were huge; other merchants and honest officials attempted to control the despicable trade.

For three years, from the time of the arrival of Jennings and the pirates from Campeche to the fall of 1718, Nassau thrived as a pirate city. Little civil authority remained, and the outlaws were able to do as they pleased. The settlement had been in a miserable condition since the attacks of the Spanish during the late war. Only two hundred had survived by making "their escape from ye Spaniards, and lived in the woods destitute of all necessarys."[3] Between 1716 and 1718, the pirates "had brought into ye Harbor of Providence about 40 sail of Merchant Shipps, where they were either burnt or sunk and had plundered great numbers in the Gulf of Florida, and the Windward Passage bound to England, out of which they had taken their gunns, small arms, provisions and ammunition, sails, anchors, cables and the best of their cargo and left them to the Mercy of the Seas which some of the shipps were lost and many of the men perished for want of necessarys."

When the situation had reached an intolerable stage and the complaints of robbed shipowners and settlers could no longer be ignored, it was determined to make the colony a royal one and abolish the proprietorship which had failed so miserably. The new governor chosen to restore civil order and establish a new administration was Woodes Rogers, one of the most able men to appear in colonial America. No better choice could have been made. In a history in which scoundrels and mediocrities parade one after another, Rogers stands as a giant of ability and wisdom. This remarkable man had been a successful privateer captain during the late war with Spain. He had captured many Spanish prizes off the Pacific coast of the Americas and had circumnavigated the globe. His importance is recognized in the account of his life in the *Dictionary of National Biography*. A Bristol man, Rogers was endowed by nature with the qualities of leadership—intelligence, a real interest in his profession, a charming way with his fellows, and not the least, a great sense of humor, which is really a sense of balance in the way one looks at life. Rogers was kindly as well, in an age when that quality was seldom found in military and political leaders. An insight into his character is provided in his own account of an incident that occurred on the coast of Brazil. He wished to land at the town of Angra dos Reis for information and supplies, but the boat he had sent toward the town was fired on. A short time before, French pirates had raided the place, and the Portuguese governor thought that Rogers's ship was more of the same. Rogers's diplomatic reaction to the unfriendly reception won him the governor's friendship and a delightful week of festivities. Rogers and his company, with musicians from the ships, were invited to take part in a religious program:

> We waited on the Governour, Signior Raphael de Silva Lagos, in a body, being ten of us, with two trumpets and a hautboy, which he desir'd might play us to church, where our musick did the office of an organ, but separate from the singing, which was by the fathers well perform'd. Our musick played "Hey, boys, up go we!" and all manner of noisy paltry tunes. And after service, our musicians, who were by that time more than half drunk, march'd at the head of the company; next to them an old father and two fryars carrying lamps of incense, then an image dressed with flowers and wax candles, then about forty priests, fryars, etc., followed by the Governor of the town, myself, and Capt. Courtney, with each of us a long wax candle lighted. The ceremony held about two hours; after which we were splendidly entertained by the fathers of the Convent, and then by the Governour. They unanimously told us they expected nothing from us but our Company, and they had no more but our musick.[4]

The cruise around the world which brought Rogers national fame in Great Britain also brought his qualities of leadership to the attention of Crown officials, and when it was determined to answer the rising problem of piracy in the West Indies and the English colonies to the north with a pronged offensive, he was the man selected for the most important job. In 1717 the Crown ministers decided to send a royal governor to Nassau to take over that "pirate republic" and organize an effective civil administration, thereby depriving the pirates of their principal base of operations. And at the same time, a general amnesty would be declared by the King to give pirates wishing to reform the opportunity to do so. Rogers was to go to Nassau armed with the King's amnesty, the confidence of the King's ministers, and the authority to set up a royal colonial government. His reception was an exciting one as he describes it in his first report to the Lords Commissioners for Trade and Plantations:

I take leave to acquaint Your Lordships I arriv'd in this Port on the 26 July last in Company with the Men of Warr ordered to assist me. I met with little opposition in coming in, but found a French ship (that was taken by the Pirates of 22 Guns) burning in the Harbour—which we were told was set on Fire to drive out His Majestys Ship the Rose who got in too eagerly the evening before me, and cut her cable and run out in the Night for fear of being burnt by one Charles Vane who command'd the Pirates and at our [approach] and His Majestys Ship—the Milfords near approach the next morning, they finding it impossible to escape us, he with about ninety men fled away in a Sloop wearing the black Flag, and Fir'd guns of Defiance when they perceiv'd their Sloop out Sayl'd the Two—that I sent to chase them hence.[5]

When Rogers arrived he was visited on board his ship by several men from Harbor Island, who told him that unlike Vane, many pirates were interested in receiving the King's amnesty. Thus, when Rogers landed the next day, he had some knowledge of the state of things ashore. He was received with joy by some three hundred persons. The repentant pirates formed a military guard of honor in two lines and fired off their muskets in celebration. Among the pirates accepting amnesty were Henry Jennings and Benjamin Hornigold. Rogers read his commission from the King and took formal possession of the islands. After this, he set about organizing a council to help him govern in the English manner. He inquired about for the names of persons who had not been pirates and who had not traded with them to any extent. From this list, he chose six people—Nathaniel Taylor, Richard Thompson, Edward Holmes, Thomas Barnard, Thomas Spencer, and Samuel Watkins. To them he added six worthy gentlemen he had brought with him—Robert Beauchamp, William Salter, William Fairfax, William Walker, Wingate Gale, and George Hooper—and appointed these twelve the members of the first council. Between the date the council was appointed in July and the date of the letter in which Rogers reported the appointments to the Lords Commissioners for Trade and Plantations (October 31), Salter and Walker died in an epidemic, which some of the local people attributed to a great pile of rawhides the pirates had stolen and had piled up near the town. The epidemic had raged before Rogers and his party arrived, but "as if fresh European blood could only draw the Infection, the Inhabitants and People quickly became free and our Poor attendants on every hand seized so violently that I have had above one hundred sick at one time—and not a healthfull officer, till now We begin to recover. The air being Purged I trust in God shall not see such another Season; this last being such an Extraordinary Fatality unknown before to Persons who have lived here these Forty Years past." Christopher Gale and Thomas Walker were chosen to replace the dead councillors.

Officials in the new government were chosen from the council, including a chief justice and a first lieutenant of the militia, who was also to be secretary general. William Fairfax was appointed judge of the admiralty. Having gotten the rudiments of his government organized, Rogers now turned to the fortifications of the town, since he feared an attack by the Spanish (Spain and Great Britain were then fighting a naval war in the Mediterranean):

> Here we found the ruins of the former Fort which we are Employ'd in rebuilding, One Bastion fronting the Sea last week fell down having only a Crazy crack'd wall in its Foundation. The wages of hired Workmen are Extravagantly dear, and I have buried most of those I brought with Me. If his Majesty would please to contribute towards the Fortification Necessary to be erected in two more places in the harbour of Nassau when I have workmen here, the charge would be much less then at any other place in the West Indies . . . here is the best stone, lime & Timber, every where on this Island, but at present the excessive laziness of the People and Sickly Season has been the only cause, I have not put the place by this time in a better posture of Defence, I shall continue doing all I can for fear of a Sudden Rupture wth. either France or Spain, it lying so advantageous to annoy their Trade that they would dread the consequence of this Place more then any other English Settlement in America.

Rogers had arrived in the *Delicia,* escorted by the Royal Navy vessels *Rose* and *Milford.* The two naval vessels were to return to Great Britain in a short period, leaving only the *Delicia* as guardship, and Rogers was anxious to get the fortifications in order before the warships left. When the construction of the forts was delayed by the sickness of the people, Rogers asked the commanders of the warships to remain in Nassau Harbor for a month or two more to give him protection, but they would not stay longer than a few weeks and left the colony practically defenseless when they sailed. This led Rogers later to recommend that the governor have authority over naval vessels stationed in the colony, a recommendation not followed.

When Rogers landed, he had published the King's amnesty for pirates who turned themselves in and took an oath never to engage in piracy again. Most of the pirate community at Nassau took advantage of the King's offer (the notable exceptions were Vane and his chief mate, Edward Teach). Rogers now attempted to whip this motley and

Governor Woodes Rogers with his family. From an eighteenth-century
engraving

undisciplined crew into the semblance of a trained militia to augment
the regular troops and artillery he had brought. In a few weeks, he
could muster a company of men armed with muskets and hangers to
help defend the town against attack, and the guardship could furnish
some support to the artillery that had come with him. But the guns in
the fortifications were in deplorable condition, with few of the pieces
mounted and serviceable. Rogers prepared a long and complete list of
the ordnance and stores necessary to put the fort in proper condition
for defense, but little if anything was furnished him, and two years
after he left the island to return to Great Britain, many of the guns in
the fort and in the magazine were still unserviceable.

One of Rogers's first acts in cleaning up the activity of the pirates
was to appoint officers to go aboard the ships in the harbor and inventory the ladings. The crews were brought ashore and lived for some
time in tents made from the sails of their vessels until houses could be
built. During the first months, Rogers had a real fear that Charles Vane
would return and attack Nassau. On hearing that Vane was expected
to come to Green Turtle Cay near Abaco, Rogers armed a sloop, put
the reformed pirate Hornigold in command, and sent it on a reconnaissance mission to see what Vane was up to. The outcome is best described in Rogers's own words:

In the meantime I kept a very Strick't watch for fear of any Surprize, and not hearing from Capt. Hornigold I was afraid he was either taken by Vaine or begun his old Practice of Pirating again wch. was the General opinion here in his absence but to my great Satisfaction he return'd in about three weeks having lain most of that time concealed & view of Vaine the Pirate in order to Surprize him or some of his men that they expected would be near them in their Boats, but tho they failed in this Capt. Hornigold brought wth. him a Sloop of this Place that got leave from me to go out a turtling but had been trading wth. Vaine who had then wth. him two Ships and a Brigantine, his Sloop that he escaped hence in being run away with by another set of new Pirates, the two Ships he took coming out of Carolina one of Four hundred & the other of Two hundred Tons loaded wth. Rice, Pitch & Tarr and Skins bound for London the Neptune Capt. King being the largest he sunk and the Emperour Capt. Arnold Powers he left wthout doing her any damage except taking away their Provisions. I have secured the Mercht. that traded wth. Vaine and having not yet a Power to make an Example of him here he remains in Irons to be sent home to England by the next Ship.

Vane got away because Hornigold was not strong enough to attack him, and Rogers blamed the escape on the fact he did not have support from a Royal Navy vessel. Rogers then requested that any naval vessel sent to the islands in the future be placed under the authority of the governor. He suggested that the assignment of a small royal sloop like the *Shark* would enable him to put together a small flotilla manned with local people which could join the Royal Navy vessel and drive the pirates from Bahamian waters. Rogers then told their lordships of the threat of Vane: "This Vaine had the Impudence to Send me word that he designs to burn my Guard Ship and visit me very soon to return the affront, I gave him on my arrival in sending two Sloops after him instead of answering the Letter he sent me. He expects soon to joyne Maj. Bonner or some other Pirate and then I am to be attack'd by them."

With the coming of cooler weather in October, the people recovered their health, and work on the fortifications speeded up. The defenses of the island were greatly improved by the end of the year, with two new emplacements at both entrances to the harbor as well as the main fort guarding the town.

Rogers now had time to turn his attention to more productive matters and devised a scheme to establish trade with Puerto Príncipe on the south coast of Cuba. The country thereabouts produced much meat and other fresh provisions, which were very scarce in Nassau, and Rogers saw an opportunity to stimulate trade, improve the health of his people by enabling them to eat fresh food, and to import breeding stock for raising local herds of cows and pigs. Working with some of the merchants in Nassau, he had three vessels fitted out with general cargo and merchandise in much demand in the Spanish colonies. These were the schooner *Bachelor's Adventure*, commanded by Captain Henry White; the sloop *Lancaster*, commanded by Captain William Greenway; and the sloop *May*, commanded by Captain John Auger. The little flotilla set sail October 5, 1718, with high expectations. The next day they came to Green Cay in the late afternoon. What happened to it is told in the anonymously written *History of the Pirates*, from which the following account is drawn.

As the island was overrun with hogs, two of the sailors went ashore to shoot one for supper. They returned with a large specimen, which was divided among the ships and cooked for supper. After this, Captains Greenway and White came aboard Captain Auger's sloop to talk over the plans for sailing. It was agreed that if they sailed at ten or eleven o'clock that night they would reach the dangerous shoals the next morning and could pass through them in daylight. The two visiting captains then returned to their ships, and shortly afterwards, two ex-pirates, Phineas Bunch and Dennis Mackarthy, with a large number of their companions, came from Captain White's sloop and boarded Captain Auger's.

Their pretence was, that they came to see Richard Turnley and Mr. James Carr, who had formerly been a midshipman in the Rose man of war, under Capt. Whitney, and being a great favorite of Governor Rogers, he had appointed him supercargo of this voyage. They desired to be treated with a bottle of beer, for they knew Mr. Carr had some that was very good in his care, which had been put on board, in order to make presents of, and to treat the Spanish merchants with.

As it was not suspected they had any thing else in view, Mr. Carr readily went down, and brought up a couple of bottles of beer. They sat upon the poop with Capt. Augur in their company, and were drinking their beer; before the second bottle was out, Bunch and Mackarthy began to rattle, talk with great pleasure, and much boasting of their former exploits when they had been pirates, crying up a pirate's life to be the only life for a man of any spirit. While they were running on in this manner, Bunch on a sudden started up, and swore he would be captain of that vessel. Augur answered him the vessel did not want a captain, for he was able to command her himself, which seemed to put an end to the discourse for that time.

Soon after Bunch began to tell what bright arms they had on board their sloop; upon which, one of Augur's men handed up some of their cutlasses which had been cleaned that day. Among them was Mr. Carr's silver-hilted sword. Bunch seemed to admire the sword, and asked whose it was? Mr. Carr made answer, it belonged to him. Bunch replied it was a very handsome one, and drawing it out, marched about the poop, flourishing it over his head, and telling Mr. Carr he would return it to him when he had done with it. At the same time he began to vapour again, and to boast of his former piracies, and coming near Mr. Carr, struck him with the sword. Turnley bid him take care what he did, for Mr. Carr would not take such usage. As they were disputing upon this matter, Dennis Mackarthy stole off, and, with some of his associates, seized upon the great cabin, where all the arms lay. At the same time several of the men began to sing a song with these words. *Did you not promise me, that you would marry me*—which it seems was the signal agreed upon among the conspirators for seizing the ship. Bunch no sooner heard them, but he cried out aloud, *that I will, for I am parson*, and struck Mr. Carr again several blows with his own sword. Mr. Carr and Turnley both seized him, and they began to struggle, when Dennis Mackarthy, with several others, returned from the cabin with each a cutlass in one hand, and a loaded pistol in the other, and running up to them said, *What! do the governor's dogs offer to resist?* And beating Turnley and Carr with their cutlasses, threatened to shoot them, at the same time firing their pistols close to their cheeks, upon which Turnley and Carr begged their lives.

When they were thus in possession of the vessel, they hailed Capt. Greenway, and desired him to come on board about urgent business. He, knowing nothing of what had passed, jumped into his boat, and with two hands only, rowed on board. Dennis Mackarthy led him into the cabin, and, as soon as he was there, laid hold of him, telling him he was now a prisoner, and must submit. He offered to make some resistance; upon which, they told him all resistance would be vain, for his own men were in the plot; and, indeed, seeing the two hands who rowed him aboard, now armed, and joining with the conspirators, he thought it was time to submit.

As soon as this was done, they sent some hands on board to seize his sloop, or rather to acquaint his men with what had been done, for they expected to meet with no resistance, many of them being in the plot, and the rest, they supposed, not very averse to it; after which, they decoyed Captain White on board, by the same stratagem they used with Greenway, and likewise sent on board his sloop, and found his men, one and all, well disposed for the design; and what was most remarkable was, that Captain Augur, seeing how things were going, joined with them, showing himself as well inclined for pirating as the worst of them.[6]

With the ships in their possession, the pirates now had to decide what to do with those not in the plot. Some were for killing Richard Turnley, having some grudge against him, but they decided to maroon him and several others, including Carr, the other captains, and some of the sailors who would not join in the piracy. These unfortunates were put into a small oarless boat and sent to Green Cay, some of them being stripped naked before departure. A paddle that had been left in the boat provided the only means of reaching the island. The next morning, the marooned men were persuaded to come aboard again, being told they would be given clothes. The true reason was to force them to reveal the hiding places of certain valuables known to be aboard. Once on the ship, they were beaten until the information was forthcoming and the pirates found what they were looking for. The prisoners asked if they might have some food, to which they were told, "Such dogs should not ask such questions."[7]

The pirates worked very hard to persuade Captain Greenway to join them, for he was an excellent navigator and commander, and being a Bermudian, he knew how to swim, an art of which many sailors were ignorant at that time. Besides, the pirates were concerned he might swim to another island and arrange the rescue of the marooned men before the pirates could clear out of the area. The captain protested that his swimming could not harm them. He secured the release of himself and other officers, and they joined the marooned men ashore. The next day, the third at Green Cay, the pirates examined Captain Greenway's sloop, decided she was unseaworthy, and transferred her cargo and supplies to the other two ships. Greenway swam to his ship but found it stripped. Seeing him on board, the pirates returned and again tried to persuade him to join them. Finally, being full of wine and in a good humor, they told Greenway he could keep his sloop and departed. Searching the hold, Greenway managed to find an "old main-sail, an old fore-sail, four small pieces of Irish beef, in an old beef barrel, and about twenty biscuits, with a broken bucket which was used to draw water in." He then swam ashore to tell his companions the good news that his sloop was back and the bad news of finding it empty. The pirates still lay offshore in the two ships. Their indecisive and capricious nature is disclosed by the way they handled the whole affair. While the marooned men were waiting for the pirates to leave so they could go aboard Greenway's sloop, they were surprised to see a boat put off for the island: "Bunch with several others went on shore, carrying with them six bottles of wine and some biscuits. Whether this was done to tempt Greenway again, or no, is hard to say; for though they talked to him a great deal, they drank all the wine themselves to the last bottle, and then gave each of the poor creatures a glass a-piece, with a bit of biscuit, and immediately after fell to beating them, and so went on board."

While all this was going on, a turtling sloop owned and sailed by Benjamin Hutchins appeared and anchored. The sloop was immediately taken, being known to the pirates as a good sailing vessel. Hutchins was importuned to join but at first refused; later, when faced with marooning, he gave in. On October 9, the pirates ordered the marooned men to come aboard Greenway's sloop. The men paddled out to the vessel in the boat that had been left them and found some of the pirates already aboard. The pirates ordered them to rig the two sails remaining in the sloop improperly, which the men did without protesting. Then Phineas Bunch and Dennis Mackarthy came aboard with more pirates, "who being either mad or drunk, fell upon them, beating them, and cutting the rigging and sails to pieces with their cutlasses, and commanding them not to sail, till they should hear from them again, threatening if they did, they would put them all to death, if ever they met them again; and so they went off, carrying with them the boat, which they sent them first ashore in, and sailed away."

Now the men were faced with a really desperate situation, neither being able to sail nor to go back ashore:

> as self preservation put them upon exerting themselves, in order to get out of this deplorable state, they began to rummage and search the vessel through every hole and corner, to see if nothing was left which might be of use to them; and it happened by chance that they found an old hatchet, with which they cut some sticks sharp to serve for marling-spikes. They also cut out several other things, to serve instead of such tools as are absolutely necessary on board a ship.
>
> When they had proceeded thus far, every man began to work as hard as he could; they cut a piece of cable, which they strung into rope yarns, and fell to mending their sails with all possible expedition; they also made a kind of fishing lines of rope yarns, and bent some nails crooked to serve for hooks; but as they were destitute of a boat, as well for the use of fishing as for going on shore, they resolved to make a bark log, that is, to lay two or three logs together, and lash them close, upon which two or three men may sit very safely in smooth water.
>
> As soon as this was done, some hands went on shore, upon one of the logs (for they made two of them) who employed themselves in cutting wild cabbage, gathering berries, and a fruit which the seamen call prickly pears, for food, while some others went a fishing upon another.

Those who went ashore also carried the old bucket with them, so that whilst some were busy in gathering things to serve for provision, one hand was constantly employed in bringing fresh water aboard in the bucket, which was tedious work, considering how little could be brought at a time, and that the sloop lay near a mile from the shore.

For five days they continued their preparations to escape. They then weighed anchor, but as they came to the harbor entrance, they saw the pirates returning:

They were much frightened at this unexpected return, because of the threatenings they had used to them at parting, not to sail without further orders; wherefore, they tacked about, and ran as close in to the shore as they could, then throwing out their bark logs, they all put themselves upon them, and made to land, as fast as they could; but before they quite reached it, the pirates got so near that they fired at them, but were too far to do execution. However, they pursued them ashore; the unhappy exiles immediately took to the woods, and for greater security climbed up some trees, whose branches were very thick, and by that means concealed themselves. The pirates not finding them, soon returned to their boat, and rowed on board the deserted sloop, whose mast and boswprit they cut away, and towing into deep water, sunk her; after which, they made again for shore, thinking that the fugitives would have been out of their lurking holes, and that they should surprize them; but they continued still on the tops of the trees and saw all that passed, and therefore thought it safest to keep their posts.

The pirates not finding them, returned to their vessels, and weighing their anchors, set sail, steering eastward.

The desperate men now were in the depths of despair, having no means of starting a fire, no means of fishing or hunting the hogs on the island, and no prospects for food but small shellfish and wild berries and roots, and no means of getting word to Providence. For eight days they lived in this way, but the cat-and-mouse game of the pirates was not over. On the ninth day they returned and seeing the marooned men ashore took pity on them. In tune with their fickle and unpredictable natures, they sent a boat ashore and some of the pirates went through the woods calling out to the marooned men who had hidden there when they saw the pirate boat start for shore. The pirates apologized for the rough treatment the men had been given and offered to provide them with food and wine if they would come out of hiding. Their bellies growling with hunger and now desperate, the men came out of the woods and went on board one of the sloops. Here the pirates "were as good as their word, for they gave them as much beef and biscuit as they could eat, during two or three days they were on board, but would not give them a bit to carry on shore."

On board the sloop was the turtler George Redding, who had been forced to join the pirates when they took his ship. Unbeknown to the pirates, he was an old friend of Richard Turnley, one of the prisoners. Redding knew that Turnley would eventually go ashore again rather than be forced to piracy, and he laid a plan to help him. When the pirates were off guard, he slipped Turnley a small tinder box which Turnley concealed. At the end of the three days the prisoners were again asked if they would join with the pirates or go ashore. They all chose to be marooned. The masters Greenway and White were forced to remain with the pirates, and the others were sent ashore. The pirates set sail for Pudden Point, a small islet near Long Island, where they careened and cleaned their vessels.

The men back on Green Cay set about for a long stay but now had the comfort of fire to dress their food. Land crabs and snakes abounded on the island, and for fourteen days the men fared well on this food, with berries and some shellfish. Then the pirates returned a third time. Again, the poor men took to the woods to avoid the abuse they feared, but this time the fickle pirates were in a compassionate mood and brought them some provisions and other things. Calling through the woods, the pirates could not persuade their victims to show themselves, so they left the goods on the beach and went away.

> The poor islanders had got to their retreat, the tops of the trees, and saw the pirates go off; upon which they ventured down, and going to the water side, were agreeably surprized to find a small cask of flour, of between twenty and thirty pounds, about a bushel of salt, two bottles of gunpowder, several bullets, besides a quantity of small shot, with a couple of muskets, a very good axe, and also a pot and a pan, and three dogs, which they took in the turtle sloop; which dogs are bred to hunting, and generally the sloops which go turtling, carry some of them, as they are very useful in tracing out the wild hogs. Besides all these, there were a dozen horn handled knives, of that sort which are usually carried to Guinea.

Richard Turnley, the best hunter of the group, took the muskets and dogs and went off hunting the wild hogs, while the rest of the men cut poles with the hatchets and set about building a hut. Soon they had a fire going with pork over it and some pork salted away for the time they could escape. Vastly comforted, the men settled down to a reasonably pleasant living while they awaited rescue. But the pirates were to make one more call. After a few days, they returned to fill their water casks, and seeing the hut, they burned it down just for the amusement of it. Turnley came back from a hunting trip with a large hog while the pirates were still in the camp, and they immediately availed themselves of this fresh meat and roasted it over the fire. When they had finished, being in a better humor, they gave the marooned men a bottle of rum and left, saying they would not return. Not until after the men on the island were rescued did they see the pirates again.

The pirates immediately sailed to Long Island, where they spotted three vessels in a harbor. Supposing the ships to be Bermudian or American, and there to load salt from the salt works nearby, the pirates attacked. The surprising outcome is told in the account from which we have been quoting:

> The turtle sloop taken from Benjamin Hutchins, was by much the best sailer; however, it was almost dark before she came up with them, and then coming close alongside of one of them, she gave a broadside, with a design to board the next minute, but received such a volley of small shot in return, as killed and wounded a great many of the pirates, and the rest, in great surprize and fright, jumped overboard, to save themselves by swimming ashore.
>
> The truth is, these sloops proved to be Spanish privateers, who observing the pirates to bear down upon them, prepared themselves for action. The commander in chief of these three privateers was one who was called by the name of Turn Joe, because he had once privateered on the English side. He had also been a pirate, and now acted by virtue of a commission from a Spanish governor. He was by birth an Irishman, a bold enterprising fellow, and was afterwards killed in an engagement with one John Bonnavee, captain of a privateer belonging to Jamaica.
>
> But to return to our story. The sloop was taken, and on board her was found, desperately wounded, Phineas Bunch, who was the captain. By and by a second of the pirate sloops came up; she heard the volley, and supposed it to be fired by Bunch, when he boarded one of the sloops; she came also alongside of one of the Spaniards, and received the welcome that was given to Bunch, and submitted as soon. A little after, came up the third, which was taken with the same ease, and in the same manner, as many of the pirates as could swim, jumping overboard to save themselves on shore, there not being a man lost on the side of the Spaniards.
>
> The next day Turn Joe asked them many questions, and finding out that several amongst them had been forced men, he, with the consent of

the other Spanish officers, ordered all the goods to be taken out of a Spanish launch, and putting some of the wounded pirates into the said launch, with some provision, water, and other liquors, gave it to the forced men, to carry them to Providence.

George Redding, Thomas Betty, Matthew Betty, and Benjamin Hutchins set sail with the wounded pirates and in two days arrived in New Providence. They went immediately to Governor Rogers and told him what had happened. This was the first word Rogers had received from the commercial enterprise in which he and the merchants had placed such high hopes and his discouragement must have been profound. Nevertheless, he set his discouragement aside and turned his attention to the problems at hand. First, he sent out a sloop to rescue the men marooned on Green Cay and then made plans to capture the remaining pirates. Phineas Bunch lay severely wounded in the launch in the harbor. The governor and some of his officers went to the launch and there heard Bunch confess to his crimes. With this, preparations were made to hang him, a trial being unnecessary. Bunch had accepted the King's amnesty and had returned to piracy: the amnesty act provided for execution in this event. Bunch was to be hanged forthwith, but fate had other plans for him, and he died from his wounds before he could be brought to the gallows. Rogers immediately set about fitting out a sloop to send after the pirates who had escaped the privateers at the salt ponds on Long Island. Captains Cockram and Hornigold went in command and were joined by Richard Turnley, for the marooned men had been returned to New Providence before the sloops sailed in quest of the pirates.

When the sloop reached the spot where the pirates were thought to be hiding, the captains were careful to keep most of their men below decks, so they could not be seen from shore and so the pirates would think the sloop a trading ship come to load salt. The pirates took the bait:

> The pirates seeing them, came only two or three of them near the shore, the rest lying in ambush, not without hopes of finding an opportunity to seize the sloop, which sent her boat out towards the shore, with orders to lay off at a little distance, as if she was afraid. Those in ambush seeing the boat so near, had not patience to stay any longer, but flocked to the water side, calling out to them to come on shore, and help them, for they were poor shipwrecked men, perishing for want. Upon which the boat rowed back again to the sloop.
>
> Upon second thoughts they sent her off again and with two bottles of wine, a bottle of rum, and some biscuit, and sent another man, who was

a stranger to those ashore, with orders to pass for master of the vessel. As soon as they approached them, the pirates called to them as before, begging them, for God's sake to come on shore; they did so, and gave them the biscuit, wine and rum, which he said he brought ashore on purpose to comfort them, because his men told him they were cast away. They were very inquisitive to know where he was bound. He told them, to New-York, and that he came in there to take in salt. They earnestly entreated him to take them on board, and carry them as passengers to New-York; they being about sixteen in number, he answered, he was afraid he had not provision sufficient for so great a number; but that he would go on board and overhaul his provision, and if they pleased, some of them might go with him, and see how his stock stood; that at least he would carry some of them, and leave some refreshment for the rest, till they could be succored another way, but that he hoped they would make him some recompence when they should arrive at New-York.

They seemed wonderfully pleased with his proposal, and promised to make him ample satisfaction for all the charges he should be at, pretending to have good friends and considerable effects in different parts of America. Accordingly he took several of them with him in the boat, and as soon as they got on board he invited them into the cabin, where, to their surprize, they saw Benjamin Hornygold, formerly a brother pirate; but what astonished them more, was to see Richard Turnley, whom they had lately marooned upon Green Key. They were immediately surrounded by several with pistols in their hands, and clapped in irons.

The same ruse was repeated with the pirates who remained on shore, and all were captured. The sloop then set sail for Providence, and when it arrived there, the governor had the pirates confined in the fort under heavy guard. He now had a vital decision to make. He had not been empowered to convene an admiralty court to try pirates, and as yet there was no adequate jail in which they could be held until they could be sent to the mainland for trial. In addition, the true temper of the former pirates in the population was not exactly known to Rogers and his councillors, so the matter had to be carefully considered, and this was done in "Private Consultation" convened in the office of the secretary on November 28, 1718. At the consultation were discussed all aspects of the problem facing the government. Rogers was not legally empowered to convene an admiralty court, he could not spare his ship to send the pirates to the mainland for trial, and he was uneasy about keeping them under guard for any length of time in a community where half the people were former pirates and former friends of the accused. He and his officers also considered the danger of pirates' coming from the outside and attempting a rescue. Then there was the larger problem of getting the defenses of the island ready for the hostilities that were expected with Spain. Rogers and his advisers felt they could not spare men to guard the pirates when all hands were desperately needed to work on the fortifications.

Since many of the pirates had accepted the King's amnesty and then had reverted to their former ways, legally strengthening the hand of the governor, it was concluded that the best course was to convene a special court and try the pirates as soon as possible. The court duly convened December 9 and 10 in the guard room of the fort. Sitting with Governor Rogers were William Fairfax and six other members of the council. After a thorough examination of the evidence presented by the testimony of those who had been marooned on Green Cay and after consideration of the pleas of the pirates themselves, the prisoners were found guilty and sentence was pronounced:

> THE COURT having duly considered of the evidence which hath been given both for and against you the said John Augur, William Cunning-ham, Dennis Mackarthy, William Dowling, William Lewis, Thomas Morris, George Bendall, William Ling, and George Rounsivel; and having also debated the several circumstances of the cases, it is ad-judged, that you the said John Augur, William Cunningham, Dennis Mackarthy, William Dowling, William Lewis, Thomas Morris, George Bendall, William Ling, and George Rounsivel, are guilty of the mutiny, felony, and piracy, wherewith you and every of you stand accused. And the Court doth accordingly pass sentence, that you the said John Augur, William Cunningham, Dennis Mackarthy, William Dowling, William Lewis, Thomas Morris, George Bendall, William Ling, and George Rounsivel, be carried to prison from whence you came, and from thence to the place of execution, where you are to be hanged by the neck till you should be *dead, dead, dead;* and God have mercy on your souls. Given under our hands this 10th day of December, A.D. 1718. [signed]
>
> | | |
> |---|---|
> | WOODES ROGERS, | WINGATE GALE, |
> | WILLIAM FAIRFAX, | NATHANIEL TAYLOR, |
> | ROBERT BEAUCHAMP, | JOSIAS BURGISS, |
> | THOMAS WALKER, | PETER COURANT.[7] |

The governor and the court ordered that the execution take place on Friday, December 12:

> Whereupon the prisoners pray'd for longer time to relent & prepare for Death, the Governour told them that from the time of their being Apprehended, which was the 15th of November, they ought to have

accounted themselves as condemned by the laws all Nations, which was only sealed now, And that the securing them hitherto and the favour the Court had allowed them in making as long a Defence as they could and wholy took up that time which the Affairs of the Settlement required in working the Fortifications, besides the Fategue thereby occasion'd to the whole Garrison the necessary Guards set over them thro. want of a Gaol, and the Garrison have been very much lessen'd by death and sickness, since his arrival, and that he was obliged to employ all his People to assist in mounting the great Guns, & in finishing the present works, with all possible dispatch, because of the expected War with Spain, & there being many more pyrates amongst these Islands, and this place left destitute of all Relief, from any Man of War, or Station'd Ship much wanted which with other Reasons, he knew too long to enumerate in the Court, He thought himselfe indispensable obliged for the wellfare of the Settlement to give them no longer time.

Then the Prisoners were ordered back to the Place of their Imprisonment in the Fort, where leave was given, them to send for any Persons to read & to pray with them.

On Fryday morning each of the Prisoners were call'd in Private to know if they had any Load upon their Spirits, for actions committed as yet unknown to the World the Declaring of which is absolutely required to prepare themselves for fitt Repentance. But they each refus'd to declare any thing as well as making known to the Governour if they knew of any farther Conspiracy against the Governmt. but this they also denie[d].

Wherefore about ten a Clock the Prisoners were released of their Irons & Comitted to the charge and care of Thos. Robenson Esq. Commissioned provost Marshall for that day, who according to custome in such Cases pinion'd them & ordered the Guards appointed to assist him, to lead them to the top of the Ramparts fronting the Sea, which was well Guarded by the Governour, Soldiers & People to the Numb. of about one hundred, At the Prisoners request severall prayers & psalms selected were read in which all present joyn'd, When the Service was ended, Orders was given to the Marshall, & he conducted the prisoners down a ladder, provided on purpose to the foot of the wall, where was a Gallows erected, & a black Flagg hoisted theron & under it a Stage, supported by three Butts, on which they assended by another Ladder, where the hangman fastned the Cords as dextreously as if he had been a servitour at Tybourne, they had ¾ of an houre allow's under the Gallows which was spent by them in Singing of Psalm, & some exhortations to their old Consorts, & the other sort of Spectators who got as near to the foot of the Gallows, as the Marshalls Guard would suffer them, Then the Governour ordered the Marshall to make ready, & all the prisoners expecting the launch, The Governour thought fitt to order Geo. Rounsivel to be untied, & when brought off the stage, the Butts having Ropes about them, were hauld away, upon which the stage fell & the Eight Swang off.

So ended the captured pirates. Rogers had gone to great lengths to explain into the record the reasons for holding the court which lacked a formal legal basis, and he had the clerk add an account of the pirates hanged, possibly to demonstrate to the Lords Commissioners for Trade and Plantations the sort of people he had to deal with and to further justify his extraordinary action. These descriptions furnish us with an insight into the kind of person that turned to piracy:

John Augur, being about 40 years of age, had been a noted ship-master at Jamaica, and since among the pirates; but on his accepting of His Majesty's act of grace, and recommendations to the governor, he was, notwithstanding, entrusted with a good vessel and cargo, in which, betraying his trust, and knowing himself guilty of the indictment, he all along appeared very penitent, and neither washed, shaved or shifted his old clothes, when carried to be executed, and when he had a small glass of wine given him on the rampart, drank it with wishes for the good success of the Bahama Islands, and the governor.

The third, Dennis Mackarthy, aged 28, had also been formerly a pirate, but accepted of the king's act of grace; and the governor had made him an ensign of the militia, being recommended as a sober, discreet person, which commission he had at the time of his joining the pirates, which very much aggravated his other crimes. During his imprisonment he behav'd himself well enough, but when he thought he was to dye, and the morning come without his expected repreve, he put on a clean shift of cloaths adorn'd at neck, wrists, knees and capp with long blew ribbons, when on the Rampart lookt cheerfully around him, saying he knew the time when there was many brave fellows on the Island that would not suffer him to dye like a dog, at the same time pull'd off his shoes kicking them over the Parapet of the fort saying he had promised not to dye with his shoes on, & he descended the fort wall, & assended the Stage with as much agility, and in a dress as if he was to fight a prize, when mounted He exhorted the people who were at the foot of the Walls to have compassion on him but their wills saw two much power over their heads to practice anything.

William Dowling of about 24 years had been a considerable time amongst the pyrates and of a wicked life, which his Majesty Act of Grace would not reform his behaviour was very loose on the stage, & after his death, some of his acquaintance declared he had confessed to them of his having murder'd his mother before he left Ireland.

William Lewis age about 34 years, as he had been a hardy pyrate & a prize fighter, scorn'd to shew any fear to dye, but heartily desired liquors to drink with his fellow sufferers on the stage, & with the standers by.

Thomas Morris aged about 22 had been a very incorragable youth & pyrate and seem'd to have little reluctancy by his frequent smiles when at the bar being dress'd with red Ribbans in the same manner as Mc-Karthy was blew, when he was going over the Rampart, he openly said that we have a new Governour but a harsh one, and a little before he was turn'd off, said aloud that he might have been a greater plague to these Islands, & now wisht he had been so.

The clerk then ended the report with the wry comment: "It was observable that few men besides the Governour Adharents and Spectators of the Tragedy, but what had lately deserv'd the same Fate; tho were several who behav'd very well, & were firm to the Governour ever since his arrival; and as they have been pardoned by the Gracious Act of his Majesty."

Thus ended Rogers's first six months as governor at Nassau. He had accomplished much in laying out the town, planning plantations, and suppressing the pirates who chose to stay, and had work on the fortifications well along. He had made other proposals to the Lords Commissioners for Trade and Plantations that were farsighted, such as settling some fifteen hundred persons in the Leeward Islands to establish a more sober and industrious people in the area, and had attempted to start a trade with Cuba, with the results we have seen. While he failed in some things, he had succeeded in laying the foundation for stability in a colony where nothing but anarchy and confusion had prevailed. In his conscience, he could take satisfaction with his first accomplishments, but the lack of word from the government and the refusal of the navy to aid him brought him mounting frustration. The commanders of the men-of-war were profiting from the raids on the pirates, as Rogers pointed out in a letter to Sir Richard Steele, dated at Nassau, January 30, 1718/19:

Every capture made by the pirates aggravates the apparent inclinations of the Commanders of our men-of-war; who having openly avowed that the greater number of pirates makes their suitable advantage in trade; for the Merchants of necessity are forced to send their effects in the King's bottoms, when they from every part hear of the ravages committed by the pirates.

There is no Governor in these American parts who has not justly complained of this grand negligence; and I am in hopes the several representations will induce the Board of Admiralty to be more strict in their orders.[8]

On May 29, 1719, he wrote the Lords Commissioners for Trade and Plantations of the continuing need for a vessel of war and of the danger in which the colony lay until the fortifications and garrison were put into fighting condition. By this time, the indifference of the people was becoming a chronic aggravation to him:

> I hope your Lordships will pardon my troubling you, but a few instances of those people I have to govern, who, though they expect the enemy that has surprised them these fifteen years thirty-four times, yet these wretches cant be kept to watch at night, and when they do they come very seldom sober, and rarely awake all night, though our officers or soldiers very often surprise their guard and carry off their arms, and I punish, fine or confine them almost every day.
>
> Then for work they mortally hate it, for when they have cleared a patch that will supply them with potatoes and yams and very little else, fish being so plentiful . . . they thus live, poorly and indolently, with a seeming content, and pray for wrecks or pirates; and few of them have any opinion of a regular orderly life under any sort of Government, and would rather spend all they have at a Punch house than pay me one-tenth to save their families and all that's dear to them.[9]

Rogers wasn't the only one writing letters. On December 3, 1719, Samuel Buck, as spokesman for the townspeople and tradesmen of Nassau, wrote the Lords Commissioners of the expenses they had to support for the defense of the island, listing £20,000 as expended on the fortifications, maintaining the garrison of troops and artillery which came with Rogers and the guardship while it was there, as well as for fitting out sloops to chase pirates, and maintaining a party of Palatine Germans the governor had brought over to settle the island. The merchants and planters ended their letter with a plea: "We humbly pray your Lordships that you'll be speedy in your representations of ye estimates being laid before Parliament and that some allowances may be made for ye building of ye forts which was done purely for yea public service and that another Independent Company be sent thither with provisions for 12 months and all necessary stores, without which your petitioners cannot support ye said expense, but must quitt ye said island, they having made no advantage either in planting or commerce."

By April 1720, Rogers had not had any instructions from the Lords Commissioners and practically no response from the Secretary of State later than July 1719, and his despair is evident in a letter dated April 20, 1720, addressed to the Lords Commissioners:

It's about twenty one Months since my first arrival here attended with as great Disappointments, Sickness & other Misfortunes as almost can be imagin'd of which I have continually advis'd in the best manner I could, and I have yet no Account from Home what is or will be done for the Preservation of this Settlemt. . . .

I have been at a great Expence to support the People here under Arms & to supply the Garrison & arm'd Vessells wth. proper necessary. for our Defence all which shall be transmitt'd home attested by the Council as soon as the Embargo is off or We know our selves out of Danger of the Enemy the place is so wretchedly Poor and having yet no assembly I can by no means raise any Part here & I beg your Lordship. intercession that the Load may not lye on me who have sacrifis'd all I can raise here wth.

Rogers finally gave up and resolved to return to London, leaving the government in the hands of William Fairfax. Rogers had given the colony all he had in energy and ability. He had ruined his health and had contracted debts that wiped out the small fortune he had acquired as a result of his voyage around the world in 1708–1711. He had been betrayed by British officialdom, by the stupidity and indifference of the government boards at home. When he left Nassau in March 1721, he took with him a memorial from his council and the leading citizens which attested to his personal sacrifices for the colony:

We thought it a duty incumbent on us, as well to the Country, as to his Excellency the Governor, and his Majesty's garrison here to put these things in a full and true light . . . that we might as much as in us lies, do our Governor justice, and prevent any farther ungrateful usage being offered him at home, to frusterate his good endeavours when please God he arrives there, for the service of his country, to preserve this settlement; for next to the Divine protection, it is owing to him, who has acted amongst us without the least regard for his private advantage or separate interest, in a scene of continual fatigues and hardships.[10]

Compare this record with that of Rogers's contemporary, Archibald Hamilton, governor of Jamaica, who had to be recalled because of collusion with the pirate Jennings. Rogers was unsuccessful in arousing interest in the colony in London, and he was not to return for several years. The Bahamas fell into a period of bad times and bad administration, while piracy again thrived in the out islands, if not openly in Nassau.

Rogers's successor, Governor Phenney, had neither the organizing ability nor the charm and persuasiveness of his predecessor, and things went from bad to worse. Phenney himself was accused of having exploited the people for his own gain, and a petition asking his recall went to London. In 1727, Rogers petitioned the King to reappoint him governor of the islands, and at the same time another petition was submitted, signed by twenty-nine prominent men, including several former colonial governors, asking His Majesty the same favor. The bad conditions in the colony and Rogers's evident qualifications tipped the scales, and Rogers was appointed, with a salary of £400 a year and the titles of governor in chief and captain general. His commission was dated in December 1728. Early in the summer of the next year, Rogers, now a widower, sailed for Nassau with his son and daughter. He arrived in the fall, and an assembly was elected. On September 30, 1728, it met and proceeded to pass several acts designed to give the colony a better economic base. These included acts to encourage the planting of cotton and sugar cane. The acts were well conceived but difficult to put into practice since many of the people Rogers had hoped to attract to the islands as planters did not come—the poor condition of the islands was well known abroad. In addition to this, Rogers now had an enemy in one Colebrook, the speaker of the assembly, who led the opposition to defeat any progressive schemes Rogers attempted to present to the body. Colebrook finally went too far and incited the garrison to mutiny, which led to his arrest and trial. He was fined £750, confined, and held until he had given security for good behavior, but the demagogue undoubtedly continued to exert a disruptive influence on the population. Just as before, Rogers set about strengthening and rebuilding the fortifications, which had been allowed to fall into ruin during the years of his absence. He built a new barracks and twenty new gun carriages to replace those that had been allowed to rot. His accounts were all but a repetition of those he gave the home government after his first arrival ten years before, for the colony was in great disorder. The only difference was that the pirate community had gone.

The affairs of the colony and the frustrations of trying to drag the population into a better condition bore heavily on the devoted Rogers. He had not lost his faith in the potential of the islands, and he was still ready with schemes that would have given the colony a firm basis for prosperity, but the nature of the inhabitants, living on tropical islands where a poor living could be made easily, was such that few wanted to make the effort to better themselves. Rogers's health began to fail, and his decline was speeded by the disappointments and abuse he had received in office. Near the end, he must have realized the futility of trying to build a prosperous colony in such a place with such a people.

Rogers died in Nassau on July 15, 1732, a few months after a boy named George Washington had been born in Virginia. After his death, the island again fell into confusion, with a rebellion of the population and a mutiny of the garrison marking the first years of Rogers's successor. Pirates did again resort to Nassau, but covertly and not in great numbers. The out islands were another matter, for here the pirates came to water their vessels, to fish for turtles, and to relax on the beaches after a cruise.

The pirates Rogers caught and executed were the incompetents of the profession, who were largely ignorant of offshore navigation and confined by their ignorance to sailing small vessels in the shallow waters and small islands of the Bahamas. Not so the pirates like Charles Vane, who had defied Rogers on his first arrival at Nassau. Vane and his equals were able to range over the whole of the West Indies and the Atlantic coast of North America, wreaking havoc on the coastal and international shipping in the generation following the peace of 1713.

XIII

Gone on Account

"I am a free prince, and I have as much authority to make war on the whole world, as he who has a hundred sail of ships at sea."

> —Words spoken by Samuel Bellamy, pirate,
> to a captured ship captain

 WHILE THE PIRATES we have seen working in the Bahamas were ignorant, capricious, and violent, many of those who followed their calling on the high seas were of a more professional cast. Some were well-educated, talented men who could not bear the restrictions of a rigidly stratified society in which the wealthy lorded it over the working classes and birth usually meant more than ability. Others were simply bored with a peaceful life and went to sea as pirates for adventure as well as for profit, especially those who had served on privateers during the frequent periods of warfare that dominated the history of the eighteenth century. In a life that was of its very nature brutal, some leaders were able to rise a cut or two above their fellows and maintain a code that, apart from their being robbers, would have gained them entrance to polite society. They were the exception, of course, for the profession of pirate required some use of violence, and violence combined with the absolute authority of the pirate captain over his victims tended to brutalize most of the leaders.

Although the natures of the pirate leaders and their followers were varied, their methods of operation were fairly standardized. Like the buccaneers of the previous century, they followed a regular code of conduct, embodied in articles of agreement. One of the codes read:

I.

Every man shall obey civil Command; the Captain shall have one full Share and a half in all Prizes; the Master, Carpenter, Boatswain and Gunner shall have one Share and quarter.

A pirate captain dressed in his finery. An eighteenth-century engraving

2.

If any Man shall offer to run away, or keep any Secret from the Company, he shall be marroon'd with one Bottle of Powder, one Bottle of Water, one small Arm, and Shot.

3.

If any Man shall steal any Thing in the Company, or game, to the Value of a Piece of Eight, he shall be Marroon'd or shot.

4.

If at any Time we should meet another Marrooner (that is, Pyrate), that Man that shall sign his Articles without the Consent of our Company, shall suffer such Punishment as the Captain and Company shall think fit.

5.

That Man that shall strike another whilst these Articles are in force, shall receive Moses's Law (that is 40 Stripes lacking one) on the bare Back.

6.

That Man that shall snap his Arms, or smoak Tobacco in the Hold, without a cap to his Pipe, or carry a Candle lighted without a Lanthorn, shall suffer the same Punishment as in the former Article.

7.

That Man that shall not keep his Arms clean, fit for an Engagement, or neglect his Business, shall be cut off from his Share, and suffer such other Punishment as the Captain and the Company shall think fit.

8.

If any Man shall lose a Joint in time of an Engagement, he shall have 400 Pieces of Eight, if a limb, 800.

9.

If at any time you meet with a prudent Woman, that Man that offers to meddle with her, without her Consent, shall suffer present Death.

The captain of a pirate company was chosen by vote and was usually the one who could navigate and had demonstrated some qualities of leadership. Having elected him and drawn up their articles of agreement, the pirates would prepare to sail. Usually they had a ship that belonged to the elected captain. Frequently a merchant captain would enter the profession and bring his ship with him. In the eighteenth century, merchant ships almost always carried guns for self-defense, and a merchant vessel could easily be converted to the warship required for piracy. The pirates would attack any ship they felt had useful loot aboard, and in the early stages of a cruise, would search a captured vessel carefully for the provisions and supplies they needed. By furnishing themselves in this way, they could keep to the sea for extended periods, until the ship needed to have the barnacles and weeds scraped from the bottom. Then the pirates would find a secluded cove or river estuary where they could careen the ship, destroy the growths with fire, and scrape and recaulk the hull. At these times, the pirates were especially vulnerable to attack.

Pirates on an extended cruise frequently sent prizes into port for sale. To do so required the cooperation of dishonest merchants who acted as fences and dishonest officials in the ports where the prizes were taken. Even some colonial governors were involved in this traffic—Governor Charles Eden of North Carolina was a notorious example—and those ports where friendly, bribable officials and equally friendly merchants waited became centers of illicit trade in pirate goods. Charleston, South Carolina; Savannah, Georgia; Providence, Rhode Island; and even staid old Boston were among them. The whole

Pirates careening their ship. Every few months a pirate captain had to find a safe beach where the crew could remove the growths which had accumulated on the ship's bottom. During this time they were vulnerable to attack by naval patrols looking for them. An eighteenth-century engraving

coast of North Carolina was infested with pirates, and the ports there received numerous cargoes of loot with the cooperation of the highest officials. Because periods of peace quickly alternated with periods of war, the pirate moved into privateering and back to piracy with frequency and ease. The line between the two often became blurred, giving the cooperating officials and merchants a good defense against charges of collusion. Piracy was, then, a big business and many a merchant prince's fortune was secretly built in dealing with the outlaws, while the merchant himself maintained an exalted social status in his own community.

Several dozen pirate captains of the first decades of the eighteenth century are known to history by name and reputation. Many of them are mentioned in Captain Johnson's *General History of the Pirates*, a book of great popularity when it was published in the early 1700's and one that contains much of the existing information we have on certain pirate leaders. We shall be quoting from this book as well as from colonial records and other contemporary literature.

After Charles Vane* defied Woodes Rogers and escaped in a sloop

* Vane is thought to have been with Jennings in his raid on the Spanish salvage camps in 1715 and apparently went to Nassau at the same time as Jennings.

across the shallows that lie off Nassau harbor, he sailed to the coast of North Carolina, where the numerous inlets offered good hiding places and the officials proved to be friendly. When it became evident to other pirates that Nassau was closed to them, they followed Vane north, and eventually the coast south of Virginia became infested. From here, the pirates attacked the shipping that sailed the main routes to and from the West Indies and to Europe by way of Bermuda. Vane had escaped with a crew of ninety men in the sloop, and two days after leaving Nassau, he captured another sloop from Barbados. To this prize, he transferred twenty-five of his crew under one Yeates, who was owner of the sloop in which they had all escaped from Rogers. After this, the pirates went to a deserted island off North Carolina, divided the loot from their prize, and held their usual drunken orgy. After a rest of some days, Vane took the two sloops to the western coast of Hispaniola, where he captured a Spanish ship bound for Havana. After removing the cargo they wanted, the pirates burned the ship and set the captured crew adrift in a small boat. Vane's next prize, a brigantine taken off St. Christopher, furnished him with much-needed provisions and ships' supplies. From the Windward Islands, he now returned to the coast of North America and took prizes off North Carolina. Here he had been preceded by Blackbeard and Stede Bonnet, who had harassed shipping there. Vane now wreaked havoc along the shipping lanes by taking, among others, several English vessels in the coastal trade, ships from Antigua and Curaçao, and a brigantine loaded with slaves that had come to North Carolina by way of the West Indies, the usual route from Africa. Vane did not keep any of these vessels, but he did take from them the provisions and stores he needed and the cargo of ninety Negroes, which he placed aboard Yeates's sloop.

Yeates had been secretly planning to go off on his own (Vane had treated him as a subordinate instead of a colleague) and with the Negroes aboard, he escaped into the Edisto River, where the water was too shallow for Vane to follow. While the furious captain sailed back and forth off the mouth of the river waiting for him to come out, Yeates sent a message overland to the governor at Charleston offering to surrender and to return the Negroes if he were given the King's amnesty. The governor agreed to Yeates's offer, and the pirates came into town, where they were pardoned and the Negroes were returned to Captain Thompson of the slaver.

Vane continued to lie off the coast waiting for Yeates and capturing ships, which he looted and released. Word soon got back to Charleston of Vane's continuing presence off the coast, and Colonel William

Rhett fitted out two vessels and went after him. But the pirate, knowing he must be soon attacked if he remained too long in the same area, had already sailed north, where he captured one small vessel off Delaware. Here Vane met a French man-of-war which his crew urged him to attack. Vane, the wise old pirate, was looking for loot, not immortality, and refused. The next day he was accused of cowardice by his crew and was deposed. Elected captain was John Rackam, one of his officers, whose career we shall soon consider. Vane, according to some accounts, was marooned; according to others, he was given a small sloop with fifteen men; in any case, having disposed of him, Rackam sailed off to the West Indies with Vane's old ship and crew.

As for the indestructible Vane, he was soon back at sea with a diminished force but just as eager as ever for captures. He sailed to the Gulf of Honduras and took three vessels out of Jamaica. One of these he kept, the others he plundered and released. These events occurred during the four months following his escape from Nassau. Near the end of the year, he engaged and captured an armed ship out of Jamaica and took another merchantman. The pirates, after going to a deserted island to divide the loot, remained there until well into February of 1719, enjoying their booty and refreshing themselves.

They had just set sail again to go cruising when a severe storm struck and drove Vane's ships onto an island beach. Most of his men died in the water, but Vane escaped to shore. Luckily for him, the island was frequently visited by turtlers, and from these men Vane was able to get enough food and water to stay alive. Thus he lived for several weeks when a merchant ship put into the island for water and the captain proved to be an old companion of Vane's, Captain Holford, who had been pardoned and had gone straight. Vane presented himself to Holford and asked to be taken aboard, but his old shipmate is supposed to have answered: "Charles I shan't have you aboard my ship unless I carry you a Prisoner; for I shall have you caballing with my Men, knock me on the Head, and run away with my Ship pyrating." Although Vane pleaded with his old shipmate and swore he had no such intentions, Holford would not give in. The most he would do was promise to return in a month, and if Vane were still there, take him prisoner and deposit him before the admiralty court in Port Royal, Jamaica. Then Holford sailed away leaving Vane on the beach.

A few days after Holford departed, another merchantman put into the island, and Vane, posing as a shipwrecked sailor, persuaded the captain to take him aboard as a seaman. Things were looking brighter for him, but unfortunately his time had run out. The ship happened to run in with Holford, an old friend of the captain who had taken Vane aboard not knowing who he was. When the captain invited Holford to come aboard for dinner, Holford readily accepted. At the time, Vane was in the hold busy at some job—he had already endeared himself to the new captain as an industrious seaman. Holford came aboard amidships and in walking past the main hatch toward the cabin glanced down into the hold and saw Vane. He immediately told his host who his industrious seaman was, and the host forthwith had Vane put in irons. Soon after, he was landed at Port Royal.

On March 22, 1720, Vane was tried before the admiralty court. The charges read to him were lengthy and covered offenses for the year 1718, some dating from as early as March 29, while Vane was enjoying the safety of Nassau before the arrival of Woodes Rogers:

> And the said *Charles Vane*, in Execution of his said Evil Designs, afterwards (*to wit*) on the 29th. Day of March, in the Year aforesaid, with Force and Arms upon the high Sea, in a certain place, distant about two Leagues from *Abbaco*,* in *America,* and within the jurisdiction of this Court; did piratically, feloniously, and in an hostile manner, attack, shoot at, and take, a certain Sloop or Vessel, call'd the John and Elizabeth, with several Hundred Spanish Pieces of Eight, and divers Goods and Merchandizes on Board her, whereof one *Benj. Bill* was Master (going from *St. Augustine* to the Island of *Providence* in *America*) then being, a Sloop or Vessel. of certain Persons, Subjects of our said Lord the King, that now is, (to the Register aforesaid unknown) and then and there, piratically, feloniously, and in an hostile manner, did make an Assault, in and upon, the said *Benj. Bill* and certain other Mariners and Persons, whose (Names to the Register aforesaid are unknown) in the same Sloop, in the Peace of God, and of our said Lord the King, then and there and then, and there, piractically, and feloniously, did put the said *Benjamin Bill,* and other the Mariners, and Persons, of the said Sloop, in the Sloop aforesaid, called *John* and *Elizabeth,* then being, in Corporal fear of their Lives, and then and there Piratically and Feloniously, did steal, take, and carry away, the said Sloop, with her Lading, Tackle, Furniture, and Apparrel, of the Value of One thousand Pounds of Current Money of Jamaica.[1]

The court then went on with charges concerning other vessels, as follows:

> April 17, 1718 a merchant ship, the *Betty,* Captain Benjamin Lee Master taken one league off Crooked Island, 200 pounds value

* Abaco Island is in the Bahamas, but since no admiralty court was commissioned for the Bahamas, the court at Jamaica claimed jurisdiction, in spite of the fact that Governor Spotswood of Virginia also seems to have claimed it.

April 22, 1718 a merchant ship, the *Fortune*, Captain George Guy Master taken 9 miles off Crooked Island, value 150 pounds

May 23, 1718 a merchant ship, the *Richard and John*, Captain Joseph Cockran Master, 12 miles from Crooked Island value 200 pounds.

October 23, 1718 a merchant ship, the *Endeavour*, Captain John Shattock Master, 6 miles from Long Island, value 250 pounds.

December 16, 1718 a merchant ship, the *Pearl*, Captain Charles Rowling Master taken in the Bay [Gulf] of Honduras.

After the charges were read, Vane was asked how he pleaded and he answered, "Not guilty." Witnesses were then called. These included some of the masters of the vessels taken, and the case against Vane was conclusive. The court retired behind closed doors, and when Vane was returned, pronounced the verdict: "That he, the said Charles Vane was guilty of the Piracy, Felony and Robbery, charged against him." The prisoner having nothing to say, the court pronounced sentence: "That he should go to the Place from whence he came, and from thence, to a place of Execution, where he [is] to be Hanged by the neck, 'till he [is] dead and the Lord have Mercy upon his Soul." On March 29, Vane and two other pirates already sentenced were taken to Gallows Point at Port Royal and there hanged, and afterwards Vane's body was hung on a gibbet in chains on Gun Key.

John Rackam, who took over Vane's command, was a pirate of some years' experience. He had a long record of piracies committed in the West Indies and was well known to his fellow pirates, who called him Calico Jack from his custom of wearing calico shirts and trousers. When Woodes Rogers drove Vane out of Nassau harbor, Rackam was Vane's first mate. Although Rackam had some success as a pirate, his notoriety in the profession is not based on his record but rather on two of his crew who shipped with him. They were women disguised as men, the only female pirates known to have worked in the Western Hemisphere.

Mary Read was born in England near the end of the seventeenth century, supposedly the daughter of a sailor's wife. The sailor had left home to go on a voyage shortly after the marriage, and never returned. He left his wife pregnant, and in due time she gave birth to a son. Then the lonesome wife had a love affair, and less than a year later she produced a vigorous daughter, in contrast to the son who was sickly. After the birth of the daughter, the son died, and the mother was able to substitute the girl for him. In a couple of years, she went calling on her late husband's mother with two-year-old Mary dressed in boy's clothes. The kindly old lady, knowing the poverty into which they had fallen, offered to rear her "grandson," but the mother refused, asking instead that the grandmother, a woman of some small means, give her five shillings a week for expenses in keeping the child. When Mary was old enough to understand the deception, she was told and cooperated with her mother to keep the allowance coming in.

The grandmother died when Mary was thirteen or fourteen years old, and the spirited young girl now left home and entered the service of a Frenchwoman as a page boy. This dull career soon bored her, and she ran away and shipped on a man-of-war as common sailor. One wonders how she was able to conceal her sex from her shipmates, but the mores of the period easily explain this. No one, not even persons of the same sex, normally appeared naked before each other at this time, for it was considered a great sin to do so. And in an age when sailors seldom bathed and habitually slept in their clothes on a dimly lighted gun deck, such a ruse could be easily maintained.

After a hitch on the man-of-war, Mary is found in the military service in Flanders as a cadet in the Flemish army. First she served in an infantry regiment and then with mounted troops, and she served in both with distinction. The young woman was now about twenty and soon found herself falling in love with one of her fellow soldiers, a young Fleming. For a while Mary endured passion alone while her odd behavior convinced her companions that she had lost her mind. But at last she confided her secret to the young man she loved and he, admiring her courage and other qualities, finally asked her to marry him. At the end of the campaign when the troop was disbanded, the young soldier and Mary were made man and wife in a ceremony attended by the whole regiment. The two had been favorites of the officers, who generously gave them a purse as a wedding present. With the money the couple went into business as operators of a tavern named the Three Horseshoes at Breda. But no sooner did they start on what appeared to be a normal, happy marriage than the young husband fell sick and died. The peace that came about the same time took away Mary's customers, and she found herself an impoverished widow in her early twenties. She again enlisted in an infantry regiment, but the memories of her marriage and the dull life in a peacetime garrison soon drove her to take passage for the West Indies to start her life over.

On the voyage, her ship was captured by English pirates, and Mary, still disguised as a man, was forced to join her fellow countrymen. She seems to have adjusted to the life well enough and continued in it until she and her shipmates accepted the King's pardon brought by Woodes Rogers to Nassau in 1718. Hostilities with Spain breaking out again, Mary shipped from Nassau as a sailor on a privateersman. Before they

Ann Bonney and Mary Read. From an eighteenth-century engraving

had lost sight of land, the crew mutinied and the privateer was taken over as a pirate. From here she transferred somehow to the ship of the pirate Vane, with John Rackam as mate. When Rackam took over as captain and sailed for the West Indies, Mary was in the crew still disguised. Rackam had taken command of Vane's ship in November. For the next six weeks or so he cruised in the islands. Possibly at the same time, another young "man" joined the crew. By a strange stroke of fate, the only other woman pirate known to American waters was to serve on the same ship as Mary Read. Her name was Anne Bonney.

Anne had been born in Ireland, the illegitimate daughter of a serving maid and a prominent barrister. When the barrister's wife left him, he took the maid as his mistress openly, creating a scandal in Cork that began to affect his career. Consequently, he decided to emigrate to South Carolina, taking his mistress and daughter with him. Here he succeeded in his profession, engaged in some trading, and finally purchased a plantation near Charleston. When Anne's mother died, she took over the household and ran it for her father. She was an intelligent and spirited girl but headstrong as well. When she fell in love with a poor young sailor, her father refused to give permission for them to marry, assuming correctly that the sailor was interested in the family fortune rather than in Anne. The father turned Anne out of the house because of the liaison, and the suitor, though disappointed in seeing a fortune escape him, took her to New Porvidence while the town was still the pirate capital.

Anne was attracted to Calico Jack Rackam, who was somewhat of a hero about town. Eventually they eloped and Anne became pregnant, at which time she was sent by her lover to friends in Cuba. While she was in Cuba, Rackam was almost trapped by Rogers's cruisers with two prizes as he lay in a cove in the Bahamas. He managed to escape, but his prizes were retaken. From here he went to Cuba to see his mistress and was almost captured again while lying in a creek. Careless as usual about posting a lookout, he was cornered by a Spanish cruiser and the English sloop it had taken. As darkness fell, the Spanish captain moved his ship across the entrance of the creek, trapping Rackam's vessel, but he made the mistake of postponing capture until morning. In the pitch-black night, the wily Rackam quietly loaded his men in a longboat, and with the oars muffled, they rowed past the Spanish cruiser and boarded the prize sloop, which lay down the creek toward the sea. The startled prize crew gave up without a sound, being told they would all be killed if any cried out. Rackam and his men then quietly slipped out to sea leaving the Spanish commander to assault an empty ship in the morning. After the birth of her child (which was left with friends in Cuba) Anne rejoined her lover.

A year or so later, Rackam was found in a weak condition, with only a small crew, including both Anne Bonney and Mary Read. Anne had discovered Mary's true sex, and they had become close friends, much to the chagrin of Calico Jack who, of course, thought the attractive young sailor a man. When he threatened to cut the sailor's throat if his Anne had anything more to do with "him," Anne revealed Mary's secret. Mary was secretly in love with another young sailor who had been forced to join the pirates, and now she could reveal her secret to him. He returned her affection and they became lovers. (In one adventure, Mary is supposed to have fought a duel to save her lover whom she knew was incapable of defeating the challenger. Before the duel took place, Mary picked a quarrel with the other man and killed him in the ensuing fight.)

It was now late in September 1720. Rackam and his crew were raiding around Harbor Island, near Eleuthera in the Bahamas, capturing fishing vessels and taking provisions and gear from them. From here, they went to Hispaniola, where they stole cattle and kidnapped two French hunters. They then started to Jamaica and on October 1, 1720, captured a sloop from which they took forty pounds' worth of merchandise. On the seventeenth of the month, they captured a Jamaican sloop owned by Captain Thomas Spenlow, who had been taken by pirates only a few months before.

By now the governor of Jamaica and the merchants of Port Royal were thoroughly aroused and on the way to preparing a surprise for the pirates. The governor armed and commissioned a sloop, giving the command of it to Captain Jonathan Barnet, who was known for his experience, courage, and efficiency. Barnet set sail from Port Royal, convoying a merchant ship bound for Cuba by way of the western end of Jamaica. Here, off Point Negril, Barnet encountered Rackam and hailed him. Rackam identified himself by name, giving his home as Cuba. Barnet called on the pirates to surrender, and Rackam replied with a blast from a swivel gun. Barnet's crew responded with a broad- side, and the pirate asked for quarter without further defense. It was said that only the two women fought with any courage, and that in one instance Mary fired into the cowardly crew, killing one of the men and wounding another. The pirates had given up without any serious resistance and were now bound for Spanish Town and justice. After a brief imprisonment, they were brought before the admiralty court, which included Captain Edward Vernon, the future admiral, and most of them were tried on Wednesday, November 16, 1720. The charges were read, the pirates pleaded innocent, the witnesses were called, and with doors shut the court deliberated. The verdict was reached with- out difficulty, the evidence being conclusive:

> Then the Court-House Doors being opened, the prisoners before- named were set at the Bar, and his Excellency the President, acquainted them, That the Court had unanimously found them Guilty of the Piracy, Robbery, and Felony, charged against them, in the said Article.
>
> Then His Excellency the President, asked them, Whether they, or either of them, had any Thing to say, or offer, Why Sentence of Death should not pass upon them, for their said Offenses? And they having nothing to say, His Excellency the President, pronounced Sentence of Death upon them in the Words following, *viz.* YOU John Rackam, George Fetherston, Richard Corner, John Davies, John Howell, Patrick Carty, Thomas Earl, James Dobbin and Noah Harwood, are to go from hence to the Place from whence you came, and from thence to the Place of Execution; where you, shall severally be hanged by the Neck, 'till you are severally Dead.
>
> And God of His infinite Mercy be merciful to every one of your Souls.[2]

The next day, Thomas Brown and John Fenwick were brought to trial, found guilty, and sentenced to death. All sentences were carried out in the four days following:

On Friday the 18th. Day of *November* 1720. Five of the said Con-
demn'd Pirates, *viz.* Capt. *John Rackam, George Fetherston,* Master,
Richard Corner Quarter-Master, *John Davies* and *John Howell,* were
executed, at *Gallows-Point,* at the town of *Port-Royal,* according to the
aforesaid Sentence; and the bodies of *Rackam, Fetherston* and *Corner,*
were afterwards carried to *Plumb-point, Bush-Key,* and *Gun-Key;*
where they were hung on Gibbits in Chains, for a publick Example,
and to terrify others from such-like evil Practices.

And the next Day, *Noah Harwood, James Dobbin, Patrick Carty,*
and *Thomas Earl,* were executed, at the Town of *Kingston.*

And on Monday following, *Thomas Brown,* alias *Bourn,* and *John
Fenwick,* were also executed at Gallows-point, at *Port Royal* aforesaid.

Rackam and his men had been dead over a week when Mary Read
and Anne Bonney were brought to the court for trial:

John Besneck, and *Peter Cornelian,* two Frenchmen, were produced
as Witnesses, against the prisoners at the Bar, and were sworn.

Mr. *Simon Clarke* was sworn Interpreter;

Then the said Two Witnesses declared, That the Two Women,
Prisoners at the Bar, were on Board Rackam's Sloop, at the Time that
Spenlow's Scooner and *Dillon*'s Sloop, were taken by Rackam; That
they were very active on Board, and willing to do any Thing; That
Ann Bonny, one of the Prisoners at the Bar, handed Gun-powder to the
Men, That when they saw any Vessel, gave Chase, or Attacked, they
wore Men's Cloaths; and, at other Times, they wore Women's Cloaths;
That they did not seem to be kept, or detain'd by Force, but of their
own Free-Will and Consent.

Thomas Dillon, being sworn, declared, That on or about the Twentieth Day of *October* last, he was lying at Anchor, with the Sloop *Mary*
and *Sarah,* whereof he was Master, in Dry-Harbour, in *Jamaica;* and
that a strange Sloop came into the said Harbour, which fired a Gun at
the Deponent's Sloop; whereupon the Deponent and his Men went
ashoar, in order to defend themselves, and Sloop; And that after several
Shot had been fired at them, by the said Sloop, the Deponent hailed
them, and one *Fetherston* (as the Deponent believed) answer'd, That
they were English Pirates, and that they need not be afraid, and desired
the Deponent to come on Board; whereupon the Deponent went on
Board, and found that the said Sloop was commanded by one John
Rackam; afterwards the said Rackam, and his Crew, took the Deponent's Sloop, and her Lading, and carried her with them to Sea; and
further said, That the two Women, Prisoners at the Bar, were on Board
Rackam's Sloop; and that Ann Bonney, one of the Prisoners at the Bar,
had a Gun in her Hand, That they were both very profligate, cursing

Torturing a pirate by pressing to make him plead guilty. An engraving of the eighteenth century

A pirate being hanged at Execution Dock, Wapping, London. An eighteenth-century engraving

Blackbeard the Pirate from Johnson's *General History of the Pirates*, 1724

and swearing much, and very ready and willing to any Thing on Board.

When asked how they pleaded, they answered, "Not guilty." The court again deliberated behind closed doors. When the doors opened and the two women were brought to the bar, a sentence of death by hanging was passed on them. The startled court now heard new evidence: "After Judgement was pronounced, as aforesaid, both the Prisoners informed the Court, that they were both quick with Child, and prayed that Execution of the Sentence might be stayed. Whereupon the Court ordered, that Execution of the said Sentence should be respited, and that an Inspection should be made."

The women had cheated the gallows, but Mary was to die in jail from a fever. Anne Bonney may have been hanged after the birth of her child, but according to legend she was reprieved and later went to England. There she ran a pub on the south coast, living to a ripe old age and regaling her customers with tales of her adventures in the West Indies. Much of the story of the two women pirates is conjecture; only the record of the trial gives us solid documentation of their lives. But their chronicle has entered the body of history and legend the pirates left us, and even in the present century whole books of fiction, some of it highly imaginative, have been written about them.

Of all the pirates who had frequented Nassau and had attacked shipping off the coast of North America and the West Indies, none was more picturesque, more of a scoundrel, or better remembered than Edward Teach, called Blackbeard. His very name has come to mean "pirate." His particularly colorful appearance, violent habits, and complete lack of scruple have perpetuated his memory in the history of piracy. Teach was born in Bristol and came to Jamaica as a young man. While there, he sailed as a privateersman of the ranks. With the end of the War of Spanish Succession, he "went on account," joining Captain Benjamin Hornigold and commanding a sloop under him. They went to New Providence almost a year and a half before the arrival of Woodes Rogers and made Nassau their base as so many others did. In 1717 Hornigold and Teach cruised off the coasts of Virginia and the Carolinas, where they took several mediocre prizes and sailing to the West Indies they took a rich French ship bound for Martinique. The French prize being much larger than his own vessel, Teach now transferred his company to her and armed her with forty guns, renaming her *Queen Anne's Revenge*. This was the start of a career that made him a legend in his own day and a synonym for pirate in our time. Charles Johnson's *General History of the Pirates* describes the fierce appearance of the man:

> Captain Teach assumed the cognomen of Blackbeard from that large quantity of hair which, like a frightful meteor, covered his whole face, and frightened America more than any comet that had appeared there a long time. . . . This beard was black, which he suffered to grow of an extravagant length; as to breadth, it came up to his eyes. He was accustomed to twist it with ribbons, in small tails, after the manner of our Ramilie wigs, and turn them about his ears. In time of action he wore a sling over his shoulders, with three brace of pistols hanging in holsters like bandoliers, and stuck lighted matches under his hat, which, appearing on each side of his face, his eyes naturally looking fierce and wild, made him altogether such a figure that imagination cannot form an idea of a fury from Hell to look more frightful.[3]

After he had acquired *Queen Anne's Revenge*, Blackbeard cruised in the West Indies and captured several ships. Each time he put the crews ashore unharmed and burned the prizes. On this cruise he was attacked by the man-of-war *Scarborough*, of thirty guns. The battle lasted several hours but the warship finally withdrew without seriously damaging the pirate. One fragment of a log Blackbeard kept has survived and gives a picture of life aboard the *Queen Anne's Revenge* under his command: "such a day, rum all out—our company somewhat sober—a damn'd confusion amongst us! Rogues a plotting—great talk of separation—so I look'd sharp for a prize—such a day, took one, with a great deal of liquor on board, so kept the company hot, damned hot, then all things well again."[4]

In the late spring of 1718, he took his ship to the Gulf of Honduras, a pirate rendezvous. Off Crab Island, he captured a merchantman loaded with hogs and cattle, all of which he took, along with the captain, the small arms, the library, and the navigating instruments. Two men of the merchantman's crew were forced to stay with the pirates, and one chose of his own free will to do so. Captain Henry Bostock, the master of the prize, later stated that he and the rest of the crew were not abused and that when he told Blackbeard of the Act of Grace, which announced the King's amnesty, the pirate was not interested. That act, promulgated at Hampton Court Palace on September 5, 1717, read as follows:

By the King
A PROCLAMATION FOR SUPPRESSING
OF PYRATES

GEORGE R.

Whereas we have received Information, that several persons, Subjects of GREAT BRITAIN, have, since the 24th Day of June, in the Year of our Lord, 1715, committed divers Pyracies and Robberies upon the High Sea, in the West Indies or adjoining our Plantations, which hath and may Occasion great Damage to the Merchants of GREAT BRITAIN and others trading into those Parts; and tho' we have appointed such Force as we judge sufficient for suppressing said Pyrates, yet the more effectually to make an End to the Same, we have thought fit, by and with the Advice of our Privy Council, to Issue this our Royal Proclamation; and we do hereby promise and declare, that in Case any of the said Pyrates shall on or before, the 5th of September, in the Year of our Lord, 1718, surrender him or themselves, to one of our Principal Secretaries of State in GREAT BRITAIN or IRELAND or to any Governor or Deputy Governor of any of our Plantations beyond the Seas; every such Pyrate and Pyrates so surrendering him or themselves, as aforesaid, shall have our gracious Pardon, of and for such, his or their Pyracy, or Pyracies, by him or them committed, before the 5th of JANUARY, next ensuing. And we do hereby strictly charge and command all our Admirals, Captains, and other Officers at Sea, and all our Governors and Commanders of any Forts, Castles, or other Places in our Plantations, and all our Officers, Civil and Military, to seize and take such of the Pyrates, who shall refuse or neglect to surrender themselves accordingly. And we do further hereby declare, that in Case any Person or Persons, on or after, the 6th Day of SEPTEMBER, 1718, shall discover or seize, or cause or procure to be discovered and seized, any one or more of the said Pyrates, so refusing or neglecting to surrender themselves as aforesaid, so as they may be brought to Justice and convicted of the said Offense such Person or Persons, so making such Discovery and Seizure, or causing or procuring such Discovery and Seizure to be made, shall have and receive as a Reward for same, viz., for any Commander of any private Ship or Vessel, the sum of 100 £ for every Lieutenant, Master, Boatswain, Carpenter and Gunner the sum of 40 £ for every inferior Officer the sum of 30 £ and for every Private Man the Sum of 20 £. And if any Person or Persons, belonging to, and being Part of the Crew, of any such Pirate Ship and Vessel, shall on or after the said sixth Day of SEPTEMBER, 1718, seize and deliver, or cause to be seized and delivered, any Commander or Commanders, of such Pyrate Ship or Vessel, so that he or they may be brought to Justice, and convicted of said Offence, such Person or Persons, as a

Reward for same, shall receive for such Commander the Sum of 200 £ which said Sums, the Lord Treasurer, or the Commissioners of our Treasury for the Time being, are hereby required and desired to pay accordingly.

Given at our Court, at HAMPTON-COURT the fifth Day of SEPTEMBER, 1717, in the fourth Year of our Reign.
God save the King.

In the Gulf of Honduras Blackbeard captured the *Adventure*. The sailing master of the prize and most of her crew consented to join Blackbeard's growing fleet. Other prizes were captured, and Blackbeard now commanded a small flotilla, which he took to the coast off Charleston. Here the pirates lay, controlling traffic in and out of the harbor. While there, they took several prizes, including a rich one carrying 6,000 spanish pieces of eight in silver and gold, and passengers bound for England. One of the passengers was Samuel Wragg, a member of the governor's council.

Needing medical supplies, Blackbeard now decided to blackmail Governor Johnson into giving them to him. His surgeon prepared a list of the medicines, instruments, and dressings required, to the value of £300 to £400, and it was sent to Charleston with two pirates and a Mr. Marks, one of the passengers from the London-bound ship. With them went a message that if the governor didn't furnish the medical supplies immediately, the pirates would kill all their prisoners, including Samuel Wragg, burn the ships in the harbor, and knock the town down with fire from their cannon. Marks gave his message to the governor, who immediately called his council. They had no alternative but to yield, there being no forces at hand to defend the town. The supplies were sent. On the first trip out, the boat overset, but on the second attempt, it reached Blackbeard's ship and the prisoners were released unharmed. Why the pirates needed medical supplies at this time is a mystery. They apparently had a supply from the ships they had captured but perhaps their needs were more specialized. One author suggests that they were suffering from venereal disease: "Brothel casualties were usually higher than battle casualties among the pirates."[5]

In January 1718, Blackbeard went to the waters off St. Christopher, where he captured several sloops and created a furor on the little island. Before the month was out, Blackbeard, having reconsidered the Act of Grace, went to North Carolina and turned himself in to Governor Charles Eden. Not only was he pardoned for his piracies but he and the governor went into business together. Now Blackbeard could operate with impunity from a well-protected base. As well, Blackbeard

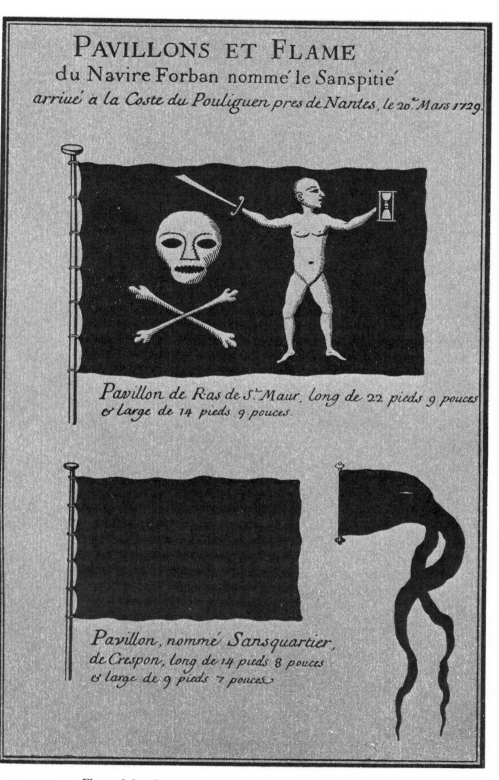

Flags of the pirates. From an eighteenth-century woodcut

now had a ready market for his goods which he could sell directly to the customers, giving the governor a commission.

After remaining on the coast of North Carolina for a time, Blackbeard sailed to Bermuda and he captured two French ships out of Martinique that were carrying sugar and cacao. Emptying one prize, he abandoned it and brought the other back to North Carolina, where he claimed he had found it derelict at sea. It was duly condemned, and Blackbeard shared the loot with Governor Eden and Tobias Knight, the collector of customs at Bath, the port which served Blackbeard. The governor received sixty hogsheads of sugar and Knight was awarded twenty. After this, Blackbeard burned his prize, fearing someone would recognize her, and cruised about the neighborhood for three or four months preying on the trade of the area—it was poor—and extracting provisions from landowners along the coast.

By this time, Blackbeard's arrogance knew no bounds. Repeatedly shippers and merchants suffering from his depredations complained to Governor Eden, but their pleas for help were fruitless. They then decided to appeal to Governor Alexander Spotswood of Virginia for help and, in secret, sent a deputation to him. When Spotswood heard of the crimes of Blackbeard and how he had corrupted Governor Eden and the collector of customs at Bath, he was horrified. Spotswood had heard some of the facts before from correspondents in North Carolina, but the emissaries furnished him with more detail and new facts about the events occurring to the south of the Virginia border. Spotswood decided to act.

He was one of the more energetic and able colonial governors serving in the English colonies at the time. Since there was no admiralty court in the Bahamas, he actually had admiralty jurisdiction over the islands. Back in 1716, when he heard rumors that the pirates were settling there after Jennings's raid on the Spanish salvage camp, he had sent a captain to investigate and report to him. Unfortunately, the captain was captured on the way home and didn't return to Virginia until August of 1717. In his belated report he told the governor of the wave of pirates that had inundated Nassau and of the domination of the local authorities by the outlaws. He also related how the local merchants traded openly with the pirates, buying stolen goods which were then smuggled into North Carolina to supply a hungry illicit market. Spotswood's subsequent report to London was apparently the first account of the actual situation in New Providence and probably played an important part in the decision to send Woodes Rogers to the Bahamas as the first royal governor.

This same energy and interest Spotswood applied to the problem of

Blackbeard and his neighboring governor to the south. After meeting with his council, he posted substantial rewards for Blackbeard and his men. Then, with the help of the commanders of two Royal Navy frigates lying in the James River, he organized an expedition to pursue them. It was decided that small armed sloops must do the job, since Blackbeard was now sailing such a vessel himself and would run into the coastal shallows of North Carolina, where a frigate could not follow him. Two merchant sloops were obtained, and Spotswood fitted them out at his own expense with heavily armed crews of experienced seamen. One of the sloops, the *Pearl*, he placed under the command of Lieutenant Robert Maynard of the Royal Navy. The other, the *Lyme*, he gave to Captain Ellis Brand. To lighten the sloops' draft, no guns were placed aboard them. The battle, when it came, was to be fought with muskets, pistols, cutlasses, and boarding axes. The sloops sailed on November 27, 1718. Four days later in the evening, they approached Ocracoke Inlet on the North Carolina coast, where the *Pearl* sighted Blackbeard's eight-gun ship *Adventure*. After he had held Charleston to ransom, Blackbeard had split up his fleet and was now alone except for an unarmed trading sloop that lay near and with which he had been doing business. He had been warned of the preparations in Virginia, one warning even coming from Tobias Knight, the collector of customs at Bath, but he ignored them, apparently confident he could handle anything that could get into shallow coastal waters and attack him. So while the sloops were preparing in Virginia, Blackbeard went on with his leisurely looting.

When he saw the masts of the *Pearl*, he was not panic-stricken or even aroused as he should have been. Instead of preparing for the battle he knew must come in the morning, he spent the night in a wild carousal.

Maynard anchored for the night. He feared to attack in the dark since the inlet was full of shallow sandbars on which he might run aground. At the first light of morning, he weighed anchor and went after Blackbeard with all sails set and the crew manning oars. Blackbeard cut his anchor cable, and turning his ship, opened fire with heavy guns loaded with ball and grapeshot. To this Maynard replied with a shower of shot from muskets which had little effect. Blackbeard's ship was now hard aground. To come alongside and board her, Maynard had to lighten his own ship, which drew even more than the pirate's. He ordered all the ballast and even some water casks thrown overboard. Presently, the ships were close enough to hail each other. Blackbeard called out, "Damn you for villains, who are you? And whence came you?" Maynard answered, "You may see by our colors we are no pirates." Blackbeard then asked Maynard to send his boat alongside so he could see who his enemy was. Maynard answered, "I cannot spare my boat, but I will come aboard of you as soon as I can with my sloop." At this, Blackbeard took a glass of rum and drank a toast to Maynard: "Damnation seize my soul if I give you quarter, or take any from you." Maynard answered calmly that he expected none and would give none.

These "civilities" exchanged, Blackbeard opened up with more shot and grape, which killed or wounded twenty men on the *Pearl* and nine on the *Lyme*. At this the *Lyme* withdrew and Maynard was left alone with his adversary. As his sloop drew alongside Blackbeard's vessel, Maynard ordered his twelve remaining men to hide themselves in the hold while he remained on the deck with only the helmsman. Through the smoke of broadsides and the hand grenades the pirates were now throwing, Blackbeard could see only Maynard and his companion. Thinking all the rest had been killed or wounded, Blackbeard boarded the *Pearl* followed closely by his crew. At this, Maynard signaled his men below and they rushed from the forward hatch on the startled pirates. Blackbeard had fallen squarely into the trap.

A bloody, confused struggle with pistols, cutlasses, and axes followed. Blackbeard had fourteen men to Maynard's thirteen, and the battle would have been evenly drawn except that the Virginia men had the advantage of surprise and were better disciplined than Blackbeard's unruly mob. Pistols were fired at point-blank range, cutlasses and axes thudded into flesh and bone amidst the curses and cries of the wounded and dying. The decks became slick with blood as the melee raged on. Maynard had singled out Blackbeard for himself, and their battle became a personal duel to the death. They both fired their pistols, and Maynard's aim was the better: Blackbeard was wounded. At this they seized their cutlasses and at the first cross Maynard's broke off at the hilt. Snatching a pistol from a holster, Maynard fired point-blank. The ball traveled through Blackbeard's body, but he stood without apparent injury and aimed a tremendous blow at Maynard's head with his cutlass. Maynard was saved from certain death by a companion who at that moment struck Blackbeard across the neck with his cutlass and caused the pirate's blow to miss. Again Maynard fired into Blackbeard's body with no apparent effect. The raging pirate fought on until he had received twenty severe wounds by cutlass and by pistol balls. At last, as he was cocking a pistol, he suddenly fell dead on the deck from loss of blood and shock. Eight other pirates were now dead and the survivors, all wounded, cried for quarter when they saw their leader die. The battle was over, but at a terrible price. Miraculously,

Blackbeard in combat with Lieutenant Robert Maynard of the Royal Navy. From a nineteenth-century woodcut

The head of Blackbeard hanging from the British sloop commanded by Lieutenant Robert Maynard as it entered Portsmouth, Virginia, harbor. From a nineteenth-century woodcut

Maynard had escaped without a serious wound. The great scourge of the Carolina coast was dead. Unlike the cowardly Rackam, Blackbeard had fought to the very end with furious courage. Though a brutal and unscrupulous man, he had undeniable ability. He did not abuse his prisoners as some of his colleagues were known to have done, and much of the fierceness of his nature was showmanship, which he used as a sort of psychological warfare. In another profession he would have been an outstanding leader.

After the battle, Maynard buried the dead while his surgeon patched up the wounded, and then he did a brutal thing, which tarnishes his gallant action. He cut off Blackbeard's head and hung it from the bowsprit of the *Pearl*. With this, he returned to Bath, where he was received with joy by the honest merchants and with anxiety by Tobias Knight. After tending to his wounded crew and prisoners, he proceeded to raid Governor Eden's warehouse, removing the hogsheads of sugar Blackbeard had given the governor out of the condemned French prize. On Blackbeard's ship, Maynard had found letters from Eden, Tobias Knight, and certain New York merchants, evidence which had given him the confidence to raid the governor's stores. When his men were well enough to continue, Maynard returned to Williamsburg, with Blackbeard's head still dangling from the bowsprit of the *Pearl*. He was received as a hero. The whole coast north to Boston was overjoyed at the news of Blackbeard's death except for the merchants who had traded with him on very favorable terms, particularly those of North Carolina. To that neglected colony, Blackbeard had brought a little prosperity with his stolen goods and many there were sad to hear of his end, not the least of whom were Governor Eden and Collector of Customs Knight. Blackbeard's death was followed by litigation between Governors Eden and Spotswood over certain of the goods the pirate left behind. Eden charged that Spotswood had violated the rights of the Carolina proprietors by sending a force into Carolina waters to destroy Blackbeard. Spotswood replied that the destruction of the pirate was possible only because of the secrecy with which the expedition had been prepared, pointing out the obvious fact that such an expedition would not have been fitted out in North Carolina.

In the dispute between the governors, Eden had the benefit of advice from Thomas Pollack, president of the North Carolina Council, who took Eden's side even though he probably realized that some suspect dealings had been going on. With Pollock's advice, Eden prevailed over a local faction of honest men who were eager to turn the governor out for his traffic with Blackbeard. A letter found on Blackbeard's ship definitely incriminated Tobias Knight and strongly suggested the complicity of Eden, who nevertheless remained for four more years as governor of North Carolina. Knight escaped punishment by dying. The fifteen captured pirates were tried and hanged in Virginia.

Before Blackbeard left on his first voyage to the Bay of Honduras, he had fallen in with Major Stede Bonnet, a real curiosity among his fellows. Bonnet had had no experience at seafaring but had served with credit in the King's forces, retiring with the rank of major. He had become a successful planter in Barbados, where he apparently enjoyed a comfortable life. He had a fine home, a good wife, and a prosperous plantation, and he was regarded by his fellow gentry as a model citizen. All of this ended suddenly and not without shock to his wife and friends when the major procured a ship and suddenly went to sea as a pirate. Johnson in his *General History of the Pirates* says that Bonnet's friends attributed this sudden strange behavior to mental derangement: "He was afterwards rather pitty'd than condemned, by those that were acquainted with him, believing that this Humour of going a-pyrating proceeded from a Disorder in his Mind, which had been but too visible in him, some Time before this wicked Undertaking; and which is said to have been occasioned by some Discomforts he found in a married State; be that as it will, the Major was but ill qualified for the Business, as not understanding maritime Affairs."[6] Thus some of his friends attributed his dementia to the fact that his marriage was failing and that he was subjected to the constant nagging of his disaffected wife. Whatever the reason, which has never been clearly determined, Bonnet took up piracy. Perhaps the name he gave his ship—*Revenge*— gives us an inkling. Apart from his genteel background, Bonnet was unique in another respect. He bought his first ship and is the only pirate known to history who didn't steal his vessel. His sloop was fitted out with ten guns of small caliber and manned with a crew of seventy men. As for his assembling a crew when he didn't have a reputation as a pirate leader, we must assume that there were enough desperate unemployed men around the waterfront at Bridgetown to take a chance on this prominent citizen with a fine well-armed sloop. There must have been some experienced pirates in the crew Bonnet recruited, for he was surprisingly successful in his first forays. In a short time off the Virginia coast, Bonnet took the *Anne* of Glasgow, the *Turbet* of Barbados, the *Endeavour* and the *Young* of Leith, Scotland. His unexplained resentment of his experiences on Barbados is demonstrated by the fact that he burned the *Turbet* and every Barbadian vessel he captured. The loot from all these ships he sold to merchants on Gardiners Island, New York. After this, Bonnet cruised off the Carolinas, where he took other prizes, and here his inexperience began to show. He started to have trouble with his crew: they defied him and disobeyed orders. At this juncture, Bonnet fell in with Blackbeard, who sensed the major's troubles and saw an opportunity to get another ship and crew into his flotilla. He got Bonnet aboard his own ship and then sent a lieutenant to command the *Revenge* while the major was forced into a subordinate position. This state of affairs lasted until Blackbeard decided to turn himself in to Governor Eden and accept the King's amnesty. At this point he returned Bonnet's ship, but when Bonnet went aboard her (he had decided to take advantage of the King's offer himself and made the trip to Bath to do so) he found Blackbeard had stolen everything of value on the vessel and had marooned seventeen of his crew. Bonnet rescued the men, resupplied his ship, and then went in search of Blackbeard to get revenge. Failing to find him, he decided to return to cruising as a pirate under the name of Captain Thomas, since he had used his real name when he was pardoned. In a very successful run, he captured several valuable prizes off Virginia and in Delaware Bay, where he transferred his flag to one of them, a larger ship than his own. His new vessel required recaulking, and Bonnet went to a beach at the mouth of the Cape Fear River to careen, recaulk and tallow her. When word of this reached Governor Johnson of South Carolina, Colonel William Rhett came forward and offered to fit out armed sloops to take the pirate before he could finish work on his vessel. The colonel sailed with two eight-gun sloops, the *Henry*, with seventy men, and the *Sea Nymph*, with sixty men. They approached the river mouth and caught Bonnet riding at anchor. Bonnet had finished work on the bottom of his ship and had refloated her but was not prepared for action. With him were three sloops, prizes, or traders. Rhett attacked at once. Bonnet tried to escape but ran aground instead. The pursuing sloops also ran aground nearby and for five hours the ships bombarded each other with their heavy guns. Finally Bonnet surrendered and he and his ship were brought into Charleston. Rhett was astonished to find that Captain Thomas was the Major Bonnet who had accepted the King's pardon. This sealed Bonnet's fate. He escaped once to Sullivans Island but was caught and tried before Chief Justice Nicholas Trott. He and his crew were condemned to death. When Trott sentenced Bonnet, he did so with a long-winded oration that must have been almost as painful to the pirate as the sentence itself:

The Lord Chief Justice's SPEECH *upon his pronouncing Sentence on Major* STEDE BONNET

MAJOR *Stede Bonnet,* you stand here convict'd upon 2 Indictments of Pyracy; one by the Verdict of the Jury, and the other by your own Confession.

Altho' you were indicted but for *two* Facts, yet you know that at your Tryal it was fully proved even by an unwilling Witness, that you *pyratically* took and rifled no less than *thirteen* Vessels since you sailed from *North-Carolina.*

So that you might have been Indicted, and convicted of *eleven* more Acts of *Piracy,* since you took the Benefit of the King's *Act of Grace,* and pretended to leave that wicked Course of Life.

Not to mention the many *Acts of Pyracy* you committed before; for which if your Pardon from *Man* was never so authentick, yet you must expect to answer for them before God.

You know that the Crimes you have committed are *evil* in themselves, and contrary to the *Light* and *Law* of *Nature,* as well as the *Law* of God, by which you are commanded that *you shall not steal,* Exodus 20.15. And the Apostle St. *Paul* expressly affirms, That *Thieves shall not inherit the Kingdom of God,* 1 Cor. 6.10.

But to *Theft,* you have added a greater Sin, which is *Murder.* How many you may have *killed* of those that resist'd you in the committing your former *Piracies,* I know not: But this we all know, that besides the Wounded, you kill'd no less than *eighteen* Persons out of those that were sent by lawful Authority to suppress you, and put a stop to those Rapines that you daily acted.

And however you may fancy that that was killing Men fairly in open *Fight,* yet this know, that the Power of the *Sword* not being committ'd into your Hands by any lawful Authority, you were not impower'd to use any *Force,* or *fight* any one; and therefore those Persons that fell in that Action, in doing their Duty to their King & Country, were *murder'd, &* their *Blood* now cries out for *Vengeance* and *Justice* against you: For it is the *Voice of Nature* confirmed by the *Law* of God, That *whosoever sheddeth Man's Blood, by Man shall his Blood be shed.* Gen. 9.6.

And consider that Death is not the only Punishment due to *Murderers;* for they are threatened to have *their Part in the Lake which burneth with Fire & Brimstone, which is the second Death,* Rev. 21.8. See *Chapter* 22.15. Words which carry that Terror with them, that considering your Circumstances & your Guilt, surely the Sound of them must make you tremble; *for who can dwell with everlasting Burnings?* Chap. 33.14.

As the *Testimony* of your *Conscience* must convince you of the great & Many Evils you have committ'd, by which you have highly offend'd God, & provok'd most justly his Wrath and Indignation against you, so I suppose I need not tell you that the only Way of obtaining Pardon & Remission of your Sins from God, is by a true and unfeigned *Repentance* and *Faith* in Christ, by whose meritorious Death and Passion, you can only hope for Salvation.

You being a Gentleman that have had the Advantage of a *liberal Education,* and being generally esteemed a Man of *Letters,* I believe it will be needless for me to explain to you the Nature of *Repentance* and *Faith* in Christ, they being so fully and so often mentioned in the Scriptures, that you cannot but know them. And therefore, perhaps, for that Reason it might be thought by some improper for me to have said so much to you, as I have already on this Occasion; neither should I have done it, but that considering the Course of your Life & Actions, I have just Reason to fear, that the Principles of Religion that had been instilled into you by your *Education,* have been at least corrupted, if not entirely defaced, by the *Scepticism* and *Infidelity* of this wicked Age; and that what Time you allow'd for Study, was rather apply'd to the *Polite Literature, &* the vain *Philosophy* of the Times, than a serious Search after the *Law & Will* of God, as revealed unto us in the Holy *Scriptures:* For *had your Delight been in the Law of the Lord,* & *that you had meditated therein Day and Night,* Psalms 1.2. you would then have found that God's *Word was a Lamp unto your Feet,* & *a Light to your Path,* Psal. 119.105, and that you would account all other Knowledge but *Loss,* in Comparison of *the Excellency of the Knowledge of Christ Jesus,* Philistines 3.8. *who to them that are called is the Power of God, and the Wisdom of God,* 1 Cor. 1.24. *even the hidden Wisdom which God ordained before the World,* Chapters 2.7.

You would then have esteem'd the *Scriptures* as the *Great Charter* of Heaven, and which delivered to us not only the most perfect *Laws* and *Rules* of Life, but also discover'd to us the Acts of *Pardon* from God, wherein they have offended those righteous Laws: For in them only is to be found the great *Mystery* of fallen Man's *Redemption, which the Angels desire to look into,* 1 Pet. 1.12.

And they would have taught you that *Sin* is the debasing of *Human Nature,* as being a *Derivation* from that *Purity, Rectitude, and Holiness,* in which God created us, and that *Virtue* and *Religion,* and walking by the Laws of God, were altogether preferable to the Ways of *Sin* and *Satan;* for that the *Ways* of Virtue are *Ways of Pleasantness, and all their Paths are Peace,* Prov. 3.17.

But what you could not learn from God's Word, by reason of your *carelessly,* or but *superficially* considering the same, I hope the Course of his *Providence,* & the present *Afflictions* that he hath laid upon you, hath now convinc'd you of the same: For however in your seeming Prosperity you might make a *Mock of your Sins* Prov. 3.17. yet now that you see that God's Hand hath reached you, and brought you to publick Justice, I hope your present unhappy Circumstances hath made you seriously reflect upon your past Actions and Course of Life; and that you are now sensible of the Greatness of your Sins, and that you find the Burden of them is intolerable.

And that therefore being thus *labouring, & heavy laden with Sin,* Mat. 11.28. you will esteem that as the most valuable *Knowledge,* that can shew you how you can be reconciled to that Supreme God that you have so highly offended; and that can reveal to you Him who is not only the powerful *Advocate with the Father for you,* 1 John 2.1. but also who hath paid that Debt that is due for your Sins by his own Death upon the Cross for you; & thereby made full Satisfaction for the Justice of God. And this is to be found no where but in God's Word, which discovers to us that *Lamb of God which takes away the Sins of the World,* John 1.29. which is *Christ* the Son of God: For this know, & be assured, *that there is none other Name under Heaven given among Men, whereby we must be sav'd,* Acts 4.12. but only by the Name of the Lord *Jesus.*

But then consider how he invites all Sinners to come unto him, and, *that he will give them rest,* Matthew 11.28. for he assures us, *that he came to seek and to save that which was lost,* Luke 19.10. Matt. 18.11. and hath promised, *that he that cometh unto him, he will in no wise cast out,* John 6.37.

So that if now you will sincerely turn to him, tho' late, even at the *eleventh Hour,* Matthew 20.6.9. he will receive you.

But surely I need not tell you, that the *Terms* of his *Mercy* is *Faith* & *Repentance.*

And do not mistake the *Nature* of Repentance to be only a bare Sorrow for your Sins, arising from the Consideration of the *Evil* and *Punishment* they have now brought upon you; but your Sorrow must arise from the Consideration of your having offended a gracious and merciful God.

But I shall not pretend to give you any particular Directions as to the Nature of Repentance: I consider that I speak to a Person, whose Offences have proceeded not so much from his not *knowing,* as his *slighting* & *neglecting* his *Duty:* Neither is it proper for me to give Advice out of the Way of my own Profession.

You may have that better delivered to you by those who have made Divinity their particular Study; and who, by their Knowledge, as well as their Office, as being the *Ambassadors of Christ,* 2. Corinthians 5.20. are best qualified to give you Instructions therein.

I only heartily wish, that what, in Compassion to your Soul, I have now said to you upon this sad and solemn Occasion, by exhorting you in general to *Faith* & *Repentance,* may have that due Effect upon you, that thereby you may become a true *Penitent.*

And therefore having now discharg'd my Duty to you as a *Christian*, by giving you the best Counsel I can, with respect to the Salvation of your Soul, I must now do my Office as a *Judge.*

The *Sentence* that the Law hath appointed to pass upon you for your Offences, and which this Court doth therefore award, is,

That you, the said Stede Bonnet, *shall go from hence to the Place from whence you came, & from thence to the Place of Execution, where you shall be hang'd by the Neck till you are dead.*

And the God of infinite Mercy be merciful to your Soul.[7]

Bonnet was hanged at White Point in Charleston in November 1718, taking with him his reason for having turned pirate.

Like Charles Vane, Samuel Bellamy had fished the wrecks of the Spanish plate fleet. It is possible that he had also been with Henry Jennings on Jennings's raid. In any case, finding the business of fishing the wrecks unrewarding, Bellamy and his companion, Paul Williams, decided to "go on account." Somehow Bellamy joined Captain Benjamin Hornigold, of whom we have already heard, when he sailed in company with another vessel under the command of a Frenchman named Leboose. Early in the summer of 1716, Hornigold and Leboose were cruising west of Havana when they sighted a ship commanded by a Captain Kingston bound from Honduras to Holland with a cargo of logwood. Hornigold and Leboose, each having seventy men, easily took the merchant ship and detained her for over a week while they relieved her of her supplies, arms, and equipment. After this, they gave the ship back to Kingston and let him proceed. One seaman from the merchantman was retained by Leboose and kept aboard his vessel for four months. This seaman, John Brown, has left us a deposition that furnishes the details of the voyage of Hornigold and Bellamy. After releasing Kingston's ship, they cruised off Cape Corrientes near the western tip of Cuba and there took two Spanish brigantines loaded with cacao. Demanding ransom which their victims could not pay, the pirates set the Spaniards ashore and burned their ships. The pirate captains now needed to overhaul their vessels and sailed to the Isle of Pines. Here they found several empty sloops lying at anchor and took them for use while they careened their own ships. This finished, they returned the sloops to their owners and sailed for Hispaniola, where they cruised for about three months. During this period, Hornigold's crew ousted him because he refused to capture any more English ships. In his place they put Samuel Bellamy, an officer with a talent for oratory and leadership ability. Hornigold sailed away in a small vessel to Nassau where, on the arrival of Woodes Rogers, he turned himself in and accepted the King's pardon. He subsequently cruised against the pirates in the service of Governor Rogers. Bellamy now found himself in command of a crew of about ninety men, most of them English. At this point, John Brown transferred to Ballamy's ship.

With Hornigold gone, Bellamy and Leboose sailed to the Virgin Islands, where they captured several prizes and secured some needed provisions. Then cruising off Saba they fell in with two ships bound for the Gulf of Honduras. One, the *Sultana*, commanded by Captain James Richards, was manned and fitted out as a man-of-war. Bellamy took her as his command. The other, a sloop commanded by a Captain Tover, was taken over by Bellamy's old companion Paul Williams. The flotilla of three now captured a ship bound to the West Indies from Ireland, and after taking the food they needed, they let her go. Shortly after, Bellamy and Williams left Leboose and stood for the Windward Passage. Here in the latter part of February 1717, they met with a large well-appointed ship and gave chase. For three days the pursuit lasted, with the pirates gradually gaining on their victim, and off the eastern side of Long Island in Crooked Island Passage, they brought her to. The ship gave up without a struggle after having fired her stern guns at the pirates. She proved to be the *Whidah*, under the command of Captain Laurence Prince and bound from Jamaica to Great Britain with a cargo of sugar, indigo, Jesuits' bark (cinchona, the source of quinine) and some gold and silver. Since the ship was fitted with eighteen guns, the pirates decided to take her as their flag, and Bellamy and his crew transferred to her. Captain Prince was given the *Sultana* and as much of the best and finest goods she could carry plus twenty pounds in silver and gold, and set free with most of his crew, although his bosun and two seamen were forced to join the pirates. After this, turning south, they took, off Petit Goave, an English vessel loaded with sugar and indigo. From her they stole what supplies they needed, forced more men, and then released her.

Bellamy now had 130 men aboard the *Whidah* and decided to go north to the Virginia Capes. The day before he arrived, he lost sight of Williams, and according to a prearranged plan, cruised back and forth for ten days waiting for him. During this period, Bellamy took three ships and a snow.* All the ships were plundered and one was sunk. Having lost the sloop, Bellamy now determined to man the prize snow and take it with him. He put eighteen pirates aboard and the original crew of the snow were forced, giving his new consort a crew of

---

* A brig with a trysail mast set close abaft the main mast, on which a boom trysail is set.

twenty-eight. Bellamy now set sail for New England. Off the coast there they harassed shipping and made several captures in the late winter and early spring. On April 26 at about nine o'clock in the morning, the *Whidah*, with the snow following, pursued and brought to the *Mary Ann*, an Irish pink* outbound from Nantucket to New York, under the command of a Captain Crumpsty. Two seamen on the *Mary Ann* later described the incident in a deposition:

> On the twenty fourth day of April last past, they sailed from Nantasket harbour bound for New York, and on the twenty sixth day of the said month, being friday, in the morning about nine of the clock, they discovered a large Ship, and her Prize, which was a Snow, astern, and the large Ship came up with the said Pink *Mary Ann*, between nine and ten, and ordered us to strike our Colours, which accordingly we did, and then they shot ahead of us, and braced too, and hoisted out her boat and sent seven Men on board, Armed with their Musquets, pistols and Cutlashes . . . and they commanded the said Capt. Crumpsty to take his Papers, and go aboard the said Ship with five of his hands and accordingly the said Crumpsty with five of his Men rowed aboard the said Pyrates Ship, and the seven Men tarryed aboard the Pink, and soon after the Pyrates sent their boat on board the said pink with four hands to get some of the Wine which they were Informed was on board the Pink, and accordingly they hoisted the pinks boat off of the hatches and opened the hatches and then went into the hold, but the Cable being Quoiled in the hatchway, they found it difficult to Come to the Wines in the hold, and so returned to their own Ship without any wine, Except five bottles of green wine which they found in the pinks Cabbin and carried away, with some of the Cloaths which belonged to the pinks Company, and presently after the pyrates had hoisted their boat on board the great Ship, they gave Orders to the Pyrates on board the pink to steer North Northwest after them, which Course they followed.[8]

The ships were enfolded in thick fog and were nearing the shallows off Wellfleet on Cape Cod. Bellamy, coming up with a sloop, sent her master ahead to lead the way as they neared the coast. The deposition from which we have just quoted tells the story as seen from the deck of the pink:

> then the large Ship whereof Capt. Samuel Bellame was Commander, and the snow and pink lay [to], it being very thick foggy weather, And about half an hour after four a Clock a sloop came up with Capt.

---

* A small trading vessel with a narrow stern and upward curving deck aft.

Bellames Ship and he hoisted out his boat and sent several men on board the Sloop and soon afterwards, Vizt. about five a Clock, the Commander of the snow bore away, and came under the stern of Capt. Bellames Ship and told him that they saw the Land; And thereupon Capt. Bellame Ordered the Pyrates on board the Pink to steer away North, which they did, and as soon as it began to be dark the sd Capt. Bellames Ship put out a light astern and also the snow and the sloop and the pink had their lights out; and about ten a Clock the weather grew thick and it lightned and rained hard and was so dark, that the pinks Comp. Could not see the shore till they were among the Breakers, when the Depon't Fitz Gerald was at helm, and had lost sight of the Great Ship, Snow and Sloop; and being among the breakers we thought it most proper and necessary to weere the Pink,* and before we could trim the head sails we run ashoar opposite to Sluts bush† at the back of Stage harbour to the southward of Cape Codd between ten and Eleven a Clock at night, And the seven Pyrates together with the Depon't and a young man named James Donovan tarryed on board the said Pink till break of day and then found the shoar side of the Pink dry and so all of them went on shoar upon the Island called Poachy [Pocket] beach, and there tarryed till about ten a Clock.

The *Whidah* had been wrecked in the breakers; both the snow and the sloop leading Bellamy's ship had run aground. It was later said that the captain of the sloop, knowing Bellamy and his crew were pirates, deliberately ran his sloop close to shore so the *Whidah* would be wrecked. If this is true, he did his work well, for only two men escaped alive from the *Whidah*. Bellamy and the rest of his crew were all drowned in the raging surf. The seven pirates and the two crewmen on the pink waited until morning aboard the grounded vessel and stepped ashore unharmed. The pirates were taken into custody and jailed in Boston. The snow escaped unharmed. The wreck had occurred at midnight on April 26.

One of the survivors from the *Whidah*, Thomas Davis, reached the house of Samuel Harding, two miles from the wreck, at five o'clock in the morning. Harding returned to the wreck with Davis on a horse and they are believed to have salvaged a quantity of treasure. The two men made several trips between the wreck and Harding's house before other locals arrived. By ten o'clock in the morning, almost a dozen other men were working on the wreck and beach, picking up treasure and valuable goods which were washed in. By the time a local official arrived two days later, there was little left to salvage for the King. The

---

* That is, to come about before the wind.
† Sluts bush was near an island now under water.

Crown had claim to the goods, since the treasure on the *Whidah* had been acquired by piracy and did not come under the ordinary salvage laws as "wreck of the sea."

A local captain, Cyprian Southack, busied himself in trying to round up the treasure and in cleaning up as necessary. His letters to Governor Samuel Shute, while hardly models of the English language, do give us much information on the aftermath of the wreck and events at the site. In a letter of May 8, 1717, Southack reported that sixty-two dead pirates had washed ashore from the *Whidah* and the coroner had seen to the burying of the bodies and intended to withhold £83 from the treasure to pay for the services. Captain Southack objected strongly to this, saying that the coroner knew the men were pirates and was not due such a fee. The search for treasure went on along the beach and among the local inhabitants and with the greatest of difficulty some was recovered for the Crown. Of the eight pirates taken on the pink, six were tried, convicted, and hanged in Boston, Cotton Mather himself seeing to the preparation of their souls for the event. Davis, who convinced the court of his being forced and who had turned state's evidence, and one of the men from the pink were acquitted. The other man who had escaped with Davis from the *Whidah*, an Indian, was apparently freed. Even today men are searching for the treasure of the *Whidah*, and coins of the period are known to wash up on the beach near the site of the wreck.

So ended the career of Samuel Bellamy. He had treated his victims dispassionately, refraining from unnecessary cruelty; at times he was even generous. He was known widely for his oratorial talents and today is remembered as much for a speech he once made as he is for his piratical exploits. In the oration he summed up the pirate's philosophy with a flair that none of his colleagues and few of his contemporaries could command. Speaking to a captain whose sloop he had captured and wished to return, Bellamy explained that his crew would not let him return it:

> I am sorry they won't let you have your sloop again, for I scorn to do any one a mischief, when it is not for my advantage; damn the sloop, we must sink her, and she might be of use to you. Though you are a sneaking puppy, and so are all those who will submit to be governed by laws which rich men have made for their own security; for the cowardly whelps have not the courage otherwise to defend what they get by their knavery; but damn ye altogether: damn them for a pack of crafty rascals, and you, who serve them, for a parcel of hen-hearted numskulls. They vilify us, the scoundrels do, when there is only this difference, they rob the poor under the cover of law, forsooth, and we

plunder the rich under the protection of our own courage. Had you not better make one of us, then sneak after these villains for employment?[9]

When the unfortunate captain replied that his conscience would not let him break the laws of God and man, Bellamy continued: "You are a devilish conscience rascal, I am a free prince, and I have as much authority to make war on the whole world, as he who has a hundred sail of ships at sea, and an army of 100,000 men in the field; and this my conscience tells me: but there is no arguing with such snivelling puppies, who allow superiors to kick them about deck at pleasure."

As their bases in America were denied them with the closing of New Providence, Jamaica, and North Carolina, some of the pirates resorted to the wild Mosquito Coast on the Gulf of Honduras, while the more daring and able moved their bases to the coast of Africa and finally to Madagascar, where they set up another "pirate republic" and preyed on the rich trade from the East.

Epilogue

 Five more wars in Europe found counterparts in America before the end of Spanish rule there: the War of the Austrian Succession in Europe, called King George's War in America; the Seven Years War, known in America as the French and Indian War; the American War of Independence, which spread to Europe as allies joined the struggling colonies against Britain; the wars of the French Revolution, which found a counterpart in a brief naval war between the United States and its recent ally France; and finally, the War of 1812, a counterpart of the Napoleonic conflicts. Each of these wars brought naval warfare to the Caribbean, the Gulf of Mexico, and the Florida Straits.

The climax was the British attack on Havana in 1762, with a powerful naval and military force under Admiral Sir George Pocock and the earl of Albemarle. After a siege of two months the city fell and was occupied, the British exacting a high tribute. For half a year the city was controlled by the British, and during this brief period the commerce of the place greatly increased, much to the city's benefit. But this lesson was lost on the officials at the Spanish court, and when the British left in February 1763, the old commercial controls were restored and the city again sank into comparative poverty. And thus it went, the Spanish seeking to the last to enforce their outdated system, while the commerce and prosperity of their colonies were stifled.

As a result of the treaty ending the Seven Years War in 1763, Great Britain gained control of Florida, and now both sides of the Straits were in British hands. This change was of little importance to Spain, for the great flood of treasure that had once passed through the Straits was now reduced to a trickle.

The Treaty of Paris, which ended the American Revolution, also led to the return of Florida to the Spanish. Again, this had little strategic significance, for the Spanish colonies were soon in rebellion. The revolution to the north had demonstrated what a grown child could do against an oppressive parent, and in Mexico and South America the Spanish Americans rose in revolt. By 1825 Spain had lost all of her mainland territory, which was now organized into republics patterned on that of the United States. Only a pitiful remnant in the West Indies—Cuba and Puerto Rico—remained to tell of the glorious days when Spain controlled all the land of the New World except Brazil.

At the time the colonies did throw off Spanish rule, they were still agrarian nations organized on the old colonial system of privilege for the few and suppression for the many—sixteenth-century nations facing life in the rapidly expanding industrial and commercial age of the nineteenth century.

Spain, like the other European nations, had opened up a "wilderness" and in so doing had destroyed numerous indigenous peoples whose history extended back as far as the ancient civilizations in the Near East. The destruction had taken several forms: outright slaughter when resistance was met with; otherwise, suppression and absorption by the Spanish, and segregation and eventual elimination by the English and French. These policies have left our age a legacy of human problems staggering in their complexity.

Today, after almost five centuries, the Caribbean, the Gulf of Mexico, and the Florida Straits remain one of the great centers of the world's commerce. The cruise ship, tanker, and freighter have replaced the galleon, frigate, merchantman, and slave trader. Where Spanish colonists or foreign enemies once poured ashore, tourists flood the ports to buy many of the same products that made the Caribbean famous in Europe centuries ago: pottery, woodenware, and textiles, whose designs go back to the period before the Spanish came. The more curious take a stroll through the massive ruins of Spanish fortifications that still dot the coasts like sleeping giants breathing of another era, the most apparent remnants of Spanish power. In Spain herself, magnificent Renaissance buildings survive as monuments to an age when she was the center of the world's richest commerce and arbiter of affairs in Europe. Other monuments to Spanish failure and misfortune are the shipwrecks that dot the seas her ships once sailed and that are today providing us with a rich legacy of antiquities. Through archaeology, we are able to understand better the true nature of colonial commerce and life at sea in the colonial era.

It seems entirely fitting that these seas, which were the center of man's last great exploratory adventure on earth—the opening of the New World—should be the stage for his latest great adventure: the exploration of the moon and the planets. And when a giant rocket leaves the earth for the moon in a volcano of flame and thunder, perhaps the restless spirit of a Columbus or a Drake—the astronauts of their age—is there to wish godspeed to their successors as they leave on another voyage into the unknown.

Chapter References

The following abbreviations are used in citing the sources of quotations:

ADM: Admiralty Records
AIS: Archives of the Indies, Seville
Aud. Mex.: Audiencia de México
BM Add MSS: British Museum Additional Manuscripts
Casa: Casa de Contratación
CO: Colonial Office Records
Escr. Cam.: Escribanía de Cámara
PRO: Public Record Office, London

I. THE GATE IS OPENED

1. Bernal Díaz del Castillo, *The Discovery and Conquest of Mexico*, trans. by A. P. Maudslay, p. 28.
2. Díaz del Castillo, p. 74.
3. This quotation and the two following are from Cortés's first letter to Charles V, *Fernando Cortés, His Five Letters of Relation to Emperor Charles V*, I, 155–170.

II. TREASURE

1. Clarence H. Haring, *Trade and Navigation Between Spain and the Indies*, pp. 177–178.
2. *Fernando Cortés, His Five Letters of Relation to Emperor Charles V*, I, 170–171.
3. Bernal Díaz del Castillo, *The Discovery and Conquest of Mexico*, trans. by A. P. Maudslay, pp. 248–249.
4. Antonio Vázquez de Espinosa, *Compendium and Description of the West Indies* (1622), p. 629.
5. Vázquez de Espinosa, pp. 625–629.
6. Alberto F. Pradeau, *Numismatic History of Mexico*, p. 21.
7. Pradeau, p. 21.

8. Vázquez de Espinosa, p. 631.

9. Thomas Gage, *The English-American: A New Survey of the West Indies* (1648), pp. 84–85. The quotations in the next three paragraphs are also from these pages.

10. Antonio de Alcedo, *The Geographical and Historical Dictionary of America and the West Indies* (1787), IV, 114.

11. Gage, p. 85.

12. Vázquez de Espinosa, p. 328.

13. Vázquez de Espinosa, pp. 48–51.

III. GALLEONS, FLOTAS, AND SHIPS OF REGISTER

1. Clarence H. Haring, *Trade and Navigation Between Spain and the Indies*, p. 4.

2. Haring, p. 10.

3. Haring, p. 8.

4. Haring, p. 14.

5. Haring, p. 24.

6. Haring, pp. 30–31.

7. Haring, pp. 33–34.

8. Haring, p. 207.

9. Alonzo Enríquez de Guzmán, *The Life and Acts*, p. 81.

10. Haring, pp. 210–211.

11. Thomas Gage, *The English-American: A New Survey of the West Indies* (1648), p. 14.

12. Haring, p. 208.

13. Deposition of Edward McIver, an English mariner who had seen the fleet in Havana (PRO CO 5/362).

14. Antonio Vázquez de Espinosa, *Compendium and Description of the West Indies* (1622), pp. 1–2.

15. Gage, p. 18.

16. Gage, p. 377.

17. Gage, p. 363.

18. Gage, p. 206.

19. Vázquez de Espinosa, p. 244.

20. Gage, pp. 342–344.

21. This quotation and the next one are from Gage, pp. 365–366.

22. William L. Schurz, *The Manila Galleon*, p. 216.

23. Quoted in Schurz, p. 253.

24. This quotation and the three following are from Gage, pp. 12–15.

25. This quotation and the next one are from Enríquez de Guzmán, pp. 80–83.

26. Gage, pp. 16–17.

27. Enríquez de Guzmán, p. 81.

28. Gage, p. 27.

29. This quotation and the next one are from Gage, pp. 373–374, 377.

30. Gage, pp. 29, 32.

31. This quotation and the next two are from Gage, pp. 367–369.

32. Antonio de Alcedo, *The Geographical and Historical Dictionary of America and the West Indies*, IV, 200–201.

33. *The Fugger News Letters*, 2d ser., pp. 198–199.

IV. THE POACHERS

1. Depositions taken November 26–December 9, 1527, at Santo Domingo before Licentiates Cristóbal Lebrón and Alonso Zuazo, judges of the High Court of

Chapter References

Justice and Equity, in Irene A. Wright, trans. and ed., *Spanish Documents Concerning English Voyages to the Caribbean, 1527–1568*, p. 29.

2. Deposition of Antonio Martín, pilot, in Wright, p. 30.
3. Deposition of Francisco de Prado, in Wright, p. 40.
4. Wright, p. 31.
5. The King to the judges of the High Court in Santo Domingo, March 27, 1528, in Wright, p. 57.
6. Licentiate Alonso Arias de Herrera to the King, May 20, 1563, in Wright, pp. 61–62.
7. Wright, p. 60.
8. Licentitae Echegoyan to the King, July 28, 1563, in Wright, pp. 64–65.
9. Licentiate Echegoyan to the King, November 4, 1563, in Wright, pp. 74–75.
10. John Sparke the Younger, *The Voyage made by M. John Hawkins Esquire* . . . , in Richard Hakluyt, *The Principal Navigations* . . . (Glasgow, 1903–1905), X, 9–63. The quotations in the next four paragraphs are also from this source.
11. Antonio de Barrios to Governor Alonso Bernáldez, April 4, 1565, in Wright, pp. 76–77.
12. Wright, pp. 80–81.
13. Wright, p. 82.
14. Sparke, p. 36.
15. Wright, p. 94.

V. THE DRAGON

1. Letter from the Council of Río de la Hacha to the Crown, July 9, 1567, in Irene A. Wright, trans. and ed., *Spanish Documents Concerning English Voyages to the Caribbean, 1527–1568*, p. 104.
2. John Hawkins's account of his voyage of 1567–1568 is in Richard Hakluyt, *The Principal Navigations* . . . , X, 64–74. All quotations in Hawkins's words are from this account.
3. Wright, *Spanish Documents,* pp. 116–117.
4. Don Martín Enríquez to John Hawkins, dated aboard the Spanish flagship off San Juan de Ulúa, September 18, 1568, in Wright, *Spanish Documents,* p. 128.
5. Statement of Don Martín Enríquez at San Juan de Ulúa, September 27, 1568, in Wright, *Spanish Documents,* pp. 132–133.
6. Interrogatory presented at Nombre de Dios, May 15, 1571, in Irene A. Wright, trans. and ed., *Documents Concerning English Voyages to the Spanish Main, 1569–1580,* p. 24.
7. Wright, *Documents,* p. 23.
8. Letter from Licentiate Carasa (first name not given), a judge in the high court at Panama to the King, dated at Panama, March 27, 1570, in Wright, *Documents,* p. 9.
9. The account of the voyage and the raid on Nombre de Dios, which is quoted extensively in this chapter, is from Philip Nichols's *Sir Francis Drake Revived* (1628), which is reprinted in Wright, *Documents,* pp. 245–326.
10. Pedro de Ortega Valencia, royal factor at Nombre de Dios, to the King, February 22, 1573 (the day the English reached the coast on their return from Venta Cruz), in Wright, *Documents,* p. 46.
11. Letter of the Audiencia of Panama to the Crown, May 4, 1573, in Wright, *Documents,* p. 66.
12. Depositon of Juan Bautista Manuel and Alvaro Flores, made at Seville, September 28–October 6, 1573, in Wright, *Documents,* p. 77.
13. Letter of the royal officials of Panama to the Crown, May 9, 1573, in Wright, *Documents,* p. 69.

14. Julian S. Corbett, *Drake and the Tudor Navy*, II, 3.
15. Letter of Hieronymo Lippomano to the Doge of Venice, quoted in Corbett, II, 4.
16. The English source for this voyage of Drake's, which is quoted extensively, is the contemporary account published by Thomas Cates, *A Summarie and True Discourse of Sir Francis Drakes West Indian Voyage, Begun in the Year 1585*, in Hakluyt, *The Principal Navigations*, X, 97–120.
17. The city of Santo Domingo to the Crown, February 26, 1586, in Irene A. Wright, trans. and ed., *Further English Voyages to Spanish America, 1583–1594*, p. 40.
18. Letter from Governor Pedro Fernández de Busto to the Audiencia of Panama, March 12, 1586, in Wright, *Further English Voyages*, p. 53. The next quotation is also from this source.
19. An anonymous account of the sack of Cartagena, in Wright, *Further English Voyages*, p. 49.

VI. LUTHERAN INFECTION AND CATHOLIC CURE

1. Jean Ribaut, *The Whole & True Discovery of Terra Florida*, pp. 65 and 85. The next quotations and the ones in the following five paragraphs are also from Ribaut, pp. 66–91, 96.
2. Report of Manrique de Rojas through his scrivener, quoted in Charles E. Bennett, *Laudonnière and Fort Caroline*, pp. 123–124.
3. This quotation is from one of three long letters that Laudonnière wrote describing his experiences. Richard Hakluyt was instrumental in having the letters published first in French, as part of a work entitled *L'Histoire notable de la Floride* (Paris, 1586). He then translated the work into English, called it "A Notable Historie Containing Foure Voyages Made by Certaine French Captaynes into Florida," and included it in the 1600 edition of his *Principal Navigations*. All the quotations from Laudonnière given in this chapter are from the "Notable Historie" as given in the Glasgow edition of the *Principal Navigations* (1903–1905), IX, 1–99.
4. This and the next quotation are from Ruiz Manso's deposition, September 24, 1565, in Bennett, pp. 104–105.
5. Pedro Menéndez de Avilés to Philip II, dated "In this Province of Florida," September 11, 1565, in *Proceedings of the Massachusetts Historical Society*, 2d ser., VIII, 420.
6. Pedro Menéndez de Avilés to Philip II, dated "From this Province of Florida," October 15, 1565, in *Proceedings of the Massachusetts Historical Society*, 2d ser., VIII, 425–426.
7. This and the next two quotations are from Jacques Le Moyne de Morgues, *Narrative*, trans. by Frederick B. Perkins, pp. 18–19.
8. This and the next four quotaions are from Menéndez' letter to Philip II, October 15, 1565, in *Proceedings of the Massachusetts Historical Society*, 2d ser., VIII, 425–429, 438.
9. This and the next two quotations are from Le Moyne, pp. 21–23.
10. Jeanette T. Conner, Introduction to Jean Ribaut's *The Whole & True Discouerye of Terra Florida*, p. 30.
11. *Proceedings of the Massachusetts Historical Society*, 2d ser., VIII, 425–426.
12. When M. M. Basanier published *L'Histoire notable de la Floride* in Paris in 1586, he included an abridged version of "La Reprinse de la Floride par le captaine Gourgues." This abridged version was published by Richard Hakluyt in London in 1587. However, a much longer and comprehensive version existed in five variant manuscripts in the Bibliothèque Nationale in Paris. Jeanette T. Conner translated one of these manuscripts, carefully collating it with the other four.

Chapter References

This translation is in the collections of the Library of Congress and was first published by Charles E. Bennett in his *Settlement of Florida*, pp. 202–227. This and the remaining quotations in this chapter are from this source.

VII. GREAT STORMS AND SHIPWRECKS

1. Francisco Carreño to Philip II, 1578, in Jeanette T. Conner, ed. and trans., *Colonial Records of Spanish Florida*, II, 341.
2. Barcia, *Chronological History*, p. 25.
3. Barcia, p. 30.
4. Hernando d'Escalente Fontaneda, *Memoir . . . Respecting Florida*, pp. 18–19.
5. Fontaneda, p. 22.
6. John Sparke, *The Voyage made by M. John Hawkins Esquire . . .*, in Richard Hakluyt, *The Principal Navigations . . .* (Glasgow, 1904), X, 57–58.
7. Antonio Vázquez de Espinosa, *The True Story of the Voyage and Sea Trip of 1622 . . .*, Discourse II.
8. This quotation and the three following are from Vázquez, Discourse V.
9. Charles May, *An Account of the Wonderful Preservation of the Ship* Terra Nova *of London*, p. 359.
10. This quotation and those in the next paragraph are from May, pp. 360–361.
11. This quotation and the two following are from Vázquez, Discourse VII.
12. This quotation and the four following are from Vázquez, Discourse X.
13. Vázquez, Discourse XIIII.
14. Vázquez, Discourse XV.
15. This quotation and the five following are from Vázquez, Discourse XVIII.

VIII. DUTCH TREAT

1. Thomas Gage, *The English-American: A New Survey of the West Indies* (1648), pp. 370–371.
2. Gage, pp. 374–375.
3. This quotation and the next are from Gage, p. 376.
4. Piet Pieterzoon Heyn, "Missive to Our Lords and Masters [the directors of the Dutch West India Company], sent September 26, 1628, with the yachts *Vos* and *Oijevaar*," in *Werken Hist. Gemmtsch*, 3d ser., No. 53.
5. Jacob de Liefde, *The Great Dutch Admirals*, pp. 57–58.
6. Don Juan Benavides to Philip IV, October 7, 1628, AIS-Casa 5117.
7. Don Juan de Leoz to Philip IV, October 7, 1628, AIS-Casa 5117. The next quotation is also from this letter.

IX. BERMUDA, A STUDY IN CORAL AND GOLD

1. From the translation by Richard Eden, first published in 1555. A reprint of 1577 is included by Henry Lefroy in *Memorials of the Discovery and Early Settlement of the Bermudas . . .*, I, 2–3.
2. John Smith, *General Historie of Virginia*, Bk. V, in Lefroy, 1, 7.
3. Henry May's narrative, in Lefroy, I, 7–9.
4. Sir George Somers to the earl of Salisbury, June 20, 1610, in Lefroy, I, 10–11.
5. This and the next quotation are from Silvanus Jordan's narrative, in Lefroy, I, 14–18.
6. Strachy's narrative, in Lefroy, I, 48–50.
7. Smith, *General Historie*, in Lefroy, I, 156–157. The next two quotations are also from these pages.

Chapter References

8. Deposition by Simon Day, master of the *Joseph,* given in England, February 22, 1621, in Lefroy, I, 242.
9. Governor Nathaniel Butler to William Seymour, n.d., in Lefroy, I, 248.
10. Lefroy, I, 245.
11. Contemporary translation quoted in Lefroy, I, 240–241.
12. "Company of Adventurers and Owners of the Somers Islands" to Gondomar, February 9, 1621/22, in Lefroy, I, 241–242.
13. Lefroy, I, 251–252.
14. Translated by Lawrence D. Gurrin, in "Shipwrecked Spaniards," *Bermuda Historical Quarterly,* XVIII (Spring, 1961): 14. The quotations in the next two paragraphs are also from this source.

X. THE BUTCHERS

1. Maurice Besson, *The Scourge of the Indies,* p. 8.
2. John Esquemeling [Alexander Olivier Esquemelìn], *The Buccaneers of America* (1684). Since, with two exceptions, all the quotations in the chapter are from this book, it seems simplest and best to cite the references as follows:
The career of Pierre le Grand: pp. 54–56.
The profession of buccaneering after Le Grand's coup: pp. 56–60.
The activities of Bartholomew Portugués: pp. 65–69.
The career of Roche Brasiliano: pp. 70–74.
John Scot's assault on Campeche: p. 74.
Henry Morgan's "intelligence" mission to Cuba: pp. 134–137.
Morgan's raid on Porto Bello: pp. 140–147.
Morgan's expedition to the Spanish Main: pp. 150–179.
Morgan's raid on Panama: pp. 193–238.
The career of L'Ollonais: pp. 79–117.
3. Clarence H. Haring, *The Buccaneers in the West Indies in the XVII Century,* p. 160.

XI. TWO LOST TREASURE FLEETS

1. Depositon of Captain Nicolás de Inda, pilot, given at Havana, August 16, 1715 (AIS-Escr. Cam. 55c).
2. Admiral Francisco Salmón to the Marqués de Casatorres, governor of Cuba, dated at Barra de Ayz, August 4, 1715 (AIS-Escr. Cam. 55c).
3. Admiral Salmón to Casatorres, dated from Florida, September 2, 1715 (AIS-Escr. Cam. 55c).
4. Admiral Salmón to Casatorres, September 16, 1715 (AIS-Escr. Cam. 55c).
5. Admiral Salmón to Philip V, dated from Florida, September 20, 1715 (AIS-Escr. Cam. 55c).
6. PRO CO 137/10.
7. Juan Francisco del Valle to the Marqués de Monteleón, dated at Jamaica, March 18, 1716 (PRO-CO 137/11).
8. Governor Archibald Hamilton to the Lords Commissioners for Trade and Plantations, dated at Jamaica, June 12, 1716 (PRO-CO 137/11).
9. Captain Balchen to Mr. Burchet of the Admiralty, dated at the Nore, May 13, 1716 (PRO-CO 137/11).
10. Copy of a representation of the merchants of Jamaica to the Lords Commissioners for Trade and Plantations (PRO-CO 137/11).
11. Memorial of Juan Francisco del Valle to Governor Archibald Hamilton, undated copy, received by the Lords Commissioners for Trade and Plantations on May 19, 1716 (PRO-CO 137/11).

12. Juan Francisco del Valle to the Marqués de Monteleón, dated at Jamaica, March 18, 1716 (PRO-CO 137/11).

13. Governor Archibald Hamilton to the Lords Commissioners for Trade and Plantations, dated at Jamaica, June 12, 1716 (PRO-CO 137/11).

14. The Royal Officials at Havana to the King, August 19, 1733 (AIS-Aud. Mex. 2977). The other quotations in the paragraph are also from this letter.

15. Depositon made by John Calcock, given before Governor Robert Johnson at Charleston, S.C., September 17, 1733, and transmitted to the Lords Commissioners for Trade and Plantations by Governor Johnson with a letter of the same date (PRO-CO 5/362).

16. The Court Officials in Madrid to Admiral Rodrigo de Torres, December 25, 1733 (AIS-Aud. Mex. 2977).

17. The Court Officials in Madrid to the Deputies of Commerce at Havana, December 25, 1733 (AIS-Aud. Mex. 2977).

18. Admiral Rodrigo de Torres to Don José Patiño at Madrid, dated from Havana, November 8, 1733 (AIS-Aud. Mex. 2977). The next quotation is also from this letter.

XII. HOUSECLEANING IN PROVIDENCE

1. Official memorandum of Alexander Spotswood, governor of Virginia, February 26, 1714 (PRO-CO 37/9 and 249).

2. Minutes of a council held in Virginia (PRO-CO 37/9 and 249).

3. Letter of Samuel Buck to the Lords Commissioners for Trade and Plantations, Providence, December 3, 1719 (PRO-CO 23/1). The next quotation is also from this source.

4. Woodes Rogers, *A Cruising Voyage Around the World*, pp. 31-32.

5. Woodes Rogers, governor of the Bahamas, to the Lords Commissioners for Trade and Plantations, October 31 and November 4, 1718, and received by the Lords, December 17, 1718 (PRO-CO 23/1). The next four quotations are also from this source.

6. All quotations are from pp. 224-240 of this work.

7. Record of a special Admiralty session (PRO CO 23/1). The next three quotations are also from this source.

8. Letter addressed "To the Honorable Sir Richard Steele; to be left at Bartram's Coffee House in Church Court, opposite Hungerford Market in the Strand, London. Via Carolina." (BM Add MSS 5145, fols. 123-126).

9. PRO-CO 23/1. The next two quotations are also from this source.

10. News item, *London Magazine*, August 12, 1721.

XIII. GONE ON ACCOUNT

1. *The Tryals of Captain John Rackam, and Other Pirates*, p. 37.

2. *The Tryals of . . . John Rackam*, pp. 12, 15. The next three quotations are from pp. 15, 18-19.

3. Charles Johnson, *A General History of the Pirates*, I, 33.

4. Johnson, I, 34.

5. Patrick Pringle, *Jolly Roger*, p. 195.

6. Johnson, I, 36.

7. Johnson, I, 47-51.

8. Deposition of Thomas Fitzgerald and Alexander Mackonochie, given on May 6, 1717, in John F. Jameson, *Privateering and Piracy in the Colonial Period*, pp. 296-297.

9. *The History of the Pirates*, p. 124. The next quotation is also from this source.

Bibliography

BIBLIOGRAPHICAL WORKS

Bolton, Herbert E. *Guide to Materials for the History of the United States in the Principal Archives of Mexico.* Washington, D.C.: Carnegie Institution, 1913.

Manwaring, G. E. *Bibliography of British Naval History.* London, 1930.

Schafer, Ernesto. *Indice de la Colección de Documentos de Indias.* 2 vols. Madrid, 1946–47.

Shepherd, William R. *Guide to Materials for the History of the United States in the Spanish Archives, Simances and Seville.* Washington, D.C.: Carnegie Institution, 1907.

Wroth, Lawrence C. *Source Materials of Florida History in the John Carter Brown Library.* Jacksonville, 1941.

MANUSCRIPTS

In the Public Record Office, London (PRO), are the Admiralty Records (ADM) and Colonial Office Records (CO), which have been cited extensively in this book, especially those concerned with the loss of the fleet of New Spain in 1733; conditions in the Bahamas in the early eighteenth century; the piracy committed by Bermudians in 1714; and Henry Jennings's raid on the Spanish salvage camp in 1715.

In the British Museum, the repository Additional Manuscripts (BM Add MSS) yielded correspondence of Woodes Rogers, governor of the Bahamas.

In the Archives of the Indies, Seville (AIS) are the records and correspondence of the Audiencia de México (Aud. Mex.), which contain material on the loss of the fleet of New Spain in 1733; the records of the Casa de Contratación (Casa) on the capture of an entire plate fleet by the Dutch in 1628; and records of the Escribanía de Cámara (Escr. Cam.) on the loss of the combined fleet in 1715.

PRIMARY SOURCES

Acosta, José de. *The Natural and Moral History of the Indies* (1590). Trans. by Edward Grimston (1604). London: Hakluyt Society, 1880.

Bibliography

Alcedo, Antonio de. *The Geographical and Historical Dictionary of America and the West Indies* (1787). Trans. by G. A. Thompson. 5 vols. London, 1812.

Andrews, Kenneth R., ed. *The Last Voyage of Drake and Hawkins.* Hakluyt Society Publications, 2d ser., No. 142. Cambridge: Hakluyt Society, 1972.

Barcia, Andrés González de. *Barcia's Chronological History of the Continent of Florida* (1723). Trans. by Anthony Kerrigan. Gainesville, Fla.: University of Florida Press, 1951.

Bennett, Charles E. *Laudonnière and Fort Caroline.* Gainesville, Fla.: University of Florida Press, 1964.

––––––. *The Settlement of Florida.* Gainesville, Fla.: University of Florida Press, 1968.

Besson, Maurice, ed. *The Scourge of the Indies.* Trans. by Everard Thornton. New York: Random House, 1929.

Bradford, William. *Correspondence of the Emperor Charles V.* London, 1850.

Carroll, B. R., comp. *Historical Collections of South Carolina.* 2 vols. New York, 1836.

Catsby, Mark. *The Natural History of Carolina, Florida and the Bahamas Islands.* London, 1731–43.

Champlain, Samuel de. *Narrative of a Voyage to the West Indies and Mexico in the Years 1599–1602.* Trans. by Alice Wilmer. Hakluyt Society Publications, 1st ser., No. 23. London: Hakluyt Society, 1857.

Conner, Jeanette T., ed. *Colonial Records of Spanish Florida.* Vol. II. Deland, Fla.: Florida State Historical Society, 1930.

Cortés, Hernando. *Fernando Cortés, His Five Letters of Relation to Emperor Charles V.* Ed. and trans. by Francis A. MacNutt. 2 vols. Cleveland: A. Clark, 1908.

Dampier, William. *A New Voyage Round the World.* London, 1697.

Díaz del Castillo, Bernal. *The Discovery and Conquest of Mexico, 1517–1521.* Trans. by A. P. Maudslay. New York: Farrar, Straus & Cudahy, 1956.

Enríquez de Guzmán, Alonzo. *The Life and Acts.* Trans. by Clements R. Markham. London: Hakluyt Society, 1862.

Esquemeling, John. *The Buccaneers of America* (1684). New York: Dover, 1967.

Fontaneda, Hernando d'Escalente. *Memoir of Hernando d'Escalente Fontaneda Respecting Florida.* Trans. by Buckingham Smith. Washington, D.C., 1854. Reprinted with revisions: David True, ed. Miami, Fla.: University of Miami Press, 1944.

Fugger News Letters, The. 2d ser. (1568–1605). Ed. by Victor von Klarwell. Trans. by L. S. R. Byrne. New York: Putnam's, 1926.

Gage, Thomas. *The English-American: A New Survey of the West Indies* (1648). London: Routledge, 1928.

Garcilaso de la Vega (el Inca). *The Florida of the Inca.* Trans. by John G. and Jeannette J. Varner. Austin, Tex.: University of Texas Press, 1951.

Gurrin, L. D., trans. "Shipwrecked Spaniards in 1639," *Bermuda Historical Quarterly,* XVIII (Spring 1961): 13–28.

Hakluyt, Richard. *Divers Voyages Touching the Discovery of America . . .* (1582). Ed. by John Winter Jones. New York: Burt Franklin, n.d.

––––––. *The Principal Navigations, Voyages, Traffics and Discoveries of the English Nation.* 12 vols. Glasgow: James MacLehose, 1903–1905. (The first edition was published in 1589; the second, enlarged, in 3 vols., 1598–1600.)

Heyn, Piet Pieterzoon. "Missive to our Lords and Masters [the directors of the Dutch West India Company] sent 26 September 1628 with the yachts the *Vos* and the *Oijevaar.*" In *Werken Hist. Gemmtsch,* 3d ser., No. 53. Translated for the author by Dr. Lipke Holthuis of the University of Leyden.

History of the Pirates, The. Haverhill, Mass., 1825.

Bibliography

Hoover, Herbert C. and Lou Henry, trans. *Georgius Agricola de re metallica.* New York: Dover, 1950.

Jameson, John F. *Privateering and Piracy in the Colonial Period: Illustrative Documents.* New York: Macmillan, 1923.

Jefferys, Thomas. *A Description of the Spanish Islands and Settlements on the Coast of the West Indies.* London, 1762.

Johnson, Charles. *A General History of the Robberies and Murders of the Most Notorious Pirates* (1724). Reprinted as *A General History of the Pirates.* 2 vols. London: Philip Sainsbury, 1925, 1927.

Lefroy, J. Henry, ed. *The History of the Bermudaes.* From a manuscript in the Sloan Collection, British Museum. 1882. Reprint: New York: Burt Franklin, n.d.

———, ed. and trans. *Memorials of the Discovery and Early Settlement of the Bermudas or Somers Islands, 1515–1685.* 2 vols. Bermuda: Government Library, 1932.

Le Moyne de Morgues, Jacques. *Narrative of Le Moyne.* Trans. by Frederick B. Perkins. Boston, 1875.

Lives and Bloody Exploits of the Most Noted Pirates, The. Hartford, Conn., 1839.

McKinnen, Daniel. *A Tour Through the British West Indies.* London: T. White, 1804.

May, Charles. *An Account of the Wonderful Preservation of the Ship* Terra Nova *of London.* London: printed for Henry Lintot and John Osborn at the Golden Bell Paternoster Row, n.d. (The work was written in 1699.)

Maynarde, Thomas. *Sir Francis Drake, His Voyage, 1595.* London: Hakluyt Society, 1849.

Menéndez de Avilés, Pedro. "Translation of Several Letters from Pero [sic] Menéndez de Avilés to the King of Spain." In *Proceedings of the Massachusetts Historical Society,* 2d ser., VIII (1894): 416–468.

Nichols, Philip. *Sir Francis Drake Revived* (1628). Reprinted in Irene A. Wright, trans. and ed., *Documents Concerning English Voyages to the Spanish Main, 1569–1580,* Hakluyt Society Publications, 2d ser., LXXI, 245–341 (London: Hakluyt Society, 1932).

Priestley, Herbert I. *The Luna Papers.* 2 vols. Deland, Fla.: Florida State Historical Society, 1928.

Ribaut, Jean. *The Whole & True Discouerye of Terra Florida* (1563). With notes by H. M. Biggar and an introduction by Jeanette T. Conner. Deland, Fla.: Florida State Historical Society, 1927.

Rogers, Woodes. *A Cruising Voyage Round the World* (1712). New York: Dover, 1970.

Romans, Bernard. *History of East and West Florida.* New York, 1775.

———. *New and Enlarged Book of Sailing Directions.* London, 1794.

Smith, A. *The Atrocities of the Pirates.* London, 1824.

Sparke the Younger, John. *The Voyage made by M. John Hawkins Esquire . . . to the coast of Guinea, and the Indies of Nova Hispania, begun in An. Dom. 1564.* In Richard Hakluyt, *The Principal Navigations . . .* (Glasgow, 1903–1905), X:9–63.

Stock, Leo. *Proceedings and Debates of the British Parliaments Respecting North America.* Washington, D.C.: Carnegie Institution, 1924–26.

Tryals of Captain John Rackam, and Other Pirates, The. Printed by Robert Baldwin. Jamaica, 1721. The one copy known is in the Public Record Office, London (Colonial Office Records, CO 137/14).

Vásquez (or Vázquez) de Espinosa, Antonio. *Compendium and Description of the West Indies* (1628). Trans. by Charles Upson Clark. Washington, D.C.: Smithsonian Institution, 1942.

———. *Tratado Verdadero del Viage y Navegación deste Año de 1622, que hizo la flota de Nueva España, y Honduras* . . . [*The True Story of the Voyage and Sea Trip of 1622, Which the Fleets of New Spain and Honduras Made* . . .]. Malaga, 1623. A rare pamphlet in the John Carter Brown Library, Providence, R.I. Translated for the author by William Snyder of the Smithsonian Institution.

Wafer, Lionel. *A New Voyage and Description of the Isthmus of America.* London, 1699.

Wright, Irene A., trans. and ed. *Documents Concerning English Voyages to the Spanish Main, 1569–1580.* Hakluyt Society Publications, 2d ser., Vol. LXXI. London: Hakluyt Society, 1932.

————. *Further English Voyages to Spanish America.* Hakluyt Society Publications, 2d ser., Vol. XCIX. London: Hakluyt Society, 1951.

————. *Spanish Documents Concerning English Voyages to the Caribbean, 1527–1568.* Hakluyt Society Pubilcations, 2d ser., Vol. LXII. London: Hakluyt Society, 1929.

SECONDARY SOURCES

Andrews, Kenneth R. *English Privateering During the Spanish War, 1585–1603.* Cambridge, Eng.: Cambridge University Press, 1964.

Bell, H. MacLachlan. *Bahamas: Isles of June.* New York: McBride, 1934.

Benson, E. F. *Sir Francis Drake.* New York: Harper, 1927.

Bolton, Herbert E. *Spanish Borderlands.* Chronicles of America Series, Vol. 23. New Haven: Yale University Press, 1921.

————, and Marshall, Thomas M. *Colonization of North America, 1492–1783.* New York: Macmillan, 1921.

Bonnycastle, Richard. *Spanish America.* Philadelphia, 1819.

Bourne, Edward G. *Spain in America.* New York, 1904.

Boxer, Charles R. *The Dutch Seaborne Empire, 1600–1800.* New York: Knopf, 1965.

Brinton, Daniel G. *Notes on the Floridian Peninsula.* Philadelphia, 1859.

Burney, James. *History of the Buccaneers of America* (1816). London, 1891.

Carse, Robert. *The Age of Piracy.* New York: Rinehart, 1957.

Chapin, H. M. *Privateer Ships and Sailors, 1625–1725.* Toulon, 1926.

Clowes, William L. *The Royal Navy.* 7 vols. Boston, 1897–1903.

Corbett, Julian S. *Drake and the Tudor Navy.* 2 vols. London, 1898.

————. *The Successors of Drake.* London, 1900.

Crump, Helen T. *Colonial Admiralty Jurisdiction in the Seventeenth Century.* London: Longmans, Green, 1931.

Del Mar, Alexander. *A History of the Precious Metals.* New York, 1902.

Elliott, J. H. *Imperial Spain, 1469–1716.* New York: St. Martins, 1964.

Ellms, Charles. *Pirates Own Book.* Portland, Me., 1844.

Fairbanks, George R. *History of Florida.* Philadelphia, 1871.

Fernández Duro, Cesareo. *Disquisiciones náuticas.* 6 vols. Madrid, 1877–1881.

Fisher, Lillian. *Viceregal Administration in the Spanish American Colonies.* Berkeley: University of California Press, 1926.

Folmer, Henry. *Franco-Spanish Rivalry, 1524–1763.* Glendale, Calif.: A. N. Clark, 1953.

Forbes, James G. *Sketches, Historical and Topographical of the Floridas.* New York, 1821.

Gosse, Philip. *The Pirates' Who's Who.* Boston: Charles E. Lauriat, 1924.

————. *Sir John Hawkins.* London: Lane, 1930.

Hamilton, Earl J. *American Treasure and the Price Revoluton in Spain, 1501–1650.* Cambridge, Mass.: Harvard University Press, 1934.

Haring, Clarence H. *The Buccaneers in the West Indies in the XVII Century.* London: Methuen, 1910.

————. *Trade and Navigation Between Spain and the Indies in the Time of the Hapsburgs.* Cambridge, Mass.: Harvard University Press, 1918.

Hart, Francis Russell. *Admirals of the Caribbean.* Boston: Houghton Mifflin, 1922.

————. *The Siege of Havana, 1762.* Boston: Houghton Mifflin, 1931.

Hurd, Sir Archibald. *The Reign of the Pirates.* London: Heath Cranton, 1925.

Karraker, Cyrus H. *The Hispaniola Treasure.* Philadelphia: University of Pennsylvania Press, 1934.

————. *Piracy Was a Business.* Rindge, N.H.: R. R. Smith, 1953.

Liefde, Jacob de. *The Great Dutch Admirals.* London, n.d.

Lindsay, Philip. *The Great Buccaneer: Being the Life, Death and Extraordinary Adventures of Sir Henry Morgan.* New York: Funk and Wagnalls, 1951.

Lockhart, James. *Spanish Peru, 1532–1560: A Colonial Society.* Madison, Wis.: University of Wisconsin Press, 1968.

Lowery, Woodbury. *The Spanish Settlements in North America.* New York, 1911.

————. *The Spanish Settlements Within the Present Limits of the United States.* New York: Russell & Russell, 1959.

Lucas, C. P. *A Historical Geography of the British Colonies.* Oxford, 1890.

Marx, Robert. *Shipwrecks of the Western Hemisphere.* New York: World, 1971.

Maury, Matthew F. *Physical Geography of the Sea.* London, 1855.

Morison, Samuel Eliot. *Admiral of the Ocean Sea.* Boston: Little, Brown, 1942.

Newton, Arthur P. *The European Nations in the West Indies, 1493–1688.* New York: Barnes & Noble, 1967.

Norton, Charles L. *A Handbook of Florida.* New York, 1890.

Ober, Frederick A. *Aborigines of the West Indies.* Worcester, Mass., 1894.

Pares, Richard. *War and Trade in the West Indies, 1739–1763.* New York: Oxford, 1936.

Parry, J. H. *The Age of Reconnaissance.* Cleveland: World, 1963.

Peterson, Mendel L. *History Under the Sea.* Washington: Smithsonian Institution, 1965.

Pradeau, Alberto F. *Numismatic History of Mexico.* Los Angeles: privately printed, 1938.

Pringle, Patrick. *Jolly Roger: The Story of the Great Age of Piracy.* New York: Norton, 1953.

Pyle, Howard, ed. *The Buccaneers and Marooners of America.* London, 1892.

Rippy, J. Fred, and Jean T. Nelson. *Crusaders of the Jungle.* Chapel Hill: University of North Carolina Press, 1936.

Rodway, James. *West Indies and the Spanish Main.* New York, 1896.

Roscher, W. *The Spanish Colonial System.* Trans. by E. G. Bourne. New York, 1904.

Sauer, Carl O. *The Early Spanish Main.* Berkeley, Calif.: University of California Press, 1966.

Seitz, Don C. *Under the Black Flag.* New York: Dial, 1925.

Shea, John G. *Catholic Missions Among the Indian Tribes of the United States.* New York, 1854.

Simpson, Lesley B. *The Encomienda in New Spain, 1492–1550.* Berkeley, Calif.: University of California Press, 1929.

Sternbeck, Alfred. *Filibusters and Buccaneers.* Trans. by Elizabeth Hill and Doris Mudie. New York: McBride, 1930.

Van Middeldyk, R. A. *The History of Puerto Rico.* New York, 1903.

Waters, D. W. *The Art of Navigation in England in Elizabethan and Early Stuart Times.* New Haven: Yale University Press, 1958.

Wilgus, A. Curtis. *Histories and Historians of Hispanic America*. New York: H. W. Wilson, 1942.

Wilkinson, Henry C. *The Adventurers of Bermuda*. New York: Oxford, 1958.

————. *Bermuda in the Old Empire: A History of the Island from the Dissolution of the Somers Island Company Until the End of the American Revolutionary War, 1684–1784*. London: Oxford, 1950.

Williamson, J. A. *Maritime Enterprise, 1485–1558*. London: Oxford, 1913.

Wilson, T. W. *Piratical Descents upon Cuba*. Havana, 1851.

Winsor, Justin, ed. *Narrative and Critical History of America*. 8 vols. Cambridge, Mass., 1884–1889.

Woodbury, George. *The Great Days of Piracy in the West Indies*. New York: Norton, 1951.

Wright, Irene A. *The Early History of Cuba, 1492–1586*. New York, 1916.

Yolen, Jane H. *Pirates in Petticoats*. New York: McKay, 1963.

Index

American, pirate raids on, 389. *See also* Bahama Islands; Bermuda
Enríques de Guzmán, Alonzo. *See* Guzmán, Alonzo Enríquez de
Espinosa, Antonio Vázquez de. *See* Vázquez de Espinosa, Antonio
Esquemelin, Alexander Olivier (John Esquemeling), 298–300; accounts of buccaneers, 300–357 *passim*
Esteban de Ubilla, Juan. *See* Ubilla, Juan Esteban de
Explorers Research Corp., 284*n*

Fairfax, William, 394, 406, 411
fairs, trade. *See* trade
falconet (cannon), 238
Far East trade, 51, 81–82, 88, 285
farming. *See* plantations
featherwork, 171
Ferdinand, king of Spain, 7, 9, 14, 19, 38
Fernández de Busto, Pedro, 164
Fernández de Oviedo, Gonzalo. *See* Oviedo, Gonzalo Fernández de
finances, of Spanish Crown, 51, 65, 95, 195, 359–360, 385
fleet, treasure, 52–96; establishment and organization, 36, 60–64; reports on, 51, 95; raids on, 51, 58–61, 154, 171, 250, 252, 300–301; financing, 51, 65, 95; risks, 52, 58–60, 95–96, 246–247, 284; departures and arrivals, 52, 82–84, 87–88, 94–95, 363–364; shipping regulations, 53–57, 93–96, 363–364; convoy system, 60–64, 93; sailing schedules and patterns, 61, 62, 66–69, 93, 140*n*, 144; ships and armament, 62–64, 69–73, 95, 275; cargo, 62, 66, 96, 284, 362, 379–382; peak of development, 64; size of, 65–68; officials, 65; foreign-built ships, 70, 385; provisions, 85–87, 89, 143, 232, 363; intelligence reports on, 93, 369–370; success, 96; capture of, by Dutch, 252, 258–266; end of, 376. *See also* Flota of New Spain; Galeones; Manila Galleon; routes; shipwrecks; voyages
fleets: of Drake (1585), 155–157; French, to Fla. (1565), 195; Dutch war fleets (1623; 1626), 253, 256, 257; buccaneer (L'Ollonois), 354–355
Flores de Valdés, Diego, 134–135, 149, 214
Flores Island, Azores, 243

Florida: discovery and exploration, 4, 12, 14–20; Spanish settlement, 30, 195; lack of fortification, 30, 230; English exploration, 116–118, 194–195; description, 116–118, 176–178 *passim*, 180–181; French in, 116, 118, 132, 171, 176–224; geographical boundaries, 124*n*, 219*n*; British control, 451; Spanish recontrol, 452. *See also* Florida Keys; Florida, Straits of; Indians; St. Augustine, Fla.
Florida Current. *See* Florida, Straits of
Florida Keys (Los Mártires), 14, 116, 231*n*
Florida, Straits of (Florida Current; New Bahama Channel): discovery, 4, 14–19; as treasure fleet route, 19, 20, 30, 52, 75, 227–228, 298, 364, 451–452; vulnerability, 30, 230, 387; dangers of, 77, 227–228, 365, 385; use by Drake and Hawkins, 115, 116, 167; advantages, 228; pirate attacks, 388, 389; naval warfare (1740–1812), 451; in twentieth century, 452
Flota of New Spain (Mexican fleet): organization and function, 62–66, 68–69, 77, 81; encounters with English and Dutch, 126–127, 251–252; shipwrecks and salvage, 228–229, 231–236, 240–247, 361–385
Fonseca, Juan Rodríguez de, 56–57
Fontaneda, Hernando d'Escalente, 228*n*, 229–230
food: aboard ship, 85–87; price of, 88–89; of buccaneers, 302, 340
Fountain of Youth, 14
Fourquevaux, Ambassador, 214
France: raids on the Spanish, 51, 58–60, 134, 149–151 *passim*, 171, 173, 174–175, 300–301; claims in America, 97, 170–175, 179, 226; trade with Spanish America, 113, 123, 132; settlement in Florida, *see* Florida; atrocities, 132–134, 141; hostilities with Spain, 134, 174–175, 183; Protestantism (Huguenots), 149, 170, 174–176, 182–184, 224; in West Indies, 226; settlement in Tortuga, 298; expulsion from Lesser Antilles, 298; wars of Louis XIV (1688–1715), 357, 359–360; attack on Nassau, 388; wars (1740–1812), 451; treatment of natives, 452. *See also* buccaneers; Caroline, Fort
Francis I, king of France, 34*n*, 51, 60, 61, 171–174, 175

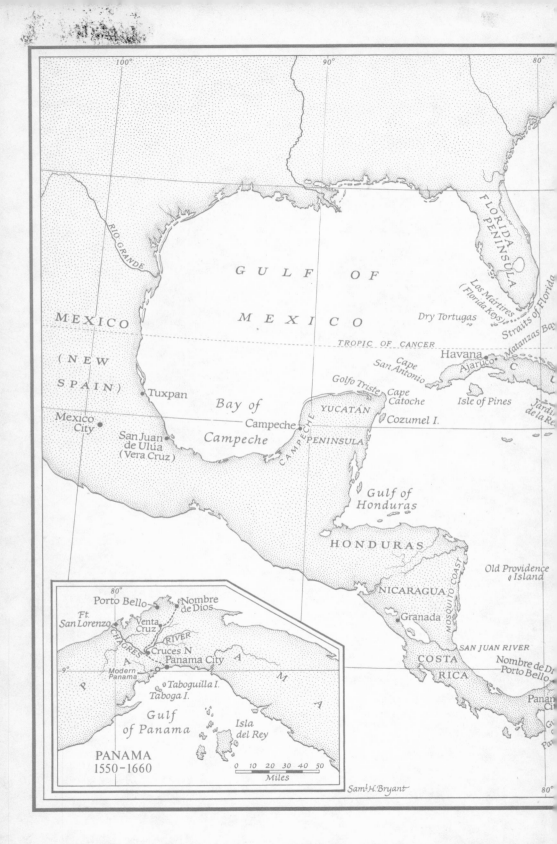

G U L F   O F

M E X I C O

MEXICO

(NEW

SPAIN)

RIO GRANDE

Tuxpan

Mexico
City

San Juan
de Ulúa
(Vera Cruz)

Bay of

Campeche

Campeche

TROPIC OF CANCER

Golfo Triste

YUCATÁN

CAMPECHE   PENINSULA

Cape
San Antonio

Cape
Catoche

Cozumel I.

Dry Tortugas

Havana

Ajaruco

Isle of Pines

FLORIDA
PENINSULA

Los Mártires
(Florida Keys)

Straits of Florida

Matanzas Bay

C U

Jardí
de la Re

Gulf of
Honduras

H O N D U R A S

Old Providence
Island

NICARAGUA

Granada

MOSQUITO COAST

SAN JUAN RIVER

COSTA

RICA

Nombre de Di
Porto Bello

Panan
Ci

80°

Porto Bello

Ft.
San Lorenzo

Nombre
de Dios

Venta
Cruz

CHAGRES

RIVER

Cruces N

Panama City

Modern
Panama

Taboguilla I.

Taboga I.

Gulf
of Panama

Isla
del Rey

PANAMA
1550-1660

0 10 20 30 40 50
Miles

P   A   M   A

Saml H. Bryant

100°

90°

80°

9°

80°

80°